Measures
for
Clinical Practice

A SOURCEBOOK

Measures
for
Clinical Practice

A SOURCEBOOK

Kevin Corcoran
Joel Fischer

THE FREE PRESS
A Division of Macmillan, Inc.
NEW YORK

Collier Macmillan Publishers
LONDON

The Free Press
A Division of Macmillan, Inc.
866 Third Avenue, New York, N. Y. 10022

Collier Macmillan Canada, Inc.

Printed in the United States of America

printing number
2   3   4   5   6   7   8   9   10

Library of Congress Cataloging-in-Publication Data

Corcoran, Kevin (Kevin J.)
    Measures for clinical practice.

    Bibliography: p.
    Includes index.
    1. Psychological tests.   I. Fischer, Joel.
II. Title. [DNLM: 1. Psychological Tests—
instrumentation. WM 145 C793m]
BF176.C66   1987   616.89′075   86–25819
ISBN 0–02–906681–6

To Geneviese Olivetti,
for an immeasurably fun-filled
and loving relationship,
and to the memory of Virgil and Bunkey

CONTENTS

PART
I MEASUREMENT AND PRACTICE

PART
II   INSTRUMENTS FOR PRACTICE

INSTRUMENTS FOR ADULTS

INSTRUMENTS FOR ADULTS (CONTINUED)

INSTRUMENTS FOR ADULTS (CONTINUED)

INSTRUMENTS FOR ADULTS (CONTINUED)

INSTRUMENTS FOR CHILDREN

INSTRUMENTS FOR CHILDREN (CONTINUED)

INSTRUMENTS FOR COUPLES AND FAMILIES

INSTRUMENTS FOR COUPLES AND FAMILIES (CONTINUED)

INSTRUMENTS CROSS-INDEXED BY PROBLEM AREA

Problem Area

Instrument

Alcoholism

Michigan Alcoholism Screening Test 227

Anger
(also see Hostility)

State-Trait Anger Scale 336

Anxiety
(also see Phobia and Mood)

Achievement Anxiety Test 81
Children's Cognitive Assessment Questionnaire 375
Clinical Anxiety Scale 123
Cognitive-Somatic Anxiety Questionnaire 128
Costello-Comrey Anxiety Scale 135
Death Anxiety Scale 141
Interaction and Audience Anxiousness Scales 195
Mathematics Anxiety Rating Scale—Revised 221
Self-Consciousness Scale 292
Self-Rating Anxiety Scale 300
Social Avoidance and Distress Scale 324
Fear of Negative Evaluation Scale 153
Social Anxiety Thoughts Questionnaire 326
Social Fear Scale 328
Social Interaction Self-Statement Test 331
Stressful Situations Questionnaire 342

Assertiveness
(also see Anxiety and Interpersonal Behavior)

Assertion Inventory 88
Assertive Job-Hunting Survey 92
Assertiveness Scale for Adolescents 355
Assertiveness Self-Report Inventory 94

FOREWORD

In the year 2000 historians will inevitably review the progress of the human race in the twentieth century. Historians of behavioral science reviewing progress in the provision of human services will have to confront a curious issue. They will note that the twentieth century witnessed the development of a science of human behavior. They will also note that from mid-century on clinicians treating behavioral and emotional disorders began relying more heavily on the systematic application of theories and facts emanating from this science to emotional and behavioral problems. They will make observations on various false starts in the development of our therapeutic techniques, and offer reasons for the initial acceptance of these "false starts" in which clinicians or practitioners would apply exactly the same intervention or style of intervention to every problem that came before them. But in the last analysis historians will applaud the slow but systematic development of ever more powerful specific procedures and techniques devised to deal successfully with the variety of specific emotional and behavioral problems. This will be one of the success stories of the twentieth century.

Historians will also note a curious paradox which they will be hard pressed to explain. They will write that well into the 1980s few practitioners or clinicians evaluated the effects of their new treatments in any systematic way. Rather, whatever the behavioral or emotional problem, they would simply ask clients from time to time how they were feeling or how they were doing. Sometimes this would be followed by reports in an official chart or record duly noting clients' replies. If families or married couples were involved, a report from only one member of the interpersonal system would often suffice. Occasionally, these attempts at "evaluation" would reach peaks of quantifiable objectivity by presenting the questions in somewhat different ways such as "how are you feeling or doing compared to a year ago when you first came to see me?"

Historians will point out wryly that this practice would be analogous to physicians periodically asking patients with blood infections or fractures "how are you feeling" without bothering to analyze blood samples or take X rays. "How could this have been?" they will ask. In searching for answers they will examine records of clinical practice in the late twentieth century and find that the most usual response from clinicians was that they were simply too busy to evaluate what they were doing. But the real reason, astute historians will note, is that they never learned how.

Our government regulatory agencies, and other institutions, have anticipated these turn-of-the-century historians with the implementation of procedures requiring practitioners to evaluate what they do. This practice, most often subsumed under the rubric of "accountability," will very soon have a broad and deep hold on the practice of countless human service providers. But more important than the rise of new regulations in an era of deregulation will be the full realization on the part of all practitioners of the ultimate logic and wisdom of evaluating what they do. In response to this need, a number of books have appeared of late dealing with methods to help practitioners evaluate what they do. Some books even suggest that this will enable clinicians to make direct contributions to our science. Using strategies of repeated measurement of emotional and behavioral problems combined with sophisticated case study procedures and single case experimental designs, the teaching of these methods is increasing rapidly in our graduate and professional schools. But at the heart of this process is measurement, and the *sine qua non* of successful measurement is the availability of realistic and practical measures of change. Only through wide dissemination of realistic, practical, and accurate measures of change will practitioners be able to fulfill the requirements of accountability as well as their own growing sense of personal obligation to their clients to evaluate their intervention. Up until now this has been our weakness, not because satisfactory measures did not exist, but because so many widely scattered measurement tools existed that it was impossible for any one practitioner to keep track of these developments, let alone make a wise choice of which measures might be useful.

Now Corcoran and Fischer have accomplished this task and the result is this excellent book that not only describes the essentials of measurement but also presents the most up-to-date and satisfactory measures of change for almost any problem a practitioner might encounter. Concentrating on what they call rapid assessment instruments (RAIs), they present a series of brief questionnaires most of which fulfill the criterion of being under 45 items, thereby requiring no more than several minutes to fill out. By cross-referencing these RAIs by problem areas, no practitioner need take more than a few minutes to choose the proper questionnaire for any problem or combination of problems with which he or she might be confronted. With its well-written and easy-to-read chapters on what makes a brief questionnaire measure satisfactory or unsatisfactory, this book should be on the shelf of every practitioner working in a human service setting. Through the use of this book practitioners will not only be able to meet growing demands for accountability, but also satisfy their own desires for objective quantifiable indications of progress in a manner that can be accomplished in no more than several minutes. As this activity becomes an integral part of the delivery of human services, the value of this book will increase.

David H. Barlow, Ph.D.
Center for Stress and Anxiety Disorders
Department of Psychology
State University of New York at Albany

PREFACE

The purpose of this book is to provide for practitioners and students a number of instruments that they can use to help them monitor and evaluate their practice. These instruments were specifically selected because they measure most of the common problems seen in clinical practice, they are relatively short, easy to score and administer, and because we believe they really will help you, the reader, in your practice.

We know through our own practice, and the practice of our students and colleagues, how difficult it sometimes is to be clear about where you are going with a client and whether or not you actually get there. We also realize the frustrations of trying to help a client be specific about a particular problem rather than leaving the problem defined in some global, vague—and therefore, unworkable—way.

These essentially are problems in *measurement*: being able to be as clear as possible about what you and the client are working on. Without a clear handle on the problem, the typical frustrations of practice are multiplied many times. We believe the instruments we present in this book will help relieve some of the frustrations you may have experienced in attempting to be precise about clients' problems. We also hope that we will be able to overcome the old myth of clinical practice that "most of our clients' problems really aren't measureable." We plan to show you that they are, and just how to go about doing it.

Practitioners in all the human services—psychology, social work, counseling, psychiatry, and nursing—increasingly are being held accountable for monitoring and evaluating their practice. One of the simplest yet most productive ways of doing this is to have available a package of instruments that measure the wide range of problems that practitioners typically face. Then, you simply would select the instruments most appropriate for the problem of the client (individual, couple, or family) and use those to monitor practice with that client or system.

There are a number of such instruments available. Unfortunately, they are widely scattered throughout the literature. With this book, we hope to save you the time and energy required to go into the literature to find and select the appropriate instrument. We not only provide information about those instruments, we include copies of them so that you can immediately assess their utility for your practice. We also provide information as to where you can obtain copies of the instruments if you want to use them.

This book is addressed to members of all the helping professions who are engaged in clinical or therapeutic work with individuals, couples, or families. Further, we believe the instruments contained in this book will be useful to practitioners from all theoretical orientations who are interested in monitoring or evaluating their practice. Indeed, one of the great appeals of these instruments is that they are not limited to use by adherents of only one or even a few clinical schools of thought or theoretical orientations. If you believe that it is useful to be able to keep track of changes in your client's problem as your intervention proceeds, then we think this book is for you.

Although we don't mean to oversimplify the task, we believe this book can be useful to students and practitioners with very little experience in using measures such as we have included here. Of course, we will provide information on how to use these instruments, including relevant data on their reliability and validity and other characteristics. Indeed, we believe this book also will be useful to researchers who will be able to use these instruments to help them conduct their studies in a wide range of problem areas.

This book is organized into two parts. Part I, consisting of six chapters, provides the necessary background for you to review, analyze, select, and administer measures for use in your own practice. Part II—the heart of the book—provides copies of actual instruments along with information about each instrument and how to use it.

We hope this book will prove useful to you. Most of all, we hope it will help you enhance the efficiency and effectiveness of your practice.

ORGANIZATION OF INSTRUMENTS

The instruments in Part II are organized into three sections: Instruments for Adults, for Children, and for Couples and Families. Within each section, the instruments are presented in alphabetical order. However, for more help in finding an instrument that is specially designed for a particular problem area, consult the third part of the Table of Contents. We have presented a list of instruments cross-indexed by problem area. Thus, if you need an instrument for evaluating your client's anxiety, you could look under Anxiety in the Table of Contents and see which instruments are designed for measurement of anxiety. We hope this will facilitate the selection process.

ACKNOWLEDGMENTS

We are very grateful to several people who have helped us in developing this book. Hisae Tachi, Nancy Young, and Cathy Cabalce have provided a tremendous amount of help and support. Laura Wolff, our editor at the Free Press, was a delight to work with. And while the order of authors for this book was determined by a flip of a coin, we are both convinced that each of us did most of the work.

PART
I

Measurement
and Practice

1

INTRODUCTION

Your client has come to you with a number of
complaints. "I just feel lousy. I don't have any energy,
I just never want to go out anymore. Sometimes,
especially at night, I find myself crying over nothing. I
don't even feel like eating. My boss pushes me around
at work; he makes me do all kinds of things that the
other employees don't have to do. But I can't tell him
I won't do the work. Then I feel even worse." After a
good deal of exploration, you help the client focus the
complaints until you see certain patterns. Among
them, the client seems to be depressed, have low
self-esteem, and to be very unassertive. You devise an
intervention program to work with all of these areas,
but one thing is missing. Although you're pretty sure
your interventions will be the right ones, other than
asking the client how she feels and maybe making a
few observations on your own, you don't have a clear
way of assessing accurately whether or not there will
be real improvement in each of these areas. After all,
they are pretty hard to measure with any degree of
objectivity. Or are they?

This book will help you answer that question. Al-
though we don't pretend to have all the answers to all the questions
you might have on how to measure your client's problems, we hope to
be able to help you grapple with a most important issue for clinical
practice: how we can more or less accurately and objectively, and without a lot of aggravation and extra work, measure some of the most commonly encountered clinical problems.

In the short case example at the beginning of this chapter, there
actually are several ways a practitioner could have measured the client's
problems. We will briefly examine several methods of measurement in
this book, but the main focus is on one: the use of instruments that the
client can fill out himself or herself, and that give a fairly clear picture

of the intensity or magnitude of a given problem. In the case example presented earlier, the practitioner might have selected one of several readily accessible, easy-to-use instruments to measure the client's degree of depression, level of self-esteem, or assertiveness. Indeed, instruments to measure each of these problems are included in Part II of this book.

ACCOUNTABILITY IN PRACTICE

The last decade or so has seen increasing pressure brought to bear on practitioners to be "accountable" for what they do in practice. Although the term accountability has several meanings, we believe the most basic meaning of accountability is this: we have to be responsible for what we do with our clients. The most crucial aspect of that responsibility is a commitment to delivering effective services.

There are very few in the human services who would deny the importance of providing effective services to clients as a major priority. Where the differences come about is in deciding how to go about implementing or operationalizing this commitment to providing effective services. Conscientious monitoring and measurement of one's practice and the client's functioning is a primary way to fulfill this commitment.

Use of Research in Practice

Let's face it. Many human services practitioners are not very enamored with research, often because they do not see its value—how it can really make a difference in practice.

Part of the problem may be that researchers have not done their best to demystify the research process. Most research texts reflect a way of thinking about many phenomena that is very different from the way many practitioners view the world. After all, most of us in the helping professions are there because we want to work with people, not numbers.

But research does offer some very concrete ways of enhancing our practice. First of all, recent years have seen a tremendous increase in the number of studies with positive outcomes. Many hundreds of studies point to a wide range of clinical techniques and programs that have been successful in helping clients with a multitude of problems (Fischer, 1981). Thus, practitioners can now select a number of intervention techniques or programs on the basis of their demonstrated success with one or more problem configurations as documented in numerous studies (e.g., see Barlow, 1985).

A second practical value of research is the availability of a range of methods to help us *monitor* how well we are doing with our clients, that is, to keep track of our clients' problems over time and, if necessary, make changes in our intervention program if it is not proceeding as well as desired. This is true whether our clients are individuals, couples, families, or other groups.

And third, we also have the research tools to *evaluate* our practice, to make decisions about whether or not our clients' problems are actually changing, and also whether or not it was our interventions that helped them change. Both of these areas—the monitoring and the evaluating of practice—are obviously of great importance to practitioners, and the practical relevance of the research tools is what makes recent developments in research so exciting for all of us.

By and large, the recent developments that have made research more accessible to practitioners have come about in two areas: research designs for practice, and new measurement tools. While the focus of this book is on measurement, we will provide a brief review of designs for practice, and the relation of these designs to measurement.

RESEARCH DESIGNS FOR PRACTICE

There is a wide variety of research designs that can provide useful information for practice. The most common—the ones most practitioners learned about in their educational programs—are the experimental designs, field studies, and surveys in which the researcher collects data on large groups of people or events and then analyzes those data using a variety of mathematical and statistical techniques. Some of these designs (e.g., those using random assignment, control and contrast groups) are best suited for informing our practice about which interventions work best with what clients with what problems in what situations. But despite their value these designs are rarely used by practitioners, because they often require more sophisticated knowledge, time, or resources than are available to most practitioners.

A second set of designs that can be of value to practitioners are the *single system designs*. These designs, which allow practitioners to monitor and evaluate each case, have been called by a number of terms: single case experimental designs, single subject or single N designs, time series designs, and single organism designs. While all these terms basically refer to the same set of operations, we prefer the term single system design because it suggests that the designs do not have to be limited to a single client but can be used with couples, families, groups, organizations, or larger collectivities.

These designs, elaborated in several recent books (Bloom and

Fischer, 1982; Jayaratne and Levy, 1979; Kazdin, 1982; Barlow et al., 1984; Barlow and Hersen, 1984; Kratochwill, 1978), are a relatively new development for the helping professions. And while this new technology is increasingly being made available to practitioners, a brief review of the basic components of single system designs is in order.

The first component of single system designs is the specification of a problem which the practitioner and client agree needs to be worked on. This problem can be in any of the many areas of human functioning—behavioral, cognitive, affective, or the activities of individuals or groups.

The second component is selecting a way to measure the problem. In the past, finding ways to measure problems has been a major stumbling block for many practitioners. But there are now a wide variety of ways to measure problems—some of which were once thought to be "unmeasurable"—available to practitioners of diverse theoretical orientations. These will be discussed throughout the rest of this book.

The third component is the implementation of the design itself—the systematic collection of information about the problem on a regular basis. This generally starts before the intervention proper is begun—the baseline—and continues over time until the intervention is completed. This use of "repeated measures"—collecting information on a problem over time—is a hallmark of single system designs, and provides the basis for the monitoring and evaluation functions described earlier.

The essence of single system designs is the comparison of the intensity, level, magnitude, frequency, or duration of the problem at different phases of the research. These comparisons are typically plotted on a graph, as shall be illustrated below, to facilitate visual examination. For example, one might conduct an elementary study of a client's progress by comparing information collected during the baseline on the client's level of depression with information collected during the intervention period to see if there is any change in the problem. A graphed example of such a design, called an A-B design (A = baseline; B = intervention), is presented in Figure 1.1. As with all single system designs, the level of the problem is plotted along the vertical axis and the time period is plotted along the horizontal axis. In this case, the client was assessed using a self-administered depression scale once a week. During a three-week assessment period (the baseline) the client filled out the questionnaire three times. The intervention was begun the fourth week and the steady decline in scores shows that the level of the client's depression was decreasing.

A more sophisticated design, combining or alternating different intervention or nonintervention (baseline) phases, can indicate not only whether the client's problem changed, but whether the practitioner's

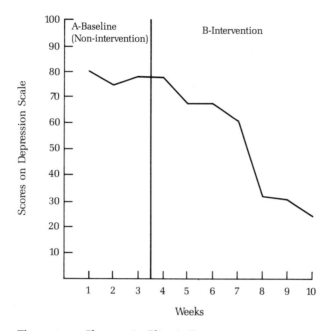

Figure 1.1. Changes in Client's Depression Scores over a Period of 10 Weeks

intervention program is responsible for the change. An example of one of several designs that can provide evidence of the relationship between the intervention and the change in the client's problems is presented in Figure 1.2. This example, in which the goal is to increase the client's assertiveness, is called an A-B-A-B (reversal or withdrawal) design. Evidence of the link between intervention and a change in the problem is established by the fact that the problem diminishes only when the intervention is applied and returns to its previous level when the intervention is withdrawn or applied to another problem.

As the practitioner collects information on the problem, he or she also is getting feedback on whether the intervention is producing the desired effects and therefore should be continued, or should be changed—this is the monitoring function. An example of the effects of such monitoring is presented in Figure 1.3. In this example, the practitioner was not satisfied with the slow progress shown in the first intervention period (Phase B) and changed his intervention to produce a more positive result (Phase C).

Finally, a review of all the information collected will provide data on success in attaining the desired goal—the evaluation of the outcome.

Single system designs seem to offer excellent opportunities for ac-

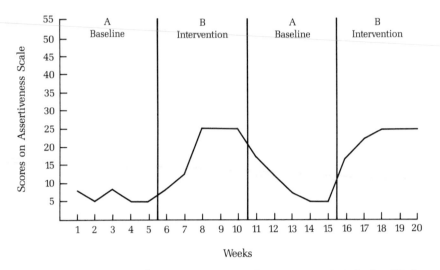

Figure 1.2. Changes in Client's Assertiveness Scores over a Period of 20 Weeks

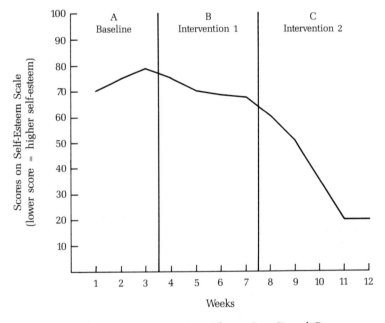

Figure 1.3. Changes in Intervention (Phases B & C) and Concurrent Change in Client's Self-Esteem Scores

tual utilization. They can be built into practice with each and every case; they provide direct feedback enabling the practitioner to readily assess, monitor, and evaluate the case; and they allow the practitioner to make changes in the intervention program if it appears not to be working. Thus, the instruments described in this book will probably find their most frequent use in the context of single system designs.

However, the same instruments can be—and have been—used in classical research. The selection of a design depends on the question one is asking: for some questions, a classical design is more appropriate; for others, one of the single system designs would be the design of choice. (A comparison of the characteristics, advantages, and disadvantage of classical and single system designs is available in Bloom and Fischer, 1982). The use and administration of the measure would vary with the design, from once in a cross-sectional survey to pre- and post-test administration in a classical experiment, to repeated administration—perhaps once or twice weekly—in a single system design that lasts for several weeks.

The Role of Measurement

One of the key challenges of all types of research, and practice as well, is finding a way to measure the problem. Measurement helps us be precise in defining problems and goals. It is measurement of the client's problems that allows feedback on the success or failure of treatment efforts, indicating when changes in the intervention program are necessary. Measurement procedures help standardize and objectify both research and practice. Using procedures that can also be used by others provides a basis for comparing results of different intervention programs. In a word, measurement of our clients' problems helps us know where we are going and when we get there.

Because formal measurement procedures provide the best basis for evaluating what we do, they are essential components of responsible, accountable practice. In Chapter 3 we will review a range of measurement procedures available to practitioners. However, the focus of this book is on one type of measure: standardized paper-and-pencil questionnaires that can be filled out by the client in a relatively short period of time, that can be easily administered and scored by the practitioner, and that give fairly accurate pictures of the client's condition at any point in time and/or over a period of many administrations. These types of measures have been called rapid assessment instruments (RAIs) by Levitt and Reid (1981).

We believe that these are among the most useful of all measurement tools for reasons that will be discussed throughout this book. Suffice it to say at this point that although there are many examples of these instruments, until now they have not been available in a single source. It is our hope that by compiling these instruments in this book, we will encourage far greater utilization of them in the everyday practice of the helping professions.

2

BASIC PRINCIPLES
OF MEASUREMENT

In this chapter we will review some basic principles of measurement. The major purpose of this review is to acquaint you with some of the terms we use in Part II in describing the instruments there, and to help you in selecting measures. Since the topic can be difficult, we will try to present it in an understandable way by dividing the material into four areas: a definition of measurement, the research principles defining a "good" measure, the statistical principles involved in interpreting scores, and the practice principles involved in using measures.

MEASUREMENT DEFINED

Measurement can actually be defined simply, although some writers have developed complex, technical, and intimidating definitions. Moreover, researchers in measurement are like other scientists as they, too, create a new vocabulary for concepts most of us already know. For example, a mathematician works with "integers," while the rest of us use "numbers."

Most simply, measurement is the systematic process of assigning a number to "some thing" (Nunnally, 1978, p. 3). The "thing" is known as a variable. The variables of concern to clinical practice tend to be a client's behavior, thoughts, feelings or situation (the dependent or outcome variable); treatment goals; and theoretical concepts such as self-esteem. The number assigned represents a quantified attribute of the variable.

This simple definition of measurement is the process of quantifying the "thing." Quantification is beneficial in work with clients because it allows you to monitor change mathematically. The mathematical procedures of interest to us are addition, subtraction, multiplication and division. For example, suppose you have successfully treated "an explosive personality" such that at the end of therapy you conclude the "explosive personality is in remission." By assigning a number to, say, the symptom of anger by using Spielberger's (1982) State Trait Anger Scale, you can mathematically monitor how this symptom has changed during treatment. It would be impossible, on the other hand, to subtract an explosive personality in remission from an explosive personality.

In determining which math procedures to use, the first consideration is known as the "level of measurement," of which there are four: nominal, ordinal, interval, and ratio. These four levels differ from each other by the presence or absence of four characteristics: exclusiveness, order, equivalency, and absoluteness.

The nominal level of measurement possesses only exclusiveness, which means the number assigned to an attribute is distinct from others as it represents one and only one attribute. With a nominal level the number is essentially the same as a name given to the attribute. An example of a nominal variable is "sex" with the attributes of "male" and "female." It is impossible to use mathematics with nominal measures, just as it is with terms like "explosive personality."

The ordinal level of measurement possesses exclusiveness, but is also ordered. To say the numbers are ordered means the numbers have a ranking. An example of an ordinal level of measurement is the severity of a client's problems or the ranking of a client's social functioning, as described in the DSM III (American Psychiatric Association, 1980). With ordinal measures you can compare the relative positions between the numbers assigned to some variable. For example, you can compare "poor functioning"—which is assigned the number 5—in relation to "superior functioning"—which is assigned the number 1. While you can compare the relative rankings of an ordinal level of measurement, you cannot determine how much the two attributes differ by using the mathematic procedures of addition, subtraction, multiplication, and division. In other words, you cannot subtract "superior" from "poor."

The use of math procedures is appropriate with measures at the interval level. An interval measure possesses exclusiveness and is ordered, but differs from ordinal measures in having equivalency. Equivalency means the distances between the numbers assigned to an attribute are equal. For example, the difference, or distance, between 2 and 4 on a seven-point scale is equal to the difference between 5 and 7.

With interval level measures, however, we do not have an absolute zero. This means either that complete absence of the variable never occurs or that our tool cannot assess it. For example, self-esteem is never completely absent as illustrated with the Index of Self Esteem (Hudson, 1982). Consequently, we really should not multiply or divide scores from interval level measures since a score of 30 on an assertiveness questionnaire, for example, may not reflect twice as much assertion as a score of 60. Another example of this issue is temperature; 90 degrees is not twice as hot as 45 degrees.

The problem caused by not having an absolute zero is resolved by assuming the measurement tool has an arbitrary zero. By assuming there is an arbitrary score which reflects an absence of the variable we can use all four mathematical procedures: addition, subtraction, multiplication, and division.

The fourth level of measurement is ratio. Measures that are at a ratio level possess exclusiveness, order, equivalency, and have an absolute zero. The only difference between a ratio and an interval level of measurement is this characteristic. With an interval level measure, we had to *assume* an arbitrary zero instead of actually having and being able to measure an absolute zero. This means there is an absolute absence of the variable which our measurement tool can ascertain. Ratio measures are fairly rare in the behavioral and social sciences, although numerous everyday variables can be measured on a ratio scale, such as age, years of marriage, and so on. However, the assumption of an arbitrary zero allows us to use all the mathematical procedures to monitor our practice.

The benefits of measurement, namely our ability to better understand what is happening in treatment, is a result of our using math to help us monitor practice. The levels of measurement which result from how a number is assigned to something determines which math you will be able to use. As the remainder of this book will show you, measures at the interval and ratio levels allow the practitioner to determine the effects of treatment most clearly and, therefore, to be a more accountable professional.

RESEARCH PRINCIPLES UNDERLYING MEASUREMENT

A good measure essentially is one that is reliable and valid. Reliability refers to the consistency of an instrument in terms of the items measuring the same entity and the total instrument measuring the same way every time. Validity pertains to whether the measure accurately assesses what it was designed to assess. Unfortunately, no instrument available for clinical practice is completely reliable or valid. Lack of reliability and lack of validity are referred to as random and systematic error, respectively.

Reliability

There are three basic approaches to determining an instrument's reliability: whether the individual items of a measure are consistent with each other; whether scores are stable over time; and whether different forms of the same instrument are equal to each other. These approaches to estimating reliability are known as internal consistency, test-retest reliability, and parallel forms reliability.

Internal consistency. Items of an instrument that are not consistent with one another are most likely measuring different things, and thus do not contribute to—and may detract from—the instrument's assessment of the particular variable in question. When using measures in practice you will want to use those tools where the items are all tapping a similar aspect of a particular construct domain.

The research procedure frequently used to determine if the items are internally consistent is Cronbach's coefficient alpha. This statistic is based on the average correlations among the items. A correlation is a statistic reflecting the amount of association between variables. In terms of reliability, the alpha coefficient has a maximum value of 1.0. When an instrument has a high alpha it means the items are tapping a similar domain, and, hence, that the instrument is internally consistent. While there are no hard and fast rules, an alpha coefficient exceeding .80 suggests the instrument is internally consistent.

In addition to Cronbach's alpha, there are other similar methods for estimating internal consistency. The essential logic of the procedures is to determine the correlation among the items. There are three frequently encountered methods. The "Kuder-Richardson formula 20" is an appropriate method for instruments with dichotomous items, such as true-false and forced-choice questions. "Split-half reliability" is a method that estimates the consistency by correlating the first half of the items with the second half; this method can also divide the items into two groups by randomly assigning them. A special form of split-half reliability is known as "odd-even." With odd-even reliability the odd items are correlated with the even items. Any method of split-half reliability underestimates consistency because reliability is influenced by the total number of items in an instrument. Because of this, you will often find references to the "Spearman-Brown formula," which corrects for this underestimation.

Test-retest reliability. Reliability can also be assessed in terms of the consistency of scores from different administrations of the instrument. If in actuality the variable has not changed between the times you measure it, then the scores should be relatively similar. This is known as test-retest reliability. Test-retest reliability is also estimated from a correlation. A strong correlation, say above .80, suggests that the instrument is stable over time.

When you use an instrument over a period of time—namely before, during, and after therapy—test-retest reliability becomes very important. How, after all, can you tell if the apparent change in your client's problem is real change if the instrument you use is not stable? Without some evidence of stability you are less able to discern if the observed change was real or simply reflected error in your instrument. Again, there are no concrete rules for determining how strong the test-retest coefficient of stability needs to be. Correlations of .69 or better for a one-month period between administrations is considered a "reasonable degree of stability" (Cronbach, 1970, p. 144). For shorter intervals, like a week or two, we suggest a stronger correlation, above .80, as an acceptable level of stability.

Parallel forms. A third way to assess reliability is to determine if two forms of the same instrument are correlated. When two forms of the same measure exist, such as the Rathus Assertiveness Inventories (Rathus, 1973; McCormick, 1985), then the scores for each should be highly correlated. Here, correlations of above .80 are needed to consider two parallel forms consistent.

Error. All three approaches to reliability are designed to detect the absence of error in the measure. Another way to look at reliability is to estimate directly the amount of error in the instrument. This is known as the standard error of measurement (SEM), and is basically an estimate of the standard deviation of error. As an index of error, the SEM can be used to determine what change in scores may be due to error. For example, if the instrument's SEM is 5 and scores changed from 30 to 25 from one administration to the next, this change is likely due to error in the measurement. Thus, only change greater than the SEM may be considered real change.

The SEM is also an important way to consider reliability because it is less easily influenced by differences in the samples from which reliability is estimated. The SEM has limitations because the number reflects the scale range of the measurement tool. You cannot directly compare the SEM from different instruments unless they have the same range of scores. For example, Zung's (1965) Self-Rating Depression scale has a range of 20 to 80. Hudson's (1982) Generalized Contentment scale, however, has a range of zero to 100. The size of the SEM of both scales is affected by their respective ranges. However, in general, the smaller the SEM, the more reliable the instrument (the less measurement error).

One way to solve this problem is to convert the SEM into a percentage, by dividing the SEM by the score range and multiplying by 100. This gives you the percentage of scores which might be due to error. By making this conversion you will be able to compare two instruments and, all other things being equal, use the one with the least amount of error.

Validity

The validity of an instrument refers to how well it measures what it was designed to measure. There are three general approaches to validity: content validity, criterion validity, and construct validity. The literature, however, is full of inconsistent—and occasionally incorrect—use of these terms.

Content validity.   Content validity assesses whether the substance of the items taps the entity you are trying to measure. More specifically, since it is not possible to ask every question about your client's problem, content validity indicates whether these particular scale items are a representative sample of the content area.

There are two basic approaches to content validity, face and logical content validity. Face validity asks if the items appear on the surface to tap the content. Face validity is determined by examining the items and judging if they appear to represent the content. To illustrate this, select any instrument from Part II and look at the items. In your judgment do they look like they measure the content they are supposed to? If so, you would say the instrument has face validity.

This exercise demonstrates the major problem with face validity: it is basically someone's subjective judgment. Logical content validity, however, is more systematic. It refers to the procedure the instrument developer used to evaluate the content of the items and whether they cover the entire content domain. When this information is available, it will be presented by the researcher in a manual or in the research article on the instrument. While you will want to use an instrument that has logical content validity, the necessary information is frequently not available. Consequently, you will often have to settle for your own judgment of the face validity.

Criterion validity. This approach to validity has several different names, and therefore generates a great deal of confusion. It is also known as empirical validity or predictive validity, among other terms. In general, criterion validity asks whether the measure correlates significantly with other relevant variables. Usually, these other variables are already established as valid measures. There are two basic types of criterion validity: *predictive validity* asks whether the instrument is correlated with some event that will occur in the future. *Concurrent validity* refers to an instrument's correlation with an event that is assessed at the same time the measure is administered.

These approaches to validity are empirically based and are more sophisticated than content validity. Quite simply, both approaches to criterion validity are estimates of an instrument's association with some other relevant measure where you would most likely expect to find a correlation. When such information is available, you can be more confident that your instrument is accurately measuring what it was designed to measure.

Another approach to criterion validity is known-groups validity. This procedure (sometimes called discriminant validity) compares scores on the measure for a group that has the problem and one that does not. If the measure is valid, then these groups should have significantly different scores. Different scores support the validity by suggesting that the measure actually taps the presence of the variable.

Construct validity. The third type of validity asks whether the instrument taps a particular theoretical construct. For example, does the Splitting Scale (Gerson, 1984) really measure this defense mechanism? The answer can be partially determined from criterion validity, of course, but a more convincing procedure is construct validation. In order to consider an instrument as having construct validity, it should be shown to have convergent validity *and* discriminant validity, although some authors use the terms as if they were separate types of validity.

Convergent validity asks if a construct, such as loneliness, correlates with some theoretically relevant variable, such as the amount of time a person spends by him or herself. Other examples could be whether the measurement of loneliness correlates with the number of friends or feelings of alienation. In other words, do scores on a measure converge with theoretically relevant variables? With convergent validity you want to find statistically significant correlations between the instrument and other measures of relevant variables. Discriminant validity, on the other hand, refers to the way theoretically nonrelevant and dissimilar variables should not be associated with scores on the instrument. Here you would want to find instruments that are not significantly correlated in order to believe the score is not measuring something theoretically irrelevant.

Another approach to construct validity is factorial validity, by which researchers determine if an instrument has convergent and discriminant validity (Sundberg, 1977, p. 45). Factorial validity can be determined with a statistical procedure known as factor analysis designed to derive groups of variables that measure separate aspects of the problem, which are called "factors." If the variables were similar, they would correlate with the same factor and would suggest convergent validity. Since this statistical procedure is designed to detect relatively uncorrelated factors, variables not associated with a particular factor suggest discriminant validity.

This approach to factorial validity is often a statistical nightmare. First of all, one needs a large number of subjects to use the statistic appropriately. Moreover, the statistical procedure has numerous variations which are frequently misapplied, and the specific values used for decision making—known as eigenvalues—may not be sufficiently stringent to actually indicate the variables form a meaningful factor. Consequently, the construct validity findings can be misleading (Cattell, 1966; Comrey, 1978).

A second way to estimate factorial validity is to determine if individual items correlate with the instrument's total score and do not correlate with unrelated variables. This procedure, nicely demonstrated by Hudson (1982), again tells you if the instrument converges with relevant variables and differs from less relevant ones. Factorial validity, then, helps you decide if the theoretical construct is indeed being measured by the instrument.

Let us now summarize this material from a practical point of view. First of all, to monitor and evaluate practice you will want to use instruments that are reliable and valid. You can consider the instrument to be reliable if the items are consistent with each other and the scores are stable from one administration to the next; when available, different forms of the same instrument need to be highly correlated in order to consider the scores consistent.

Additionally, you will want to use measures that provide relatively valid assessments of the problem. The simplest way to address this issue is to examine the content of the items and make a judgment about the face validity of the instrument. More sophisticated methods are found when the researcher correlates the scores with some criterion of future status (predictive validity) or present status (concurrent validity). At times you will find measures that are reported to have known-groups validity, which means the scores are different for groups with and without the problem. Finally, you may come across instruments that are reported to have construct validity, which means that within the same study, the measure converges with theoretically relevant variables and does not correlate with nonrelevant ones.

It is important to look beyond these validity terms in assessing research or deciding whether to use a scale, because many researchers use the terms inconsistently. Moreover, we must warn you that you will probably never find all of this information regarding the reliability and validity of a particular instrument. Since no measure in the behavioral and social sciences is completely reliable and valid, you will simply have to settle for some error in measurement. Consequently, you must also be judicious in how you interpret and use scores from instruments. However, we firmly believe that a measure without complete substantiation is usually better than no measure at all.

STATISTICAL PRINCIPLES OF INTERPRETATION

We are now at a point to discuss the next of our four basic sets of principles, namely how to make meaningful the number assigned to the variable being measured.

In order for a number to be meaningful it must be interpreted by comparing it with other numbers. This section will discuss different scores researchers may use when describing their instruments and methods of comparing scores in order to interpret them. If you want to understand a score, it is essential that you be familiar with some elementary statistics related to central tendency and variability.

Measures of Central Tendency and Variability

In order to interpret a score it is necessary to have more than one score. A group of scores is called a sample, which has a distribution. We can describe a sample by its central tendency and variability.

Central tendency is commonly described by the mean, mode, and median of all the scores. The mean is what we frequently call the average (the sum of all scores divided by the number of scores). The mode is the most frequently occurring score. The median is that score which is the middle value of all the scores when arranged from lowest to highest. When the mean, mode, and median all have the same value, the distribution is called "normal." A normal distribution is displayed in Figure 2.1.

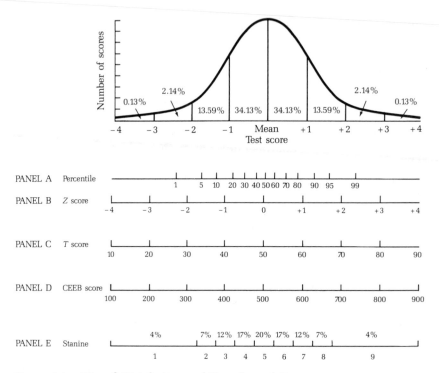

Figure 2.1. Normal Distribution and Transformed Scores

By itself, a measure of central tendency is not very informative. We also need to know how scores deviate from the central tendency, which is variability. The basic measures of variability are range, variance, and standard deviation. The range is the difference between the lowest and highest scores. The number tells us very little, besides the difference between the two extreme scores. The variance, on the other hand, is a number representing the entire area of the distribution, that is, *all* the scores taken together, and refers to the extent to which scores tend to cluster around or scatter away from the mean of the entire distribution. Variance is determined by the following formula:

$$\Sigma (X - M)^2 \div n - 1$$

In this formula X represents each score, from which the mean (M) is subtracted. The result is then squared and added together (Σ); this number is then divided by the sample size (n) minus one.

The square root of the variance is the standard deviation, which reflects the deviation from the mean, or how far the scores on a measure are from the mean. The standard deviation can also indicate what percentage of scores is higher or lower than a particular score. With a normal distribution, half of the area is below the mean and half is above. One standard deviation above the mean represents approximately 34.13% of the area away from the mean. As Figure 2.1 illustrates, an additional standard deviation incorporates another 13.6% of the distribution, while a third standard deviation includes approximately 2.1% more, and a fourth represents about .13%.

These concepts are important because you will need to use them with different types of scores, as well as with some methods of comparing scores.

Raw scores and transformed scores. We now consider some of the different types of scores you might obtain yourself or come across in the literature. The basic types are raw scores and transformed scores, of which we will consider percentile ranks, standard scores, and three different standardized scores. Raw scores are the straightforward responses to the items on a measure. In your use of an instrument to monitor your practice you will most likely only need to use raw scores.

Raw scores from instruments with different possible ranges of scores, however, cannot be compared with each other. Consider the same issue we discussed earlier in terms of comparing different SEMs. A score of 30 on a 20 to 80 scale cannot be compared with a score of 35 on a zero to 100 scale. In order to compare scores from such measures you will need to transform the scores so that the ranges are the same.

Probably the most widely used transformed score—although not the best for our purposes—is a percentile rank. A percentile rank represents the proportion of scores which are lower than a particular raw score. With percentile ranks the median score is the 50th percentile, which is displayed in Panel A of Figure 2.1. Because percentile ranks concern one person's score in comparison to others' scores in the same sample, its use in single system evaluation is infrequent. Rather, you will be concerned with your client's score in relation to his or her previous scores.

You could use percentile rank, however, by comparing the percentile rank at the end of treatment with that at the beginning of treatment. To do so, you would simply count all scores with values less than the one you are interested in, divide by the total number of scores, and then multiply by 100. If you did this with two instruments with different ranges, you could compare the performances as reflected in percentile ranks.

A more useful transformed score is the standard score. Standard scores are also known as "Z scores." Standard scores convert a raw score to a number that reflects its distance from the mean. This transformed score derives its name from the standard deviation as it is essentially a measure of the score in terms of the extent of its deviation from the mean. The standard score, therefore, usually has a range from −4 to +4. A standard score of +1 would indicate that the score was 34.1% above the mean. With standard scores the mean is always zero. The standard score is displayed in Panel B of Figure 2.1.

Standard scores are derived from the following formula:

$$Z = (X - M) \div Std.$$

where Z is the transformed score, X is the raw score, M is the sample mean, and std. is the standard deviation. By using this formula you can transform raw scores from different instruments to have the same range, a mean of zero and a standard deviation of one. These transformed scores, then can be used to compare performances on different instruments. They also appear frequently in the literature.

Raw scores can also be transformed into standardized scores. Standardized scores are those where the mean and standard deviation are converted to some agreed-upon convention or standard. Some of the more common standardized scores you'll come across in the literature are T scores, CEEBs, and stanines.

A T score has a mean of 50 and a standard deviation of 10. This is seen in Panel C of Figure 2.1. A CEEB, which stands for College Entrance Examination Board, has a mean of 500 and a standard deviation of 100. The CEEB score is found in Panel D of Figure 2.1. The stanine, which is abbreviated from *standard nine*, has a mean of 4.5, and a range of one to nine. This standardized score is displayed in Panel E of Figure 2.1.

To transform a raw score to one of these standardized scores, or any other standard you might want, you do the following:

1. Decide on a mean and standard deviation you want for your standardized scores.
2. Multiply the raw score by the standard deviation which you selected in step 1.
3. Add the results of step 2 to the mean you selected in step 1.

By following these procedures your raw score is transformed into a standardized score.

To summarize, transformed scores allow you to compare instruments which have different ranges of scores; many authors will report data on the instruments in the form of transformed scores.

Methods of comparing raw and transformed scores. As we stated earlier, in order for a score to be interpreted it must be compared with other scores. We will consider two basic procedures for comparing scores: norm-referenced comparisons and self-referenced comparisons.

Norm-referenced comparisons allow you to interpret a score by comparing it with an established "norm." Ideally, these normative data should be representative of a population. When you compare your client's score with a norm, you can interpret it in terms of how the performance relates to the sample mean and standard deviation, in other words, how much above or below the mean your client is in relation to the norm.

Unfortunately, we do not have many instruments for rapid assessment that have well-established norms. Norm-referenced comparisons also have many limitations. One limitation is that the samples used to develop instruments are frequently not representative of a larger population. Secondly, even if the sample is representative, it is quite possible that your client is dissimilar enough to make the norm-referenced data nonrepresentative. Consider two examples. The Selfism scale (Phares and Erskine, 1984) was designed to measure narcissism and was developed with undergraduates; these data might not be an appropriate norm with which to compare a narcissistic client's scores. It would make sense, though, to make norm-referenced comparisons between an adult client whose problem is due to irrational belief on Shorkey's Rational Behavior Scale (Shorkey & Whiteman, 1977), since these normative data are more representative of adult clients. Additionally, norms represent performance on an instrument at a specific point in time. Old normative data, say ten years or older, may not be relevant to clients you measure in 1987.

To avoid these and other problems with normative comparisons, an alternative method of interpreting scores is to compare your client's scores with his or her previous performance. This is the basis of the single system research designs we discussed in Chapter 1 as an excellent way to monitor practice.

When used in single system evaluation, self-referenced comparison means you interpret scores by comparing performance throughout the course of treatment. Clearly, this kind of comparison indicates whether your client's scores reveal change over time.

There are several advantages to self-referenced comparisons. First of all, you can usually use raw scores. Additionally, you can be more certain the comparisons are relevant and appropriate since the scores are from your own client and not some normative data which may or may not be relevant or representative. Finally, self-referenced comparisons have the advantage of being timely—or not outdated—since the assessment is occurring over the actual course of treatment.

PRACTICE PRINCIPLES INVOLVED IN MEASUREMENT

Having discussed what a "good" instrument is and how to statistically interpret scores, we turn now to the actual use of measures to monitor your client's progress and evaluate your effectiveness. In choosing to use a particular instrument you need to consider several factors which determine its practical value. These include utility, suitability and acceptability, sensitivity, directness, nonreactivity, and appropriateness. All of these issues concern the practical value of using instruments in your practice.

Utility

Utility refers to how much practical advantage you get from using an instrument (Gottman & Leiblum, 1974). In clinical practice, an instrument which helps you plan—or improve upon—your services, or provides accurate feedback regarding your effectiveness would be considered to have some utility (Nelson, 1981).

Certain features of an instrument influence its utility. Chief among these are the measure's purpose, length, your ability to score it, and the ease of interpreting the score. Instruments that tap a clinically relevant problem, are short, easy to score, and easy to interpret are the most useful for practice.

Suitability and Acceptability

A second element of an instrument's practical value is how suitable its content is to your client's intellectual ability and emotional state. Many require fairly sophisticated vocabulary or reading levels and may not be suitable for clients with poor literacy skills or whose first language is not English. Similarly, instruments may require the ability to discriminate between different emotional states, a set of skills which may not be developed in young children or severely disturbed clients. Psychotic clients, for example, are usually unable to accurately fill out most instruments.

If the scores are not accurate reflections of your client's problem, then the use of the instrument has little practical advantage. Furthermore, in order for an instrument to have practical value, your client will need to perceive the content as acceptable (Haynes, 1983), and the process of measuring the problem throughout treatment as important. If your client does not realize that measuring his or her problem is important, then the instrument may not be given serious attention—or even completed at all. Similarly, if your client sees the content as offensive, which might occur with some of the sexuality instruments, the responses may be affected. As we will discuss later, in these circumstances you will need to familiarize your client with the value of measurement in practice, and select an instrument with an understanding of your client's point of view.

Sensitivity

Since measurement in practice is intended to observe change over time, you will need to use instruments that are sensitive to tapping those changes. Without a sensitive instrument your client's progress may go undetected. You might ask, though, "Aren't scores supposed to be stable as an indicator of reliability?" Yes, and in fact, you will want an instrument that is both stable and sensitive. In other words, you will want to use instruments that are stable unless actual change has occurred. When real change does occur you will want an instrument that is sensitive enough to reveal that change.

Directness

Directness refers to how the score reflects the actual behavior, thoughts, or feelings of your client. Instruments that tap an underlying disposition from which you make inferences about your client are considered indirect. Direct measures, then, are *signs* of the problem, while indirect ones are *symbols* of the problem. Behavioral observations are considered relatively direct measures, while the Rorschach Inkblot is a classic example of an indirect measure. Most instruments, of course, are somewhere between these extremes. When deciding which instrument to use you should try to find ones that measure the actual problem as much as possible in terms of its manifested behavior or the client's experience. By avoiding the most indirect measures, not only are you preventing potential problems in reliability, but you can more validly ascertain the magnitude or intensity of the client's problem.

Nonreactivity

You will also want to try to use instruments that are relatively nonreactive. Reactivity refers to how the very act of measuring something changes it. Some methods of measurement are very reactive, such as the self-monitoring of cigarette smoking (e.g. Conway, 1977), while others are relatively nonreactive. Nonreactive measures are also known as unobtrusive. Since you are interested in how your treatment helps a client change, you certainly want an instrument that in and of itself, by the act of measurement, does not change your client.

At first glance, reactivity may seem beneficial in your effort to change a client's problem. After all, if measuring something can change it, why not just give all clients instruments instead of delivering treatment? However, the change from a reactive measure rarely produces long-lasting change, which therapeutic interventions are designed to produce. Consequently, you should attempt to use instruments that do not artificially affect the results, that is, relatively nonreactive instruments. If you do use instruments that could produce reactive changes, you have to be aware of this in both your administration of the measure—and try to minimize it—and in a more cautious interpretation of results.

Appropriateness

This final criterion of an instrument's practical value is actually a composite of all the previous principles. Appropriateness refers to how compatible an instrument is for single system evaluation. In order for it to be appropriate for routine use it must require little time for your client to complete and little time for you to score. Instruments that are lengthy or complicated to score may provide valuable information, but cannot be used on a regular and frequent basis throughout the course of treatment because they take up too much valuable time.

Appropriateness is also considered in the context of the information gained from using an instrument. In order for the information to be appropriate it must be reliable and valid, have utility, be suitable and acceptable to your client, sensitive to measuring real change, and measure the problem in a relatively direct and nonreactive manner. Instruments that meet these practice principles can provide important information which allows you to more fully understand your client as you monitor his or her progress.

3

TYPES OF MEASUREMENT TOOLS

For many years, a large number of practitioners in the human services thought that many of the problems they worked with were "unmeasurable." How, went the question, can you really measure what a person thinks or feels about himself or herself? How can you measure affect, attitudes, qualities of life, and so on?

But in recent years, there has been a gradual shift in thinking among human service professionals. More and more of us are convinced that most if not all of the problems with which we work are indeed measurable—in terms that lead to increased precision and objectivity in our practice. In fact, one practitioner/researcher put the issue bluntly: "If you cannot measure the client's problem, it does not exist" (Hudson, 1978).

The point, perhaps, is that while it may be difficult to measure our client's problems, it is not impossible. Many of our clients do indeed bring us problems that are globally or vaguely defined at first. The task for the practitioner is to help the client define (or redefine) the problem in terms that are amenable to measurement. This is not because measurement is an end in itself. Rather, it is because once a problem is measurable, it will also be clear enough to work with in an intervention program. Thus, your job as a practitioner is to find some *indicator* of the problem that can be measured so that you will know just how well you are doing with your intervention program. Examples of such indicators abound: a score on a self-esteem questionnaire can be an indicator of how a person feels about himself or herself, a score on a depression scale is an indicator of the intensity of one's depression, and so on.

Again, the goal here is not measurement for the sake of measurement. The goal is responsible, accountable practice. From the point of view of measurement, this means finding some indicator of the problem that is representative, that will be accessible to measurement, and that will provide leads for both conducting your intervention and evaluating its effects. Without these dimensions, we never could lay claim to being accountable practitioners.

The remainder of this chapter provides an overview of a number of ways to measure clients' problems. Although the central concern of this book is standardized rapid assessment instruments, we do not believe these instruments are the only way clients' problems can be measured. There are other complementary methods of measurement, to be selected depending on the needs of the individual case. The methods we will be discussing here include behavioral observations, self-anchored and rating scales, client logs, unobtrusive measures, electromechanical measures, and of course, standardized questionnaire measures. Since each of these sections will simply be an overview of the area, we hope you will be encouraged to pursue the literature for further information on each method. (Some comprehensive references on measurement of practice problems include Goldstein & Hersen, 1984; Hudson, 1982; Barlow, 1981; Mash and Terdal, 1981; Haynes and Wilson, 1979; Cone and Hawkins, 1977; Ciminero et al., 1977; Kendall and Hollon, 1981; Haynes, 1978; Nay, 1979; Hersen and Bellack, 1981; Bloom and Fischer, 1982.) We also hope that by the end of this chapter, you will agree that just about any problem—behavior, feeling, attitude, thought, activity—can be measured.

BEHAVIORAL OBSERVATIONS

When you think of observing behaviors, you probably think of behaviors that you actually can see. But we have a broader definition. By behavior, we mean just about anything people do, whether it is overt (kissing, walking) or covert (thinking or feeling). The key here is that the behavior must be measurable and countable by someone, whether it is the client counting his negative thoughts, or number of cigarettes smoked, or someone else observing the number of times a child swears.

Behavioral measures, based on observation of the client's actual functioning, are particularly useful because they typically are the most direct expression of the problem and therefore tend to have a great deal of validity. Also, because behavior can be counted and defined fairly specifically, this form of measurement can add a good deal to the precision and reliability of one's assessment. Moreover, the behaviors can be a ready target for intervention efforts.

There are three basic ways of measuring or counting behavior: frequency, duration, and interval counts. Frequency measures involve simply counting how often a problem behavior occurs. The key consideration in deciding to use a frequency count is that the problem occurs too often and needs to be decreased (say, negative self-thoughts, anxiety, number of cigarettes smoked), or the problem does not occur often enough and needs to be increased (number of chores completed, number of meetings attended).

The second type of behavioral measure is a duration count. Duration counts are used when the problem involves time, that is, a problem occurs for too long a period (tantrums, crying, tension, headaches), or does not occur for a long enough period (studying, exercise, maintenance of penile erections). Duration counts require a timepiece such as a stop watch to keep track of how long a behavior lasts. It is, of course, crucial to be absolutely clear about when a behavior begins and ends to be certain about how long it lasts.

The third type of behavior observation is an interval measure. This might be used when a behavior occurs so often or for so long a period, or is so difficult to break into discrete units, that it becomes problematic to use frequency or duration recording. In interval recording, a period of observation is selected and then divided into equal blocks of time. Then all the observer has to do is record whether or not the behavior is displayed at all during each of the recording intervals. The behavior is recorded as occurring only once per interval no matter how long or how many times it has occurred.

With all three forms of behavior observation, it is very important for the practitioner and whoever is doing the counting to have the problem specifically defined and to be clear about the time period involved in the recording. To this end, it is particularly important to have two observers, say the practitioner and the person who will be doing the observing, engage in "reliability checks." In these, the two recorders observe the problem behavior and then compare their observations. To obtain a reliability coefficient (a measure of how much or little the score depends on the particular scorer) one observer's figures are divided into the other's (always the largest into the smallest). For frequency measures, you would divide the largest number of observed behaviors (say 12) into the smallest (say 10) and come up with a figure of .83 or 83 percent reliability. For duration measures, the same method is used, dividing the smaller duration by the larger (10 minutes of observed problems divided by 12 minutes equals .83). For interval measures, you would divide the number of intervals in which two observers agreed the problem did or did not occur by the total number of intervals to get your reliability figure.

Behavioral observation is often accompanied by the use of coding forms or other tools, such as prepared checklists, 3 × 5 cards to keep track of behavior, stop watches, golf counters to tally up everything from calories to negative thoughts, cassette tape recorders, coins to move from one pocket to another, and so on. The methods of counting are limited only by your own imagination, as long as they are portable and relatively unobtrusive. Behavioral observation is one of the most flexible, useful, and important types of measurement you can implement in order to monitor and evaluate your client's progress.

SELF-ANCHORED AND RATING SCALES

The self-anchored scale is so flexible and can be used with so many problems and in so many situations that it has been dubbed "the all purpose measurement procedure" (Bloom, 1975). The practitioner and client together can construct a self-anchored scale to measure any given problem (Bloom & Fischer, 1982). All you do is establish a range that focuses on the intensity of the problem as perceived by the client, that is, the degree or extent to which the client experiences some feeling, thought, or condition. Any number of problems can be measured by this procedure: thoughts and feelings, the intensity of pain, fear, sexual excitement, and so on. These scales are very easy to construct and can be used as many times per day as the occasion calls for. Indeed, for many problems that only the client himself or herself can report on, this may be the only kind of measurement available.

The process of developing a scale is relatively straightforward. Once the problem area is defined, you present to the client a picture of a social or psychological thermometer, with one end being the most intense end of the problem and the other the least intense. Then you select the number of points for the scale. We usually recommend 0–10 or 1–9, although if the client has difficulty in discriminating among that many points, you can collapse the scale to 1–7 or 1–5 points. Make sure you are clear with the client that they are equal intervals, so that the difference between 1 and 2 on the scale is no greater than the difference between 5 and 6. Finally, you and the client attempt to anchor the scale points using as much concrete detail to define each point as possible. Thus, if level 9 is the most intense level of the problem, you would try to help the client describe what he or she is experiencing at that level. A self-anchored scale measuring intensity of cognitions of sadness might look like this:

1 ——— 2 ——— 3 ——— 4 ——— 5 ——— 6 ——— 7 ——— 8 ——— 9

No cognitions
of sadness
(feel mellow,
happy, glad to
talk with friends
and colleagues)

Moderate
sadness
(feel unhappy,
prefer to be
left alone)

Intense sadness
(crying all day,
thoughts of
suicide, locked
in my room all day)

Rating scales are constructed pretty much the same way as self-anchored scales, with one difference: the client does not rate himself or herself. Instead, someone else uses the scale to rate the client. These scales have a number of uses. They can be used when the client is unable to rate himself or herself or when an additional perspective on the problem is needed. They can even be used as "analogue measures," for example, to rate an artificially created situation such as a structured role play which the practitioner sets up to evaluate the progress of clients on selected behaviors (say, in the learning of job interview skills).

Both self-anchored and rating scales are very easy to use and their flexibility and face validity recommend them highly.

CLIENT LOGS

One of the most important tasks of the practitioner is to collect from the client as much systematic and accurate information as possible in order to develop and evaluate the optimal intervention plan. One way of facilitating this process is through use of client logs. These essentially are journals kept by clients of events they consider relevant to their problem. The logs are more or less formal records of these events that can be used to minimize distortion when the client presents information to the practitioner.

Client logs have two purposes. The first one is to aid in the overall assessment by helping pinpoint problems. Part of this process is to use the material collected in the log as a source for hypotheses about events that seem related to the client's problems as well as the client's reaction to these events.

The second purpose is for evaluation. Client logs provide an on-going record of the client's activities involving the problem being worked on. The value of the client logs can be greatly expanded by, first, using each incident recorded as a behavioral count of the occurrence of the problem and second, adding a self-anchored scale on which the client records the intensity of his or her feelings about the recorded event.

You can use the same format for all client logs. This consists of a prepared form which lists across the top of the page the types of information that should be collected. This information, of course, varies with the nature of the problem, but usually includes a brief description of the event, what preceded or followed it, who was present, and what the client did, thought, or felt about it. Along the left-hand side of the page, the time of each event is recorded. A general model for client logs is presented in Figure 3.1.

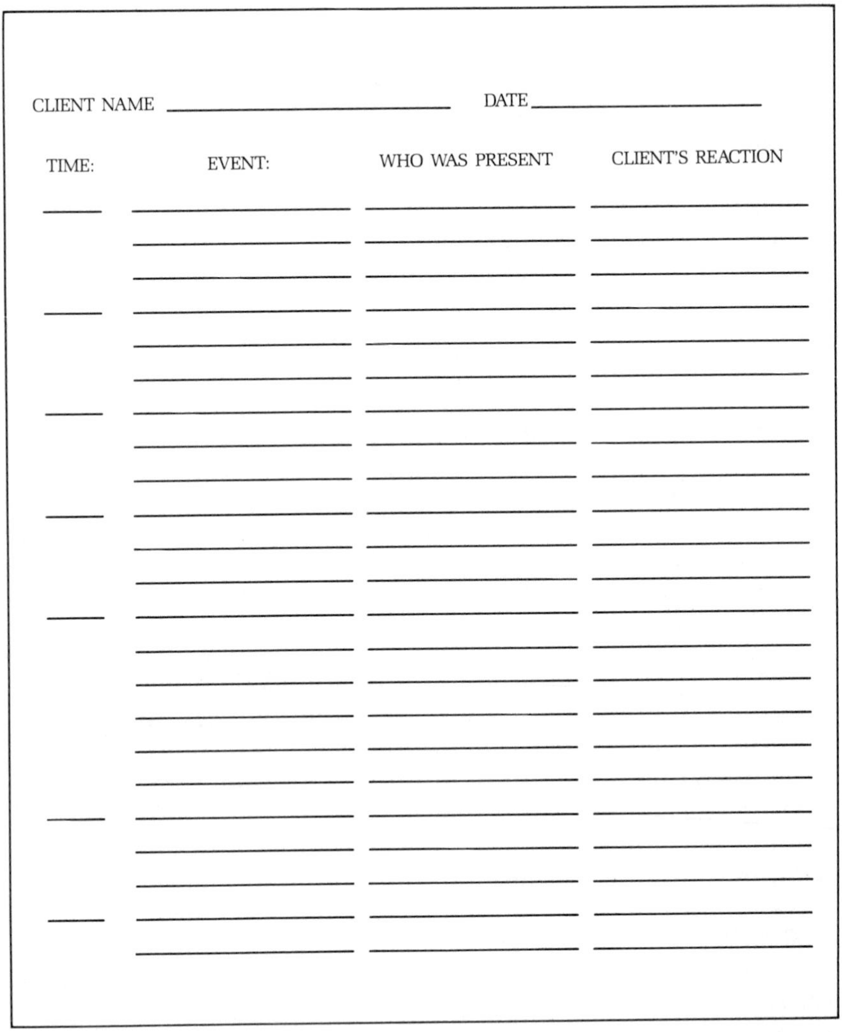

CLIENT NAME _____ DATE _____

TIME:	EVENT:	WHO WAS PRESENT	CLIENT'S REACTION
___	_____	_____	_____
	_____	_____	_____
	_____	_____	_____
___	_____	_____	_____
	_____	_____	_____
	_____	_____	_____
___	_____	_____	_____
	_____	_____	_____
	_____	_____	_____
___	_____	_____	_____
	_____	_____	_____
	_____	_____	_____
___	_____	_____	_____
	_____	_____	_____
	_____	_____	_____
	_____	_____	_____
___	_____	_____	_____
	_____	_____	_____
	_____	_____	_____
___	_____	_____	_____
	_____	_____	_____

Figure 3.1. General Model for Client Logs (*Adapted From Bloom and Fischer, 1982*)

Client logs essentially vary according to the time and the category of the problem. Regarding time, the client can be asked to record whenever an event occurs or at specifically preset intervals. Categories of problems can also vary from relatively open (record any event you think is critical) to very specific including a number of different categories (e.g., who was present, what did he or she say, what did you say, what was their reaction, and so on). A number of examples of these different types of logs are available in Bloom and Fischer (1982) and Schwartz and Goldiamond (1975).

UNOBTRUSIVE MEASURES

An obvious concern you might have in using measurement procedures with your client is that the actual act of measurement might affect or change the client's problem before you even begin your intervention, thereby distorting your results. We discussed this in Chapter 2 as reactivity, and indeed, the potential for change due to measurement itself is an ever-present danger. There are procedures for overcoming reactivity in some measures and even using it to clinical advantage (see, e.g., Nay, 1979), which we will discuss further in Chapter 6. But there are also some measures that were designed specifically to avoid the problem of reactivity; these are called unobtrusive measures (Webb et al., 1966). Essentially, these are measures where the client is not aware of being measured so that there is little chance that the act of measurement itself can produce change.

There are several types of unobtrusive measures that might be useful. Behavioral products enable one to measure the effects of behavior (e.g., items left on the floor or the number of cigarette butts in an ashtray). Physical traces are evidence left by an individual or group without the knowledge it will be used for other purposes. Simple observation involves the act of observing the client without being seen or noticed (e.g., through a one-way mirror).

One other unobtrusive measure that is particularly useful is the archival record, involving data that are kept for one purpose, but can be used to help evaluate an intervention program. Indeed, in some instances, these records might directly reflect the problem on which the practitioner is working (school attendance, school grades, recidivism rates, agency record data, etc.).

It is important to be aware of the fact that archival data can also present some frustrations because often they are incomplete, lost, or difficult to gain access to, but because they do overcome problems of reactivity they can be a particularly valuable measurement tool.

ELECTRO-MECHANICAL MEASURES

One area of measurement that usually receives fairly scant attention in the practice literature is the use of electro-mechanical devices for psychophysiological assessment. This oversight may be due to a natural aversion on the part of many human service practitioners to hook clients up to mechanical devices. Further, these devices tend to be expensive and/or complicated to use, and are usually not available to practitioners.

On the other hand, in certain circumstances these devices may be the measurement procedure of choice. This obviously is in a situation when the physiological measures are clearly related to the social or psychological problem. The broad range of electro-mechanical devices available and their increasing utilization in areas such as behavioral medicine, sex therapy, and treatment of anxiety and stress suggest their potential importance for practitioners.

Among the most commonly used devices are the electromyogram (EMG) to measure muscle action; the electrocardiogram (EKG) for cardiac reactions; blood pressure readings; skin resistance level (SRL) and response (SRR) to measure sweat gland activity; electroencephalogram (EEG) to monitor brain functions; and strain gauges and plethysmographs to monitor sexual arousal. These devices are most useful when one can be relatively certain the devices possess an adequate degree of reliability and validity, and when there appears to be a unique physiological response that can provide information on social or psychological variables that would permit an appropriate intervention plan (Kallman and Feuerstein, 1977). Some additional sources that can be reviewed for information include Rugh and Schwitzgebel (1977), Lang (1977), Epstein (1976), Haynes (1978), and Ray and Raczynski (1984).

STANDARDIZED MEASURES

Our main reason for this discussion of other measurement procedures is that they *are* available, they have important uses, and just because we are focusing on standardized, self-report instruments, we don't mean to exclude other methods. In fact, our basic recommendations for measuring client problems are first, use the best (most direct, valid, reliable, sensitive) measure available every time you can; and second, whenever possible, try to use more than one measure because problems usually are not confined to only one area of human functioning. Two measures can provide a far broader and more accurate picture of changes in a client's problem than one. And standardized, self-report instruments are only one of several measures available.

In fact, though, just about all of the rest of the book will be concerned with the use of standardized measures. A standardized measure is one that has uniform procedures for administration and scoring, and contains a series of structured questions or statements designed to elicit information from the client. These statements do not vary each time the questionnaire is administered. In addition, standardized measures usually provide a numerical score for estimating the magnitude, intensity, or degree of the client's problem (Levitt and Reid, 1981). There is usually information available about the psychometric properties of the measure, the purpose and interpretation of the measure, its reliability and validity, scoring and administration, and sometimes norms for comparison of individual scores with the scores of groups who have been scored on the measure previously.

There are literally thousands of standardized measures available for just about any type of problem a practitioner might have to deal with in practice. Similarly, there are many different types of standardized measures including scales, checklists, inventories, indexes, and so on. Further, these measures have been developed to be filled out not only by the client (self-report), but by professionals and significant others. However, many of these measures are excessively long, complicated, difficult to score and/or interpret, and have weak or questionable psychometric information available about them. Indeed, precisely because there are so many of these measures available, we consider the primary purpose of this book the selection of those instruments that would be most useful to you in your practice.

Our effort to select from the many thousands of available instruments and develop a useful set of measures focused on rapid assessment instruments (RAIs). Several characteristics distinguish RAIs from other forms of standardized measures (Levitt and Reid, 1981):

1. They are self-report measures, filled out by the client.
2. They tend to be short (one to two pages), easy to administer, and easy to complete (usually in less than 15 minutes).
3. They are generally written in a clear simple language that the client can understand.
4. They can be scored rapidly, often in the presence of the client.
5. The interpretation of the measure is straightforward and clear.
6. Use of the measure by the practitioner does not require extensive knowledge of testing procedures.
7. They do not require subscription to a particular theoretical perspective.
8. They provide a systematic overview of the client's problem as well as information on individual aspects that may be discussed in the interview.

9. The overall score provides an index of the degree, intensity, or magnitude of the client's problem.
10. They can provide a structured means for collecting data that is standardized and comparable across applications of the measure, both for individual clients, and across all clients.
11. They can be used on a one-time basis, or as repeated measures, thereby producing information on changes in the client's problem over time by comparing scores from one administration to another. The scores obtained can be plotted on a single system design chart such as those illustrated in Chapter 1, allowing easy visual inspection of changes.

As you can see, these instruments have a great deal of potential for adding immensely useful information to practice. They can be used as a guide to treatment planning, can provide feedback regarding progress, can provide evidence as to overall effectiveness, and can even provide information that will be useful to the practitioner in the give and take of the clinical interview. All of this can be accomplished within the context of the interview; very little additional time is required for the client to complete and practitioner to score the measure.

Now while it might seem as though these instruments are the answer to the practitioner's dream, even a panacea for all measurement problems, in fact, some problems do exist in using these measures. In the remainder of Part I, we will discuss standardized measures in more detail, including their strengths and limitations, and particularly, how you can administer them in a way that will provide you with optimal results.

The Issue of Standardization

Because there are so many measures available, it is important to have clear criteria for selecting a measure. In this section we explain the criteria we used in selecting the instruments included in this book. Essentially, just about all of the measures we examined can be considered standardized. There are two main aspects of standardization. The first is that a standardized measure has uniform items, scoring procedures, and method of administration that do not change no matter how many times you administer the instrument or to whom you administer it. (The one exception to this might be the extra care you would want to take to explain the instrument to people who have trouble in understanding its application.)

Secondly, standardized measures generally have certain types of information available about them. That is, it is the responsibility of the developer of an instrument to provide sufficient information about it to allow a potential user to make a sound judgment about the measure's value. The areas of information include purpose and interpretation, reliability, validity, scoring, administration, and norms. (Norms refer to interpreting the meaning of a score on an instrument in relation to scores of other groups of people who have taken it, or in relation to achievement of some preset criterion, e.g., qualifying for some type of license; these areas are discussed in more detail in Chapter 2, and in publications by the American Psychological Association, 1974; Anastasi, 1982; Cronbach, 1970).

Just because a measure does not have all of this information does not mean it is not standardized. Instruments vary on the extent to which complete information is available, especially concerning validity, because of the difficulty of developing such information. This is particularly true if the measure is relatively new. On the other hand, to the extent that information from all or most of these categories is available for any given measure, you can make a more rational decision and select a better instrument than if only some of this information is available.

Standardization is not the same thing as "objectivity" (Cronbach, 1970). If a measure is "objective," then every observer who sees a performance arrives at exactly the same report. The more two observers disagree, the more subjective is the observation and evaluation.

Problems Addressed

As we indicated earlier, there are standardized measures available for just about any area of human functioning. Measures are available that examine general or broadly defined dimensions such as environments, including ward, treatment, and correctional environments (Moos, 1974, 1975a & b, 1979); personality; adjustment; competence; and mental health (see, e.g., the collection of measures in Buros, 1978, and listed in Part II of this book). But standardized measures also address just about any specific problem area you might conceivably face in practice. One sourcebook alone (Comrey et al., 1973) lists 45 categories of measures in specific problem areas ranging from alcoholism to juvenile delinquency to sex to vocational tests. The measures available span the full range of human functioning including behaviors, cognitions, attitudes, and feelings.

Of course, most of these measures are not included in this book for reasons indicated earlier: some are too sophisticated or require too much training to be easily used in practice, many are simply too long or difficult for the client to fill out readily, many do not have sufficient psychometric data to allow a reasoned judgment about their practical advantages, and many are not feasible for use in single system design as repeated measures.

Focus of Measures

There are a number of different dimensions that characterize an instrument. One is the degree to which the measure assesses a range, from the client's global perceptions to more specific reactions. The client may be asked to describe his or her feelings in general about some state of affairs ("Do you feel depressed?"), or at the other end of the continuum, might be asked to indicate how many hours he or she cries per day.

Another related dimension distinguishes broad personality measures from measures of specific problem areas. Some of the broader personality measures, such as the Rorschach Test or the Thematic Apperception Test (TAT), focus on the client's reaction to ambiguous visual stimuli and produce broadly based diagnostic categories regarding the client's psychological functioning. At the other end of the continuum, some instruments are focused around specific problem areas, for example, a scale on sexual satisfaction which provides a specific index of the level of the client's sexual satisfaction with his or her partner.

Instruments may also be categorized as state versus trait measures. In essence, a "trait" is viewed as a relatively enduring or stable characteristic of an individual, and is broadly defined. A "state," on the other hand, is seen as a more transitory emotional condition typically elicited by a particular stimulus or environmental condition. Though controversy continues over whether human personality and functioning are best conceptualized in terms of traits or states, both kinds of measures have value to the extent that they facilitate the prediction and modification of individual behavior (Mischel, 1968). And while we cannot hope to resolve this controversy here, we do want you to be aware that a few of the instruments in Part II do make this distinction.

Yet another dimension of standardized measures is their directness. As we discussed in Chapter 2, directness refers to the extent to which you have to make an inference regarding the behavior, cognition, or feelings being assessed. All things being equal (which they rarely are), we believe that the more direct the measure, the more potential value it has for your practice. Thus, in choosing between two instruments, if one produces a score from which you need to make an inference about the client's condition, and the other produces a score that directly reflects the client's problem, we would suggest the latter measure is a more useful one.

More or less direct measures can include observations of specific behaviors, self-reports of clients of their thoughts and feelings, and any other method of measurement that requires minimal inference about the client's condition. Although we have attempted to locate as many direct measures as possible, we actually have provided a broad range—from more or less direct to more or less indirect—because many standardized measures do require some degree of inference about the client's condition yet contain reliability and validity information that is as good as the more direct measures.

Standardized measures also differ in who is to fill them out. Some are designed to be filled out by practitioners or significant others about someone else (e.g., a parent or counselor checking items on an inventory about a child's behavior). Others, including all those in Part II of this book, are designed as self-report measures, in that the person filling out the questionnaire responds with his or her thoughts or feelings to items on the instrument that typically refer to the respondent's own condition, problem, or circumstances.

Some standardized measures have cutting scores. These are scores, based on the norms for that measure, which distinguish different groups of respondents. Thus, if research on a particular measure has shown that people who score above a certain point can be distinguished from people below that point with regard to possession of certain characteristics, that would be a cutting point. For example, based on extensive research on the Clinical Measurement Package (Hudson, 1982), scores above 30 on each instrument tend to distinguish people who have a clinically significant problem on that particular measure from those who do not. Other instruments may have cutting scores that distinguish different categories of respondents, for example, not depressed, moderately depressed, and severely depressed. While cutting scores can be a great advantage to the practitioner in interpreting a given measure, they generally should be used with caution and not too rigidly; a few-point difference in one person's score as compared to someone else's may not, in reality, reflect a true difference between those two people, even though one may be on one side of the cutting score and the other person on the other side.

Finally, standardized measures also vary according to the age of the target group of users. Some measures are designed for children and adolescents, some for both children and adults, and a few target the elderly. We have tried to include a cross-section of available measures for all groups. However, because there are natural limitations on children's abilities to fill out questionnaires, there are fewer instruments available for them. Most measures for children are actually rating scales which are filled out by adults about children, and this type of instrument is not included in this book.

Procedures for Developing
Standardized Measures

In this section we will try to provide a little clarity about some of the terms used to describe a variety of different types of measure. Although we will be using standard references as guides (e.g., Anastasi, 1982; Cronbach, 1970; Miller, 1977), we must admit that there is not universal acceptance of all these terms.

Standardized measures are developed in any number of ways: The author may intuitively think up items that could be included on an instrument, he or she may select items based on a review of the literature (both of these using a face validity criterion), or by using more empirically oriented methods. Instruments developed empirically have been described by Golden et al. (1984) as having three basic methodologies: (1) developing items on the basis of their ability to discriminate between two other groups (say, between depressed and nondepressed clients); (2) using items that show a high correlation with an external variable of interest (e.g., correlation of items on a depression scale with psychiatric ratings); (3) using items that group together empirically on the basis of factor analysis (i.e., intercorrelations of certain items from a pool of items).

Standardized measures also vary according to the number of dimensions included within one measure. The scores on some measures reflect only one dimension, such as overall magnitude of depression. While unidimensionality generally is considered desirable, some measures are multidimensional; they include subdimensions (often based on factor analysis). For example, an overall score dealing with self-esteem may encompass subscales reflecting feelings of self-worth under different circumstances. Most experts believe unidimensional measures are more desirable because they are more efficient—easier to use—and because multidimensional measures, to some extent, consist of several unidimensional measures collected on one instrument. On the other hand, if all subdimensions of a multidimensional measure have good reliability and validity, the multidimensional instrument can be at least as useful as several unidimensional measures, and perhaps more efficient.

Finally, there are different categories of measures including inventories, indexes, and scales, although the terms are often used interchangeably. The most generic term for these measures is "questionnaire" because they all require someone to write responses on a piece of paper. Inventories and checklists typically include a range of behaviors, thoughts, or feelings and the respondent indicates whether or not these appear to be present.

Indexes and scales, the most commonly used (and confused) terms, are really variations of the same phenomenon. Both are composite measures constructed from two or more indicators or items. Some observers believe the distinction between the two is that indexes produce ordinal levels of measurement while scales produce interval levels (Hudson, 1981). Others claim that both indexes and scales are ordinal measures, but distinguish between the two according to the manner in which their scores are assigned. Indexes are said to be constructed through the simple accumulation of scores assigned to individual attributes, while scales are constructed by assigning scores to patterns of attributes (Babbie, 1983). Thus, scales are seen as taking advantage of the intensity structure that may exist among attributes.

Basically, though, both indexes and scales are developed using logical inference and a numerical scale which assumes some underlying continuity and which the respondent can realistically act upon in self-rating (Miller, 1977). However, there are so many different types of measures that are differentiated on a technical basis that a brief review of these measures, based on the work of Miller (1977), follows. The most commonly used standardized measures fall into the following categories:

Thurstone equal appearing scale. This is a scale comprising a number of items whose position on the scale is determined by ranking operations, i.e., in its development experts make judgments as to the order of the items. The respondent then selects the responses that best describe how he or she feels.

Likert-type scale. This commonly used scale is comprised of a series of items to which the client responds. The scores on each item are summed to produce an overall score. The client indicates agreement or disagreement with each item on an intensity scale. It is particularly useful in ordering people regarding attitudes.

Guttman scale-analysis. This technique is an attempt to describe the unidimensionality of a scale. Only items meeting a criterion of reproducibility are acceptable (i.e., if we know a respondent's extreme position, we should be able to reproduce all of his or her responses). If this scale is unidimensional, a person who has a more favorable attitude about some variable than another person should respond to each item with equal or greater favorableness than the other. Each score on the scale corresponds to a response pattern or scale type; thus, the score can be used to predict the response of all items.

Scale discrimination techniques. These techniques also seek to develop a set of items that are unidimensional, have equal-appearing intervals, and measure intensity. Aspects of the first three types of scales described above and, hence, their advantages are combined here.

Rating scales. This type of procedure is an attempt to obtain an evaluation or quantitative judgment about personality, group, or institutional characteristics based upon personal judgments. The respondent or rater places the person or object being rated at a point along the continuum or in one of an ordered series of categories, and then a numerical value is assigned to the point or category. Rating scales can be used to assess a wide variety of attitudes, values, and social activities.

Paired comparison. This procedure attempts to assess psychological values of qualitative stimuli without knowledge of any corresponding respondent values. Respondents are asked to select the more favorable of a pair of statements or objects over a set of several pairs, and an attempt is made to order the statements or objects along a continuum. This procedure is often called "forced choice."

Semantic differential. This type of measure attempts to assess the meaning of an object to the respondent. The respondent is asked to rate a given concept on a series of seven-point, bipolar rating scales. The rating is made according to the respondent's perception of the relatedness or association of the adjective (e.g., good-bad, fair-unfair) to the concept being rated.

Other available techniques include multidimensional scaling (Miller, 1977) and item-response theory (Reckase, 1984). These are more complicated and beyond the scope of this book. However, some of the procedures described above are represented in Part II; hence, their brief description here.

THE RAI: FULL CIRCLE

Rapid Assessment Instruments—as standardized measures—are not limited to one type of scale or index. Any measure we could locate that was standardized, short, easy to administer and score, based on self-reports, focused on a problem which you might see in clinical practice, and contained relatively useful psychometric properties was reviewed for inclusion in Part II, as long as it was available from the authors.

4

ADVANTAGES AND DISADVANTAGES OF RAPID ASSESSMENT INSTRUMENTS

In Chapter 3 we discussed a variety of tools for measuring your practice. Though rapid assessment instruments (RAIs) are most amenable to routine use with most clients, their use is not without limitations. In this chapter we will discuss some of the advantages and disadvantages of using RAIs to monitor your client's progress and evaluate practice.

ADVANTAGES

We believe, as do others (e.g., Bloom and Fischer, 1982; Wittenborn, 1984), that using RAIs in practice has enormous value in terms of enhancing effectiveness and accountability. Among the advantages of particular importance to your clinical practice are efficiency, accessibility, disclosure, comparability, and the potential for theoretical neutrality.

Efficiency

Perhaps the major strength of RAIs is their efficiency. Rapid assessment instruments are efficient because they are easy to administer, do not require extensive training, and tend to be short in length; thus, they do not require much time for scoring. RAIs are efficient also because they are readily available from the professional literature and are usually inexpensive to use. Any clinician can easily have available right at his or her desk a number of RAIs to apply with a given client depending on the problem and situation.

Accessibility

RAIs can provide access to information about the client that may be hard to observe overtly. As this volume illustrates, RAIs have been developed to measure a large variety of attitudes, feelings, and behaviors, and self-anchored scales can easily be developed by you for those problems without a standardized instrument. RAIs also have the potential of providing information about certain behaviors that are only observable through self-reports, such as magical thinking or a client's feelings. In addition, self-report instruments indicate how important a problem is to the client in terms of its level or magnitude.

Disclosure

RAIs enable the client to disclose sensitive information that he or she might find difficult to verbalize (Fischer & Gochros, 1975; Hudson, 1982). This is particularly advantageous during the initial phases of treatment before you and your client have developed a trusting relationship. For example, during an initial interview a client may be relucent to discuss particular sexual behaviors or dissatisfaction (Wincze & Lange, 1982). This type of information, however, may be disclosed by completing the Sexuality Arousability Inventory (Hoon and Chambless, 1987) or the Index of Sexual Satisfaction (Hudson, 1982).

Comparability

Another advantage of RAIs is comparability. You can make comparisons two ways: by comparing scores with some established norm or by comparing a client's performance with previous scores. The advantage of self-referenced comparison, you will remember, is that you can monitor your client's progress throughout treatment.

Neutrality

A final advantage to consider is that many RAIs have the potential of being theoretically neutral. We say potential because many instruments are germane to a theory and most of our knowledge in clinical practice is derived from theoretical constructs. Nonetheless, many instruments do not require that you adhere to a particular theory in order to use them to help you monitor treatment.

Clearly, neutrality is not an absolute characteristic of instruments. In fact, many are designed to assess a problem from a specific theoretical perspective, such as the Rational Behavior Inventory (Shorkey and Whiteman, 1977). On the other hand, instruments like Hudson's scales (Hudson, 1982) or Stiles' (1980) Session Evaluation Questionnaire are not theoretically based. More importantly, even those instruments that have been developed within a particular theoretical framework may be used to monitor practice even if you do not adhere to the theory, or are using a treatment approach derived from a different theoretical orientation.

DISADVANTAGES

In spite of their many advantages, RAIs are not a panacea. In fact, clinical measures have several limitations. These disadvantages tend to relate to psychometrics, practical utility, and the agency context in which you might work. As we shall discuss, however, many of these limitations may be minimized by the way you use the RAIs.

Psychometric Disadvantages

Four of the basic disadvantages of using RAIs pertain to psychometrics. First of all, while many instruments have reliability and validity data, these research findings are only estimates based on particular groups. The psychometric data come from a group and it is difficult to determine if, indeed, the instrument would be reliable and valid for your particular client. In clinical practice your client's problem would probably not be reflective of the norm for, say, a group of college sophomores. The focus of your practice is most likely a single system, such as an individual or a family.

One way to minimize the adverse effect of this issue is to be judicious about accepting scores as "truth." Any score is simply an estimate of some attribute, and should not be accepted uncritically. Moreover, scores contain error, which means that decisions about practice can be incorrect if based strictly on any instrument. You should never, for example, terminate treatment simply based on the score from a rapid assessment instrument. In other words, we suggest you use scores as indicators in monitoring practice but never rely on a score too much. In this respect, rapid assessment instruments should be used in conjunction with other methods of evaluating progress, such as supervision and case consultations.

RAIs also tend to be obtrusive and may cause some reactive effect in your client. As explained above, reactivity occurs when the assessment process alters the actual problem. While reactivity is more often found in self-monitoring behavioral observations (e.g., Johnson & Bolstad, 1973; Kazdin, 1982), RAIs can induce reactivity by sensitizing your client toward the content.

Similarly, RAIs are susceptible to distorted responses by your client. A client may distort the truth to provide socially desirable responses, or to suggest that it is too early to terminate treatment or that clinical services are not needed.

As we will discuss more fully in Chapter 6, you can minimize these potential disadvantages by informing your client of the importance of measurement in practice. Moreover, you must reassure your client that his or her honest responses will be helpful to treatment. After all, as Mischel (1981) has noted, "We cannot expect honest self reports unless people are convinced that their honesty will not be used against them" (p. 482). This reassurance will need to be presented explicitly, and evidenced throughout the course of treatment.

A fourth disadvantage related to reliability and validity is that while many instruments focus on a particular problem, most are not specific enough to measure its nuances. Depression, for example, has many dimensions relating to social behavior, cognitions, biochemistry, and affect. Many instruments, although certainly not all, are simply too general to tap these subtleties. Consequently, you may not find an instrument that addresses the specific aspect of your client's problem.

The most feasible way to minimize this limitation is to use RAIs that are as specific and direct as possible. This will allow more confidence in the validity of the scores, although you should always remain somewhat critical. Additionally, we suggest you use more than one instrument whenever possible. The use of multiple measures can further increase your confidence in the scores.

Practical Disadvantages

Another set of disadvantages pertains to how RAIs are used in your practice. One limitation is that since RAIs are so easy to administer, score, and interpret they can be overused. This can occur by administering a scale too frequently or by relying too much on what you think the score means.

The most direct way to minimize this is to allow sufficient time to elapse between administrations. We suggest about one week between administrations for most rapid assessment instruments, though some can be administered twice a week. Finally, you can minimize overuse of an instrument by using parallel forms when they exist. For example, you could use the Rathus Assertion scale and the Simplified Rathus Assertion scale on alternating weeks. However, using parallel forms may mean you have to transform the scores in order to compare them, and parallel forms frequently are not available.

Another practical disadvantage is that rapid assessment instruments are relatively new to the literature. Consequently, instruments may not exist to measure a client's problem, or even more likely, its nuances. In such circumstances you may very well have to use a measure you consider second choice, one that may not be as direct or specific as you would like.

You may also find practical limitations due to your client's abilities and/or awareness of the problem. For example, a young child's reading level may not be sufficient for RAIs, or the child's awareness and memory may not be adequate to provide valid information.

The most obvious way to minimize these potential problems is to find instruments that are appropriate for your client's ability. You should also try to be creative in solving each unique problem as it arises, such as reading the instrument to the child or administering it frequently enough to allow the child to be able to respond accurately. When you do apply creative ways of resolving these types of problems, you also should remember that these instruments are standardized, and in order to keep scores as valid as possible you should follow the same procedures each time you use the instrument with the client.

Agency Disadvantages

You may encounter other obstacles to the use of RAIs in an agency setting (Thomas, 1978; Toseland & Reid, 1985). There may be open opposition from colleagues and supervisors who are unfamiliar with the value of monitoring practice. Or demanding caseloads and paper work may take up too much of your time.

The latter restraint is minimized, as you know, by the fact that RAIs are short and do not take much time to complete and score. Moreover, the administration of RAIs is flexible enough so that your client can complete them outside the office or prior to the interview with you.

Open opposition to monitoring and evaluating your practice may be more difficult to overcome. In part it may necessitate taking a leadership role and educating your colleagues about the benefits of measurement in practice. (You might even consider giving them copies of this book; your colleagues—and the authors—will thank you for it, too.)

On the other hand, agencies can provide a context in which the use of measurements is enhanced (Austin, 1981). For example, you can encourage your agency to use RAIs by obtaining a variety of different measures that assess the clinical problems most frequently seen in your agency. Agencies can also arrange for release time for you to search for additional instruments to add to your repertoire, as well as providing group supervision to improve staff ability to use instruments to monitor and evaluate practice.

RAIs are like all other assessment procedures, including clinical judgments: they are not perfect. But, like clinical judgment, when used wisely in the context of the entire therapeutic relationship and all the information available about the client, they can be invaluable to effective practice.

5

SELECTING MEASURES FOR PRACTICE

While this book provides many of the instruments you will need in your evaluation of practice, there will be many times when you will want additional ones or even other types of measures. This is especially true since the field of measurement is growing very rapidly and more and more instruments are becoming available. In this chapter we will discuss how you can go about selecting RAIs. We will consider what you will be measuring within certain important contexts and will show you how to locate measures. We will also suggest questions you can ask to help you evaluate which measure to use. Our emphasis is on short, standardized RAIs but we will mention additional types of measurement tools when appropriate.

DEFINING WHAT YOU NEED TO MEASURE

By the end of your assessment interviews you will probably have a pretty good idea about your client's problem and some of the objectives of treatment. It is helpful to have the problem or treatment goals narrowed down in fairly concrete terms. You will then not only be more likely to effect change, but you will have a better chance of finding an appropriate tool to measure this change. Thus, one guideline to consider as you define your measurement need is to be concrete and specific about what your client is to change and the goals of treatment.

Once you have decided what you intend to measure, whether it is a specific client behavior—like the length of a temper tantrum—or a less direct construct, such as self-esteem or marital discord, you will need to decide which type of measurement tool to use.

First consider the source of the observations. Who should complete a behavioral rating scale, or is it better to have the client use a self-report instrument? You have three choices here: the client, a significant other, or you as the clinician.

With children you might very well need a significant other, such as a parent or teacher. The reason for this is that children are not the most reliable and valid sources of observations; plus, they may be limited by reading ability, recall, and awareness. Consequently, you might very well need to use behavioral rating scales. For example, you might consider having a teacher complete the Teacher's Self-Control Rating Scale to use in conjunction with the Children's Perceived Self-Control Scale (Humphrey, 1982). Using more than one measure will enhance the validity of your observations, and allow you to be more certain about the change you are monitoring in your client.

You can also measure the problem or treatment goals yourself. We usually do this anyway, and call it clinical judgment. By using a standardized measurement tool your accuracy may substantiate the clinical judgment as well as improve it. Another tool to help evaluate your own practice is the Session Evaluation Questionnaire (Stiles, 1980). This instrument assesses the depth and smoothness of a therapy session and can serve as an indicator of the quality of each treatment session. Such instruments give you more feedback on how well your clinical work is progressing.

We believe a very good observer of the client's problem and treatment goals is the client. In fact, as we mentioned before, some clinical problems can only be measured by the client. But clearly clients are not the only source of information. In deciding which source to use you should first consider which person will be the most reliable and valid observer. Then, if it is at all possible to use more than one source, do so. This will increase the amount and quality of information you receive and enable you to be more confident about what you are measuring.

Another factor in defining what is to be measured is your practice approach. While we argued earlier that one advantage of RAIs is the potential of being theoretically neutral, you may very well want a measure consistent with a particular theory, or you may want to avoid certain theoretically based instruments. For example, the clinician working with a borderline personality may want a theoretically based instrument like the Selfism Scale (Phares & Erskine, 1984) or the Ego Identity Scale (Tan et al., 1977). The cognitive-behaviorist, on the other hand, might prefer the Ellis Irrational Values Scale (McDonald and Games, 1972). In deciding what to measure, then, you should ask if the specific problem or treatment goal implies a certain theoretical perspective. Also, consider whether what you are measuring can be tapped by measurement tools from different theories. This may broaden not only your clinical orientation, but the range of possible instruments from which to select.

In deciding what to measure you should also consider where the measurement will occur. This is important because many client problems differ across various settings (Kazdin, 1979; Wicker, 1981). Similarly, observations in one environment may not generalize to other environments (Bellack and Hersen, 1977; Mischel, 1968). One guideline in deciding where to make the observations is whether the clinical problem is seen as a state or trait. As we mentioned in Chapter 3, state problems are considered more transitory and tend to be more apparent in specific settings. Trait behaviors, on the other hand, are believed to be more stable characteristics of an individual's general behavior (Levy, 1983), and therefore should be evident in a variety of settings.

If you consider your client's problem as a state, we suggest you use measurement tools that are completed in the appropriate environment, such as in a classroom or at the family dinner table if these are the specific places the problem occurs. If you believe the problem is more of a trait of your client, then you can be more flexible in where the measure is used. But you will need to be consistent, and make certain that the measurement is always recorded in the same setting, a topic we'll discuss more fully in the following chapter.

Whenever possible, the selection of instruments for monitoring practice should not be limited to one type of measurement tool, or even one source of observations. An optimal assessment package includes a self-report rapid assessment instrument, observations by significant others, a behavioral observation if possible, and perhaps a client log. Admittedly, it may be difficult to include all of these in daily practice with each and every client. You should, however, try to use as many as possible, provided they give you information you think relates to the client problem or treatment goals. This not only allows for more reliable and valid observations, but enables you to assess different aspects of the same problem.

How, though, do you decide on particular instruments for a particular client with a particular problem? The first step, of course, is to have a concrete and observable definition of the problem. Secondly, make sure the measures you are considering are relatively reliable and valid, and suitable to the respondent's reading level and ability to understand and complete the instruments. Next, familiarize yourself with the different self-reports and other types of measurement devices by completing them yourself. You should consider each item in terms of whether it is a sample of the client's problem. This will not only give you an understanding of the instruments, but will allow you to select the one that is most reflective of the subtleties of your client's problem. Once you have familiarized yourself with the different measurements, consider using as many as possible. The entire time for any individual respondent to complete the instruments should not exceed ten to fifteen minutes. Before asking a significant other (spouse, parent, roommate) to make some observations, make certain the person is invested in the client's progress and willing to comply with the task. Finally, consider if the measures are appropriate for your treatment approach; many are theoretically neutral, so this may not be much of a problem.

These considerations are illustrated by the following case example. Therapy was initiated for a family who sought treatment from one of the authors because of disciplinary problems with the teenage daughter who reportedly was "not herself." The child was "doing as she pleased," was truant from school for weeks at a time, and was arguing with her parents. At times she would lose control and hit or shove the mother. The assessment suggested that the mother, father, and daughter did not have age appropriate interpersonal boundaries (Minuchin, 1974), and that the child—not the parents—was in control of the family. Since most of the discord was between the mother and daughter, the former completed the Index of Parental Attitudes and the latter completed the Child's Attitude Toward Mother Scale (Hudson, 1982). To further evaluate the treatment the father was instructed to complete the Index of Family Relations (Hudson, 1982), and the school registrar reported the frequency of attendance. These theoretically neutral measures were assessed weekly over the course of treatment using structural family therapy techniques. This assessment package provided a sound picture of the family members' interpersonal relationships and one manifestation of the child's disciplinary problem.

LOCATING MEASUREMENT TOOLS

Once you have a good idea about what specifically you want to measure and with what type of tool, you have to find the measurement device. This book, of course, is designed to be one source of locating appropriate instruments. There may be occasions when you will need different types of measurement tools or additional instruments. Consequently, we offer some suggestions about where to start looking.

There are two general outlets for measurement tools: publishing houses and the professional literature. Publishing houses market measurement tools for profit. The cost may vary considerably, although most instruments are relatively inexpensive. In fact, an agency may be able to purchase a large number of instruments at a substantial savings. A list of some of the major publishers is presented in Table 5.1.

You can also find instruments in the journal literature, but this may require an expensive computer literature search. Consequently, you may decide to manually search reference indexes like Buros's (1982) *Mental Measurement Yearbook,* or review some of the seminal volumes on measurement. A list of works available since 1970 is presented in Table 5.2. All of these books either discuss different methods of measurement or present measurement devices, many of which are relevant to clinical practice. Another alternative is to examine the abstracts in certain journals that tend to emphasize measurement. Table 5.3 lists several journals that frequently publish instruments.

QUESTIONS TO ASK IN EVALUATING INSTRUMENTS

Between the publishing houses, books, and journals you will probably find an instrument or two for your measurement need. The question becomes, then, which measurement tool to use and how to select it. This issue actually addresses much of what we have considered throughout this book. On a general level, you will want to select the most reliable, valid, and practical instrument for your purpose. If no instrument meets these criteria, remember you can always construct a self-anchored scale.

While there are no definitive rules for evaluating measures, we suggest you consider instruments in the context of the research principles and practice principles we discussed in Chapter 2. To facilitate your evaluation of instruments from this perspective, we have categorized the research and practice criteria into 20 questions relating to the sample, reliability, validity, and practicality of an instrument. These questions are presented in Table 5.4, which can be used to facilitate your evaluation of measures.

Questions Regarding the Sample

When evaluating a measure consider the sample or samples from which the instrument was developed. If you intend to compare your client's scores with the normative data available, you should ask if the population is appropriate for your client. By appropriate we mean that your client could be considered a member of the population. It will be of little value for you to compare your client to a norm from a dissimilar population or with outdated data. Many times instruments are devel-

TABLE 5.1

Partial List of Publishers Marketing Measurement Devices

Academic Therapy Publications, 20 Commercial Boulevard, Novato, California 94947; (415) 883-3314

Associates for Research in Behavior, Inc. (ARBOR), The Science Center, 34th & Market Streets, Philadelphia, Pennsylvania 19104; (215) 387-5300

Behavior Science Press, P.O. Box BV, University, Alabama 35486; (205) 759-2089

Biometrics Research, Research Assessment and Training Unit, New York State Psychiatric Institute, 722 West 168th Street, Room 341, New York, New York 10032; (212) 960-5534

Bureau of Educational Measurements, Emporia State University, Emporia, Kansas 66801; (316) 343-1200

Center for Epidemiologic Studies, Department of Health and Human Services, 5600 Fishers Lane, Rockville, Maryland 20857; (301) 443-4513

Clinical Psychometric Research, P.O. Box 425, Ridgewood, Maryland 21139; no business phone

Consulting Psychologists Press, Inc., 577 College Avenue, P.O. Box 11636, Palo Alto, California 94306; (415) 857-1444

CTB/McGraw-Hill, Del Monte Research Park, Monterey, California 93940; (408) 649-8400, (800) 538-9547, in California (800) 682-9222

Educational and Industrial Testing Service (EDITS), P.O. Box 7234, San Diego, California 92107; (619) 222-1666

Family Life Publications, Inc., Box 427, Saluda, North Carolina 28773; (704) 749-4971

Institute for Personality and Ability Testing, Inc. (IPAT), P.O. Box 188, 1062 Coronado Drive, Champaign, Illinois 61820; (213) 652-2922

Institute for Psychosomatic & Psychiatric Research & Training/ Daniel Offer, Michael Reese Hospital and Medical Center, 29th Street and Ellis Avenue, Chicago, Illinois 60616; (312) 791-3826

Merrill (Charles E.), Publishing Company, 1300 Alum Creek Drive, Box 508, Columbus, Ohio 43216; (614) 258-8441

Monitor, P.O. Box 2337, Hollywood, California 90028; no business phone

Nursing Research Associates, 3752 Cummings Street, Eau Claire, Wisconsin 54701; (715) 836-4731

Personnel Research Institute (PRI), Psychological Research Services, Case Western Reserve University, 11220 Bellflower Road, Cleveland, Ohio 44106; (216) 368-3546

Person-O-Metrics, Inc., Evaluation & Development Services, 20504 Williamsburg Road, Dearborn Heights, Michigan 48127; no business phone

Professional Examinations Division/The Psychological Corporation, 7500 Old Oak Boulevard, Cleveland, Ohio 44130; no business phone

Psychodiagnostic Test Company, Box 859, East Lansing, Michigan 48823; no business phone

Psychological Assessment and Services, Inc., P.O. Box 1031, Iowa City, Iowa 52240; no business phone

Psychological Assessment Resources, Inc., P.O. Box 98, Odessa, Florida 33556; (813) 920-6357

Psychological Services, Inc., Suite 1200, 3450 Wilshire Boulevard, Los Angeles, California 90010; (213) 738-1132

Research Concepts, A Division of Test Maker, Inc., 1368 East Airport Road, Muskegon, Michigan 49444; (616) 739-7401

Research Press, Box 317760, Champaign, Illinois 61820; (217) 352-3273

Research Psychologists Press, Inc., P.O. Box 984, Port Huron, Michigan 48060; (313) 982-4556

Science Research Associates, Inc. (SRA), 155 North Wacker Drive, Chicago, Illinois 60606; (800) 621-0664, in Illinois (312) 984-2000

Scott, Foresman and Company, Test Division, 1900 East Lake Avenue, Glenview, Illinois 60025; (312) 729-3000

United States Department of Defense, Testing Directorate, Headquarters, Military Enlistment Processing Command, Attn: MEPCT, Fort Sheridan, Illinois 60037; (312) 926-4111

United States Department of Labor, Division of Testing, Employment and Training Administration, Washington, D.C. 20213; (202) 376-6270

University Associates, Inc., Learning Resources Corporation, 8517 Production Avenue, P.O. Box 26240, San Diego, California 92126; (714) 578-5900

Western Psychological Services, 12031 Wilshire Boulevard, Los Angeles, California 90025; (213) 478-2061

Reprinted from Corcoran, 1988, with permission from R. M. Grinnell, Jr. and F. E. Peacock Press.

Selected Volumes Since 1970 on Measurement Devices

Volumes Reprinting Measures

>Cautela (1977)
>Cautela (1981)
>Hudson (1982)
>Robinson and Shaver (1973)
>Mash and Terdal (1976)

Volumes Describing and Referencing Measures

>Anastasi (1982)
>Beere (1979)
>Buros (1978)
>Chun, Cobb and French (1975)
>Goldman and Busch (1978 and 1983)
>Goldman and Sanders (1974)
>Johnson and Bommarito (1971)
>Lake, Miles, and Earle (1973)
>McReynolds (1981)
>Miller (1977)
>Scholl and Schnur (1976)
>Southworth, Burr, and Cox (1981)
>Sweetland and Keyser (1983)

Volumes Discussing Measurement Methods

>Barlow (1981)
>Ciminero, Calhoun, and Adams (1977)
>Cone and Hawkins (1977)
>Goldman, Stein, and Guerry (1983)
>Goldstein and Hersen (1984)
>Haynes (1978)
>Haynes and Wilson (1979)
>Hersen and Bellack (1981)
>Lambert, Christensen, and DeJulio (1983)
>Lauffer (1982)
>Mash and Terdal (1981)
>MerLuzzi, Glass, and Genest (1981)
>Waskow and Parloff (1975)
>Woody (1980)

Reprinted from Corcoran, 1988, with permission from R. M. Grinnell, Jr., and F. E. Peacock Press.

TABLE 5.3

Journals Frequently Publishing New Measurement Tools

Applied Behavioral Measurement
Behavior Assessment
Behavior Therapy
Educational and Psychological Measurement
Journal of Behavioral Assessment and Psychopathology
Journal of Clinical Psychology
Journal of Consulting and Clinical Psychology
Journal of Personality Assessment
Measurement and Evaluation in Counseling and Development

---

oped on undergraduates, a group that really may not be clinically relevant for your purposes. This does not mean you should necessarily reject the instrument. However, you can be more comfortable with the reliability and validity of an instrument if the sample is sufficiently large and representative of a pertinent population, and the data are fairly current.

Questions Regarding Reliability

In order for an instrument to be helpful to your practice, you must be convinced it is a fairly reliable measure of the problem. Of course there will be times when you do not have information on a measure's reliability and you will need to be more critical when interpreting the scores. When possible, though, we suggest you use an instrument that has internal consistency coefficients of at least .80.

Another reliability question is whether an instrument is appropriate for repeated measurement throughout the course of treatment. As we have discussed before, you will want to try to find instruments that are stable over time. Unstable measures introduce mistakes or error in the information you use to monitor your clients. It is not possible to evaluate practice if the information contains too much error. We suggest you look first for those instruments that have test-retest reliability correlations of around .80. This is high enough to suggest the instrument is sufficiently free of error.

Infrequently you may be fortunate enough to have two forms of the same instrument, enabling you to alternate the administration of the instruments as you monitor your client. By doing so you minimize error due to such factors as memory, practice, and instrument decay (Kazdin, 1980). You will remember from our previous discussion in Chapter 2

TABLE 5.4

Questions to Consider in Evaluating Measurement Tools

Questioning the Sample
  1. Are the samples sizes sufficiently large?
  2. Are the samples representative of a relevant population?
  3. Are the data from the samples current or up-to-date?

Questioning the Reliability

  4. Is there sufficient evidence of internal consistency, say above .80?
  5. Is there stability over a relevant period of time?
  6. If more than one form is available, are they parallel?

Questioning the Validity

  7. Do the items appear to have face validity?
  8. Is there evidence of predictive or current validity?
  9. Are the criterion variables themselves reliable and valid?
  10. If there is known-groups validity, do the samples have different scores?
  11. Are scores correlated with relevant variables *and* uncorrelated with irrelevant ones.
  12. Are there cross-validation studies that also support the measure?

Questioning the Practicality

  13. Is the instrument short enough for rapid completion?
  14. Is the content socially acceptable to your client?
  15. Is the instrument feasible for your client to complete?
  16. Does the instrument seem to have utility?
  17. Is the instrument sensitive to measuring change?
  18. Does the instrument tap the problem in a relatively direct manner?
  19. Is the instrument relatively nonreactive?
  20. Is the instrument easy to score?

that the two instruments are called parallel forms or alternate forms. These two forms should correlate at a high magnitude, say above .80.

There will be times when no instrument tested for reliability is available and you will need to use an instrument that has no reliability data. In such cases you should be even more judicious in your reliance on the scores.

Questions Regarding Validity

Once you are satisfied with the instrument's reliability you should consider its validity. You will undoubtedly not find a measure that provides all the validity data you might desire, but at a minimal level the content of the instrument should have face validity. In other words, the instrument should appear to measure what it was designed to.

A more important validity consideration concerns criterion validity, either concurrent or predictive. When considering the criterion validity of an instrument we recommend that you also question whether the criterion itself is reliable and valid. Evidence of criterion validity is of little value if those variables are unreliable or invalid. In general, when predictive or concurrent validity data are available you would expect to find moderate to high correlations between the instrument and the criterion variable.

Alternatively, you might find instruments that are reported to have known-groups validity. Here you should consider if the subjects with the particular problem have scores that are different from a group of subjects without the problem. For example, scores on the Bulimia Test (Smith and Thelen, 1984) are different for people with an eating disorder compared to those without such a problem.

Finally, you might come across a measure that is reported to have construct validity. Often, this information is misleading because construct validity requires both convergent and discriminant estimates. When evaluating your instruments for construct validity, you will be looking for evidence that scores converge with theoretically relevant variables, such that statistically significant correlations are reported. Additionally, you may find evidence that the instrument is not associated with nonrelevant variables. Here you would hope to find instruments that are uncorrelated with the nonrelevant variables, that is, are not statistically significant.

Your review of an instrument's validity, whether one of the criterion validity procedures or construct validity, will probably be based on only one study. There is nothing wrong with selecting a measure based on just one study. However, some instruments have received a lot of attention and may have cross-validation studies. If the findings from these studies attest to the instrument's validity, they enable you to select the instrument for your use with greater confidence.

Questions Regarding Practicality

Another set of questions to ask in evaluating instruments concerns practice principles. Here you will find it helpful to consider the practical advantages of using a particular measure with a particular client who has a particular problem.

The first three practicality questions will help you determine the likelihood that your client will complete the instruments you have selected to measure the problem. Even the most reliable and valid instrument is of no practical value if your client leaves it unanswered.

There are three major aspects of an instrument that can influence whether you should select it for measuring your practice: its length, the social acceptability of its content, and the ability of your client to complete it. Lengthy instruments that are not acceptable or comprehensible to your client might cause him or her to become frustrated, offended, and less committed to observing the problem with rapid assessment instruments. This complicates the treatment process instead of complementing it, preventing you from determining whether change is actually occurring. Consequently, we recommend you select instruments that are short, that ask questions your client will consider socially acceptable, and that your client can readily comprehend.

You will also want to consider the practical advantage of the information gained from using an instrument, and whether the information would be available otherwise. Here we are speaking of an instrument's utility, and the point of concern is that the measure provide you with information useful to monitoring practice. For example, in treating a client complaining of feeling depressed because of too few dates you might consider measuring his or her social isolation, feelings of loneliness, depression, or dating and assertion skills. Feelings of isolation, loneliness, and depression may very well be the consequence of too few dates, while the lack of dating and assertiveness may be the actual reason he or she is not getting dates. If this were the case, then you would want to select a measure of these social skills, such as the Dating and Assertion Questionnaire (Levenson and Gottman, 1978) which appears in this book. By using these instruments you will gain valuable information about how well you and your client are treating the actual problem.

Since the purpose of measuring your practice is to determine when change is occurring, you will need to ask if the instrument also is sensitive. When data on sensitivity are available, they are often in the form of change scores before and after a clinical intervention. This information is frequently not available on measurement tools; thus, you might have to use the instrument to see if it indeed registers change in your client's behavior.

When selecting a measure we recommend you use those that seem relatively direct. Instruments differ in their degree of directness, and while you will rarely find an instrument that is as direct as you might like, we recommend that you try not to use measures that clearly consider the score to be a symbol of some problem as opposed to a sign of the problem. Most of the instruments in this volume are not totally direct, but only a few assume indirect dispositions of the problem. Measures that ask for responses about the frequency, intensity, or experience of a clinical problem are considered direct because the items are a sample of the problem. Instruments that assume some underlying cause or disposition to the problem, are indirect. The essential feature of our recommendation for using as direct a measure as possible is to select instruments which are not one step removed from what you are measuring. We recommend that you try to use instruments containing items that are considered examples or samples of the problem, and thus require less inference in interpreting the scores.

Additionally, in your evaluation of instruments, you should ask if a measure is nonreactive. Unfortunately, few measurement tools are totally nonreactive, so you will have to settle for the possibility of some change in your client due to the act of measurement. This is less of a problem with RAIs than with other tools, such as self-monitoring of specific behaviors like smoking. When selecting an instrument, consider whether it will appear to induce change in your client when none is occurring and use the tool which appears the most nonreactive. For example, does the client appear to be changing before the treatment has actually begun, such as during the baseline phase. If so, we would suggest you consider using another type of measurement tool or at least interpret the results with caution.

An additional practicality question to ask when deciding whether to use a measure is how easy it is to score. Those tools that are difficult and time consuming to score may be less feasible for your purpose of measuring practice. Consider for example, how frequently you would actually use an instrument that required anything more than ten or fifteen minutes to score. Thus, the size and structure of rapid assessment instruments, which make them fairly easy to score, are significant advantages.

6

ADMINISTERING THE INSTRUMENTS

Selecting the right measure for your client is only a first step. Like everything else in practice, if the measure isn't *used*, whatever effort you've put in to this point will amount to nothing. Perhaps even more important than selecting the right instrument is gaining the client's cooperation in completing it. This chapter presents some guidelines for administering measures that we hope will help you utilize them in an optimum way. The chapter is divided into two sections—the mechanics of administration and the skills of administration.

MECHANICS OF ADMINISTRATION

Several aspects of administering measures involve such "mechanics" as when, where, and how often they should be used. While we consider these to be the mechanics of administration, it is especially important to note here, as we will later in the chapter, the way you *present* the mechanics may be more important than the mechanics themselves.

Knowledge of Your Measure

There can be no substitute for the practitioner being well informed about the instrument. One suggestion we have is for you to administer to yourself any instrument you plan to use with clients. Get a feel for what it is like. In addition, you want to be knowledgeable about the meaning and interpretation of the instrument, its scoring, and its varied uses. Try to be prepared for any question the client could ask you about the measure. The best way to do this is to try to locate the original reference sources on the instrument so that you can be familiar with its functions. Once you read this material, take the instrument yourself, and interpret your own score, you will be better prepared to deal with the client's questions.

Where to Administer Your Measure

The instrument can be completed by the client in your office (or wherever your interview is conducted) or elsewhere. If you administer the instrument in your office, you again have two choices: it can be administered prior to your interview, say by a receptionist or intake worker, or by you during the interview. Part of the consideration here is time and the availability of other personnel. If someone else presents the instrument to the client, he or she should be able to answer questions about it. If you do the administering of the instrument, you should be sure you have the time available during the interview so that the client won't feel rushed. In both circumstances, you should attempt to provide the client with a quiet place to fill out the instrument so the client won't feel that others are observing his or her completion of the instrument. This can be embarrassing and may lead to distorted results.

On the other hand, having the client fill out the instrument at home can serve as a successful "homework" assignment, a task the client takes responsibility for completing on a regular basis. This can provide structure for your intervention program. Also, the client will be able to complete the instrument without the feeling of being watched. Filling out the instrument at home also may give the client more time to think about his or her responses, providing more thoughtful answers and possibly even additional material for your interview session.

Time of Administration

It should be clear to both you and the client that the instrument should be filled out at roughly the same time and place each time it is completed. If the client is to complete the instrument at home, and you have seen a pattern in the most likely times for the client to experience the problem, you might instruct the client to fill out the instrument in those circumstances at that time each week. This should minimize the possibility that the client's responses will change only because the conditions in which he or she completes the instrument change.

Number of Administrations

You, of course, have to decide how often the instrument should be administered, though some instruments come with instructions on this point. In general, the longer or more difficult the instrument is, the less frequently you would ask the client to complete it. An obvious consideration is how willing the client is to complete it. If he or she appears bored, annoyed, or reluctant to complete the instrument, or appears to be answering in patterned or repetitious ways, this is pretty clear feedback that you might be asking the client to fill it out too many times. It is important to get feedback on this each time the client turns in the questionnaire. You simply might ask, "How's the questionnaire going? Are you having a hard time in filling it out?"

Another consideration is the extent to which you rely on the instrument as your sole source of feedback on the client. The more you rely on it as a major source of information, the more often you would want to administer the instrument. As we mentioned earlier, whenever possible multiple measures should be the rule rather than the exception.

A general rule of thumb for most of the instruments included in Part II of this book is that they be used no more than twice per week, with once a week being the most typically recommended frequency of administration. In any case, the goal is to make completion of the measure as unaversive as possible.

Scoring

Unfortunately, though there are some similarities among many of the instruments included in this book as to how they are scored (just about all of them total the individual items to come up with an overall score), there also are many differences among them. Thus, we cannot provide you with one or two clear guidelines on how these instruments are scored except to say most can be done in just a few minutes with little or no training and no need for advanced mathematical skills. However, specific instructions for scoring the instruments in Part II are provided in the comments accompanying each instrument.

On the other hand, you do have some options regarding when and where you score an instrument. The first option is to score the instrument when the client is not there. This is most obvious when the client mails the instrument in to you or the instrument cannot be readily scored in just a few minutes.

The second option is to score the intrument while the client is watching. This, of course, provides the most rapid feedback to the client (we suggest providing feedback on the score and the meaning of the score as soon as possible no matter when the scoring is done). But scoring while the client is watching does have its drawbacks. You might become flustered and make an error in your scoring, or the silence while you are scoring or the experience of watching you score could make the client uncomfortable and anxious. In these circumstances, you might make a few remarks to the client while you are scoring, suggest that he or she does not have to remain seated, or provide some reading material (a good time for bibliotherapy) for the client.

Once you have scored the instrument, we suggest plotting the scores on a chart such as those illustrated in Chapter 1. Not only does this allow easy visual analysis of changes, but if the client is comfortable posting it in a conspicuous place in his or her residence, it can serve as a motivating factor as well.

USE OF COMPUTERS IN ADMINISTERING MEASURES
(by Paul R. Raffoul and Walter W. Hudson)

Throughout this book we have focused on the use of formal assessment tools that are completed and scored manually. In addition, we have described RAIs as paper-and-pencil devices that are completed by clients or practitioners. However, we should not overlook the growing number of clinical applications for microcomputers.

Almost twenty-five years ago, systems of computer-based test interpretation (CBTI) were utilized for scoring aptitude and interest tests and to provide profiles and grade predictions in academic settings. Personality tests such as the MMPI, the Sixteen Personality Factor Questionnaire (16PF), and the Rorschach were also the early focus of CBTI systems (Fowler, 1985).

Many benefits of computer interviews stem from their program standardization and reliability of administration. "In contrast to human-administered interviews, computer interviews are 100% reliable; computers never forget to ask a question, and given the same pattern of responses by a client, the computer will always ask the same questions in the same way" (Erdman et al., 1985, p. 761).

Another attractive feature of these systems is the computer's ability to perform many different functions at very high speeds. This relieves both the practitioner and the client from any involvement with scoring details thereby allowing more time to focus on information that is useful to clinical work.

Collecting certain types of sensitive information using computers is also often less uncomfortable or embarrassing to the client, and may provide an increased sense of privacy and objectivity in certain situations. Many of the advantages of a computer over a human being in certain situations have been summarized by Colby (1980):

> It [the computer] does not get tired, angry, or bored. It is always willing to listen and to give evidence of having heard. It can work at any time of the day or night, every day of the week, every month of the year. It does not have family problems of its own. It is never sick or hung over. Its performance does not vary from hour to hour or from day to day. It is very polite. It has a perfect memory. It need not be morally judgmental. It has no superior social status. It does not seek money. It can provide the patient with a copy of the interview to study. It does what it is supposed to and no more (and no less). (p. 114)

With computers' increasing capability for branching questions, the additional feature of flexibility can extend beyond paper-and-pencil questionnaires. Thus, a computer interview can be programmed for a specific individual's unique demands and information. Finally, computer administration of questions can increase data integrity by virtually eliminating incomplete responses since it calls the client's attention to items not completed.

Computerized measurement is not without disadvantages as well. One cited most often concerns the perceived impersonal and inhumane aspects associated with a machine rather than another human being. While research remains to be done in this regard, the literature to date suggests that "although there are clearly some individuals who do not like the idea of a computer interview and although individuals who are receptive to computers would not want to use them in every circumstance, the overwhelming majority of respondents report positive attitudes" (Erdman et al., 1985, p. 762).

A final consideration in computerizing aspects of clinical practice must include the cost of such a system. This cost is not limited to the machine(s) and necessary peripheral equipment, but includes the necessary cost of software for professional programs and/or the programming cost of having a program written for a particular practice setting.

In any case, it is very likely that the microcomputer will be used in even more novel ways in which clients participate in the evaluation of their problems and assessment of progress through direct interaction with the computer. An example of this use is the new professional software program called the Clinical Assessment System (CAS) which Hudson (1985) has produced to administer, score, and interpret any one of the Clinical Measurement Package (CMP) scales that are reproduced in Part II of this book. In this computer-based system, clients actually work at the keyboard of a microcomputer. The CAS program instantly checks client responses for consistency and provides an immediate opportunity to correct mistakes that might otherwise be undetected. This package also produces immediate graphic results of the client's progress whenever one or more of the CMP scales is completed on a regular or periodic basis.

Another way the microcomputer can relieve the practitioner of considerable labor is also illustrated by the CAS program. That is, the practitioner can use a word processor in conjunction with the CAS program to maintain all client notes and files in a single computer environment.

Many clinicians would like to use single systems designs as a means of monitoring and evaluating client progress over the course of their treatment. Unfortunately, some practitioners believe that they do not have the time or administrative supports needed to do such things as design, prepare, and maintain the charts and graphs that are needed for the effective use of single system designs in clinical practice. Microcomputers can solve some of these problems because of their ability to process information very accurately and rapidly. Again, for example, the CAS program automatically applies a single system design, specified by the practitioner, to the scores that are obtained when clients complete any of the CMP scales on a regular or periodic basis, and produces a graph of the scores with the specified single system design.

THE SKILLS OF ADMINISTERING MEASURES

A number of key principles underlie the smooth and effective administration of instruments. Essentially, these are all interpersonal skills; good rapport and a good relationship with the client will provide tremendous advantages to your work by facilitating cooperative give-and-take between you and the client.

Be Confident

We can't think of a more important piece of advice. Few, if any, clients will be willing to participate in any program (let alone fill out some strange questionnaire) with a practitioner who stumbles or makes apologies to the client for administering one of these measures. It is essential to appear confident to a client who may be very unsure of himself or herself or anxious and insecure in a new situation. Part of your confidence will come from familiarity with the instrument and experience in administering it. But we also urge you to engage in some structured role playing with colleagues prior to your first administration of one of these instruments; this practice experience may be just what it takes to provide you with the confidence to inspire the client to really want to cooperate with you.

Structure the Situation

In all therapeutic endeavors, it is very important that you explain to the client what you are doing, why you are doing it, how important it is, and, in the case of one of these instruments, how the scores will be used. Many people have built-in mistrust of questionnaires (they see them as "tests") and it is important for you to overcome that lack of trust. A good way of doing it is to provide the client with a clear rationale for the use of the measure. Assure the client of confidentiality of his or her scores (within organizational constraints). Perhaps use a medical analogy: "Just as your physician has to take your blood pressure to monitor how well you are doing, we have to have this information to insure we are on the right track." This kind of structure has been shown to be very effective in a whole range of situations when introducing new material to the client. Further, it is very important to explain to the client that this is not a "test" and that there are no right or wrong answers.

Sensitivity

Just as with any interview situation, you have to be very sensitive to the nuances in the client's response to your request to fill out the questionnaire. Perhaps this is just part of good interviewing behavior—the interpersonal skills that form the heart of therapeutic work anyway. This includes being sensitive to your client's reaction to determine whether he or she finds the content socially acceptable. But you have to be aware that some people may be concerned about what the questionnaire means, but will not voice their questions or objections uninvited. Therefore, unless you give them an opportunity to express themselves, your entire effort may be undermined. The guideline here: encourage the client to express his or her doubts, fears, and concerns about use of the measure.

Ethnic and Cultural Differences

Most of the measures in this book have been used largely with a white, middle-class American population. Thus, we urge that you use extreme care in utilization and interpretation of these instruments with clients from other ethnic or socioeconomic groups. This does not mean that these measures are inappropriate for nonwhite or extremely poor clients; only that data are not always available to attest to the utility of the measure for those groups.

If you do decide to use one of these instruments with a nonwhite or poor client, we urge again that you be especially sensitive. First of all, the whole context of use of questionnaires may have a different meaning to someone from a minority ethnic group. It is crucial to explore this with the client. Second, it is important to ascertain with each client whether he or she understands how to use the questionnaire and the meaning of every item. You would be shocked to find how many presumably "simple" words are not understood even by middle-class, white Americans. Imagine then the complications of using these measures with someone whose English vocabulary may be even more limited.

You might go over some or all of the items orally with your client to make sure he or she understands it. In fact, some practitioners, with some of the briefer instruments, routinely read each item aloud to the client, after which the client provides the responses orally. This can also be done in work with children. The problem with this method is that it may have a serious effect on the reliability and validity of the questionnaire because the practitioner could subtly influence responses by the way he or she presents the items.

Response Problems

All questionnaires are subject to certain types of bias. The first is called *response bias* in which the client responds to each item in a questionnaire in the same or patterned way (for example, all fours on a six-point scale). Another problem is called *social desirability response set* in which the client responds on the basis of what he or she thinks the response should be rather than on what he or she actually thinks or feels.

Some questionnaires are structured with an eye toward addressing these problems. For example, response bias can be handled by varying the directionality of items so that a four on one item might mean something negative and a four on another item might mean something positive. Some questionnaires attempt to control for social desirability response set by wording items in such a way that they do not obviously reflect social values.

But let's face it. Our clients are only human. There are many characteristics of a therapeutic setting that could encourage them to provide distorted answers on their questionnaires. These so-called demand characteristics include subtle cues from the practitioner which lead the client to think he or she "has" to improve. Or the client's payment of fees may lead him to focus on what he or she is getting for the money. Another related bias is the client's deliberate falsification of information on the questionnaire in order to achieve some goal—such as release from a court order or from prison, change in job or school status, or even a child or spouse falsifying information for fear that a parent or spouse might be hurt.

Unfortunately, there are no easy solutions to these problems. Perhaps the most important way to deal with them is for the practitioner to be "up front" about them. All of these questionnaires are indeed easy to falsify. It is very important for the practitioner to let the client know that he or she is well aware of how the measure can be distorted. In the context of a sensitive and trusting relationship and confidentiality regarding the client's responses, the practitioner might say:

> Look, I realize just how easy it is to put just about anything you want on these questionnaires to make yourself look better (or worse as the case might be). But it is very important that you and I have as honest and accurate answers as possible in this questionnaire. Otherwise, I just won't be able to know how well we're doing, and this means I won't be able to develop the best possible program to help you with your problems.

Clinical Uses

One advantage of these instruments is that they can provide "grist for the therapeutic mill"—more information for you and the client to discuss. There are numerous examples of interactions that can be centered on the instruments your client may be filling out.

Inconsistent responses. Inconsistencies in the client's responses may appear in the form of differences between a client's verbal responses and scores on the instrument or differences between scores on similar items on the instrument. In both instances, it is the practitioner's responsibility to inquire about and discuss those inconsistencies with the client. A good deal of clinical skill is called for here, because the purpose is not to "catch" the client in an error or lie. The purpose is to help the client clarify which response is most accurate and perhaps to review items on the instruments that may not be clear. Careful, sensitive exploration with the client of these inconsistencies could enhance both the relationship and use of the instrument.

Changes in scores. It is important for the practitioner to be alert to any changes—positive or negative—in the client's scores on the instrument and to discuss these with the client. This is, in essence, the monitoring function of these measures: keeping track of changes as the relationship progresses. It is important that the practitioner not be too overenthusiastic about positive changes or too disturbed about negative changes. First, one must be alert to the fact that the changes may not be due to the practitioner's interventions, but may be due to other events, client distortion, or the client's desire to please the practitioner. Second, the practitioner by his or her response could subtly encourage the client to keep reporting progress when no progress is being made, or conversely, discourage honesty if the client is doing poorly.

On the other hand, it is crucial for the practitioner to be able to encourage the client to report changes as honestly as the client can— whether they are negative or positive changes. This can be done by being straightforward about the importance of honest recording as an aid to treatment planning. Further, when the practitioner is relatively certain that positive changes are accurate, those changes can be used to support the intervention program and motivate the client to continue participating.

Individual items. Most RAIs included in this book have fairly good reliability as a complete instrument. Often, individual items have much lower reliability. Thus, discussion of individual items with clients is somewhat risky and one should not depend heavily on their interpretation. On the other hand, examining individual items—especially if the client initiates such examination—can prove useful. It can serve as a communication tool as you and the client open up discussion about a particular topic based on scores on that item. Individual items can provide clues to problems that need further exploration; for example, when one item changes very rapidly or doesn't change at all. Looking at individual items can clarify for the client how the instrument as a whole can be used to monitor progress. And a review of individual items can also enhance the relationship between the practitioner and client because it will highlight the practitioner's sensitivity to specific components of the client's problem.

In general, when using RAIs for clinical purposes, one must be prepared for a variety of reactions from the client, including anger, defensiveness, enthusiasm, happiness over changes, reluctance to speak about the scores, and so on. Each reaction, of course, must be dealt with not only as it affects the measurement procedure, but as it affects the overall treatment process. Sensitivity and empathy about presumably small issues such as those discussed above can pay large dividends in enhancing the clinical process.

Further, it is important to remember that use of RAIs constitutes only one part of the intervention process. Many conditions can affect changes in scores on a given measure, and, therefore, one must avoid overreliance on one score on one measure as the only indicator of change. In addition to sensitive clinical observation of changes in the client, this is one of the reasons we have encouraged use of more than one measure to monitor and evaluate changes.

A Program for Cooperation

The success or failure of any measurement program—indeed any activities requiring some outside effort on the part of the client—depends on how well the practitioner is able to elicit the client's cooperation. The suggestions in this chapter are an attempt to provide some ideas specific to the administration of standardized measures that we hope will enhance that cooperation.

But there is another way to approach the problem. The clinical literature increasingly is concerned with enhancing the client's cooperation in a whole range of other tasks and activities such as homework and behavioral assignments. This literature typically uses the term "compliance"—a term borrowed from the medical literature essentially referring to the carrying out of an assignment in the manner described by the person who assigned the task. There is increasing empirical evidence about a number of effective ways to gain such compliance or cooperation from the client. Following the work of Shelton and Levy (1981), these procedures will be briefly described here.

1. Assignments should be clear. Give specific details regarding when, where, how long, and under what circumstances the questionnaire should be completed. Provide written instructions when possible.
2. Give direct skill training and practice when needed. If the client has trouble filling out a questionnaire, practice filling it out in the office.
3. Reinforce cooperation. Provide praise and support for efforts at completing the instrument. Encourage others in the client's environment to do so too.
4. Begin small. Do not ask the client to do too much too often.

You can gradually increase what you do both quantitatively and in complexity as the client masters the earlier tasks.

5. Use prompts, cues, or reminders. You might have a copy of the instrument assignment posted where the client is likely to see it. You might even give the client a call once in a while in between contacts just to keep in touch and indicate your support, inquiring at the same time how he or she is doing in filling out the questionnaire.

6. Have the client make a commitment to cooperate. This might be done in a form of a verbal commitment, or better yet, a written contract.

7. Help the client make a private commitment to cooperate. Elicit the client's thoughts and feelings about filling out the questionnaire. Find out if he or she has had experience with that type of assignment before. Give a clear rationale to the client so he or she will accept the importance of the measure. Prepare the client for potential problems. If it is possible, have the client help select which instrument he or she will use.

8. Use a cognitive rehearsal strategy. Have the client relax, visualize the task, visualize successful completion, and engage in self-reinforcing statements or images.

9. Try to anticipate any negative effects of cooperation and prepare the client to deal with them.

10. The more sources that keep track of how well the client is doing, the more likely it is that the client will cooperate. This is another reason why it might be useful to post the client's chart in a conspicuous place.

11. Make sure you have a good relationship with the client and that he or she trusts you before you assign a task. Show empathy, caring, and warmth. Present the assignment with confidence and sincerity.

PART
II

Instruments
for Practice

INTRODUCTION

So far in this book we have reviewed the role of measurement to monitor your client's progress and to evaluate your effectiveness using single system research designs. Our discussion has included an overview of the basic principles of a reliable and valid measure, the principles related to using measures in practice, and issues regarding interpreting scores. We have also discussed some of the different types of measures, including the advantages and disadvantages of rapid assessment instruments. While we clearly believe this type of measure is particularly valuable, we *know* that there may be times when you will want other measurement tools as well as additional rapid assessment instruments. To this end we have presented information on determining what to measure within the context of practice, how to locate measures, and pertinent questions you might ask when evaluating which measure to use. Finally, we have presented some guidelines for you to consider when administering instruments.

We now turn our attention to the rationale and procedures we used to locate and select the instruments presented here. We have not included all the available rapid assessment instruments, but we believe that the measures that are included cover most of the client problem areas commonly encountered in practice.

The primary rationale for including an instrument in this volume was that it measures some specific client problem or treatment goal relevant to clinical practice. Thus, we excluded certain instruments which we felt just were not relevant to treatment. For example, a measure of macho personality constellation (Mosher and Sirkin, 1984) was not included because this is not a frequently seen clinical problem.

We also excluded instruments that measure *practitioner* behaviors that might occur during your interventions. While there is indeed a growing concern for measuring what you do as a clinician (e.g., Nelsen, 1985), we believe you would more likely want to measure particular client problems or treatment goals. This, after all, is one of the best ways to monitor practice.

We also decided only to include self-report instruments that could be used for rapid assessment. While numerous other types of measurement tools are available, we believe you would be more likely to monitor your practice with those on which your client reports directly his or her perceptions, feelings, or experiences. Not only are clients often the best source of this information, but RAIs can be used in conjunction with your own clinical assessment.

In the same vein, we have included only those instruments that are relatively short. While there is no concrete agreement on how short an instrument should be in order to be used for rapid completion and scoring, we arbitrarily decided to include mainly those that are 45 items or less. There are a few, however, that are slightly longer than 45 items; we included these because shorter measures were not available for that particular problem or because the instrument has subscales that can be used for rapid assessment.

Finally, just about all of the instruments we included had some evidence of reliability and validity, and all have some practice utility as they provide information which will help you monitor your client and evaluate your effectiveness. In order to facilitate your use of instruments to monitor practice, which we hope you will do on a regular basis, we have critiqued each instrument. Like many measures in the behavioral and social sciences, some of those included here lack convincing reliability, validity, or other important data. This is not to imply that no data was available, just that more is needed to be thoroughly convincing. When you use one of these instruments, even those with sufficient reliability and validity data for that matter, we hope you will approach them with a judicious degree of criticism.

LOCATING THE INSTRUMENT

In order to locate measurement tools, we began with a computer literature search. Additionally, we identified key volumes and journals that pertained to measurement in practice and reviewed them for appropriate instruments. (See Chapter 5, Tables 5.2 and 5.3.) For the nine journals we used all volumes were reviewed from 1974, except the *Journal of Clinical Psychology* and the *Journal of Personality Assessment*, which were reviewed from 1964 through 1986. For journals that first appeared later than 1974, all volumes were reviewed.

THE FINAL SELECTION

Whenever possible, we have tried to include more than one instrument to measure a problem, not only to provide a choice, but because different instruments tap different aspects of a problem. For example, you will notice there are several measures of anxiety. Some of these may be more appropriate for your measurement need than others. Finally, there are obviously more instruments available to measure certain types of problems than others. For example, relatively few measures are available to assess entire families—perhaps because of the newness of the field, and children—because children tend to have more difficulty in filling out self-report instruments than adults. For both children and families, we included as many RAIs as we could.

In sum, while we have not included all available self-report rapid assessment instruments (e.g., a few that we would have chosen to include were not available for reproduction), we believe the instruments we have chosen cover most of the client problem areas commonly encountered in practice. Nevertheless, we must stress the fact that other measures are available, and you should consider using them in conjunction with RAIs. We hope the instruments presented in this book will get you started as you develop more and more measurement tools for use in monitoring clients and evaluating your clinical effectiveness.

INSTRUMENTS FOR ADULTS

ACHIEVEMENT ANXIETY TEST (AAT)

AUTHORS: Richard Alpert and Ralph N. Haber

PURPOSE: To measure anxiety about academic achievement.

DESCRIPTION: The AAT is a 19-item instrument designed to measure anxiety about academic achievement. The AAT consists of two separate scales, a "facilitating scale" (items 2, 9, 11, 12, 14, 16, 19, 21, 24) which assesses anxiety as a motivator, and a "debilitating scale" (remainder of items) which assesses the degree to which anxiety interferes with performance. The two scales are administered on one questionnaire but scored separately. The value of these scales is in their specificity, both in defining the two aspects of anxiety, and in measuring anxiety specifically related to academic achievement. The AAT predicts academic performance, particularly verbal aptitude, more accurately than do the general anxiety scales.

NORMS: The AAT was developed with several samples of undergraduate introductory psychology students. The total N was 323, with no other demographic data reported, although it appeared that respondents were male. The mean score on the facilitating scale was 27.28, and on the debilitating scale, 26.33.

SCORING: The two subscales are scored separately with scores on each of the items summed to produce the overall score. Each item has a different response category, although all are on 5-point scales indicating the degree to which the statement applies to the respondent. Items 8, 10, and 12 from the facilitating scale are reverse-scored as are items 3, 4, 13, 17, and 19 from the debilitating scale.

RELIABILITY: The AAT has excellent stability: 10-week test-retest correlations of .83 for the facilitating and .87 for the debilitating scale, and eight-month test-retest correlations of .75 for the facilitating scale and .76 for the debilitating scale. No internal consistency information was reported.

VALIDITY: The AAT has good criterion-related validity correlating significantly with several measures of academic performance. Both subscales also are correlated with verbal aptitude. The AAT also has good predictive validity, significantly predicting grade point averages.

PRIMARY REFERENCE: Alpert, R. and Haber, R. N. (1960). Anxiety in academic achievement situations, *Journal of Abnormal and Social Psychology* 61, 207–215. Instrument reproduced with permission of the American Psychological Association.

AVAILABILITY: Journal article.

AAT

Instructions: Please circle the number for each item that comes closest to describing you.

1. Nervousness while taking an exam or test hinders me from doing well.

   Always   Never
     1   2   3   4   5

2. I work most effectively under pressure, as when the task is very important.

   Always   Never
     1   2   3   4   5

3. In a course where I have been doing poorly, my fear of a bad grade cuts down my efficiency.

   Never   Always
     1   2   3   4   5

4. When I am poorly prepared for an exam or test, I get upset, and do less well than even my restricted knowledge should allow.

   This never   This practically
   happens to me   always happens to me

5. The more important the examination, the less well I seem to do.

   Always   Never
     1   2   3   4   5

6. While I may (or may not) be nervous before taking an exam, once I start, I seem to forget to be nervous.

   I always   I am always nervous
   forget
     1   2   3   4   5

7. During exams or tests, I block on questions to which I know the answers, even though I remember them as soon as the exam is over.

                                           I never block on
   This always   questions to which
   happens to me   I know the answers
     1   2   3   4   5

8. Nervousness while taking a test helps me do better.

   It never helps   It often helps
        1   2   3   4   5

9. When I start a test, nothing is able to distract me.

   This is always   This is never
   true of me   true of me
        1   2   3   4   5

10. In courses in which the total grade is based mainly on one exam,
    I seem to do better than other people.

    Never   Always
        1   2   3   4   5

11. I find that my mind goes blank at the beginning of an exam, and
    it takes me a few minutes before I can function.

    I almost alway   I never blank out
    blank out at first   at first
        1   2   3   4   5

12. I look forward to exams.
    Never   Always
        1   2   3   4   5

13. I am so tired from worring about an exam, that I find I almost
    don't care how well I do by the time I start the test.

    I never feel   I almost always
    this way   feel this way
        1   2   3   4   5

14. Time pressure on an exam causes me to do worse than the rest of the
    group under similar conditions.

    Time pressure always   Time pressure
    seems to make me do   never seems to
    worse than others   make me do worse than
    on an exam   others on an exam
        1   2   3   4   5

15. Although "cramming" under preexamination tension is not effective for most people, I find that if the need arises, I can learn material immediately before an exam, even under considerable pressure, and successfully retain it to use on the exam.

I am always able
to use the "crammed"
material successfully

I am never able to
use the "crammed"
material successfully

16. I enjoy taking a difficult exam more than an easy one.

Always				Never
1	2	3	4	5

17. I find myself reading exam questions without understanding them, and I must go back over them so that they will make sense.

Never				Always
1	2	3	4	5

18. The more important the exam or test, the better I seem to do.

This is true
of me

This is not true
of me

1	2	3	4	5

19. When I don't do well on a difficult item at the beginning of an exam, it tends to upset me so that I block on every easy question later on.

This never
happens to me

This almost always
happens to me

1	2	3	4	5

ARGUMENTATIVENESS SCALE (ARG)

AUTHORS: Dominic A. Infante and Andrew S. Rancer

PURPOSE: To measure argumentativeness.

DESCRIPTION: The ARG is a 20-item scale designed to measure the tendency to argue about controversial issues (or argumentativeness). Argumentativeness is viewed as a generally stable trait which predisposes the individual in communication situations to advocate positions on controversial issues and to attack verbally the positions other people take on those issues. Ten of the items indicate a tendency to approach argumentative situations and ten involve the tendency to avoid argumentative situations. The ARG is considered useful for examining communication and social conflict and dysfunctional communication. Both areas have implications for clinical practice in that high scores on the ARG may identify the incessant arguer whose behavior impairs interpersonal relations while very low scores may identify people who almost never dispute an issue and are compliant and/or easily manipulated. Thus, the ARG may prove useful particularly in couple and family counseling.

NORMS: A series of studies largely involving over 800 students in undergraduate communication courses formed the basis for much of the research on the ARG. No demographic data are reported nor are actual norms.

SCORING: Scores for each item ranging from 1 to 5 are totaled separately for the two dimensions. The total score for the tendency to avoid argumentative situations (items 1, 3, 5, 6, 8, 10, 12, 14, 16, 19) is subtracted from the total score for the tendency to approach argumentative situations (2, 4, 7, 9, 11, 13, 15, 17, 18, 20) to provide an overall score for the argumentativeness trait.

RELIABILITY: The ARG has good internal consistency, with the approach dimension (ARG ap) having a coefficient alpha of .91 and the avoidance dimension (ARG av) having an alpha of .86. The ARG also is a stable instrument with an overall ARG test-retest reliability (one week) of .91 and test-retest reliabilities of .87 for ARG ap and .86 ARG av.

VALIDITY: The ARG has fairly good concurrent validity, correlating significantly and in the expected direction with three other measures of communication predispositions. In addition, the ARG significantly correlates with friend's ratings of argumentativeness. Further, the ARG has some degree of construct validity in accurately predicting a series of behavioral choices which should and should not correlate with argumentativeness.

PRIMARY REFERENCE: Infante, D. A. and Rancer, A. S. (1982). A conceptualization and measure of argumentativeness, *Journal of Person-*

ality Assessment 46, 72–80. Instrument reproduced with permission of Dominic A. Infante and the *Journal of Personality Assessment.*
AVAILABILITY: Journal article.

ARG

This questionnaire contains statements about arguing controversial issues. Indicate how often each statement is true for you personally by placing the appropriate number in the blank to the left of the statement. If the statement is *almost never true* for you, place a "1" in the blank. If the statement is *rarely true* for you, place a "2" in the blank. If the statement is *occasionally true* for you, place a "3" in the blank. If the statement is *often true* for you, place a "4" in the blank. If the statement is *almost always true* for you, place a "5" in the blank.

____ 1. While in an argument, I worry that the person I am arguing with will form a negative impression of me.
____ 2. Arguing over controversial issues improves my intelligence.
____ 3. I enjoy avoiding arguments.
____ 4. I am energetic and enthusiastic when I argue.
____ 5. Once I finish an argument I promise myself that I will not get into another.
____ 6. Arguing with a person creates more problems for me than it solves.
____ 7. I have a pleasant, good feeling when I win a point in an argument.
____ 8. When I finish arguing with someone I feel nervous and upset.
____ 9. I enjoy a good argument over a controversial issue.
____ 10. I get an unpleasant feeling when I realize I am about to get into an argument.
____ 11. I enjoy defending my point of view on an issue.
____ 12. I am happy when I keep an argument from happening.
____ 13. I do not like to miss the opportunity to argue a controversial issue.
____ 14. I prefer being with people who rarely disagree with me.
____ 15. I consider an argument an exciting intellectual challenge.
____ 16. I find myself unable to think of effective points during an argument.
____ 17. I feel refreshed and satisfied after an argument on a controversial issue.
____ 18. I have the ability to do well in an argument.
____ 19. I try to avoid getting into arguments.
____ 20. I feel excitement when I expect that a conversation I am in is leading to an argument.

ASSERTION INVENTORY (AI)

AUTHORS: Eileen Gambrill and Cheryl Richey

PURPOSE: To measure three aspects of assertiveness.

DESCRIPTION: This versatile 40-item instrument measures three aspects of assertion: discomfort with assertion (DAI), response probability (RP) of engaging in assertive behavior, and identification of situations (IS) where assertion needs improvement. In order to calculate scores on all three scales, each item must be answered three times. However, any one of the three scores can be used. The measure can also be used to characterize a client as "assertive," "unassertive," "anxious performer," and "doesn't care." This typology is helpful in selecting an intervention which best fits the type of assertion problem of the client. Finally, in terms of known gender differences on assertion, the A1 compares favorably with other assertion instruments by having a balance between negative and positive assertive behaviors.

NORMS: Normative data are available on samples of college students in Berkeley and Seattle (N = 608). The mean DAI, RP, and IS scores were 93.9, 103.8, and 10.1, respectively.

SCORING: DAI scores and RP scores are the sums of the ratings on each item in the respective columns. The IS score is the total number of items circled. Client profiles are determined by categorizing scores from the DAI and RP scores as follows:

RP Scores

		≥ 105	≤ 104
DAI Score	≥ 96	Unassertive	Anxious performer
	≤ 95	Doesn't care	Assertive

For example, if a client's DAI score is greater than or equal to 96 and the RP score is less than or equal to 105, the client's problem would be considered unassertive. The AI can also be scored as eleven factors reflecting specific situations of discomfort (see primary reference.)

RELIABILITY: This instrument has very good reliability. Stability has been shown with test-retest correlations of .87 and .81 for DAI scores and RP scores respectively.

VALIDITY: The validity support of the AI tends to be very strong. Tests of known groups validity illustrated that scores discriminate between clinical and normal samples. The instrument also is sensitive to change, as demonstrated by differences between pre- and post-therapy scores.

PRIMARY REFERENCE: Gambril, E. D. and Richey, C. A. (1975). An assertion inventory for use in assessment and research, *Behavior Therapy* 6, 550–561. Instrument reproduced with permission of Cheryl A. Richey.

AVAILABILITY: Dr. Cheryl A. Richey, School of Social Work (JH-30), 4101 15th Avenue N.E., University of Washington, Seattle, WA 98195.

AI

Many people experience difficulty in heandling interpersonal situations requiring them to assert themselves in some way, for example, turning down a
request or asking a favor. Please indicate your degree of discomfort or
anxiety in the space provided before each situation listed below. Use
the following scale to indicate degree of discomfort.

1 = None
2 = A little
3 = A fair amount
4 = Much
5 = Very much

Then, go over the list a second time and indicate after each item the probability or likelihood of responding as described if actually presented with
the situation.* For example, if you rarely apologize when you are at fault,
you would mark "4" after that item. Use the following scale to indicate
response probability:

1 = Always do it
2 = Usually do it
3 = Do it about half the time
4 = Rarely do it
5 = Never do it

Please indicate the situations you would like to handle more assertively by
placing a circle around the item number.

*NOTE:　It is important to assess your discomfort ratings apart from your
response probability. Otherwise, one may influence the other. To
prevent this, place a piece of paper over your discomfort ratings
while responding to the situation a second time for response
probability.

Degree of Discomfort	Situation	Response Probability
___	1. Turn down a request to borrow your car	___
___	2. Compliment a friend	___
___	3. Ask a favor of someone	___
___	4. Resist sales pressure	___
___	5. Apologize when you are at fault	___
___	6. Turn down a request for a meeting or date	___
___	7. Admit fear and request consideration	___
___	8. Tell a person with whom you are intimately involved when he or she says or does something that bothers you	___
___	9. Ask for a raise	___
___	10. Admit ignorance in some area	___
___	11. Turn down a request to borrow money	___

Degree of Discomfort	Situation	Response Probability
____	12. Ask personal questions	
____	13. Turn off a talkative friend	____
____	14. Ask for constructive criticism	____
____	15. Initiate a conversation with a stranger	____
____	16. Compliment a person you are romantically involved with or interested in	____
____	17. Request a meeting or a date with a person	____
____	18. Your initial request for a meeting is turned down and you ask the person again at a later time	____
____	19. Admit confusion about a point under discussion and ask for clarification	____
____	20. Apply for a job	____
____	21. Ask whether you have offended someone	____
____	22. Tell someone that you like him or her	____
____	23. Request expected service when such is not forthcoming, for example, in a restaurant	____
____	24. Discuss openly with a person his or her criticism of your behavior	____
____	25. Return defective items in a store or restaurant	____
____	26. Express an opinion that differs from that of the person with whom you are talking	____
____	27. Resist sexual overtures when you are not interested	____
____	28. Tell a person when you feel that he or she has done something that is unfair to you	____
____	29. Accept a date	____
____	30. Tell someone good news about yourself	____
____	31. Resist pressure to drink	____
____	32. Resist a significant person's unfair demand	____
____	33. Quit a job	____
____	34. Resist pressure to use drugs	____
____	35. Discuss openly with a person his or her criticism of your work	____
____	36. Request the return of a borrowed item	____
____	37. Receive compliments	____
____	38. Continue to converse with someone who disagrees with you	____
____	39. Tell a friend or co-worker when he or she says or does something that bothers you	____
____	40. Ask a person who is annoying you in a public situation to stop	____

ASSERTIVE JOB-HUNTING SURVEY (AJHS)

AUTHOR: Heather A. Becker

PURPOSE: To measure self-reported job-hunting assertiveness.

DESCRIPTION: The AJHS is a 25-item questionnaire designed to assess assertiveness in hunting for jobs—that is, the extent to which the respondent acts on his or her environment to procure information, establish contact persons in organizations, and so on. Developed originally from a pool of 35 items based on the job-hunting literature, the items on the complete instrument were designed to reflect all aspects of job-hunting including resumé writing, contacting prospective employees, soliciting recommendations, and interviewing. The AJHS can be used in classes or assertive training groups, as an outcome measure, to stimulate discussion of job-hunting assertiveness, and as a research tool for investigating correlates of assertiveness in job hunting.

NORMS: Norms for the AJHS were established on 190 college students who had applied at a university center for career planning or job assistance. (Several hundred other students also have been studied.) The norm group included 50% men and 50% women, and represented all classifications from freshman to graduate students and a wide range of academic areas. Mean responses for each item are available in the article; the overall mean score was 105.55. Scores for subgroups of students are not provided.

SCORING: Items 1, 2, 4, 5, 7, 8, 10–12, 14, 15, 17, 19, 20, 22–25 are reverse scored on the 6-point scales, with all responses then summed. This provides a range of 25 to 150, with higher scores indicating more assertive responses.

RELIABILITY: The AJHS has very good internal consistency with a coefficient alpha of .82. The instrument also has good stability with a two-month test-retest reliability of .77.

VALIDITY: The AJHS established a form of concurrent validity with a significant correlation between previous job-hunting experience and scores on the AJHS. The AJHS also is sensitive to change, showing significant pre- to posttest changes in two assertive job-hunting classes. No other validity data were reported.

PRIMARY REFERENCE: Becker, H. A. (1980). The Assertive Job-Hunting Survey, *Measurement and Evaluation in Guidance* 13, 43–48. Instrument reproduced with permission of Heather Becker.

AVAILABILITY: Dr. Heather Becker, 2734 Trail of the Madrones, Austin, TX. 78746

AJHS

For each of the following items, please indicate to the left of the item how likely you would be to respond in a job-hunting situation using the scale below.

1 = Very unlikely
2 = Rather unlikely
3 = Unlikely
4 = Likely
5 = Rather likely
6 = Very likely

_____ 1. Would mention only paid work experience
_____ 2. Reluctant to ask for more information
_____ 3. Would ask employers if they knew of other employers
_____ 4. Downplay my qualifications
_____ 5. Would rather use an employment agency
_____ 6. Would contact employee to learn more about organization
_____ 7. Hesitate to ask questions when interviewed
_____ 8. Avoid contacting employers because they're too busy
_____ 9. Would leave or arrange another appointment
_____ 10. Experienced employment counselor knows best
_____ 11. If employer too busy, would stop trying to contact
_____ 12. Getting job largely luck
_____ 13. Would directly contact employer, rather than personnel
_____ 14. Reluctant to contact employer unless there's opening
_____ 15. Would not apply unless had all qualifications
_____ 16. Would not ask for a second interview
_____ 17. Reluctant to contact employer unless there's opening
_____ 18. Would ask employer how to improve chances for another position
_____ 19. Feel uncomfortable asking friends for job leads
_____ 20. Better take whatever job I can get
_____ 21. If personnel didn't refer me, directly contact the person
_____ 22. Would rather interview with recruiters
_____ 23. Figure there's nothing else to do
_____ 24. Check out openings before deciding what to do
_____ 25. Reluctant to contact someone I don't know for information

ASSERTIVENESS SELF-REPORT INVENTORY (ASRI)

AUTHORS: Sharon D. Herzberger, Esther Chan, and Judith Katz

PURPOSE: To measure assertiveness.

DESCRIPTION: The ASRI is a 25-item scale specifically developed to overcome criticisms of other measures of assertiveness: it is specific, in that items indicate the behavior, situation, and other people involved; it focuses on behavioral and affective dimensions of assertiveness; it is relatively short; it is broadly conceptualized; and details about development of the items for the scale are reported. The ASRI is simple to administer and to score. Items were generated by upper-level psychology students who were studying test construction and the construct of assertiveness. Those items that were not strongly endorsed in a preliminary study, that were correlated with social desirability, or that were not significantly correlated with the total score were dropped, leaving these 25 items.

NORMS: Initial work on the ASRI has been conducted with college students and not on clinical populations. A series of studies was conducted with 268 students (96 males and 172 females). Mean scores for males in different testing sessions ranged from 9.54 to 10.63 and for females from 9.81 to 10.71. There were no significant male-female differences.

SCORING: The total score is derived simply by adding the total number of "true" responses for items 1, 3, 4, 9, 13, 15, 16, 18–20, 22, 24 to "false" responses for remaining items.

RELIABILITY: The ASRI has good stability with a five-week test-retest correlation of .81. Data were not reported on internal consistency.

VALIDITY: The ASRI has good concurrent validity, correlating significantly with the Rathus Assertiveness Schedule. Further, the ASRI was not significantly correlated with subscales of the Buss-Durkee Aggression Inventory, suggesting that assertiveness and aggression are independent constructs. The ASRI also significantly predicted respondents' assertive solutions to specific dilemmas and peer-rated assertiveness, thus suggesting fair predictive validity.

PRIMARY REFERENCE: Herzberger, S. D., Chan, E., and Katz, J. (1984). The development of an assertiveness self-report inventory, *Journal of Personality Assessment* 48, 317–323. Instrument reproduced with permission of Sharon D. Herzberger and the *Journal of Personality Assessment*.

AVAILABILITY: The Free Press

ASRI

Read each question carefully and answer all 25 of them. Circle either 'True' (T) or 'False' (F), whichever most represents your viewpoint.

T F 1. When my date has acted rudely at a party, I don't hesitate to let him/her know I don't like it.

T F 2. I feel guilty after I ask my neighbor to be quiet after midnight on a weeknight.

T F 3. After eating an excellent meal at a restaurant, I do not hesitate to compliment the chef.

T F 4. If I were stood up on a date I would tell the person who stood me up that I felt angry.

T F 5. When I get a terrible haircut and my hair stylist/barber asks me how I like it, I say I like it.

T F 6. I would feel self-conscious asking a question in a large lecture class.

T F 7. I usually let my friends have a larger portion of food at social gatherings and take a smaller one for myself.

T F 8. When on a date I act cheerful, even though I am depressed, so as not to upset my date's mood.

T F 9. I feel justified when I send improperly cooked food back to the kitchen in a restaurant.

T F 10. When people I don't know wear nice outfits, I hesitate to compliment them.

T F 11. I'm not likely to tell my date that I am irritated when he/she pays more attention to others and ignores me.

T F 12. I tip a consistent percentage to a waitress despite receiving poor service.

T F 13. When an interviewer cancels an appointment for the third time I tell him/her that I am annoyed.

T F 14. When a roommate makes a mess I would rather clean it up myself than confront him/her about it.

T F 15. If I received a call late at night from a casual acquaintance, I would say I was sleeping and ask not to be called so late.

T F 16. When people use my car and don't refill the tank, I let them know I feel unfairly treated.

T F 17. I find it difficult to ask a favor of a stranger.

T F 18. If my stereo were stolen, I wouldn't regret reporting it to the police even if I suspected a friend.

T F 19. If I were going out with friends for an evening and my boyfriend/girlfriend did not want me to, I would do it anyway.

T F 20. I feel comfortable engaging in discussions in a group, even when my views are different from the majority opinion.

T F 21. I feel guilty when my boyfriend/girlfriend wants to go to a movie but we go where I wanted to instead.

T F 22. When my roommate consistently fails to take an accurate telephone message, I let him/her know I'm upset.

T   F   23.   When people use abusive language around me, I ignore it even though it bothers me.

T   F   24.   If someone makes loud noises when I am studying at the library I will express my discontent.

T   F   25.   I feel guilty telling my boyfriend/girlfriend that I have to do homework this evening instead of seeing him/her.

AUTHORITARIANISM SCALE (AS)

AUTHOR: Patrick C. L. Heaven

PURPOSE: To measure authoritarian behavior.

DESCRIPTION: The Revised F-scale is a 35-item instrument designed to measure authoritarianism. Much work has been done on the authoritarian personality using the original F-scale (Adorno et al., 1950). That scale, however, does not predict authoritarian behavior, but rather is most likely a measure of potential fascism. The Revised F-scale was developed to address this limitation and two other weaknesses: the unilateral wording of items and a response set to particular items. The Revised F-scale focuses on the multifaceted nature of authoritarianism and the items represent authoritarian behaviors. By presenting a balance of negatively and positively worded items, an acquiescent response set is controlled. The scale can be used as a short form by deleting items 3, 6, 8, 9, 10, 11, 15, 16, 17, 18, 22, 24, 26, 31 and 35.

NORMS: The Revised F-scale was developed on four separate samples from New South Wales, Australia: two samples of randomly selected adults ($n = 456$) who were in their middle 40s; 48 experienced police officers, whose average age was 31.1 with a standard deviation of 6.24 years; and a purposive sample of adults ($n = 49$). Few data are presented on the samples' F-scores except for the police officers and a subsample of adults matched with the police according to gender, age and level of education. The average F-scale score for police was 75.71 with a standard deviation of 7.37. The matched subsample's average F-scale score was 69.85 with a standard deviation of 10.98.

SCORING: Scoring is not fully described in the primary reference. Each item is rated on the degree to which the respondent agrees. A 5-item scale can be used for responses, giving a range of scores from 35 to 165. Items 5–9, 12–14, 22–24, 31 are reverse-scored. Higher scores reflect more authoritarianism.

RELIABILITY: The internal consistency of the F-scale ranged from .70 to .83 for the sample of police officers and randomly selected adults, respectively. The internal consistency for the 20-item short form was .79, which was based on the sample of adults.

VALIDITY: Research on known-groups validity suggests the F-scale discriminates police officers' scores from the matched sample of adults. The purposive sample of 49 adults had scores on the F-scale which correlated with 11 behavioral dimensions of authoritarianism as rated by two close friends.

PRIMARY REFERENCE: Heaven, P. C. L. (1985). Construction and validation of a measure of authoritarian personality, *Journal of Personality Assessment* 49, 545–551.

AVAILABILITY: Journal article.

AS

Rate each item in terms of how much you agree with the content. Please use the following scale and record your responses in the space to the left of the item.

1 = Almost Never
2 = Rarely
3 = Occassionally
4 = Frequently
5 = Almost Always

____ 1. Does the idea of being a leader attract you?
____ 2. Do you tend to feel quite confident on occasions when you are directing the activities of others?
____ 3. Do you try to get yourself into positions of authority where you can?
____ 4. Do you think you would make a good officer in the army?
____ 5. Do you think you would make a poor military leader?
____ 6. I would not vote for a political party that advocates racial discrimination.
____ 7. Is being comfortable more important to you than getting ahead?
____ 8. Are you satisfied to be no better than most other people at your job?
____ 9. I am easily convinced by the opinions of others.
____ 10. I agree with South Africa's Apartheid Policy.
____ 11. Do you tend to boss people around?
____ 12. Do you dislike having to tell others what to do?
____ 13. If you are told to take charge of some situation, does this make you feel uncomfortable?
____ 14. Would you rather take orders than give them?
____ 15. Do you tend to be the one who makes the decisions at home?
____ 16. Do you like to have the last word in an argument or discussion?
____ 17. If ever a Falkland-type situation arose in Australia, I'd volunteer to fight.
____ 18. I enjoy and feel good wearing a military uniform.
____ 19. Do you tend to plan ahead for your job or career?
____ 20. Is "getting on in life" important to you?
____ 21. Are you an ambitious person?
____ 22. Are you inclined to read of the successes of others rather than do the work of making yourself a success?
____ 23. Are you inclined to take life as it comes without much planning?
____ 24. Would it upset you a lot to see a child or animal suffer?
____ 25. Do you have enemies you want to harm you?
____ 26. Do you tend to dominate the conversation?
____ 27. Are you argumentative?
____ 28. Are there several people who keep trying to avoid you?
____ 29. I often find myself disagreeing with people.
____ 30. I can't help getting into arguments when people disagree with me.

___ 31. Even when my anger is aroused, I don't use strong language.
___ 32. If somebody annoys me, I am apt to tell him/her what I think.
___ 33. When people yell at me I yell back.
___ 34. When arguing, I tend to raise my voice.
___ 35. Would you like other people to be afraid of you?

AUTOMATIC THOUGHTS QUESTIONNAIRE (ATQ)

AUTHORS: Philip C. Kendall and Steven D. Hollon

PURPOSE: To measure cognitive self-statements of depression.

DESCRIPTION: This ATQ is a 30-item instrument that measures the frequency of automatic negative statements about the self. Such negative covert statements play an important role in the development, maintenance and treatment of various psychopathologies, including depression. ATQ taps four aspects of these automatic thoughts: personal maladjustment and desire for change (PMDC), negative self-concepts and negative expectations (NSNE), low self-esteem (LSE), and Helplessness. The instrument is particularly noteworthy as it was designed to measure change in cognition due to clinical interventions.

NORMS: The ATQ was developed on a sample of 312 undergraduates. The sample was young, with an average age of 20.22 with a standard deviation of 4.34 years. From this sample subjects were categorized as depressed or nondepressed based on scores from the Beck Depression Inventory (Beck, et al., 1961) and Minnesota Multiphasic Personality Inventory Depression scale. The average ATQ score for the depressed subsample was 79.64 with a standard deviation of 22.29. The average score for the nondepressed sample was 48.57 with a standard deviation of 10.89.

SCORING: Items are rated on the frequency of occurrence from "not at all" to "all the time." Total scores are the summation of all 30 items. Items tapping each factor are: PMDC: 7, 10, 14, 20, 26; NSNE: 2, 3, 9, 21, 23, 24, 28; LSE: 17, 18; Helplessness: 29, 30.

RELIABILITY: The instrument has excellent internal consistency with an alpha coefficient of .97. No information is presented for test-retest reliability.

VALIDITY: The 30 items of the ATQ were selected from a pool of 100, and all significantly discriminated depressed from nondepressed subjects. This finding was repeated with another sample of depressed and nondepressed subjects. The instrument also has good concurrent validity, correlating with two measures of depression, the Beck Depression Inventory and the MMPI Depression Scale. Contrary to the initial prediction, scores were highly correlated with anxiety.

PRIMARY REFERENCE: Hollon, S. D. and Kendall, P. C. (1980). Cognitive self-statements in depression: Development of an Automatic Thoughts Questionnaire, *Cognitive Therapy and Research* 4, 383–395. Instrument reproduced with permission of Philip C. Kendall.

AVAILABILITY: Dr. Philip C. Kendall, Division of Clinical Psychology, Temple University, Philadelphia, PA 19122

ATQ

Listed below are a variety of thoughts that pop into people's heads. Please read each thought and indicate how frequently, if at all, the thought occurred to you *over the last week*. Please read each item carefully and fill in the blank with the appropriate number, using the following scale:

1 = Not at all
2 = Sometimes
3 = Moderately often
4 = Often
5 = All the time

____ 1. I feel like I'm up against the world.
____ 2. I'm no good.
____ 3. Why can't I ever succeed?
____ 4. No one understands me.
____ 5. I've let people down.
____ 6. I don't think I can go on.
____ 7. I wish I were a better person.
____ 8. I'm so weak.
____ 9. My life's not going the way I want it to.
____ 10. I'm so disappointed in myself.
____ 11. Nothing feels good anymore.
____ 12. I can't stand this anymore.
____ 13. I can't get started.
____ 14. What's wrong with me?
____ 15. I wish I were somewhere else.
____ 16. I can't get things together.
____ 17. I hate myself.
____ 18. I'm worthless.
____ 19. Wish I could just disappear.
____ 20. What's the matter with me?
____ 21. I'm a loser.
____ 22. My life is a mess.
____ 23. I'm a failure.
____ 24. I'll never make it.
____ 25. I feel so helpless.
____ 26. Something has to change.
____ 27. There must be something wrong with me.
____ 28. My future is bleak.
____ 29. It's just not worth it.
____ 30. I can't finish anything.

BAKKER ASSERTIVENESS–AGGRESSIVENESS INVENTORY (AS–AGI)

AUTHORS: Cornelis B. Bakker, Marianne K. Bakker-Rabdau, and Saul Breit

PURPOSE: To measure two dimensions of assertion.

DESCRIPTION: This 36-item inventory measures assertiveness in terms of two components necessary for social functioning: the ability to refuse unreasonable requests ("assertiveness" AS), and the ability to take the initiative, make requests, or ask for favors ("aggressiveness" AG). Aggressiveness is different from hostility. It tends to relate more to being responsible and taking the initiative in social situations. The two instruments can also be used separately as 18-item measures.

NORMS: Normative data are available from seven different samples. From a sample of 250 college students, males had average AS and AG scores of 48.83 and 51.07, respectively, while female scores were 47.69 for the AS and 52.37 for the AG. A sample of 17 male city employee supervisors, with an average age of 40.1 with a standard deviation of 6.3 years, had AS scores of 43.85 and 47.88 for the AG. From a sample of students seeking assertiveness training the average AS and AG scores were 55.0 and 58.67 respectively, for males and 54.85 and 58.60 for females; the average ages of these males and females were 39.0 and 43.4, respectively. Additional normative data on nurses, X-Ray technicians and employees of a city water department are reported in the primary reference.

SCORING: Each item is rated on a 5-point scale from "almost always" to "almost never" according to the likelihood the respondent would behave in the specified manner. Each scale is scored separately. Those items with a plus sign before the alternative are reverse-scored as follows: 1 becomes 5, 2 becomes 4, 4 becomes 2, and 5 becomes 1. The item responses for each scale are summed with a range from 18 to 90. Higher scores indicate that the individual is less likely to exhibit assertiveness or aggressiveness.

RELIABILITY: These scales have been shown to be fairly reliable in terms of internal consistency and test-retest reliability. Internal consistency was estimated from a split-half procedure and was .73 for the AS scale and .80 for AG scale. Test-retest correlations were .75 for the AS and .88 for AG over a six-week period.

VALIDITY: Items analysis of all 36 items indicated that scores on each correlated highly with the score on the scale of which it is a part. Research on known-groups validity indicated that both scales discriminated between a client and college sample. The scales are sensitive to measuring change as AS and AG scores changed subsequent to assertiveness training.

PRIMARY REFERENCE: Bakker, C. B., Bakker-Rabdau, M. K., and Breit, S. (1978). The measurement of assertiveness and aggressiveness, *Journal of Personality Assessment* 42, 277–284. Instrument reproduced with permission of C. B. Bakker and the *Journal of Personality Assessment.*

AVAILABILITY: C. B. Bakker, M.D., Department of Psychiatry, Adult Development Program, Sacred Heart Medical Center, West 101 Eight Avenue, Spokane, WA 99220.

AS-AGI

Below are several different situations. Each is followed by one way
of responding. Your task is to read each question and indicate how
likely you are to respond in that way, according to the following
scale:

> 1 = Almost always
> 2 = Frequently
> 3 = Occasionally
> 4 = Sometimes
> 5 = Almost never

Record your answers in the space to the left of each item.

AS Items

____ 1. You have set aside the evening to get some necessary work done.
Just as you get started some friends drop over for a social
visit.
- You welcome them in and postpone what you had planned
to do.

____ 2. You are standing in line when someone pushes ahead of you.
+ You tell the person to get back in line behind you.

____ 3. A friend or relative asks to borrow your car or other valuable
property but you would prefer not to lend it to them.
- You lend it to them anyway.

____ 4. A person who has kept you waiting before is late again for
an appointment.
- You ignore it and act as if nothing has happened.

____ 5. Someone has, in your opinion, treated you unfairly or incorrectly.
+ You confront the person directly concerning this.

____ 6. Friends or neighbors fail to return some items they have
borrowed from you.
+ You keep after them until they return them.

____ 7. Others put pressure on you to drink, smoke pot, take drugs,
or eat too much.
+ You refuse to yield to their pressure.

____ 8. Another person interrupts you while you are speaking.
- You wait until the other is finished speaking before you
go on with your story.

____ 9. You are asked to carry out a task that you do not feel like
doing.
+ You tell the other that you don't want to do it.

____ 10. Your sexual partner has done something that you do not like.
- You act as if nothing bothersome has happened.

____ 11. A salesperson has spent a great deal of time showing you
merchandise but none of it is exactly what you want.
- You buy something anyway.

_____ 12. You are invited to a party or other social event, which you would rather not attend.
   - You accept the invitation.
_____ 13. In a concert or a movie theater a couple next to you distracts you with their conversation.
   + You ask them to be quiet or move somewhere else.
_____ 14. In a restaurant you receive food that is poorly prepared.
   + You ask the waiter or waitress to replace it.
_____ 15. You receive incorrect or damaged merchandise from a store.
   + You return the merchandise.
_____ 16. A person who seems a lot worse off than you asks you for something you could easily do without but you don't like to.
   - You give the person what he/she asks for.
_____ 17. Someone gives you -- unasked for -- a negative appraisal of your behavior.
   + You tell the other you are not interested.
_____ 18. Friends or parents try to get information from you that you consider personal.
   - You give them the information they want.

AG Items

_____ 19. You have been appointed to a newly formed committee.
   + You take a leadership role.
_____ 20. You are in a bus or plane sitting next to a person you have never met.
   + You strike up a conversation.
_____ 21. You are a guest in a home of a new acquaintance. The dinner was so good you would like a second helping.
   + You go ahead and take a second helping.
_____ 22. You are being interviewed for a job you really want to get.
   - You undersell yourself.
_____ 23. You are meeting or greeting several people.
   + You make physical contact with each other in turn either by hugging, putting an arm around their shoulders, or slapping their backs.
_____ 24. You have observed that someone has done an excellent job at something.
   - You don't tell that person about it.
_____ 25. In a store or restaurant the personnel are very busy and many customers seem to be waiting a long time for service.
   + You manage to get service ahead of other customers.
_____ 26. You observe someone behave in a suspicious manner.
   - You don't do anything because it is none of your business.
_____ 27. You have parked your car but notice that you do not have the correct change for the parking meter.
   + You ask a passer-by for the change.
_____ 28. Someone has done or said something that arouses your curiosity.
   - You refrain from asking questions.

___ 29. You have observed certain behaviors of a friend or acquaintance
that you think need to be changed.
+ You tell the other person about this as soon as possible.

___ 30. You would like to get a raise but your boss has said nothing
about it.
- You wait for your boss to bring the matter up.

___ 31. During a social visit with a group of friends everyone
participates actively in the conversation.
+ You dominate the conversation most of the time.

___ 32. During a discussion you believe that you have something
worthwhile to contribute.
+ You don't bother to state it unless the others ask you
to give your opinion.

___ 33. You have an opportunity to participate in a lively, no-holds
barred debate.
- You remain a listener rather than participate.

___ 34. You want a favor done by a person you do not know too well.
- You prefer to do without rather than ask that person.

___ 35. You have moved into a new neighborhood or started a new job
and you would like to make social contacts.
- You prefer to do without rather than ask that person.

___ 36. You see an opportunity to get ahead but know it will take a
great deal of energy.
+ You take the opportunity and forge ahead.

BECK DEPRESSION INVENTORY (BDI)

AUTHOR: Aaron T. Beck

PURPOSE: To measure the severity of depression

DESCRIPTION: The BDI is a 21-item scale that assesses the presence and severity of affective, cognitive, motivational, vegitative and psycho-motor components of depression. Each item on the BDI relates to a particular symptom of depression, and respondents indicate on a scale from 0 to 3 the severity of their current state of each symptom. Of the 21 items, 11 deal with cognition, two with affect, two with overt behavior, one with interpersonal symptoms, and five with so-matic symptoms. The BDI is one of the most widely used measures of depression in clinical practice, and has also been used in the non-clinical population. In addition, although developed for use with adults, the BDI has been used successfully with children. A short, 13-item version of the BDI, which correlates .96 with long form, is also available by using items 1–5, 7, 9, 12–15, 17, and 19.

NORMS: The BDI has been used on a wide range of groups including clinical and nonclinical populations. It was originally standardized on a group of 598 in-patients and out-patients in a psychiatric hos-pital, but has since been applied with a variety of other groups of psychiatric patients and with nonclinical groups such as college stu-dents. Clinical cutting scores are available for different degrees of depression.

SCORING: Respondents indicate the presence and severity of each symptom on a scale from 0 to 3. The item scores are then simply summed, producing a range from 0 to 63 on the long form and 0 to 39 on the short form, with higher scores reflecting greater severity of depression.

RELIABILITY: The BDI has good to excellent reliability. Split-half reli-abilities ranging from .78 to .93 have been reported indicating good to excellent internal consistency. Test-retest reliabilities have been good to very good, ranging from .48 for psychiatric patients after three weeks to .74 for undergraduate students after three months.

VALIDITY: The BDI has good to excellent validity. Research has shown significant correlations with a number of other depression measures indicating strong concurrent validity. In addition, the BDI correlates significantly with clinicians' ratings of depression and has been shown in several studies to be sensitive to clinical changes.

PRIMARY REFERENCE: Beck, A. T. (1967). *Depression: Clinical, Experi-mental and Theoretical Aspects.* New York: Harper & Row. Instru-ment reproduced by permission of the The Psychological Corpora-tion.

AVAILABILITY: The Psychological Corporation, 555 Academic Court, San Antonio, Texas 78204.

BDI

Name_____   Date _____

On this questionnaire are groups of statements. Please read each group
of statements carefully. Then pick out the one statement in each group which
best describes the way you have been feeling the PAST WEEK, INCLUDING TODAY!
Circle the number beside the statement you picked. If several statements in
the group seem to apply equally well, circle each one. *Be sure to read all
the statements in each group before making your choice.*

1 0 I do not feel sad.
   1 I feel sad.
   2 I am sad all the time and I can't snap out of it.
   3 I am so sad or unhappy that I can't stand it.

2 0 I am not particularly discouraged about the future.
   1 I feel discouraged about the future.
   2 I feel I have nothing to look forward to.
   3 I feel that the future is hopeless and that things cannot improve.

3 0 I do not feel like a failure.
   1 I feel I have failed more than the average person.
   2 As I look back on my life, all I can see is a lot of failures.
   3 I feel I am a complete failure as a person.

4 0 I get as much satisfaction out of things as I used to.
   1 I don't enjoy things the way I used to.
   2 I don't get real satisfaction out of anything anymore.
   3 I am dissatisfied or bored with everything.

5 0 I don't feel particularly guilty.
   1 I feel guilty a good part of the time.
   2 I feel quite guilty most of the time.
   3 I feel guilty all of the time.

6 0 I don't feel I am being punished.
   1 I feel I may be punished.
   2 I expect to be punished.
   3 I feel I am being punished.

7 0 I don't feel disappointed in myself.
   1 I am disappointed in myself.
   2 I am disgusted with myself.
   3 I hate myself.

8 0 I don't feel I am any worse than anybody else.
   1 I am critical of myself for my weaknesses or mistakes.
   2 I blame myself all the time for my faults.
   3 I blame myself for everything bad that happens.

9   0   I don't have any thoughts of killing myself.
    1   I have thoughts of killing myself, but I would not carry them out.
    2   I would like to kill myself.
    3   I would kill myself if I had the chance.

10 0   I don't cry anymore than usual.
    1   I cry more now than I used to.
    2   I cry all the time now.
    3   I used to be able to cry, but now I can't cry even though I want to.

11 0   I am no more irritated now than I ever am.
    1   I get annoyed or irritated more easily than I used to.
    2   I feel irritated all the time now.
    3   I don't get irritated at all by the things that used to irritate me.

12 0   I have not lost interest in other people.
    1   I am less interested in other people than I used to be.
    2   I have lost most of my interest in other people.
    3   I have lost all of my interest in other people.

13 0   I make decisions about as well as I ever could.
    1   I put off making decisions more than I used to.
    2   I have greater difficulty in making decisions than before.
    3   I can't make decisions at all anymore.

14 0   I don't feel I look any worse than I used to.
    1   I am worried that I am looking old or unattractive.
    2   I feel that there are permanent changes in my appearance that make
        me look unattractive.
    3   I believe that I look ugly.

15 0   I can work about as well as before.
    1   It takes an extra effort to get started at doing something.
    2   I have to push myself very hard to do anything.
    3   I can't do any work at all.

16 0   I can sleep as well as usual.
    1   I don't sleep as well as I used to.
    2   I wake up 1-2 hours earlier than usual and find it hard to go back
        to sleep.
    3   I wake up several hours earlier than I used to and cannot get back
        to sleep.

17 0   I don't get more tired than usual.
    1   I get tired more easily than I used to.
    2   I get tired from doing almost anything.
    3   I am too tired to do anything.

18 0   My appetite is no worse than usual.
    1   My appetite is not as good as it used to be.
    2   My appetite is much worse now.
    3   I have no appetite at all anymore.

19 0 I haven't lost much weight, if any lately.
      1 I have lost more than 5 pounds.
      2 I have lost more than 10 pounds.
      3 I have lost more than 15 pounds.

     I am purposely trying to lose weight by eating less.
     Yes_____ No _____

20 0 I am no more worried about my health than usual.
      1 I am worried about physical problems such as aches and pains; or
         upset stomach; or constipation.
      2 I am very worried about physical problems and it's hard to
         think of much else.
      3 I am so worried about my physical problems, that I cannot think
         about anything else.

21 0 I have not noticed any recent change in my interest in sex.
      1 I am less interested in sex than I used to be.
      2 I am much less interested in sex now.
      3 I have lost interest in sex completely.

BULIMIA TEST (BULIT)

AUTHORS: Marcia C. Smith and Mark N. Thelen

PURPOSE: To measure the symptoms of bulimia.

DESCRIPTION: BULIT was developed to assess the symptoms of bulimia as defined by the *Diagnostic and Statistical Manual, Third Edition* (APA, 1980). This 32-item instrument is arranged in a multiple choice format. The BULIT identifies behaviors related to extreme attempts to lose weight and provides criteria for ruling out anorexia nervosa. The instrument has a cutting score of 102, above which scores suggest bulimia; a more liberal cutting score of 88 can be used to identify clients with bulimic symptoms. The BULIT has a factor structure suggesting five subscale areas of bulimia: binges, feelings, vomiting, food, and weight. While it is recommended that the total score be used, the subscales can be used as well to monitor clients.

NORMS: Research on the BULIT involved both bulimic and non-bulimic samples. Nineteen out of 20 bulimic patients scored above 102 while 92 out of 94 normals scored less than 102. The mean score for another bulimic sample was 124, while the average BULIT for normals was 60.3.

SCORING: Response "e" on items 1, 2, 6, 10, 16, 19, 22, 23, 30, and response "a" on items 3–5, 8, 9, 11–15, 17, 18, 20, 21, 24–29, 31, 32, 35 are the most symptomatic bulimic behavior. If your respondent circled this alternative, the item is scored as a 5; all adjacent alternatives are scored 4, 3, 2, and 1 sequentially. Total scores are then the sum of all items, except for items 7, 33, 34, and 36, which are not included in the analysis. Scores range from 32 to 160 with higher scores reflecting more serious bulimic symptoms. The following items are used for factor subscales: binges: 1, 2, 3, 4, 8, 11, 12, 17, 18, 22, 24, 28, 31, 35; feelings: 5, 6, 10, 14, 16, 19, 20, 23, 26, 29; vomiting: 1, 8, 15, 27, 30; food: 9, 21; weight: 25, 32.

RELIABILITY: There is no report of internal consistency. However, the instrument has excellent test-retest reliability (.87 for a two-week period), and is considered stable.

VALIDITY: Items were selected for inclusion based on the ability to discriminate a sample of clinically identified bulimics from normals. This is essentially evidence of known-groups validity. Differences in total scores were found between bulimic and normal subjects, again supporting the instrument's validity. With a nonclinical sample of college students, scores again differed between those categorized as bulimics and normals, based on interview ratings. The BULIT has also been shown to have excellent concurrent validity, correlating with other measures of eating disorders, such as a measure of binge eating and the Eating Attitudes Test.

PRIMARY REFERENCE: Smith, M. C. and Thelen, M. H. (1984). Development and validation of a test for bulimia, *Journal of Consulting and Clinical Psychology* 52, 863–872. Instrument reproduced with permission of Mark H. Thelen and the American Psychological Association.

AVAILABILITY: The Free Press

BULIT

Answer each question by circling the appropriate letter. Please respond to each item as honestly as possible; remember, all of the information you provide will be kept strictly confidential.

1. Do you ever eat uncontrollably to the point of stuffing yourself (i.e., going on eating binges)?
   (a) once a month or less (or never)
   (b) 2-3 times a month
   (c) Once or twice a week
   (d) 3-6 times a week
   (e) Once a day or more
2. I am satisfied with my eating patterns.
   (a) Agree
   (b) Neutral
   (c) Disagree a little
   (d) Disagree strongly
3. Have you ever kept eating until you thought you'd explode?
   (a) Practically every time I eat
   (b) Very frequently
   (c) Often
   (d) Sometimes
   (e) Seldom or never
4. Would you presently call yourself a "binge eater"?
   (a) Yes, absolutely
   (b) Yes
   (c) Yes, probably
   (d) Yes, possibly
   (e) No, probably not
5. I prefer to eat:
   (a) At home alone
   (b) At home with others
   (c) In a public restaurant
   (d) At a friend's house
   (e) Doesn't matter
6. Do you feel you have control over amount of food you consume?
   (a) Most or all of the time
   (b) A lot of the time
   (c) Occasionally
   (d) Rarely
   (e) Never
7. I use laxatives or suppositories to help control my weight.
   (a) Once a day or more
   (b) 3-6 times a week
   (c) Once or twice a week
   (d) 2-3 times a month
   (e) Once a month or less (or never)

8. I eat until I feel too tired to continue.
   (a) At least once a day
   (b) 3-6 times a week
   (c) Once or twice a week
   (d) 2-3 times a month
   (e) Once a month or less (or never)
9. How often do you prefer eating ice cream, milk shakes, or puddings during a binge?
   (a) Always
   (b) Frequently
   (c) Sometimes
   (d) Seldom or never
   (e) I don't binge
10. How much are you concerned about your eating binges?
    (a) I don't binge
    (b) Bothers me a little
    (c) Moderate concern
    (d) Major concern
    (e) Probably the biggest concern in my life
11. Most people I know would be amazed if they knew how much food I can consume at one setting.
    (a) Without a doubt
    (b) Very probably
    (c) Probably
    (d) Possibly
    (e) No
12. Do you ever eat to the point of feeling sick?
    (a) Very frequently
    (b) Frequently
    (c) Fairly often
    (d) Occasionally
    (e) Rarely or never
13. I am afraid to eat anything for fear that I won't be able to stop.
    (a) Always
    (b) Almost always
    (c) Frequently
    (d) Sometimes
    (e) Seldom or never
14. I don't like myself after I eat too much.
    (a) Always
    (b) Frequently
    (c) Sometimes
    (d) Seldom or never
    (e) I don't eat too much
15. How often do you intentionally vomit after eating?
    (a) 2 or more times a week
    (b) Once a week
    (c) 2-3 times a month
    (d) Once a month
    (e) Less than once a month (or never)

16. Which of the following describes your feelings after binge eating?
    (a) I don't binge eat
    (b) I feel O.K.
    (c) I feel mildly upset with myself
    (d) I feel quite upset with myself
    (e) I hate myself
17. I eat a lot of food when I'm not even hungry.
    (a) Very frequently
    (b) Frequently
    (c) Occasionally
    (d) Sometimes
    (e) Seldom or never
18. My eating patterns are different from eating patterns of most people.
    (a) Always
    (b) Almost always
    (c) Frequently
    (d) Sometimes
    (e) Seldom or never
19. I have tried to lose weight by fasting or going on "crash" diets.
    (a) Not in the past year
    (b) Once in the past year
    (c) 2-3 times in the past year
    (d) 4-5 times in the past year
    (e) More than 5 times in the past year
20. I feel sad or blue after eating more than I'd planned to eat.
    (a) Always
    (b) Almost always
    (c) Frequently
    (d) Sometimes
    (e) Seldom, never, or not applicable
21. When engaged in an eating binge, I tend to eat foods that are high in carbohydrates (sweets and starches).
    (a) Always
    (b) Almost always
    (c) Frequently
    (d) Sometimes
    (e) Seldom, or I don't binge
22. Compared to most people, my ability to control my eating behavior seems to be:
    (a) Greater than others' ability
    (b) About the same
    (c) Less
    (d) Much less
    (e) I have absolutely no control
23. One of your best friends suddenly suggests that you both eat at a new restaurant buffet that night. Although you'd planned on eating something light at home, you go ahead and eat out, eating quite a lot and feeling uncomfortably full. How would you feel about yourself on the ride home?
    (a) Fine, glad I'd tried that new restaurant
    (b) A little regretful that I'd eaten so much
    (c) Somewhat disappointed in myself
    (d) Upset with myself
    (e) Totally disgusted with myself

24. I would presently label myself a "compulsive eater" (one who engages in episodes of uncontrolled eating).
    (a) Absolutely
    (b) Yes
    (c) Yes, probably
    (d) Yes, possibly
    (e) No, probably not
25. What is the most weight you've ever lost in 1 month?
    (a) Over 20 pounds
    (b) 12-20 pounds
    (c) 8-11 pounds
    (d) 4-7 pounds
    (e) Less than 4 pounds
26. If I eat too much at night I feel depressed the next morning.
    (a) Always
    (b) Frequently
    (c) Sometimes
    (d) Seldom or never
    (e) I don't eat too much at night
27. Do you believe that it is easier for you to vomit than it is for most people?
    (a) Yes, it's no problem at all for me
    (b) Yes, it's easier
    (c) Yes, it's a little easier
    (d) About the same
    (e) No, it's less easy
28. I feel that food controls my life.
    (a) Always
    (b) Almost always
    (c) Frequently
    (d) Sometimes
    (e) Seldom or never
29. I feel depressed immediately after I eat too much.
    (a) Always
    (b) Frequently
    (c) Sometimes
    (d) Seldom or never
    (e) I don't eat too much
30. How often do you vomit after eating in order to lose weight?
    (a) Less than once a month (or never)
    (b) Once a month
    (c) 2-3 times a month
    (d) Once a week
    (e) 2 or more times a week
31. When consuming a large quantity of food, at what rate of speed do you usually eat?
    (a) More rapidly than most people have ever eaten in their lives
    (b) A lot more rapidly than most people
    (c) A little more rapidly than most people
    (d) About the same rate as most people
    (e) More slowly than most people (or not applicable)

32. What is the most weight you've ever gained in one month?
    (a) Over 20 pounds
    (b) 12-20 pounds
    (c) 8-11 pounds
    (d) 4-7 pounds
    (e) Less than 4 pounds
33. *Females only.* My last menstrual period was
    (a) Within the past month
    (b) Within the past 2 months
    (c) Within the past 4 months
    (d) Within the past 6 months
    (e) Not within the past 6 months
34. I use diuretics (water pills) to help control my weight.
    (a) Once a day or more
    (b) 3-6 times a week
    (c) Once or twice a week
    (d) 2-3 times a month
    (e) Once a month or less (or never)
35. How do you think your appetite compares with that of most people you know?
    (a) Many times larger than most
    (b) Much larger
    (c) A little larger
    (d) About the same
    (e) Smaller than most
36. *Females only.* My menstrual cycles occur once a month:
    (a) Always
    (b) Usually
    (c) Sometimes
    (d) Seldom
    (e) Never

CENTER FOR EPIDEMIOLOGIC STUDIES— DEPRESSED MOOD SCALE (CES-D)

AUTHOR: L. S. Radloff

PURPOSE: To measure depressive symptomatology in the general population.

DESCRIPTION: The CES-D is a 20-item scale that was originally designed to measure depression in the general population for epidemiological research. However it also has been shown to be useful in clinical and psychiatric settings. The scale is very easily administered and scored and was found to be easy to use by respondents in both the clinical and general populations. The CES-D measures current level of depressive symptomatology, with emphasis on the affective component—depressed mood. The CES-D items were selected from a pool of items from previously validated depression scales, from the literature, and from factor analytic studies. Because of the extensive research conducted in its development and its broad applicability, the CES-D is a particularly useful measure.

NORMS: Extensive research on the CES-D involved 3574 white respondents of both sexes from the general population plus a retest involving 1422 respondents. In addition, 105 psychiatric patients of both sexes were involved in clinical studies. An additional unspecified number of black respondents from the general population were involved in the testing. Means for the general population of white respondents ranged from 7.94 to 9.25. The mean for 70 psychiatric patients was 24.42. All results regarding reliability and validity were reported as being confirmed for subgroups: blacks and whites, both sexes, and three levels of education. No cutting scores were reported.

SCORING: The CES-D is easily scored by reverse-scoring items 4, 8, 12, and 16 and then summing the scores on all items. This produces a range of 0 to 60 with higher scores indicating greater depression.

RELIABILITY: The CES-D has good internal consistency with alphas of roughly .85 for the general population and .90 for the psychiatric population. Split-half and Spearman-Brown reliability coefficients ranged from .77 to .92. The CES-D has fair stability with test-retest correlations that range from .51 to .67 (tested over two to eight weeks) and .32 to .54 (tested over 3 months to one year).

VALIDITY: The CES-D has excellent concurrent validity, correlating significantly with a number of other depression and mood scales. The CES-D also has good known-groups validity, discriminating well between psychiatric inpatients and the general population, and moderately among levels of severity within patient groups. The CES-D also discriminated between people in the general population who state they "need help" and those that did not, and it was shown to

118

be sensitive to change in psychiatric patients' status after treatment. There was a very small association with social desirability response bias but it does not appear to affect the utility of CES-D.

PRIMARY REFERENCE: Radloff, L. S. (1977). The CES-D scale: A self-report depression scale for research in the general population, *Applied Psychological Measurement* 1, 385–401. Instrument reproduced with permission of Dr. Ben Z. Locke.

AVAILABILITY: Edna L. Frazier, Program Assistant, Epidemology and Psychopathology branch, Division of Clinical Research, NIMH, 5600 Fishers Lane, Rm. 10C-09, Rockville, MD 20857.

CES-D

Using the scale below, indicate the number which best describes how often you felt or behaved this way--DURING THE PAST WEEK.

```
1 = Rarely or none of the time (less than 1 day)
2 = Some or a little of the time (1-2 days)
3 = Occasionally or a moderate amount of time (3-4 days)
4 = Most or all of the time (5-7 days)
```

DURING THE PAST WEEK:

___ 1. I was bothered by things that usually don't bother me.
___ 2. I did not feel like eating; my appetite was poor.
___ 3. I felt that I could not shake off the blues even with help from my family or friends.
___ 4. I felt that I was just as good as other people.
___ 5. I had trouble keeping my mind on what I was doing.
___ 6. I felt depressed.
___ 7. I felt that everything I did was an effort.
___ 8. I felt hopeful about the future.
___ 9. I thought my life had been a failure.
___ 10. I felt fearful.
___ 11. My sleep was restless.
___ 12. I was happy.
___ 13. I talked less than usual.
___ 14. I felt lonely.
___ 15. People were unfriendly.
___ 16. I enjoyed life.
___ 17. I had crying spells.
___ 18. I felt sad.
___ 19. I felt that people disliked me.
___ 20. I could not get "going."

CLIENT SATISFACTION QUESTIONNAIRE (CSQ-8)

AUTHOR: C. Clifford Attkisson

PURPOSE: To assess client satisfaction with treatment.

DESCRIPTION: The CSQ-8 is an 8-item, easily scored and administered measure that is designed to measure client satisfaction with services. The items for the CSQ-8 were selected on the basis of ratings by mental health professionals of a number of items that could be related to client satisfaction and on subsequent factor analysis. The CSQ-8 is unidimensional, yielding a homogeneous estimate of general satisfaction with services. The CSQ has been extensively studied, and while it is not necessarily a measure of client's perceptions of gain from treatment, or outcome, it does elicit the client's perspective on the value of services received. Items 3, 7, and 8 can be used as a shorter scale.

NORMS: The CSQ-8 has been used with a number of populations. The largest single study involved 3268 clients from 76 clinical facilities including inpatients and outpatients (Roberts and Attkisson, 1984). This study involved 42 Mexican Americans, 96 non-Mexican Hispanics, 361 blacks, and 2605 whites. Both sexes and a wide range of other demographic variables were included. In essence, the CSQ-8 seems to operate about the same across all ethnic groups. This also is true for a version of the CSQ-8 that was translated into Spanish. The mean scores for the four groups ranged from 26.35 to 27.23 and were not significantly different.

SCORING: The CSQ-8 is easily scored by summing up the individual item scores to produce a range of 8 to 32, with higher scores indicating greater satisfaction.

RELIABILITY: The CSQ-8 has excellent internal consistency with alphas that range from .86 to .94 in a number of studies. Test-retest correlations were not reported.

VALIDITY: The CSQ-8 has very good concurrent validity. Scores on the CSQ-8 are correlated with clients' ratings of global improvement and symptomatology, and therapists' ratings of clients' progress and likeability. Scores also are correlated with drop-out rate (less satisfied clients having higher drop-out rates). The CSQ-8 has also demonstrated moderate correlations with a number of other (but not all) outcome variables, thus suggesting a modest correlation between satisfaction and treatment gain.

PRIMARY REFERENCE: Larsen, D. L., Attkisson, C. C., Hargreaves, W. A., and Nguyen, T. D. (1979). Assessment of client/patient satisfaction: Development of a general scale, *Evaluation and Program Planning* 2, 197–207. Instrument reproduced with permission of C. Clifford Attkisson.

AVAILABILITY: Dr. C. Clifford Attkisson, Professor of Medical Psychology, Department of Psychiatry, Box 33-C, University of California, San Francisco, CA 94143.

CSQ-8

Please help us improve our program by answering some questions you have received. We are interested in your honest opinion, whether they are positive or negative. *Please answer all of the questions.*   We also welcome your comments and suggestions. Thank you very much, we really appreciate your help.

Circle your answer:

1. How would you rate the quality of service you have received?

4	3	2	1
Excellent	Good	Fair	Poor

2. Did you get the kind of service you wanted?

1	2	3	4
No, definitely	No, not really	Yes, generally	Yes, definitely

3. To what extent has our program met your needs?

4	3	2	1
Almost all of my needs have been met	Most of my needs have been met	Only a few of my needs have been met	None of my needs have been met

4. If a friend were in need of similar help, would you recommend our program to him or her?

1	2	3	4
No, definitely not	No, I don't think so	Yes, I think so	Yes, definitely

5. How satisfied are you with the amount of help you have received?

1	2	3	4
Quite dissatisfied	Indifferent or mildly dissatisfied	Mostly satisfied	Very satisfied

6. Have the services you received helped you to deal more effectively with your problems?

4	3	2	1
Yes, they helped a great deal	Yes, they helped somewhat	No, they really didn't help	No, they seemed to make things worse

7. In an overall, general sense, how satisfied are you with the service
    you have received?

4	3	2	1
Very satisfied	Mostly satisfied	Indifferent or mildly dissat-	Quite dissatis- fied

8. If you were to seek help again, would you come back to our program?

1	2	3	4
No, definitely not	No, I don't think so	Yes, I think so	Yes, definitely

Copyright © 1978, 1985 Clifford Attkisson, Ph.D.

CLINICAL ANXIETY SCALE (CAS)

AUTHOR: Bruce A. Thyer

PURPOSE: To measure the amount, degree, or severity of clinical anxiety.

DESCRIPTION: The CAS is a 25-item scale that is focused on measuring the amount, degree, or severity of clinical anxiety reported by the respondent with higher scores indicating higher amounts of anxiety. The CAS is simply worded, and easy to administer, score, and interpret. The items for the CAS were psychometrically derived from a larger number of items based upon the criteria for anxiety disorders in DSM III. The CAS has a clinical cutting score of 30 ($\pm$ 5), and is designed to be scored and administered in the same way as the scales of the Clinical Measurement Package (Hudson, 1982), also reproduced in this book. This instrument is particularly useful for measuring general anxiety in clinical practice.

NORMS: Initial study of the CAS was based on 41 women and 6 men (average age 40.9 years) from an agoraphobic support group, 51 men and 32 women from the U.S. Army who were attending courses in health sciences (average age 25.7 years), and 58 female and 15 male university students (average age 26.6 years). No other demographic information was available.

SCORING: The CAS is scored by first reverse-scoring items 1, 6, 7, 9, 13, 15–17, totaling these and the scores on the other items, and subtracting 25. This gives a potential range of scores from 0 to 100. For scoring questionnaires with missing items, see Hudson (1982) or the instructions for scoring the Index of Family Relations in this book.

RELIABILITY: The CAS has excellent internal consistency with a coefficient alpha of .94. The SEM of 4.2 is relatively low, suggesting a minimal amount of measurement error.

VALIDITY: The CAS has good known-groups validity in being able to discriminate significantly between groups known to be suffering from anxiety and lower-anxiety control groups. Using the clinical cutting score of 30, the CAS had a very low error rate of 6.9% in distinguishing between anxiety and control groups. No other validity information was available. Analysis of the CAS in relation to demographic variables such as age, sex, and education reveals that scores on the CAS are not affected by those factors (ethnicity was not examined).

PRIMARY REFERENCE: Westhuis, D., and Thyer, B. A. Development and validation of the Clinical Anxiety Scale: A rapid assessment instrument for empirical practice, unpublished ms., 1986. Instrument reproduced with permission of Bruce A. Thyer.

AVAILABILITY: Dr. Bruce A. Thyer, University of Georgia, School of Social Work, Athens, GA 30602.

CAS

This questionnaire is designed to measure how much anxiety you are
currently feeling. It is not a test so there are no right or wrong
answers. Answer each item as carefully and as accurately as you can
by placing a number beside each one as follows:

1 = Rarely or none of the time
2 = A little of the time
3 = Some of the time
4 = A good part of the time
5 = Most or all of the time

____ 1. I feel calm.
____ 2. I feel tense.
____ 3. I feel suddenly scared for no reason.
____ 4. I feel nervous.
____ 5. I use tranquilizers or antidepressants to cope with my anxiety.
____ 6. I feel confident about the future.
____ 7. I am free from senseless or unpleasant thoughts.
____ 8. I feel afraid to go out of my house alone.
____ 9. I feel relaxed and in control of myself.
____ 10. I have spells of terror or panic.
____ 11. I feel afraid in open spaces or in the streets.
____ 12. I feel afraid I will faint in public.
____ 13. I am comfortable traveling on buses, subways, or trains.
____ 14. I feel nervousness or shakiness inside.
____ 15. I feel comfortable in crowds, such as shopping or at a movie.
____ 16. I feel comfortable when I am left alone.
____ 17. I rarely feel afraid without good reason.
____ 18. Due to my fears, I unreasonably avoid certain animals, objects,
         or situations.
____ 19. I get upset easily or feel panicky unexpectedly.
____ 20. My hands, arms, or legs shake or tremble.
____ 21. Due to my fears, I avoid social situations, whenever possible.
____ 22. I experience sudden attacks of panic which catch me by surprise.
____ 23. I feel generally anxious.
____ 24. I am bothered by dizzy spells.
____ 25. Due to my fears, I avoid being alone, whenever possible.

COGNITIVE SLIPPAGE SCALE (CSS)

AUTHORS: Tracey C. Miers and Michael L. Raulin

PURPOSE: To measure cognitive impairment.

DESCRIPTION: The CSS is a 35-item scale that is designed to measure cognitive slippage, an aspect of cognitive distortion that is viewed as a primary characteristic of schizophrenia. Cognitive slippage is also viewed as central to a schizotypic personality indicative of a genetic predisposition to schizophrenia. Cognitive slippage can be manifested in several ways such as hallucinations, delusions, speech deficits, confused thinking, and attentional disorders. The CSS focuses mainly on speech deficits and confused thinking. Although the scale was developed to identify schizotypic characteristics, it may also be useful in identifying cognitive disorders among other populations.

NORMS: The scale was developed in two series of studies eventually involving 690 male and 516 female undergraduate students in introductory psychology courses. The mean score for males was 7.8 and for females 9.3; actual norms are not reported.

SCORING: The CSS is scored by assigning a score of one to the correct response and then summing these scores. The correct response is "true" on items 2, 3–5, 9, 11, 13, 15, 18, 20, 22, 24, 25, 27, 28, 30, 31, 33. The remainder are correct if answered "false."

RELIABILITY: The CSS has excellent internal consistency with alphas of .87 for males and .90 for females. No test-retest correlations are available.

VALIDITY: The CSS has good concurrent validity in correlations with several other scales measuring schizotypic characteristics (e.g., perceptual aberration, intense ambivalence, social fear, magical ideation, somatic symptoms, and distrust). The CSS also has fair construct validity, accurately predicting scores on several scales of the MMPI between high and low scorers on the CSS. The CSS is slightly correlated with social desirability response bias suggesting that this factor cannot be totally ruled out.

PRIMARY REFERENCE: Miers, T. C. and Raulin, M. L. (1985). The development of a scale to measure cognitive slippage. Paper presented at the Eastern Psychological Association Convention, Boston, Mass., March 1985. Instrument reproduced with permission of Michael L. Raulin.

AVAILABILITY: Dr. Michael L. Raulin, SUNY-Buffalo, Psychology Department, Julian Park Hall, Buffalo, NY 14260.

CSS

Please circle either T for true or F for false for each item as it applies to you.

T F 1. My thoughts are orderly most of the time.
T F 2. I almost always feel as though my thoughts are on a different wavelength from 98% of the population.
T F 3. Often when I am talking I feel that I am not making any sense.
T F 4. Often people ask me a question and I don't know what it is that they are asking.
T F 5. Often I don't even know what it is that I have just said.
T F 6. I hardly ever find myself saying the opposite of what I meant to say.
T F 7. I rarely feel so mixed up that I have difficulty functioning.
T F 8. My thoughts are usually clear, at least to myself.
T F 9. My thoughts are more random than orderly.
T F 10. The way I perceive things is much the same as the way in which others perceive them.
T F 11. Sometimes my thoughts just disappear.
T F 12. I can usually keep my thoughts going straight.
T F 13. My thoughts are so vague and hazy that I wish that I could just reach up and pull them into place.
T F 14. I usually feel that people understand what I say.
T F 15. There have been times when I have gone an entire day or longer without speaking.
T F 16. I ordinarily don't get confused about *when* things happened.
T F 17. It's usually easy to keep the point that I am trying to make clear in my mind.
T F 18. My thoughts speed by so fast that I can't catch them.
T F 19. I usually don't feel that I'm rambling on pointlessly when I'm speaking.
T F 20. Sometimes when I try to focus on an idea, so many other thoughts come to mind that I find it impossible to concentrate on just one.
T F 21. I have no difficulty in controlling my thoughts.
T F 22. My thinking often gets "cloudy" for no apparent reason.
T F 23. I think that I am reasonably good at communicating my ideas to other people.
T F 24. I often find myself saying something that comes out completely backwards.
T F 25. My thoughts often jump from topic to topic without any logical connection.
T F 26. I'm pretty good at keeping track of time.
T F 27. Often during the day I feel as though I am being flooded by thoughts.
T F 28. The way that I process information is very different from the way in which other people do.
T F 29. I have no difficulty separating past from present.

T F   30. I often find that people are puzzled by what I say.
T F   31. My thoughts seem to come and go so quickly that I can't keep up with them.
T F   32. I can usually think things through clearly.
T F   33. I often feel confused when I try to explain my ideas.
T F   34. Usually my thoughts aren't difficult to keep track of.
T F   35. I have no difficulty in controlling my thoughts.

COGNITIVE-SOMATIC ANXIETY QUESTIONNAIRE (CSAQ)

AUTHORS: Gary E. Schwartz, Richard J. Davidson, and Daniel J. Goleman

PURPOSE: To measure cognitive and somatic components of anxiety.

DESCRIPTION: The CSAQ is a 14-item, simply worded, easy to understand measure of the cognitive and somatic aspects of anxiety. The scale is based on the assumption that there are two different aspects of anxiety—cognitive and somatic. The importance of this for practice is that therapeutic techniques for reducing anxiety may differ in their impact on these two systems. Thus, by providing information on each aspect of anxiety, this measure allows the practitioner to be more precise in selecting intervention techniques. The CSAQ is considered to be a trait measure of anxiety in that it taps relatively enduring patterns.

NORMS: The initial study was conducted on 77 respondents consisting of 44 participants in a physical exercise class and 33 volunteers who practiced cognitively based passive meditation at least once daily. The physical exercisers were predominantly female with an average age of 27.3 years while the meditators were approximately equally divided between males and females and had an average age of 20.86 years. No real effort was made to develop norms due to the size and nature of the samples.

SCORING: The cognitive (items 1, 3, 6, 8, 9, 10, 13) and somatic items of the CSAQ appear in random order and are scored by totaling the sums of the scores on each item. Separate scores are computed for the cognitive and somatic scales with a range for each of 7 to 35.

RELIABILITY: No data reported.

VALIDITY: The CSAQ has good concurrent validity, correlating significantly with the State-Trait Anxiety Inventory. The CSAQ also demonstrated a type of known-groups validity in that respondents who were meditators reported less cognitive and more somatic anxiety than physical exercisers and the exercisers reported more cognitive and less somatic anxiety. The two groups did not differ on overall anxiety, supporting the idea that anxiety may not be a diffuse, undifferentiated state, but may be subdivided into component parts.

PRIMARY REFERENCE: Schwartz, G. E., Davidson, R. J., and Goleman, D. J. (1978). Patterning of cognitive and somatic processes in the self-regulation of anxiety: Effects of meditation versus exercise, *Psychosomatic Medicine* 40, 321–328. Instrument reproduced by permission of Gary E. Schwartz and Daniel J. Goleman and the Elsevier Science Publishing Co., Inc.

AVAILABILITY: Journal article.

CSAQ

Please read the following and rate the degree to which you generally or typically experience each symptom when you are feeling anxious. Rate each item by filling in *one* number from 1 through 5 in the left-hand column, with 1 representing "not at all" and 5 representing "very much so." Be sure to answer every item and try to be as honest and accurate as possible in your responses.

1	2	3	4	5
Not at all				Very much so

____ 1. Some unimportant thought runs through my mind and bothers me.
____ 2. I perspire.
____ 3. I imagine terrifying scenes.
____ 4. I become immobilized.
____ 5. My heart beats faster.
____ 6. I can't keep anxiety-provoking pictures out of my mind.
____ 7. I nervously pace.
____ 8. I find it difficult to concentrate because of uncontrollable thoughts.
____ 9. I can't keep anxiety-provoking thoughts out of my mind.
____ 10. I feel like I am losing out on things because I can't make up my mind soon enough.
____ 11. I feel tense in my stomach.
____ 12. I get diarrhea.
____ 13. I worry too much over something that doesn't really matter.
____ 14. I feel jittery in my body.

THE COMPULSIVENESS INVENTORY (CI)

AUTHORS: Dona M. Kagan and Rose L. Squires

PURPOSE: To measure nonpathological compulsiveness.

DESCRIPTION: The 11-item CI, based on the Leyton Obsessional Inventory, is designed to measure compulsive behaviors that are common in the normal population. Pathological compulsiveness is defined in terms of extreme preoccupation with thoughts or activities, a tendency toward overorganization and difficulty making decisions. This scale focuses specifically on overconcern with decisions and tasks to be completed perfectly according to rigid well-established norms. It measures three aspects of compulsivity: indecision and double checking (IDC), order and regularity (OR), detail and perfection (DP). The total score on the CI can also be used as a general measure of compulsiveness.

NORMS: Normative data are not available from the primary references. The CI was developed on a sample of 563 college students. Three hundred and four subjects were males and 259 were female. The average age was 28.2 with a standard deviation of 7.4 years.

SCORING: The scores on the CI are the total number of "yes" responses. Items for the subscales are: IDC: 1, 2, 3, 4, 5; DT: 6, 7, 8, 9; OR: 10, 11.

RELIABILITY: The reliability of the CI is presented for each subscale using coefficient alpha. The internal consistency for the subscales was excellent and was .89 for the IDC, .88 for OR, and .85 for DP. Alpha for the total CI was .80. No information on stability was reported.

VALIDITY: Criterion validity was estimated by correlating the subscales with numerous personality measures. While the results are not separately presented, the summary indicates that the CI subscales correlate with behavioral dimensions of rigidity in men and women, compulsive eating and dieting, and several other measures.

PRIMARY REFERENCE: Kagan, D. M. and Squires, R. L. (1985). Measuring non-pathological compulsiveness, Psychological Reports 57, 559–563, and Squires, R. L. and Kagan, D. M. (1985). Personality correlates of disordered eating, International Journal of Eating Disorders, 4, 80–85. Reprinted with permission of Donna M. Kagan and John Wiley and Sons, Inc.

AVAILABILITY: Journal article.

CI

Respond to each question below by circling "yes" or "no."

Yes No 1. Do you have to turn things over and over in your mind for a long time before being able to decide what to do?
Yes No 2. Do you often have to check things several times?
Yes No 3. Do you ever have to do things over again a certain number of times before they seem quite right?
Yes No 4. Do you have difficulty making up your mind?
Yes No 5. Do you have to go back and check doors, cupboards, or windows to make sure they are really shut?
Yes No 6. Do you dislike having a room untidy or not quite clean for even a short time?
Yes No 7. Do you take great care in hanging and folding your clothes at night?
Yes No 8. Do you like to keep a certain order to undressing and dressing or washing or bathing?
Yes No 9. Do you like to put your personal belongings in set places?
Yes No 10. Do you like to get things done exactly right down to the smallest detail?
Yes No 11. Are you the sort of person who has to pay a great deal of attention to details?

COSTELLO-COMREY DEPRESSION AND ANXIETY SCALES
(CCDAS)

AUTHORS: C. G. Costello and Andrew L. Comrey

PURPOSE: To measure depression and anxiety.

DESCRIPTION: The CCDAS is a 14-item depression scale and a 9-item anxiety scale that can be administered separately or together. These scales were initially developed separately but eventually combined into a package for final psychometric analysis. Based on independent studies utilizing a large number of items and factor analysis, the "best" depression and anxiety items were combined to form the CCDAS. These scales are viewed more as trait than state scales. The depression scale measures a person's tendency to experience a depressive mood, while the anxiety scale measures a predisposition to develop anxious affective states.

NORMS: The CCDAS was developed in a number of studies involving several hundred male and female respondents with a wide age range and number of occupations. The sample included nonclinical and clinical populations. Although means are available on earlier versions of the scales, norms were not reported for the latest CCDAS.

SCORING: All items are scored on a 1 to 9 scale, with two categories of response depending on the item: "absolutely" to "absolutely not" and "always" to "never." Scores for the anxiety and depression scales are calculated separately by reverse-scoring items 1, 6, 7, 8, 9, and 10 on the depression scale and item 3 on the anxiety scale and then summing the items on each scale. This will produce a range of 14 to 126 on the depression scale and 9 to 81 on the anxiety scale, with higher scores on both scales representing greater depression or anxiety.

RELIABILITY: The depression scale has excellent internal consistency with split-half reliabilities of .90; split-half reliability for the anxiety scale was .70. Both scales are fairly stable with test-retest correlations after admission and before discharge for psychiatric patients (no time given) of .72 for anxiety and .70 for depression (it is not clear in this case if this finding means the scales are not sensitive to change).

VALIDITY: The CCDAS has fair concurrent validity; its anxiety scale is correlated with the Taylor Manifest Anxiety Scales and the depression scale is correlated with the Depression scale of the MMPI. There is a small to moderate correlation between the CCDAS and social desirability, suggesting some response bias may be present.

PRIMARY REFERENCE: Costello, C. G. and Comrey, A. L. (1967). Scales for measuring depression and anxiety, *The Journal of Psychology* 66, 303–313. Instrument reproduced with permission of *The Journal of Psychology*.

AVAILABILITY: Journal article.

CDDAS

Please circle the number that best describes your response to each item.

Depression Scale

1. I feel that life is worthwhile.

Absolutely	Very definitely	Definitely	Probably	Possibly	Probably not	Definitely not	Very definitely not	Absolutely not
9	8	7	6	5	4	3	2	1

2. When I wake up in the morning I expect to have a miserable day.

Always	Almost always	Very frequently	Frequently	Fairly often	Occasionally	Rarely	Almost never	Never
9	8	7	6	5	4	3	2	1

3. I wish I had never been born.

Absolutely	Very definitely	Definitely	Probably	Possibly	Probably not	Definitely not	Very definitely not	Absolutely not
9	8	7	6	5	4	3	2	1

4. I feel that there is more disappointment in life than satisfaction.

Absolutely	Very definitely	Definitely	Probably	Possibly	Probably not	Definitely not	Very definitely not	Absolutely not
9	8	7	6	5	4	3	2	1

5. I want to run away from everything.

Always	Almost always	Very frequently	Frequently	Fairly often	Occasionally	Rarely	Almost never	Never
9	8	7	6	5	4	3	2	1

133

6. My future looks hopeful and promising.

Absolutely	Very definitely	Definitely	Probably	Possibly	Probably not	Definitely not	Very definitely not	Absolutely not
9	8	7	6	5	4	3	2	1

7. When I get up in the morning I expect to have an interesting day.

Always	Almost always	Very frequently	Frequently	Fairly often	Occasionally	Rarely	Almost never	Never
9	8	7	6	5	4	3	2	1

8. Living is a wonderful adventure for me.

Always	Almost always	Very frequently	Frequently	Fairly often	Occasionally	Rarely	Almost never	Never
9	8	7	6	5	4	3	2	1

9. I am a happy person.

Always	Almost always	Very frequently	Frequently	Fairly often	Occasionally	Rarely	Almost never	Never
9	8	7	6	5	4	3	2	1

10. Things have worked out well for me.

Absolutely	Very definitely	Definitely	Probably	Possibly	Probably not	Definitely not	Very definitely not	Absolutely not
9	8	7	6	5	4	3	2	1

11. The future looks so gloomy that I wonder if I should go on.

Always	Almost always	Very frequently	Frequently	Fairly often	Occasionally	Rarely	Almost never	Never
9	8	7	6	5	4	3	2	1

12. I feel that life is drudgery and boredom.

Always 9	Almost always 8	Very frequently 7	Frequently 6	Fairly often 5	Occasionally 4	Rarely 3	Almost never 2	Never 1

13. I feel blue and depressed.

Always 9	Almost always 8	Very frequently 7	Frequently 6	Fairly often 5	Occasionally 4	Rarely 3	Almost never 2	Never 1

14. When I look back I think life has been good to me.

Absolutely 9	Very definitely 8	Definitely 7	Probably 6	Possibly 5	Probably not 4	Definitely not 3	Very definitely not 2	Absolutely not 1

Anxiety Scale

1. I get rattled easily.

Always 9	Almost always 8	Very frequently 7	Frequently 6	Fairly often 5	Occasionally 4	Rarely 3	Almost never 2	Never 1

2. When faced with excitement or unexpected situations, I become nervous and jumpy.

Always 9	Almost always 8	Very frequently 7	Frequently 6	Fairly often 5	Occasionally 4	Rarely 3	Almost never 2	Never 1

3. I am calm and not easily upset.

Always 9	Almost always 8	Very frequently 7	Frequently 6	Fairly often 5	Occasionally 4	Rarely 3	Almost never 2	Never 1

4. When things go wrong I get nervous and upset instead of calmly thinking out a solution.

Always	Almost always	Very frequently	Frequently	Fairly often	Occasionally	Rarely	Almost never	Never
9	8	7	6	5	4	3	2	1

5. It makes me nervous when I have to wait.

Always	Almost always	Very frequently	Frequently	Fairly often	Occasionally	Rarely	Almost never	Never
9	8	7	6	5	4	3	2	1

6. I am a tense "high-strung" person.

Absolutely	Very definitely	Definitely	Probably	Possibly	Probably not	Definitely not	Very definitely not	Absolutely not
9	8	7	6	5	4	3	2	1

7. I am more sensitive than most other people.

Absolutely	Very definitely	Definitely	Probably	Possibly	Probably not	Definitely not	Very definitely not	Absolutely not
9	8	7	6	5	4	3	2	1

8. My hand shakes when I try to do something.

Always	Almost always	Very frequently	Frequently	Fairly often	Occasionally	Rarely	Almost never	Never
9	8	7	6	5	4	3	2	1

9. I am a very nervous person.

Absolutely	Very definitely	Definitely	Probably	Possibly	Probably not	Definitely not	Very definitely not	Absolutely not
9	8	7	6	5	4	3	2	1

DATING AND ASSERTION QUESTIONNAIRE (DAQ)

AUTHORS: Robert W. Levenson and John M. Gottman

PURPOSE: To measure social competence.

DESCRIPTION: The 18-item DAQ was designed to measure social competence in two social situations: dating and assertion; the focus is on social skills. Nine items measure the general social skills of dating and nine measure assertion. The measures are sensitive to change resulting from social skills training and therefore, are clinically useful. The Dating items and Assertion items form two separate measures. One limitation of the DAT is that two, and possibly three, of the items pertain to social stituations for college students and would not be relevant to other clients.

NORMS: Normative data on the DAQ are limited. The two subscales were developed on samples of college students, including those volunteering for social skills training in dating ($n = 46$) and assertiveness training ($n = 46$). Posttest scores for the dating skills training group were 2.41 on the Dating subscale and 2.76 on the Assertion subscale; posttest scores for subjects in the assertiveness training were 3.02 for the Dating subscale and 3.02 for the Assertion subscale.

SCORING: Half of the items are rated on a 1 to 4 scale of how frequently the respondent performs the specified behavior. The other half are rated on a 1 to 5 scale according to how comfortable the respondent would feel in the specified situation. Separate scores are computed for the dating and assertion subscales, noted by an "A" or a "D" beside the items. To compute the assertion subscale score add the responses to items 1, 3, 4 and 6, then divide by 4; next add the responses to items 10, 12, 15, 16 and 18, then divide that product by 5; add these two products to get an assertion subscale score. To compute the dating subscale score add the responses to items 2, 5, 7, 8 and 9 and then divide the product by 5; next add the response to items 11, 13, 14 and 17, and then divide by 4. Add these two products together for a dating subscale score. These scoring procedures are summarized as: Assertion subscale score = [(items 1 + 3 + 4 + 6) ÷ 4] + [(items 10 + 12 + 15 + 16 + 18) ÷ 5]. Dating subscale score = [(items 2 + 5 + 7 + 8 + 9) ÷ 5] + [(items 11 + 13 + 14 + 17) ÷ 4]. Both subscale scores range from one to nine.

RELIABILITY: These subscales have good to excellent reliability. Their internal consistency using coefficient alpha was .92 and .85 for the dating and assertive subscales, respectively. The test-retest reliability correlation was also good with both scales correlating .71 over a two-week period. The subscales were only slightly less stable when tested over a six-week test-retest period.

VALIDITY: The validity of these subscales is supported by known-groups

137

validity where significantly different scores were found between a clinical sample and a non-clinical ("normal") sample of college students. Scores were also significantly different for people identified as having dating and assertive problems compared to a sample of "normal" college subjects. Both instruments have been shown to be sensitive to measuring change resulting from social skills training.

PRIMARY REFERENCE: Levenson, R. W. and Gottman, J. M. (1978). Toward the assessment of social competence, *Journal of Consulting and Clinical Psychology* 46, 453–462. Instrument reproduced with permission of Robert W. Levenson and the American Psychological Association.

AVAILABILITY: Journal article.

DAQ

We are interested in finding out something about the likelihood of your acting in certain ways. Below you will find a list of specific behaviors you may or may not exhibit. Use the following rating scale:

1 = I never do this
2 = I sometimes do this
3 = I often do this
4 = I do this almost always

Now next to each of the items on the following list, place the number which best indicates the likelihood of your behaving in that way. Be as objective as possible.

____ 1. Stand up for your rights (A)
____ 2. Maintain a long conversation with a member of the opposite sex (D)
____ 3. Be confident in your ability to succeed in a situation in which you have to demonstrate your competence (A)
____ 4. Say "no" when you feel like it (A)
____ 5. Get a second date with someone you have dated once (D)
____ 6. Assume a role of leadership (A)
____ 7. Be able to accurately sense how a member of the opposite sex feels about you (D)
____ 8. Have an intimate emotional relationship with a member of the opposite sex (D)
____ 9. Have an intimate physical relationship with a member of the opposite sex (D)

The following questions describe a variety of social situations that you might encounter. In each situation you may feel "put on the spot." Some situations may be familiar to you, and others may not. We'd like you to read each situation and try to imagine yourself actually in the situation. The more vividly you get a mental picture and place yourself into the situation, the better.

After each situation circle one of the numbers from 1 to 5 which best describes you using the following scale:

1 = I would be so uncomfortable and so unable to handle this situation that I would avoid it if possible.
2 = I would feel very uncomfortable and would have a lot of difficulty handling this situation.
3 = I would feel somewhat uncomfortable and would have some difficulty in handling this situation.

4 = I would feel quite comfortable and would be able to handle
    this situation fairly well.
5 = I would feel very comfortable and be able to handle this
    situation very well.

____ 10. You're waiting patiently in line at the checkout when a
        couple of people cut right in front of you. You feel really
        annoyed and want to tell them to wait their turn at the back
        of the line. One of them says, "Look, you don't mind do you?
        But we're in a terrible hurry." (A)

____ 11. You have enjoyed this date and would like to see your date
        again. The evening is coming to a close and you decide to say
        something. (D)

____ 12. You are talking to a professor about dropping a class. You
        explain your situation, which you fabricate slightly for effect.
        Looking at his grade book the professor comments that you are
        pretty far behind. You go into greater detail about why you
        are behind and why you'd like to be allowed to withdraw from
        his class. He then says, "I'm sorry, but it's against
        university policy to let you withdraw this late in the
        semester." (A)

____ 13. You meet someone you don't know very well but are attracted to.
        You want to ask him/her out for a date. (D)

____ 14. You meet someone of the opposite sex at lunch and have a very
        enjoyable conversation. You'd like to get together again and
        decide to say something. (D)

____ 15. Your roommate has several obnoxious traits that upset you very
        much. So far, you have mentioned them once or twice, but no
        noticeable changes have occurred. You still have 3 months
        left to live together. You decide to say something. (A)

____ 16. You're with a small group of people who you don't know too
        well. Most of them are expressing a point of view that you
        disagree with. You'd like to state your opinion even if it
        means you'll probably be in the minority. (A)

____ 17. You go to a party where you don't know many people. Someone
        of the opposite sex approaches you and introduces themself.
        You want to start a conversation and get to know him/her. (D)

____ 18. You are trying to make an appointment with the dean. You are
        talking to his secretary face-to-face. She asks you what
        division you are in and when you tell her, she starts asking
        you questions about the nature of your problem. You inquire
        as to why she is asking all these questions and she replies
        very snobbishly that she is the person who decides if your
        problem is important enough to warrant an audience with the
        dean. You decide to say something. (A)

DEATH ANXIETY SCALE (DAS)

AUTHOR: Donald I. Templer

PURPOSE: To measure death anxiety.

DESCRIPTION: The DAS is a 15-item instrument that is designed to measure respondents' anxiety about death. The DAS includes a broad range of items and concerns about death. The instrument was carefully developed from an original pool of 40 items and has been found to be relatively free of response bias and social-desirability response set. Several factor analytic studies of the DAS have identified a number of different factors, although essentially, the overall score is what is considered meaningful. A major advantage of the DAS is that it has been studied and used extensively with a variety of populations. Information is available demonstrating the relationship between the DAS and age, sex, religion, specific environmental influences, personality, physical and mental health, life expectancy, and a variety of behaviors.

NORMS: The DAS has been tested with a variety of samples including males and females, adolescents and adults, psychiatric patients, and a number of occupational groups. Respondents total in the several thousands. Norms for some groups have been reported: means of "normal" respondents vary from 4.5 to 7.0 with DAS scores being higher for females and psychiatric patients. For a cross-sectional sample of middle class people, the means reported were: 7.50 for youths, 7.25 for young adults, 6.85 for middle-aged, and 5.74 for elderly respondents.

SCORING: The DAS is scored by assigning a score of one to each item correctly answered (1 = T, 2 = F, 3 = F, 4 = T, 5 = F, 6 = F, 7 = F, 8–14 = T, 15 = F), and then totaling across items.

RELIABILITY: The DAS has fairly good internal consistency with a Kuder-Richardson formula coefficient of .76. The DAS also has good stability with a three-week test-retest correlation of .83.

VALIDITY: The DAS has good concurrent validity, correlating .74 with the Fear of Death Scale. It also has demonstrated good known-groups validity, distinguishing significantly between a group of psychiatric patients who verbalized high death anxiety and a control group.

PRIMARY REFERENCE: Lonetto, R. and Templer, D. I. (1983). The nature of death anxiety, in C. D. Spielberger and J. N. Butcher (eds.), *Advances in Personality Assessment*, Vol 3. Hillsdale, N.J.: Lawrence Erlbaum, pp. 14–174. Instrument reproduced with permission of Donald I. Templer.

AVAILABILITY: Dr. Donald I. Templer, California School of Professional Psychology, 1350 M Street, Fresno, CA 93721.

DAS

If a statement is true or mostly true as applied to you, circle "T."
If a statement is false or mostly false as applied to you, circle
"F."

T   F   1.   I am very much afraid to die.
T   F   2.   The thought of death seldom enters my mind.
T   F   3.   It doesn't make me nervous when people talk about death.
T   F   4.   I dread to think about having to have an operation.
T   F   5.   I am not at all afraid to die.
T   F   6.   I am not particularly afraid of getting cancer.
T   F   7.   The thought of death never bothers me.
T   F   8.   I am often distressed by the way time flies so very
              rapidly.
T   F   9.   I fear dying a painful death.
T   F   10.   The subject of life after death troubles me greatly.
T   F   11.   I am really scared of having a heart attack.
T   F   12.   I often think about how short life really is.
T   F   13.   I shudder when I hear people talking about a World War III.
T   F   14.   The sight of a dead body is horrifying to me.
T   F   15.   I feel that the future holds nothing for me to fear.

DYSFUNCTIONAL ATTITUDE SCALE (DAS)

AUTHOR: Arlene Weissman

PURPOSE: To measure cognitive distortion.

DESCRIPTION: The DAS is a 40-item instrument designed to identify cognitive distortions—particularly the distortions that may underlie or cause depression. Based on the cognitive therapy model of Aaron Beck, the items on the DAS were constructed so as to represent seven major value systems: approval, love, achievement, perfectionism, entitlement, omnipotence, and autonomy. Two 40-item parallel forms of the DAS which are highly correlated and have roughly the same psychometric properties, were derived from an original pool of 100 items. Although the overall score on the DAS is considered the key measure, practitioners can also examine areas where the respondent is emotionally vulnerable or strong by analyzing responses to specific items. Clinical work can then be directed at correcting the distortions underlying the depression, rather than only at the depressive symptoms per se.

NORMS: The DAS was developed in a series of studies ultimately involving some 216 male and 485 female, predominantly white undergraduate students. Other research involved 105 depressed outpatients, 30 manic-depressive outpatients and their spouses, and 107 depressed patients. No actual norms were reported since the number of DAS items varied among these studies. For nonclinical respondents, the mean score is approximately 113.

SCORING: The DAS is easily scored by using zeros for items omitted, assigning a score of 1 (on a 7-point scale) to the adaptive end of the scale, and simply summing up the scores on all items. With no items omitted, scores on the DAS range from 40 to 280 with lower scores equaling more adaptive beliefs (few cognitive distortions).

RELIABILITY: The DAS has excellent internal consistency with alphas on the form of the DAS reproduced here ranging from .84 to .92. The DAS also has excellent stability with test-retest correlations over eight weeks of .80 to .84.

VALIDITY: The DAS has excellent concurrent validity, significantly correlating with a number of other measures of depression and depressive-distortions such as the Beck Depression Inventory, the Profile of Mood States, and the Story Completion Test. The DAS also has good known-groups validity, significantly distinguishing between groups diagnosed as depressed or not depressed on the Beck Depression Inventory. The DAS also was found to be sensitive to change following clinical intervention with depressed outpatients.

PRIMARY REFERENCE: Weissman, A. N. (1980). Assessing depressogenic attitudes: A validation study. Paper presented at the 51st Annual Meeting of the Eastern Psychological Association, Hartford, Connecticut. Instrument reproduced with permission of Arlene N. Weissman.

AVAILABILITY: Dr. Arlene Weissman, Towers, Perrin, Forster, and Crosby, 1500 Market Street, Philadelphia, PA 19102.

DAS

This questionnaire lists different attitudes or beliefs which people sometimes hold. Read *each* statement carefully and decide how much you agree or disagree with the statement.

For each of the attitudes, indicate to the left of the item the number that *best describes how you think*. Be sure to choose only one answer for each attitude. Because people are different, there is no right answer or wrong answer to these statements. Your answers are confidential, so please do not put your name on this sheet.

To decide whether a given attitude is typical of your way of looking at things, simply keep in mind what you are like *most of the time*.

    1 = Totally agree
    2 = Agree very much
    3 = Agree slightly
    4 = Neutral
    5 = Disagree slightly
    6 = Disagree very much
    7 = Totally disagree

____ 1. It is difficult to be happy unless one is good looking, intelligent, rich, and creative.
____ 2. Happiness is more a matter of my attitude towards myself than the way other people feel about me.
____ 3. People will probably think less of me if I make a mistake.
____ 4. If I do not do well all the time, people will not respect me.
____ 5. Taking even a small risk is foolish because the loss is likely to be a disaster.
____ 6. It is possible to gain another person's respect without being especially talented at anything.
____ 7. I cannot be happy unless most people I know admire me.
____ 8. If a person asks for help, it is a sign of weakness.
____ 9. If I do not do as well as other people, it means I am a weak person.
____ 10. If I fail at my work, then I am a failure as a person.
____ 11. If you cannot do something well, there is little point in doing it at all.
____ 12. Making mistakes is fine because I can learn from them.
____ 13. If someone disagrees with me, it probably indicates he does not like me.
____ 14. If I fail partly, it is as bad as being a complete failure.

___ 15. If other people know what you are really like, they will think less of you.

___ 16. I am nothing if a person I love doesn't love me.

___ 17. One can get pleasure from an activity regardless of the end result.

___ 18. People should have a chance to succeed before doing anything.

___ 19. My value as a person depends greatly on what others think of me.

___ 20. If I don't set the highest standards for myself, I am likely to end up a second-rate person.

___ 21. If I am to be a worthwhile person, I must be the best in at least one way.

___ 22. People who have good ideas are better than those who do not.

___ 23. I should be upset if I make a mistake.

___ 24. My own opinions of myself are more important than others' opinions of me.

___ 25. To be a good, moral, worthwhile person I must help everyone who needs it.

___ 26. If I ask a question, it makes me look stupid.

___ 27. It is awful to be put down by people important to you.

___ 28. If you don't have other people to lean on, you are going to be sad.

___ 29. I can reach important goals without pushing myself.

___ 30. It is possible for a person to be scolded and not get upset.

___ 31. I cannot trust other people because they might be cruel to me.

___ 32. If others dislike you, you cannot be happy.

___ 33. It is best to give up your own interests in order to please other people.

___ 34. My happiness depends more on other people than it does on me.

___ 35. I do not need the approval of other people in order to be happy.

___ 36. If a person avoids problems, the problems tend to go away.

___ 37. I can be happy even if I miss out on many of the good things in life.

___ 38. What other people think about me is very important.

___ 39. Being alone leads to unhappiness.

___ 40. I can find happiness without being loved by another person.

EATING ATTITUDES TEST (EAT)

AUTHORS: David M. Garner and Paul E. Garfinkel

PURPOSE: To measure symptoms of anorexia nervosa.

DESCRIPTION: The 40-item EAT was designed to measure a broad range of behaviors and attitudes characteristic of anorexia nervosa. Each item is a symptom frequently observed in the disorder. The instrument has a rough cutting score of 30, above which scores indicate anorectic eating concerns. The EAT is helpful in identifying clients with serious eating concerns even if they do not show the weight loss classic to this disorder.

NORMS: The EAT was initially developed using two samples of patients diagnosed as manifesting anorexia nervosa (n = 32 and n = 34). The average age of the onset of the disorder was 18.4 years. Two "normal" control groups were also used which were composed of Canadian college students (n = 34 and n = 59). The normal control subjects and anorectics were from similar socioeconomic backgrounds, and the average age for the four groups was approximately 22.4 years old. Average EAT scores for one of the anorectic samples was 58.9 with a standard deviation of 13.3. The normal control sample of 59 had a mean of 15.6 with a standard deviation of 9.3. A group of clinically recovered anorectics (n = 9) had a mean of 11.4 and a standard deviation of 5.1.

SCORING: The 40 items are scored in terms of how frequently the person experiences them. Items 1, 18, 19, 23 and 39 are scored as follows: 6 = 3, 5 = 2, 4 = 1 and 3, 2 and 1 = 0. The remaining items are scored as follows: 1 = 2, 2 = 2, 3 = 1, and 4, 5 and 6 = 0. Items 2-17, 20-22, 24-26, 28-38, 40 when marked "Always" and items 1, 18, 19, 23, and 39 when marked "Never" indicate anorexia. Total scores are the sum of the item values, and range from 0 to 120.

RELIABILITY: This instrument has evidence of excellent internal consistency with a coefficient alpha of .94 for a combined sample of anorectics and normals. For the anorectic subjects alone, the coefficient was .79.

VALIDITY: A 23-item prototype of this instrument was tested for known-groups validity. Scores differed significantly for a sample of anorectics and "normals." This finding was replicated in a separate sample. The EAT was shown to be independent of the Restraint Scale, weight fluctuation, extroversion, and neuroticism. Post hoc analysis of a group of recovered anorectics indicated that scores were in the normal range, suggesting the scale is sensitive.

PRIMARY REFERENCE: Garner, D. M. and Garfinkel, P. E. (1979). The

Eating Attitudes Test: An index of the symptoms of anorexia nervosa, *Psychological Medicine* 9, 273–279. Instrument reproduced with permission of David Garner.

AVAILABILITY: Dr. David Garner, 200 Elizabeth Street, Bell Wing H-639, Toronto, Ontario M5G2C4, Canada or from this book.

EAT

Please indicate on the line at left the answer which applies best to each of the numbered statements. All of the results will be *strictly* confidential. Most of the questions directly relate to food or eating, although other types of questions have been included. Please answer each question carefully. Thank you.

1 = Always
2 = Very often
3 = Often
4 = Sometimes
5 = Rarely
6 = Never

____ 1. Like eating with other people.
____ 2. Prepare foods for others but do not eat what I cook.
____ 3. Become anxious prior to eating.
____ 4. Am terrified about being overweight.
____ 5. Avoid eating when I am hungry.
____ 6. Find myself preoccupied with food.
____ 7. Have gone on eating binges where I feel that I may not be able to stop.
____ 8. Cut my food into small pieces.
____ 9. Aware of the calorie content of foods that I eat.
____ 10. Particularly avoid foods with a high carbohydrate content (e.g., bread, potatoes, rice, etc.).
____ 11. Feel bloated after meals.
____ 12. Feel that others would prefer if I ate more.
____ 13. Vomit after I have eaten.
____ 14. Feel extremely guilty after eating.
____ 15. Am preoccupied with a desire to be thinner.
____ 16. Exercise strenuously to burn off calories.
____ 17. Weigh myself several times a day.
____ 18. Like my clothes to fit tightly.
____ 19. Enjoy eating meat.
____ 20. Wake up early in the morning.
____ 21. Eat the same foods day after day.
____ 22. Think about burning my calories when I exercise.
____ 23. Have regular menstrual periods.
____ 24. Other people think that I am too thin.
____ 25. Am preoccupied with the thought of having fat on my body.
____ 26. Take longer than others to eat my meals.
____ 27. Enjoy eating at restaurants.
____ 28. Take laxatives.
____ 29. Avoid foods with sugar in them.
____ 30. Eat diet foods.
____ 31. Feel that food controls my life.
____ 32. Display self control around food.

___ 33. Feel that others pressure me to eat.
___ 34. Give too much time and thought to food.
___ 35. Suffer from constipation.
___ 36. Feel uncomfortable after eating sweets.
___ 37. Engage in dieting behaviour.
___ 38. Like my stomach to be empty.
___ 39. Enjoy trying new rich foods.
___ 40. Have the impulse to vomit after meals.

EGO IDENTITY SCALE (EIS)

AUTHORS: Allen L. Tan, Randall J. Kendis, Judith Fine, and Joseph Porac

PURPOSE: To measure ego identity.

DESCRIPTION: The EIS is a 12-item scale that measures Erik Erikson's concept of ego identity. The authors reviewed Erikson's characterization of ego identity achievement and developed 41 pairs of forced-choice items with one item representing ego identity and one representing ego diffusion. Ego identity was defined as acceptance of self, a sense of direction. Identity diffusion implies doubts about one's self, lack of sense of continuity over time, and inability to make decisions and commitments. This pool of 41 items was reduced to 12 on the basis of their ability to discriminate between high and lower scorers across all 41 items, and imperviousness to social desirability response set.

NORMS: A series of studies to develop the EIS was conducted involving 249 undergraduate students. No other demographic data or norms were reported.

SCORING: The EIS is scored by assigning a score of 1 to each statement that reflects ego identity and that is circled by the respondent, then summing the scores. The items that reflect ego identity are 1a, 2b, 3b, 4a, 5b, 6b, 7b, 8a, 9b, 10b, 11a, 12a.

RELIABILITY: The EIS has only fair internal consistency with a split-half reliability coefficient of .68. No other reliability information was reported.

VALIDITY: The EIS correlated significantly and in predicted directions with four personality variables: internal control, intimacy, dogmatism, and extent to which an individual derives his or her values from his or her own life experiences. These correlations provide some evidence of construct validity. The EIS also correlated significantly with indices of political and occupational commitment.

PRIMARY REFERENCE: Tan, A. L., Kendis, R. J., Fine, J. T., and Porac, J. (1977). A Short Measure of Eriksonian Ego Identity, *Journal of Personality Assessment* 41, 279–284. Instrument reproduced with permission of Allen Tan, Randall Kendis, and Judith Fine.

AVAILABILITY: Journal article or Dr. Randall Kendis, 10171 Kingbird Avenue, Fountain Valley, CA 92708 (stamped, self-addressed envelope).

EIS

On these pages, you will see 12 PAIRS of statements. Each pair consists
of an *a* statement and a *b* statement. Read each of them carefully, and
choose which of the two describes *you* better. If it is statement *a*,
then encircle the letter *a* that appears before the statement. If it is
statement *b*, then encircle the letter *b* that precedes the statement.
Make sure that you make a choice on every one of the 12 pairs of
statements.

1. a. I enjoy being active in clubs and youth groups.
   b. I prefer to focus on hobbies which I can do on my own time, at
      my own pace.
2. a. When I daydream, it is primarily about my past experiences.
   b. When I daydream, it is primarily about the future and what it
      has in store for me.
3. a. No matter how well I do a job, I always end up thinking that I
      could have done better.
   b. When I complete a job that I have seriously worked on, I usually
      do not have doubts as to its quality.
4. a. I will generally voice an opinion, even if I appear to be the
      only one in a group with that point of view.
   b. If I appear to be the only one in a group with a certain
      opinion, I try to keep quiet in order to avoid feeling self-
      conscious.
5. a. Generally speaking, a person can keep much better control of
      himself and of situations if he maintains an emotional distance
      from others.
   b. A person need not feel loss of control, of himself, and of
      situations simply because he becomes intimately involved with
      another person.
6. a. I have doubts as to the kind of person my abilities will enable
      me to become.
   b. I try to formulate ideas now which will help me achieve my
      future goals.
7. a. My evaluation of self-worth depends on the success or failure of
      my behavior in a given situation.
   b. My self-evaluation, while flexible, remains about the same in
      most situations.
8. a. While there may be disadvantages to competition, I agree that it
      is sometimes necessary and even good.
   b. I do not enjoy competition, and often do not see the need for it.
9. a. There are times when I don't know what is expected of me.
   b. I have a clear vision of how my life will unfold ahead of me.
10. a. What I demand of myself and what others demand of me are often
       in conflict.
    b. Most of the time, I don't mind doing what others demand of me
       because they are things I would probably have done anyway.

11. a. When confronted with a task that I do not particularly enjoy, I
       find that I usually can discipline myself enough to perform them.
    b. Often, when confronted with a task, I find myself expending my
       energies on other interesting but unrelated activities instead
       of concentrating on completing the task.
12. a. Because of my philosophy of life, I have faith in myself, and in
       society in general.
    b. Because of the uncertain nature of the individual and society,
       it is natural for me not to have a basic trust in society, in
       others, or even in myself.

FEAR OF NEGATIVE EVALUATION (FNE)

AUTHORS: David Watson and Ronald Friend

PURPOSE: To measure social anxiety.

DESCRIPTION: This 30-item instrument was designed to measure one aspect of social anxiety, the fear of receiving negative evaluations from others. Scores on the FNE essentially reflect a fear of the loss of social approval. Items on the measure include signs of anxiety and ineffective social behaviors that would incur disapproval by others. The FNE is also available in a shorter, 12-item form (Leary, 1983). The Brief FNE is composed of the original FNE items which correlated above .50 with the total FNE score. The Brief FNE and the original FNE are highly correlated.

NORMS: The FNE was originally developed on a sample of 297 college students, of which 92 were excluded from data analysis because of attrition or missing information. No demographic data are presented. The mean FNE score was 13.97 for males (n = 60) and 16.1 for females (n = 146). The Brief FNE has a different scoring system. The mean Brief FNE score was 35.7 with a standard deviation of 8.1 for a sample of 150 college students.

SCORING: The FNE items are answered "true" or "false." Items 2, 3, 5, 7, 9, 11, 13, 14, 17, 19, 20, 22, 24, 25, 28, 29 and 30 are keyed "true" while the other items are keyed for "false" responses. A value of 1 is assigned to each item answer which matches the key and 0 for answers which do not match the key. Scores are the summation of all item values, and range from 0 to 30.

The Brief FNE is rated on a five point scale in terms of how characteristic each item is of the respondent. Items 2, 4, 7 and 10 are reverse-scored. Total scores are the sum of the item responses and range from 12 to 60.

RELIABILITY: Internal consistency of the FNE was first determined by correlating each item with the total FNE score. The average item to total score correlation was .72. Internal consistency using Kuder-Richardson formula 20 was excellent, with correlations of .94 for a sample of 205 college students and .96 for a separate sample of 154 subjects. The FNE was shown to be stable with a test-retest correlation of .78 over a one-month period and .94 from a separate sample of 29 subjects. The Brief FNE has a reported internal consistency of .90 using Cronbach's alpha. The Brief FNE is also considered stable with a test-retest correlation of .75 over a four week period.

VALIDITY: Known-groups validity has been demonstrated by comparing a sample of subjects who scored in the upper 25 percentile with subjects from the lower 25 percentile. The results, which only approximate statistical significance, suggest the high FNE group sought more approval from others and avoided disapproval. The groups also differed on measures of uneasiness. Scores on the FNE correlated with measures of social approval, locus of control, desirability, autonomy, dependence, dominance, abasement, exhibitionism, and other measures of anxiety. The Brief FNE was evaluated for validity first by correlating scores with the full length FNE, which was .96. Criterion-related validity was shown with scores on the Brief FNE correlating with anxiety, avoidance, the degree to which respondents said that they were well presented, and the degree to which respondents were bothered by an unfavorable evaluation from others.

PRIMARY REFERENCE: Watson, D. and R. Friend (1969). Measurement of social-evaluative anxiety, *Journal of Consulting and Clinical Psychology* 33, 448–457. Leary, M. R. (1983). A brief version of the Fear of Negative Evaluation scale, *Personality and Social Psychology Bulletin* 9, 371–375. Instrument reproduced with permission of D. Watson and the American Psychological Association.

AVAILABILITY: Journal articles.

FNE

For the following statements, please answer each in terms of whether it is true or false for you. Circle T for true or F for false.

T F 1. I rarely worry about seeming foolish to others.
T F 2. I worry about what people will think of me even when I know it doesn't make any difference.
T F 3. I become tense and jittery if I know someone is sizing me up.
T F 4. I am unconcerned even if I know people are forming an unfavorable impression of me.
T F 5. I feel very upset when I commit some social error.
T F 6. The opinions that important people have of me cause me little concern.
T F 7. I am often afraid that I may look ridiculous or make a fool of myself.
T F 8. I react very little when other people disapprove of me.
T F 9. I am frequently afraid of other people noticing my shortcomings.
T F 10. The disapproval of others would have little effect on me.
T F 11. If someone is evaluating me I tend to expect the worst.
T F 12. I rarely worry about what kind of impression I am making on someone.
T F 13. I am afraid that others will not approve of me.
T F 14. I am afraid that people will find fault with me.
T F 15. Other people's opinions of me do not bother me.
T F 16. I am not necessarily upset if I do not please someone.
T F 17. When I am talking to someone, I worry about what they may be thinking about me.
T F 18. I feel that you can't help making social errors sometimes, so why worry about it.
T F 19. I am usually worried about what kind of impression I make.
T F 20. I worry a lot about what my superiors think of me.
T F 21. If I know someone is judging me, it has little effect on me.
T F 22. I worry that others will think I am not worthwhile.
T F 23. I worry very little about what others may think of me.
T F 24. Sometimes I think I am too concerned with what other people think of me.
T F 25. I often worry that I will say or do the wrong things.
T F 26. I am often indifferent to the opinions others have of me.
T F 27. I am usually confident that others will have a favorable impression of me.
T F 28. I often worry that people who are important to me won't think very much of me.
T F 29. I brood about the opinions my friends have about me.
T F 30. I become tense and jittery if I know I am being judged by my superiors.

BRIEF FNE

For the following statements please indicate how characteristic each is of you using the following rating scale:

> 1 = Not at all characteristic of me
> 2 = Slightly characteristic of me
> 3 = Moderately characteristic of me
> 4 = Very characteristic of me
> 5 = Extremely characteristic of me

Please record your answers in the spaces to the left of the items.

____ 1. I worry about what other people will think of me even when I know it doesn't make any difference.

____ 2. I am unconcerned even if I know people are forming an unfavorable impression of me.

____ 3. I am frequently afraid of other people noticing my shortcomings.

____ 4. I rarely worry about what kind of impression I am making on someone.

____ 5. I am afraid that people will not approve of me.

____ 6. I am afraid that people will find fault with me.

____ 7. Other people's opinion of me do not bother me.

____ 8. When I am talking to someone, I worry about what they may be thinking about me.

____ 9. I am usually worried about what kind of impression I make.

____ 10. If I know someone is judging me, it has little effect on me.

____ 11. Sometimes I think I am too concerned with what other people think of me.

____ 12. I often worry that I will say or do the wrong things.

FEAR QUESTIONNAIRE (FQ)

AUTHORS: I. M. Marks and A. M. Mathews

PURPOSE: To measure fear in phobic patients.

DESCRIPTION: This 24-item instrument was developed in three research and treatment facilities in order to assess the outcome of work with phobic patients. The form is general enough to be useful with any phobic disorder, but has added precision because it allows the practitioner to specify the phobia that is the focus of treatment, which is called the main target phobia rating. The form includes fifteen questions on different types of phobia, which can be used as subscales measuring agoraphobia (Ag), blood-injury phobia (BI) and social phobia (SP). The FQ also includes 5 items measuring anxiety and depression symptoms (ADS) associated with phobia. Finally, along with the target phobia at the beginning of the form, the FQ ends with another global phobia index.

NORMS: Normative data are reported on all aspects of the FQ. For the main target phobia, the mean score for a sample of 20 phobic inpatients was 7. The mean score on the 15-item total phobia scale was 47 for the 20 patients. Extensive additional data on large samples are available (see Mathews, Gelder, and Johnston, 1981).

SCORING: All items are rated on a scale from 1 to 8 with higher scores reflecting more severe phobic responses. The total phobia rating is the sum of the scores for items 2 through 16. The three subscales are composed of the following items: Ag: 5, 6, 8, 12, 15; BI: 2, 4, 10, 13, 16; SP: 3, 7, 9, 11, 14. The ADS score is the sum of items 18 through 22.

RELIABILITY: This instrument has good test-retest reliability. For the three subscales combined the correlation was .82 for a one-week period. Test-retest was also excellent for the Main Target Phobia (.93), and good for the global phobia rating (.79) and the anxiety-depression subscale (.82). Internal consistency data are not reported.

VALIDITY: The validity of the FQ has been supported by several studies. The FQ has been shown to discriminate between phobics and nonphobics on all aspects of the measure. Most important for the purposes of monitoring clients, the FQ has been shown to be sensitive, with scores changing over the course of intervention.

PRIMARY REFERENCE: Marks, I. M. and Mathews, A. M. (1978). Brief standard self-rating for phobic patients, *Behavior Research and Therapy* 17, 263–267. Instrument reproduced with permission of I. M. Marks and A. M. Mathews.

AVAILABILITY: Journal article.

FQ

Choose a number from the scale below to show how much you would avoid
each of the situations listed below because of fear or other unpleasant
feelings. Then write the number you chose in the blank opposite each
situation.

| 0 | 1 | 2 | 3 | 4 | 5 | 6 | 7 | 8 |

| Would not avoid it | Slightly avoid it | Definitely avoid it | Markedly avoid it | Always avoid it |

____ 1. Main phobia you want treated (describe in your own words)

____ 2. Injections or minor surgery
____ 3. Eating or drinking with other people
____ 4. Hospitals
____ 5. Traveling alone by bus or coach
____ 6. Walking alone in busy streets
____ 7. Being watched or stared at
____ 8. Going into crowded shops
____ 9. Talking to people in authority
____ 10. Sight of blood
____ 11. Being criticized
____ 12. Going alone far from home
____ 13. Thought of injury or illness
____ 14. Speaking or acting to an audience
____ 15. Large open spaces
____ 16. Going to the dentist
____ 17. Other situations (describe)

Now choose a number from the scale below to show how much you are
troubled by each problem listed, and write the number in the blank.

| 0 | 1 | 2 | 3 | 4 | 5 | 6 | 7 | 8 |

| Hardly at all | Slightly troublesome | Definitely troublesome | Markedly troublesome | Very severely troublesome |

____ 18. Feeling miserable or depressed
____ 19. Feeling irritable or angry
____ 20. Feeling tense or panicky
____ 21. Upsetting thoughts coming into your mind
____ 22. Feeling you or your surroundings are strange or unreal
____ 23. Other feelings (describe)

How would you rate the present state of your phobic symptoms on the scale below? Please circle one number between 0 and 8.

0	1	2	3	4	5	6	7	8

No phobias present	Slightly disturbing/ not really disburbing	Definitely disturbing/ disabling	Markedly disturbing/ disabling	Very severely disturbing/ disabling

FEAR SURVEY SCHEDULE–II (FSS-II)

AUTHOR: James H. Geer

PURPOSE: To measure responses to commonly occurring fears.

DESCRIPTION: The 51-item FSS-II is designed to measure fear responses. While the instrument is slightly longer than others in this volume, it is included because it is one of three available fear schedules that have received much attention in the behavior therapy literature. The instrument lists potential fear evoking situations and stimuli. A client rates his or her level of discomfort or distress. The items included on the FSS-II were first empirically selected from a pool of 111. Each item was then examined to determine its correlation with total scores. All items, except number 15, correlated with total scores for male and female college students, with item 15 reaching .05 significance for females. Total scores on this FSS reflect general fear.

NORMS: Mean scores on the sample mentioned above were 75.78 with a standard deviation of 33.84 for males and 100.16 with a standard deviation of 36.11 for females. These means were significantly different. Additionally, Bernstein and Allen (1969) sampled 1814 college students enrolled in an introductory psychology class and report means and standard deviations of 81.81 and 33.64 for males and 108.47 and 36.78 for females. These means were also significantly different.

SCORING: Each item is rated on a 7-point scale of intensity of fear. Scores are the sum of the item scores and range from 51 to 357. Higher scores indicate greater fear.

RELIABILITY: The FSS-II is considered a very reliable instrument with an internal consistency coefficient of .94 using Kuder-Richardson formula 20. The instrument is reported to be stable, although the reliability data are not as direct as test-retest reliability data.

VALIDITY: The FSS has good concurrent validity with significant correlations between the FSS and emotionality and anxiety, while the scores are not associated with scores on measures of introversion and extroversion. Known-groups validity data indicate that groups categorized according to FSS scores differ on five relevant criteria: the time it took subjects to approach a frightening stimulus, the distance between the subjects and the stimulus, subjects' ratings of experienced fear, experimenter's rating of the fear the subjects presented, and an affect adjective checklist completed by the subjects.

PRIMARY REFERENCE: Geer, J. H. (1965). The development of a scale to measure fear, *Behavioral Research and Therapy* 3, 45–53. Instrument reproduced with permission of James H. Geer.

AVAILABILITY: Journal article.

FSS

Below are 51 different stimuli which can cause fear in people. Please rate how much fear you feel using the following rating scale and record your answer in the space provided:

1 = None
2 = Very little fear
3 = A little fear
4 = Some fear
5 = Much fear
6 = Very much fear
7 = Terror

____ 1. Sharp objects
____ 2. Being a passenger in a car
____ 3. Dead bodies
____ 4. Suffocating
____ 5. Failing a test
____ 6. Looking foolish
____ 7. Being a passenger in an airplane
____ 8. Worms
____ 9. Arguing with parents
____ 10. Rats and mice
____ 11. Life after death
____ 12. Hypodermic needles
____ 13. Being criticized
____ 14. Meeting someone for the first time
____ 15. Roller coasters
____ 16. Being alone
____ 17. Making mistakes
____ 18. Being misunderstood
____ 19. Death
____ 20. Being in a fight
____ 21. Crowded places
____ 22. Blood
____ 23. Heights
____ 24. Being a leader
____ 25. Swimming alone
____ 26. Illness

____ 27. Being with drunks
____ 28. Illness or injury to loved ones
____ 29. Being self-conscious
____ 30. Driving a car
____ 31. Meeting authority
____ 32. Mental illness
____ 33. Closed places
____ 34. Boating
____ 35. Spiders
____ 36. Thunderstorms
____ 37. Not being a success
____ 38. God
____ 39. Snakes
____ 40. Cemeteries
____ 41. Speaking before a group
____ 42. Seeing a fight
____ 43. Death of a loved one
____ 44. Dark places
____ 45. Strange dogs
____ 46. Deep water
____ 47. Being with a member of the opposite sex
____ 48. Stinging insects
____ 49. Untimely or early death
____ 50. Losing a job
____ 51. Auto accidents

FREQUENCY OF SELF-REINFORCEMENT
QUESTIONNAIRE (FSRQ)

AUTHOR: Elaine M. Heiby

PURPOSE: To measure skill at self-reinforcement.

DESCRIPTION: The FSRQ is a 30-item instrument designed to assess respondents' encouraging, supporting, and valuing themselves and their own efforts. Self-reinforcement is seen as a generalized response set with a low frequency of self-reinforcement seen as a possible causative factor in depression. Thus, use of this measure would be in conjunction with clinical work on increasing a client's skills at, and the frequency of, self-reinforcement. Items on the FSRQ were initially selected from a pool of 100 items, based on judgments of content validity by 10 clinicians. Research on the FSRQ is continuing with a shorter form currently being studied.

NORMS: Initial development of the FSRQ involved two studies of 40 undergraduates (roughly equally divided between females and males). Actual norms on the latest version of the FSRQ are not available.

SCORING: The FSRQ is easily scored by reverse-scoring negatively worded items and summing the individual items to obtain an overall score. The range of scores is from 0 to 90 with higher scores indicating greater frequency of self-reinforcement. Scores below 16 indicate serious deficits in self-reinforcement skills, dependency upon others for approval, and possible vulnerability to depression.

RELIABILITY: The FSRQ has very good internal consistency with split-half reliability of .87. The FSRQ has excellent stability with an eight-week test-retest correlation of .92.

VALIDITY: The FSRQ has good concurrent validity as demonstrated by correlations between FSRQ scores and self-monitoring of self-reinforcement and experimenter ratings of respondents' tendency to engage in self-reinforcement. The FSRQ is not correlated with social desirability response set, and is sensitive to change following training in self-reinforcement skills. The FSRQ is also reported as having good construct validity as demonstrated by negative correlations with self-punishment, the Beck Depression Inventory and measures of cognitive distortion.

PRIMARY REFERENCE: Heiby, E. M. (1983). Assessment of frequency of self-reinforcement, *Journal of Personality and Social Psychology* 44, 1304–1307. Instrument reproduced with permission of Elaine M. Heiby and the American Psychological Association.

AVAILABILITY: Dr. Elaine M. Heiby, University of Hawaii, Department of Psychology, Honolulu, HI 96822.

FSRQ

Below are a number of statements about beliefs or attitudes people have. Indicate how descriptive the statements are for yourself by rating each item, as indicated below. There are no right or wrong answers. Your answers are confidential, so do not put your name on this sheet. Thank you!

Rate each item for how much of the time it is descriptive for you. In the blank before each item, rate:

        0 = Never descriptive of me
        1 = A little of the time descriptive of me
        2 = Some of the time descriptive of me
        3 = Most of the time descriptive of me

____ 1. When I fail at something, I am still able to feel good about myself.

____ 2. I can stick to a boring task that I need to finish without someone pushing me.

____ 3. I have negative thoughts about myself.

____ 4. When I do something right, I take time to enjoy the feeling.

____ 5. I have such high standards for what I expect of myself that I have a hard time meeting my standards.

____ 6. I seem to blame myself and be very critical of myself when things go wrong.

____ 7. I can have a good time doing some things alone.

____ 8. I get upset with myself when I make mistakes.

____ 9. My feelings of self-confidence go up and down.

____ 10. When I succeed at small things, it helps me to go on.

____ 11. If I do not do something absolutely perfectly, I don't feel satisfied.

____ 12. I get myself through hard things mostly by thinking I'll enjoy myself afterwards.

____ 13. When I make mistakes, I take time to criticize myself.

____ 14. I encourage myself to improve at something by feeling good about myself.

____ 15. I put myself down so that I will do things better in the future.

____ 16. I think talking about what you've done right is bragging.

____ 17. I find that I feel better when I silently praise myself.

____ 18. I can keep working at something hard to do when I stop to think of what I've already done.

____ 19. The way I keep up my self-confidence is by remembering any successes I have had.

____ 20. The way I achieve my goals is by rewarding myself every step along the way.

____ 21. Praising yourself is being selfish.

____ 22. When someone criticizes me, I lose my self-confidence.

____ 23. I criticize myself more often than others criticize me.

____ 24. I feel I have a lot of good qualities.

____ 25. I silently praise myself even when other people do not praise me.

____ 26. Any activity can provide some pleasure no matter how it comes out.

____ 27. If I don't do the best possible job, I don't feel good about myself.

____ 28. I should be upset if I make a mistake.

____ 29. My happiness depends more on myself than it depends on other people.

____ 30. People who talk about their own better points are just bragging.

GENERALIZED CONTENTMENT SCALE (GCS)

AUTHOR: Walter Hudson

PURPOSE: To measure nonpsychotic depression.

DESCRIPTION: The GCS is a 25-item scale that is designed to measure the degree, severity, or magnitude of nonpsychotic depression. In contrast to many measures of depression, the GCS focuses largely on affective aspects of clinical depression, examining respondents' feelings about a number of behaviors, attitudes, and events associated with depression. A particular advantage of the GCS is a cutting score of 30 ($\pm$ 5), with scores above 30 indicating that the respondent has a clinically significant problem and scores below 30 indicating the individual has no such problem. Another advantage of the GCS is that it is one of nine scales of the Clinical Measurement Package (Hudson, 1982) reproduced here, all of which are administered and scored the same way.

NORMS: This scale was developed with 2140 respondents, including single and married individuals, clinical and nonclinical populations, high school and college students and nonstudents. Respondents were primarily Caucasian, but also included Japanese and Chinese Americans, and a smaller number of members of other ethnic groups. The GCS is not recommended for use with children under the age of 12.

SCORING: The GCS is scored by first reverse-scoring the items listed at the bottom of the scale (5, 8, 9, 11, 12, 13, 15, 16, 21, 22, 23, 24), totaling these and the other item scores, and subtracting 25. This gives a range of 0 to 100 with higher scores indicating more depression. For scoring questionnaires with missing items, see Hudson (1982) or instructions for scoring the Index of Family Relations in this book.

RELIABILITY: The GCS has a mean alpha of .92, indicating excellent internal consistency, and an excellent (low) S.E.M. of 4.56. The GCS also has excellent stability with a two-hour test-retest correlation of .94.

VALIDITY: The GCS has good concurrent validity, correlating in two studies .85 and .76 with the Beck Depression Inventory and .92 and .81 for two samples using the Zung Depression Inventory. The GCS has excellent known-groups validity, discriminating significantly between members of a group judged to be clinically depressed and those judged not to be depressed. The GCS also has good construct validity, correlating poorly with a number of measures with which it should not correlate, and correlating at high levels with several measures with which it should, such as self-esteem, happiness, and sense of identity.

PRIMARY REFERENCE: Hudson, W. W. (1982). *The Clinical Measurement Package: A Field Manual.* Chicago: Dorsey. Instrument reproduced with permission of Walter W. Hudson and the Dorsey Press.

AVAILABILITY: The Dorsey Press, 242 South Michigan Avenue, Suite 440, Chicago, IL 60604.

GCS

This questionnaire is designed to measure the degree of contentment that you feel about your life and surroundings. It is not a test, so there are no right or wrong answers. Answer each item as carefully and accurately as you can by placing a number beside each one as follows:

1 = Rarely or none of the time
2 = A little of the time
3 = Some of the time
4 = Good part of the time
5 = Most or all of the time

Please begin.

___ 1. I feel powerless to do anything about my life.
___ 2. I feel blue.
___ 3. I am restless and can't keep still.
___ 4. I have crying spells.
___ 5. It is easy for me to relax.
___ 6. I have a hard time getting started on things that I need to do.
___ 7. I do not sleep well at night.
___ 8. When things get tough, I feel there is always someone I can turn to.
___ 9. I feel that the future looks bright for me.
___ 10. I feel downhearted.
___ 11. I feel that I am needed.
___ 12. I feel that I am appreciated by others.
___ 13. I enjoy being active and busy.
___ 14. I feel that others would be better off without me.
___ 15. I enjoy being with other people.
___ 16. I feel it is easy for me to make decisions.
___ 17. I feel downtrodden.
___ 18. I am irritable.
___ 19. I get upset easily.
___ 20. I feel that I don't deserve to have a good time.
___ 21. I have a full life.
___ 22. I feel that people really care about me.
___ 23. I have a great deal of fun.
___ 24. I feel great in the morning.
___ 25. I feel that my situation is hopeless.

5,8,9,11,12,13,15,16,21,22,23,24

GENERALIZED EXPECTANCY FOR SUCCESS SCALE (GESS)

AUTHORS: Bobbi Fibel and W. Daniel Hale

PURPOSE: To measure locus of control of success.

DESCRIPTION: The GESS is a 30-item measure that assesses the generalized expectancy of being successful. The construct is defined as the belief that in most situations one is able to obtain desired goals. The concept is related to anxiety and the negative cognition often associated with depression, and suicidal ideation. Factor analysis suggests that the instrument is measuring three aspects of generalized expectancy: general efficacy (GE), long range career oriented expectancy (LRCOE), personal problem solving (PPS), and a fourth factor that has no consistent theme. Items were selected based, in part, on not correlating with social desirability.

NORMS: The instrument was developed with three samples of college students. The samples were reported to be predominantly middle-class Caucasian college students (207 females and 132 males). For males, the mean was 112.32 with a standard deviation of 13.8, a median of 113.14 and a mode of 112. For females, the mean was 112.15 with a standard deviation of 13.23, a median of 112.8 and a mode of 109.

SCORING: Each item is rated in terms of how much it applies to the respondent. Items reflecting failure are reverse-scored (numbers 1, 2, 4, 6, 7, 8, 14, 15, 17, 18, 24, 27, 28). Scores are the sum of the item ratings, and range from 30 to 150. Higher scores reflect an internal control of success. Items for the factors are: GE: 4, 8, 9, 10, 12, 13, 15, 16, 21, 22; LRCOE: 14, 17, 24, 25, 26, 29, 30; PPS: 3, 5, 6, 11, 19, 20, 23, 28.

RELIABILITY: The GESS has excellent reliability for the total score. Data were not presented for factors. Internal consistency using coefficient alpha was .90 for females and .91 for males. Test-retest reliability for a six-week period was .83 for both genders.

VALIDITY: The validity of the GESS has been tested primarily with concurrent validity procedures. Scores correlate significantly with depression, hopelessness, and suicidal ideation. Scores were not associated with social desirability for men, but were correlated for females.

PRIMARY REFERENCE: Fibel, B. and W. Daniel Hale (1978). The generalized expectancy for success scale—A new measure, *Journal of Consulting and Clinical Psychology* 46, 924–931. Instrument reproduced with permission of W. Daniel Hale and the American Psychological Association.

AVAILABILITY: Journal article.

GESS

Please indicate the degree to which you believe each statement would apply to you personally by indicating to the left of the item the appropriate number, according to the following key:

> 1 = Highly improbable
> 2 = Improbable
> 3 = Equally improbable and probable, not sure
> 4 = Probable
> 5 = Highly probable

In the future I expect that I will
____ 1. find that people don't seem to understand what I am trying to say.
____ 2. be discouraged about my ability to gain the respect of others.
____ 3. be a good parent.
____ 4. be unable to accomplish my goals.
____ 5. have a stressful marital relationship.
____ 6. deal poorly with emergency situations.
____ 7. find my efforts to change situations I don't like are ineffective.
____ 8. not be very good at learning new skills.
____ 9. carry through my responsibilities successfully.
____ 10. discover that the good in life outweighs the bad.
____ 11. handle unexpected problems successfully.
____ 12. get the promotions I deserve.
____ 13. succeed in the projects I undertake.
____ 14. not make any significant contributions to society.
____ 15. discover that my life is not getting much better.
____ 16. be listened to when I speak.
____ 17. discover that my plans don't work out too well.
____ 18. find that no matter how hard I try, things just don't turn out the way I would like.
____ 19. handle myself well in whatever situation I'm in.
____ 20. be able to solve my own problems.
____ 21. succeed at most things I try.
____ 22. be successful in my endeavors in the long run.
____ 23. be very successful working out my personal life.
____ 24. experience many failures in my life.
____ 25. make a good first impression on people I meet for the first time.
____ 26. attain the career goals I have set for myself.
____ 27. have difficulty dealing with my superiors.
____ 28. have problems working with others.
____ 29. be a good judge of what it takes to get ahead.
____ 30. achieve recognition in my profession.

GERIATRIC DEPRESSION SCALE (GDS)

AUTHORS: T. L. Brink and Jerome A. Yesavage

PURPOSE: To measure depression in the elderly.

DESCRIPTION: The GDS is a 15-item scale to rate depression in the elderly. The GDS is written in simple language and can be administered in an oral or written format. If administered orally, the practitioner may have to repeat the question in order to get a response that is clearly yes or no. Translations are available in Spanish and French. The main purpose for development of the GDS was to provide a screening test for depression in elderly populations that would be simple to administer and not require special training for the interviewer. The GDS has been used successfully with both physically healthy and ill samples of the elderly.

NORMS: The initial data for the GDS came from two groups of elderly people. The first (n = 40) were individuals recruited from senior centers and housing projects who were functioning well with no history of mental problems. The second group (n = 60) comprised elderly under treatment—inpatient and outpatient—for depression. No other demographic data are reported. The authors state that 0 to 10 on the GDS is normal; 11 to 20 indicates moderate or severe depression.

SCORING: Of the 30 items, 20 indicate the presence of depression when answered positively while 10 (items 1, 5, 7, 9, 15, 19, 21, 27, 29, 30) indicate depression when answered negatively. The GDS is scored by totaling one point counted for each depressive answer and zero points counted for a nondepressed answer.

RELIABILITY: The GDS has excellent internal consistency with an alpha of .94 and split-half reliability of .94. The GDS also has excellent stability with a one-week test-retest correlation of. 85.

VALIDITY: The GDS has excellent concurrent validity with correlations of .83 between the GDS and Zung's Self-Rating Depression Scale and .84 with the Hamilton Rating Scale for Depression. The GDS also has good known-groups validity in distinguishing significantly among respondents classified as normal, mildly depressed, and severely depressed. The GDS also has distinguished between depressed and nondepressed physically ill elderly and between depressed and nondepressed elderly undergoing cognitive treatment for senile dementia.

PRIMARY REFERENCE: Yesavage, J. A., Brink, T. L., Rose, T. L., and Leirer, V. O. (1983). Development and validation of a geriatric depression screening scale: A preliminary report, *Journal of Psychiatric Research* 17, 37–49. Instrument reproduced with permission of T. L. Brink and Jerome Yesavage.

AVAILABILITY: Dr. T. L. Brink, Clinical Gerontologist, 1044 Sylvan Drive, San Carlos, CA 94070 or Dr. Jerome Yesavage, V. A. Medical Center, Palo Alto, CA 94305.

GDS

CHOOSE THE BEST ANSWER FOR HOW YOU FELT OVER THE PAST WEEK

Yes	No	1. Are you basically satisfied with your life?
Yes	No	2. Have you dropped many of your activities and interests?
Yes	No	3. Do you feel that your life is empty?
Yes	No	4. Do you often get bored?
Yes	No	5. Are you in good spirits most of the time?
Yes	No	6. Are you afraid that something bad is going to happen to you?
Yes	No	7. Do you feel happy most of the time?
Yes	No	8. Do you often feel helpless?
Yes	No	9. Do you prefer to stay at home, rather than going out and doing new things?
Yes	No	10. Do you feel you have more problems with memory than most?
Yes	No	11. Do you think it is wonderful to be alive now?
Yes	No	12. Do you feel pretty worthless the way you are now?
Yes	No	13. Do you feel full of energy?
Yes	No	14. Do you feel that your situation is hopeless?
Yes	No	15. Do you think that most people are better off than you are?

GOLDFARB FEAR OF FAT SCALE (GFFS)

AUTHOR: Lori A. Goldfarb

PURPOSE: To measure the fear of gaining weight.

DESCRIPTION: The 10-item GFFS measures one of the underlying emotional experiences of eating disorders, the fear of becoming fat. The instrument can also be used to assess weight phobia. It is also useful to identify clients at risk of bulimia or anorexia as well as to assess the state of those already suffering from these disorders.

NORMS: The GFFS was developed on student and clinical samples. The mean score was 25.5 for 98 high school females. A sample of randomly selected college students had a mean of 18.33, while a small sample of anorectic patients (N = 7) had a mean of 35.0. A third sample of college females had a mean of 30 for a group of diagnosed bulimics, 23.9 for "repeat dieters," and 17.3 for nondieting females.

SCORING: Each item is rated on a scale from 1 to 4, "very untrue" to "very true." Scores are the sum of each item, and range from 10 to 40 with high scores indicating more fear of gaining weight.

RELIABILITY: The GFFS has been shown to have very good reliability. The internal consistency reliability using coefficient alpha was .85. Over a one-week period, the GFFS has excellent stability, with a test-retest correlation of .88.

VALIDITY: The validity data is generally positive. There were significantly different scores for samples of anorectic patients and college females; the scores also differed between bulimic and repeat dieters and nondieters. Both of these studies reflect known-groups validity. Correlations between the GFFS and state-trait anxiety, depression, neuroticism, maladjustment, and control and achievement orientations demonstrate concurrent validity. The GFFS was negatively correlated with self-esteem.

PRIMARY REFERENCE: Goldfarb, L. A., Dykens, E. M., and Gerrard, M. (1985). The Goldfarb fear of fat scale, *Journal of Personality Assessment* 49, 329–332. Instrument reproduced with permission of Lori A. Goldfarb and the *Journal of Personality Assessment*.

AVAILABILITY: Journal article.

GFFS

Please read each of the following statements and select the number which best represents your feelings and beliefs.

> 1 = Very untrue
> 2 = Somewhat untrue
> 3 = Somewhat true
> 4 = Very true

___ 1. My biggest fear is of becoming fat.
___ 2. I am afraid to gain even a little weight.
___ 3. I believe there is a real risk that I will become overweight someday.
___ 4. I don't understand how overweight people can live with themselves.
___ 5. Becoming fat would be the worst thing that could happen to me.
___ 6. If I stopped concentrating on controlling my weight, chances are I would become very fat.
___ 7. There is nothing that I can do to make the thought of gaining weight less painful and frightening.
___ 8. I feel like all my energy goes into controlling my weight.
___ 9. If I eat even a little, I may lose control and not stop eating.
___ 10. Staying hungry is the only way I can guard against losing control and becoming fat.

HUNGER-SATIETY SCALES (H-SS)

AUTHOR: Paul E. Garfinkel

PURPOSE: To measure the sensation of hunger and satiety.

DESCRIPTION: The H-SS is comprised of two 9-item measures developed for research on anorexia. The point of departure for the instrument is that anorectic patients have a disturbed view of hunger signals—they become unable to perceive hunger and therefore eat less frequently; and because they feel unable to stop eating, they are unable to recognize satiation. The hunger scale measures one's response to signs of hunger and the satiety scale assesses one's response to signs to stop eating. The instruments do not provide continuous scores, so comparison must be in terms of change from misperception to correct perception on each item.

NORMS: The instrument was originally developed on a sample of 11 female anorexia nervosa patients who had a weight loss greater than 25 percent. These subjects ranged in ages from 16 to 23 years. Eleven undergraduate females were selected to serve as a comparison group. These subjects were matched with the clinical sample on age, religion, social class and height.

SCORING: Scores are not summed on the H-SS. Each item is an individual index. Comparisons can be made by examining changes in the alternatives chosen as indicative of respondent's "feelings at the moment."

RELIABILITY: Reliability data are not available.

VALIDITY: Known-groups validity is evident from the fact that the anorectics and matched controls responded differently. Anorectics tended to have a stronger urge to eat and to be more preoccupied with food and more anxious when hungry. The control group experienced satiety as a fullness in the stomach while anorectic patients experienced satiety without appropriate physical sensations.

PRIMARY REFERENCE: Garfinkel, P. E. (1974). Perception of hunger and satiety in anorexia nervosa, *Psychological Medicine* 4, 309–315. Instruments reproduced with permission of Paul Garfinkel.

AVAILABILITY: Journal article.

H-SS

This questionnaire is about hunger. For each heading circle as many of the answers as are appropriate to how you feel now. You may leave a section out or answer more than once. At the end add any general comments about your usual feelings of hunger.

I. Gastric sensations:

1. feeling of emptiness
2. rumbling
3. ache
4. pain
5. tenseness
6. nausea
7. no gastric sensations to provide information for hunger

II. Mouth and throat sensations:

1. emptiness
2. dryness
3. salivation
4. unpleasant taste or sensation
5. pleasant
6. tightness

III. Cerebral sensations:

1. headache
2. dizziness
3. faintness
4. spots before the eyes
5. ringing in ears

IV. General overall sensations:

1. weakness
2. tiredness
3. restlessness
4. cold
5. warmth
6. muscular spasms

V. Mood when hungry:

1. nervous
2. irritable
3. tense
4. depressed
5. apathetic
6. cheerful
7. excited
8. calm
9. relaxed
10. contented

VI. Urge to eat:

1. no urge to eat
2. mild -- would eat if food were available but can wait comfortably
3. fairly strong -- want to eat soon, waiting is fairly uncomfortable
4. so strong you want to eat now, waiting is very uncomfortable

VII.   Preoccupation with thoughts of   VIII.   Time of day or night when
       food.   hungriest:

     1.   not at all -- no thoughts
       of food
     2.   mild -- only occasional
       thoughts of food
     3.   moderate -- many thoughts
       of food but can concentrate
       on other things   IX.   Other comments about hunger:
     4.   very preoccupied -- most
       of thoughts are of food
       and it is difficult to
       concentrate on other
       things

This questionnaire is about fullness. For each heading circle as many
answers as are appropriate to how you've felt since completing the meal.
You may leave a section out or answer more than once. At the end add
any general comments about your feelings of fullness.

I.   One most important reason for   II.   Gastric sensation at end of
     stopping eating: eating:

     1.   no more food available   1.   full stomach
     2.   eat until feeling of   2.   distended
       satisfaction   3.   bloated
     3.   "diet-limit" set for   4.   nausea
       figure or health   5.   ache
                                         6.   pain
                                         7.   feeling of emptiness
                                         8.   no stomach sensations
                                              to provide information
                                              for stopping

III.   Cerebral sensations at end   IV.   General overall sensations
       of eating: at end of eating:

     1.   headache   1.   weakness
     2.   dizziness   2.   tiredness
     3.   faintness   3.   restlessness
     4.   spots before the eyes   4.   cold
     5.   ringing in ears   5.   warmth
                                         6.   muscular spasms

V. Mood at end of eating:

1. nervous
2. irritable
3. tense
4. depressed
5. apathetic
6. cheerful
7. excited
8. calm
9. relaxed
10. contented

VI. Urge to eat at end of eating:

1. no urge to eat
2. mild -- would eat if food were available
3. moderate -- want to eat again soon, waiting is fairly uncomfortable
4. strong -- want to eat again now, waiting is very uncomfortable

VII. Preoccupation with thoughts of food:

1. not at all -- no thoughts of food
2. mild -- only occasional thoughts of food
3. moderate -- many thoughts of food but can concentrate on other things
4. very preoccupied -- most of thoughts are of food and it is difficult to concentrate on other things

VIII. Will power required to stop eating:

1. none -- stopping is an abrupt process
2. none -- stopping a gradual process
3. some -- will power required since the urge to eat is still present
4. considerable will power is required.

IV. Other comments about feeling full:

HYPOCHONDRIASIS SCALE FOR INSTITUTIONAL GERIATRIC PATIENTS (HSIG)

AUTHOR: T. L. Brink

PURPOSE: To measure beliefs about physical health in geriatric patients.

DESCRIPTION: The HSIG is a 6-item scale that can be administered in written or oral form. The practitioner may have to repeat questions in order to get a clear yes or no answer. The HSIG is actually a test of attitudes rather than behavior so that it is possible for a respondent to score high on the HSIG (higher scores indicating higher hypochondriasis), and yet have no somatic complaints. The 6 items for the scale were selected from a pool of 27 questions on the basis of their ability to distinguish between respondents known to be hypochondriacal and those known not to be. The scale is available in Spanish and French.

NORMS: Initial study was conducted on a sample of 69 patients at three extended-care facilities for the elderly. The mean score for those identified by staff as hypochondriacal was 3.9 and the mean score for nonhypochondriacal patients was 1.56. No other demographic data were available.

SCORING: Each item is answered yes or no. For each hypochondriacal answer, the item is scored as one point; these items are then summed for a total score with a range of 0 to 6. Scores under 3 are considered nonhypochondriacal.

RELIABILITY: No reliability data were reported.

VALIDITY: The HSIG significantly distinguished between geriatric patients identified by staff consensus as hypochondriacal and those not so identified. No other validity data are available.

PRIMARY REFERENCE: Brink, T. L. et al. (1978). Hypochondriasis in an institutional geriatric population: Construction of a scale (HSIG), *Journal of the American Geriatrics Society* 26, 552–559. Instrument reproduced with permission of T. L. Brink.

AVAILABILITY: Dr. T. L. Brink, Clinical Gerontologist, 1044 Sylvan Drive, San Carlos, CA 94070.

HSIG

Please circle either "Yes" or No" for each question as it applies to you.

Yes No 1. Are you satisfied with your health most of the time?
Yes No 2. Do you ever feel completely well?
Yes No 3. Are you tired most of the time?
Yes No 4. Do you feel your best in the morning?
Yes No 5. Do you frequently have strange aches and pains that you cannot identify?
Yes No 6. Is it hard for you to believe it when the doctor tells you that there is nothing physically wrong with you?

ILLNESS BEHAVIOR INVENTORY (IBI)

AUTHORS: Ira Daniel Turkat and Loyd S. Pettegrew

PURPOSE: To measure illness behavior.

DESCRIPTION: The IBI is a 20-item scale designed to assess the behaviors performed or reported by a respondent that indicate he or she is physically ill or in physical discomfort. The items were initially developed based on observations of patients in inpatient and ambulatory clinical settings. Two dimensions of illness behavior are measured by this instrument: work-related illness behavior with items related to the curtailment of work behaviors and activities when ill, and social illness behavior with items related to frequent discussion or complaints about being ill and acting more ill than one feels. This measure may be useful in work with clients who exhibit excessive or inappropriate illness behavior and as a screening device for clinical practice since it correlates well with a variety of factors related to medical utilization.

NORMS: Several different samples were used to examine aspects of this measure including 40 graduate nursing students, 32 undergraduate linguistic students, 50 lower back pain patients, a group of diabetic neuropathy patients (N unknown), 152 healthy college students and 63 female undergraduates. No other demographic information was provided. The IBI is in an early stage of development, and work on standardization is only beginning.

SCORING: Scores on each of the six-point Likert scales are simply totaled to provide a range from 20 to 120. Higher scores indicate greater illness behavior.

RELIABILITY: The IBI has excellent internal consistency: the 9 work items have an alpha of .89 and the 11 social items have an alpha of .88. No data for the measure as a whole were reported. The IBI also has excellent stability with two-week test-retest reliabilities of .97 for work-related items, .93 for social items, and .90 overall.

VALIDITY: The IBI has good concurrent validity in that it correlates significantly with a number of illness behavior measures and treatment outcome measures in chronically ill samples. The IBI also has good known-groups validity in distinguishing between patients independently assessed as either high or low illness behavior patients. Finally, the IBI also demonstrates good predictive validity by predicting several illness behaviors in a healthy sample.

PRIMARY REFERENCE: Turkat, I. D. and Pettegrew, L. S. (1983). Development and validation of the illness behavior inventory, *Journal of Behavioral Assessment* 5, 35–45. Instrument reproduced with permission of Ira D. Turkat and L. S. Pettegrew, and Plenum Press.

AVAILABILITY: Dr. Loyd S. Pettegrew, Department of Communications, University of South Florida, Tampa, FL 33620.

IBI

Please put a number beside each item indicating the extent to which you agree or disagree as follows:

> 1 = Strongly disagree
> 2 = Disagree
> 3 = Somewhat disagree
> 4 = Somewhat agree
> 5 = Agree
> 6 = Strongly agree

____ 1. I see doctors often.
____ 2. When ill, I have to stop work completely.
____ 3. I stay in bed when I feel ill.
____ 4. I work fewer hours when I'm ill.
____ 5. I do fewer chores around the house when I'm ill.
____ 6. I seek help from others when I'm ill.
____ 7. When ill, I work slower.
____ 8. I leave work early when I'm ill.
____ 9. I complain about being ill when I feel ill.
____ 10. I avoid certain aspects of my job when I'm ill.
____ 11. I take rest periods when I'm ill.
____ 12. Most people who know me are aware that I take medication.
____ 13. Even if I don't feel ill at certain times, I find that I talk about my illness anyway.
____ 14. Others often behave towards me as if I'm ill.
____ 15. Although I very seldom bring up the topic of my illness, I frequently find myself involved in conversation about my illness with others.
____ 16. Others seem to act as if I am more ill than I really am.
____ 17. My illness or aspects of it are a frequent topic of conversation.
____ 18. When I'm ill people can tell by the way I act.
____ 19. Often I act more ill than I really am.
____ 20. I have large medical bills.

ILLNESS BEHAVIOR QUESTIONNAIRE (IBQ)

AUTHORS: I. Pilowsky and N. D. Spence

PURPOSE: To measure the ways individuals experience and respond to their health status.

DESCRIPTION: The IBQ is a 62-item instrument designed to measure a respondent's attitudes, ideas, affects, and attributions in relation to illness. The IBQ consists of seven major subscales derived through factor analysis, each of which has at least 5 items. The seven scales of the IBQ are general hypochondriasis (GH), disease conviction (DC), psychologic versus somatic perceptions of illness (P/S), affective inhibition (AI), affective distrubance (AD), denial (D), and irritability (I). The IBQ also generates scores on the Whiteley Index of Hypochondriasis (WH) and two other minor factors. The IBQ is written in easily understood language, is easily scored, and translations in several languages are available. Some of the scales have cut-off points for the detection of abnormality. The IBQ is useful for examining illness behavior in general and for identifying physical complaints that are manifestations of a psychiatric disorder. A manual is available from the author.

NORMS: Data on the IBQ have been developed in several studies including 231 pain clinic patients, 147 general practice patients, 217 general hospital patients, and 540 patients from a general hospital psychiatric ward. The respondents are from both the United States and Australia. Norms are available in the manual for all these groups.

SCORING: The IBQ is very easily hand scored by using the scoring key available in the manual. The scoring key on the questionnaire describes which items on the IBQ belong to which subscale and the meaning of a "yes" or "no" on each item. The "correct" answers and the items for each subscale are shown in the right-hand column of the questionnaire. These items are summed to obtain the subscale scores. For the Whiteley Index of Hypochondriasis; a "yes" answer to items 1, 2, 9, 10, 16, 21, 24, 33, 34, 38, 39, and 41 and a "no" answer to item 8 are the "correct" scores.

RELIABILITY: The IBQ has very good stability with one- to twelve-week test–retest correlations that range from .67 to .85 for the subscales; only one correlation (for affective inhibition) is below .76. No data on internal consistency were reported.

VALIDITY: The IBQ has good face and content validity. The affective disturbance subscale has very good concurrent validity, correlating significantly with several measures of depression and anxiety. The subscales of the IBQ also have good known-groups validity, distinguishing predictably in several studies between criterion groups, for example, psychiatric versus pain patients. In addition, there were high levels of agreement between the scores of patients and the patients' responses as perceived by spouses.

PRIMARY REFERENCE: Pilowsky, I. (1983). *Manual for the Illness Behavior Questionnaire.* University of Adelaide, Department of Psychiatry. Instrument reproduced with permission of I. Pilowsky.

AVAILABILITY: Professor I. Pilowsky, University of Adelaide, Department of Psychiatry, Royal Adelaide Hospital, Adelaide, South Australia 5001.

IBQ

Scoring
Key

	Yes	No	1. Do you worry a lot about your health?
DC-Yes	Yes	No	2. Do you think there is something seriously wrong with your body?
DC-Yes	Yes	No	3. Does your illness interfere with your life a great deal?
I-No	Yes	No	4. Are you easy to get on with when you are ill?
	Yes	No	5. Does your family have a history of illness?
	Yes	No	6. Do you think you are more liable to illness than other people.
DC-No	Yes	No	7. If the doctor told you that he could find nothing wrong with you would you believe him?
	Yes	No	8. Is it easy for you to forget about yourself and think about all sorts of other things?
GH-Yes	Yes	No	9. If you feel ill and someone tells you that you are looking better, do you become annoyed?
DC-Yes	Yes	No	10. Do you find that you are often aware of various things happening in your body?
P/S-Yes	Yes	No	11. Do you ever think of your illness as a punishment for something you have done wrong in the past?
AD-Yes	Yes	No	12. Do you have trouble with your nerves?
	Yes	No	13. If you feel ill or worried, can you be easily cheered up by the doctor?
	Yes	No	14. Do you think that other people realize what it's like to be sick?
	Yes	No	15. Does it upset you to talk to the doctor about your illness?
PS-No	Yes	No	16. Are you bothered by many pains and aches?
I-Yes	Yes	No	17. Does your illness affect the way you get on with your family or friends a great deal?
AD-Yes	Yes	No	18. Do you find that you get anxious easily?
	Yes	No	19. Do you know anybody who has had the same illness as you?
GH-Yes	Yes	No	20. Are you more sensitive to pain than other people?
GH-Yes	Yes	No	21. Are you afraid of illness?
AI-No	Yes	No	22. Can you express your personal feelings easily to other people?
	Yes	No	23. Do people feel sorry for you when you are ill?
GH-Yes	Yes	No	24. Do you think that you worry about your health more than most people?
	Yes	No	25. Do you find that your illness affects your sexual relations?
	Yes	No	26. Do you experience a lot of pain with your illness?
D-No	Yes	No	27. Except for your illness, do you have any problems in your life?
	Yes	No	28. Do you care whether or not people realize you are sick?
GH-Yes	Yes	No	29. Do you find that you get jealous of other people's good health?

Scoring
Key

GH-Yes	Yes	No	30.	Do you ever have silly thoughts about your health which you can't get out of your mind, no matter how hard you try?
D-No	Yes	No	31.	Do you have any financial problems?
GH-Yes	Yes	No	32.	Are you upset by the way people take your illness?
	Yes	No	33.	Is it hard for you to believe the doctor when he tells you there is nothing for you to worry about?
	Yes	No	34.	Do you often worry about the possibility that you have got a serious illness?
DC-No	Yes	No	35.	Are you sleeping well?
AI-Yes	Yes	No	36.	When you are angry, do you tend to bottle up your feelings?
GH-Yes	Yes	No	37.	Do you often think that you might suddenly fall ill?
GH-Yes	Yes	No	38.	If a disease is brought to your attention (through the radio, television, newspapers, or someone you know) do you worry about getting it yourself?
	Yes	No	39.	Do you get the feeling that people are not taking your illness seriously enough?
	Yes	No	40.	Are you upset by the appearance of your face or body?
DC-Yes	Yes	No	41.	Do you find that you are bothered by many different symptoms?
	Yes	No	42.	Do you frequently try to explain to others how you are feeling?
D-No	Yes	No	43.	Do you have any family problems?
P/S-Yes	Yes	No	44.	Do you think there is something the matter with your mind?
	Yes	No	45.	Are you eating well?
P/S-No	Yes	No	46.	Is your bad health the biggest difficulty of your life?
AD-Yes	Yes	No	47.	Do you find that you get sad easily?
	Yes	No	48.	Do you worry or fuss over small details that seem unimportant to others?
	Yes	No	49.	Are you always a cooperative patient?
	Yes	No	50.	Do you often have the symptoms of a very serious disease?
	Yes	No	51.	Do you find that you get angry easily?
	Yes	No	52.	Do you have any work problems?
AI-Yes	Yes	No	53.	Do you prefer to keep your feelings to yourself?
Ad-Yes	Yes	No	54.	Do you often find that you get depressed?
D-Yes	Yes	No	55.	Would all your worries be over if you were physically healthy?
I-Yes	Yes	No	56.	Are you more irritable towards other people?
P/S-Yes	Yes	No	57.	Do you think that your symptoms may be caused by worry?
AI-Yes	Yes	No	58.	Is it easy for you to let people know when you are cross with them?
AD-Yes	Yes	No	59.	Is it hard for you to relax?
D-No	Yes	No	60.	Do you have personal worries which are not caused by physical illness?
I-Yes	Yes	No	61.	Do you often find that you lose patience with other people?
AI-Yes	Yes	No	62.	Is it hard for you to show people your personal feelings?

IMPACT OF EVENT SCALE (IES)

AUTHOR: Mardi J. Horowitz

PURPOSE: To measure the stress associated with traumatic events.

DESCRIPTION: The 15-item IES assesses the experience of posttraumatic stress for any specific life event and its context, such as the death of a loved one. The instructions intentionally do not define the traumatic event. This is to be done by the practitioner and the respondent during the course of treatment. The IES is a relatively direct measure of the stress associated with a traumatic event. The IES measures two categories of experience in response to stressful events: intrusive experience, such as ideas, feelings, or bad dreams; and avoidance, the recognized avoidance of certain ideas, feelings, and situations. Because the IES has been shown to be sensitive to change, it is appropriate for monitoring client's progress in treatment.

NORMS: Normative data are available on two samples. One was a sample of 35 outpatients who sought treatment to cope with the death of a parent. The second was a field sample of 37 adult volunteers who had a recently deceased parent. The average age of the outpatient sample was 31.4 with a standard deviation of 8.7 years. The mean score and standard deviation on the intrusive subscale was 21.02 and 7.9, respectively. Mean score on the avoidance subscale was 20.8 with a standard deviation of 10.2. The mean intrusive subscale score for the field sample was 13.5 with a standard deviation of 9.1. The avoidance subscale mean was 9.4 with a standard deviation of 9.6. All of the above data were assessed two months after the stressful event had occurred.

SCORING: Items are rated according to how frequently the intrusive or avoidance reaction occurred. Responses are scored from 1 to 4 with higher scores reflecting more stressful impact. Scores for the intrusive subscale range from 7 to 28 and are the sum of the ratings on the following items: 1, 4, 5, 6, 10, 11, 14. Scores range from 8 to 32 for the avoidance subscale, computed by adding the ratings on the following items: 2, 3, 7, 8, 9, 12, 13, 15.

RELIABILITY: Based on two separate samples, the subscales of the IES show very good internal consistency with coefficients ranging from .79 to .92, with an average of .86 for the intrusive subscale and .90 for the avoidance subscale. No data on stability were reported.

VALIDITY: The known groups validity of the IES has been supported with significant differences in the scores of outpatients seeking treatment for bereavement and three field samples. The subscales indicate the IES is sensitive to change as scores changed over the course of the treatment.

PRIMARY REFERENCE: Horowitz, M. J., Wilner, N., and Alvarez, W. (1979). Impact of event scale: A measure of subjective stress. *Psychological Medicine* 41, 209–218; Zilberg, N. J., Weiss, D. S., and Horowitz, M. J. (1982). Impact of event scale: A cross-validation study and some empirical evidence supporting a conceptual model of stress response syndromes, *Journal of Consulting and Clinical Psychology* 50, 407–414. Instrument reproduced with permission of M. J. Horowitz and the American Psychological Association.

AVAILABILITY: Mardi J. Horowitz, M.D., Professor of Psychiatry, University of California, 401 Parnassus Avenue, San Francisco, CA 94143.

IES

Below is a list of comments made by people about stressful life events and the context surrounding them. Read each item and decide how frequently each item was true for you during the past seven (7) days, for the event and its context about which you are dealing with in treatment. If the item did not occur during the past seven days, choose the "Not at all" option. Indicate on the line at the left of each comment the number that best describes that item. Please complete each item.

```
1 = Not at all
2 = Rarely
3 = Sometimes
4 = Often
```

____ 1. I thought about it when I didn't mean to.
____ 2. I avoided letting myself get upset when I thought about it or was reminded of it.
____ 3. I tried to remove it from memory.
____ 4. I had trouble falling asleep or staying asleep, because of pictures or thoughts that came into my mind.
____ 5. I had waves of strong feelings about it.
____ 6. I had dreams about it.
____ 7. I stayed away from reminders of it.
____ 8. I felt as if it hadn't happened or wasn't real.
____ 9. I tried not to talk about it.
____ 10. Pictures about it popped into my mind.
____ 11. Other things kept making me think about it.
____ 12. I was aware that I still had a lot of feelings about it, but I didn't deal with them.
____ 13. I tried not to think about it.
____ 14. Any reminder brought back feelings about it.
____ 15. My feelings about it were kind of numb.

INDEX OF SELF-ESTEEM (ISE)

AUTHOR: Walter W. Hudson

PURPOSE: To measure problems with self-esteem.

DESCRIPTION: The ISE is a 25-item scale designed to measure the degree, severity, or magnitude of a problem the client has with self-esteem. Self-esteem is considered as the evaluative component of self-concept. The ISE is written in very simple language, is easily administered, and easily scored. Because problems with self-esteem are often central to social and psychological difficulties, this instrument has a wide range of utility for a number of clinical problems. The ISE has a cutting score of 30 (± 5), with scores above 30 indicating the respondent has a clinically significant problem and scores below 30 indicating the individual has no such problem. Another advantage of the ISE is that it is one of nine scales of the Clinical Measurement Package (Hudson, 1982) reproduced here, all of which are administered and scored the same way.

NORMS: This scale was derived from tests of 1745 respondents, including single and married individuals, clinical and nonclinical populations, college students and nonstudents. Respondents included Caucasians, Japanese and Chinese Americans, and a smaller number of members of other ethnic groups. The ISE is not recommended for use with children under the age of 12.

SCORING: The ISE is scored by first reverse-scoring the items listed at the bottom of the scale (3, 4–7, 14, 15, 18, 21, 22, 23, 25), totaling these and the other items scores, and subtracting 25. This gives a range of 0 to 100 with higher scores giving more evidence of the presence of problems with self-esteem. For scoring questionnaires with missing items, see Hudson (1982) or instructions for scoring the Index of Family Relations in this book.

RELIABILITY: The ISE has a mean alpha of .93, indicating excellent internal consistency, and an excellent (low) S.E.M. of 3.70. The ISE also has excellent stability with a two-hour test-retest correlation of .92.

VALIDITY: The ISE has good known-groups validity, significantly distinguishing between clients judged by clinicians to have problems in the area of self-esteem and those known not to. Further, the ISE has very good construct validity, correlating poorly with measures with which it should not and correlating well with a range of other measures with which it should correlate highly, e.g., depression, happiness, sense of identity, and scores on the Generalized Contentment Scale (depression).

PRIMARY REFERENCE: Hudson, W. W. (1982). *The Clinical Measurement Package: A Field Manual.* Chicago: Dorsey. Instrument reproduced with permission of Walter W. Hudson and Dorsey Press.

188

AVAILABILITY: The Dorsey Press, 224 South Michigan Avenue, Suite 440, Chicago, IL 60604.

ISE

This questionnaire is designed to measure how you see yourself. It is not a test, so there are no right or wrong ansers. Please answer each item as carefully and accurately as you can by placing a number by each one as follows:

1 = Rarely or none of the time
2 = A little of the time
3 = Some of the time
4 = A good part of the time
5 = Most or all of the time

____ 1. I feel that people would not like me if they really knew me well.
____ 2. I feel that others get along much better than I do.
____ 3. I feel that I am a beautiful person.
____ 4. When I am with other people I feel they are glad I am with them.
____ 5. I feel that people really like to talk with me.
____ 6. I feel that I am a very competent person.
____ 7. I think I make a good impression on others.
____ 8. I feel that I need more self-confidence.
____ 9. When I am with strangers I am very nervous.
____ 10. I think that I am a dull person.
____ 11. I feel ugly.
____ 12. I feel that others have more fun than I do.
____ 13. I feel that I bore people.
____ 14. I think my friends find me interesting.
____ 15. I think I have a good sense of humor.
____ 16. I feel very self-conscious when I am with strangers.
____ 17. I feel that if I could be more like other people I would have it made.
____ 18. I feel that people have a good time when they are with me.
____ 19. I feel like a wall flower when I go out.
____ 20. I feel I get pushed around more than others.
____ 21. I think I am a rather nice person.
____ 22. I feel that people really like me very much.
____ 23. I feel that I am a likeable person.
____ 24. I am afraid I will appear foolish to others.
____ 25. My friends think very highly of me.

3,4,5,6,7,14,15,18,21,22,23,25

INDEX OF SEXUAL SATISFACTION (ISS)

AUTHOR: Walter W. Hudson

PURPOSE: To measure problems in sexual satisfaction.

DESCRIPTION: The ISS is a 25-item measure of the degree, severity or magnitude of a problem in the sexual component of a couple's relationship. The ISS measures the respondent's feelings about a number of behaviors, attitudes, events, affect states and preferences that are associated with the sexual relationship between partners. The items were written with special concern about being non-offensive and not imposing on the rights or privacy of the client. The ISS has a cutting score of 30 (±5), with scores above 30 indicating the respondent has a clinically significant problem and scores below 30 indicating the individual has no such problem. Another advantage of the ISS is that it is one of 9 scales of the Clinical Measurement Package (Hudson, 1982) reproduced here, all of which are administered and scored the same way.

NORMS: The scale was developed from tests of 1738 respondents, including single and married individuals, clinical and nonclinical populations, high school and college students and nonstudents. Respondents were primarily Caucasian, but also include Japanese and Chinese Americans, and a smaller number of members of other ethnic groups.

SCORING: The ISS is scored by first reverse-scoring the items listed at the bottom of the scale (1, 2, 3, 9, 10, 12, 16, 17, 19, 21, 22, 23), totaling these and the other item scores, and subtracting 25. This gives a range of 0 to 100 with higher scores giving more evidence of the presence of sexual dissatisfaction. For scoring questionnaires with missing items, see Hudson (1982) or instructions for scoring the Index of Family Relations in this book.

RELIABILITY: The ISS has a mean alpha of .92, indicating excellent internal consistency, and a (low) S.E.M. of 4.24. The ISS also has excellent stability with a two-hour test-retest correlation of .94.

VALIDITY: The ISS has excellent concurrent validity, correlating significantly with the Locke-Wallace Marital Adjustment Scale and the Index of Marital Satisfaction. It has excellent known-groups validity, significantly distinguishing between people known to have problems with sexual satisfaction and those known not to. The ISS also has excellent construct validity, correlating poorly with those measures with which it should not correlate and correlating highly with several measures with which it should correlate such as measures of marital satisfaction and marital problems.

PRIMARY REFERENCE: Hudson, W. W. (1982). *The Clinical Measurement Package: A Field Manual*. Chicago: Dorsey. Instrument reproduced with permission of Walter W. Hudson and The Dorsey Press.

AVAILABILITY: The Dorsey Press, 224 South Michigan Avenue, Suite 440, Chicago, IL 60604.

ISS

This questionnaire is designed to measure the degree of satisfaction you have in the sexual relationship with your partner. It is not a test, so there are no right or wrong answers. Answer each item as carefully and accurately as you can by placing a number beside each one as follows:

1 = Rarely or none of the time
2 = A little of the time
3 = Some of the time
4 = Good part of the time
5 = Most or all of the time

___ 1. I feel that my partner enjoys our sex life.
___ 2. My sex life is very exciting.
___ 3. Sex is fun for my partner and me.
___ 4. I feel that my partner sees little in me except for the sex I can give.
___ 5. I feel that sex is dirty and disgusting.
___ 6. My sex life is monotonous.
___ 7. When we have sex it is too rushed and hurriedly completed.
___ 8. I feel that my sex life is lacking in quality.
___ 9. My partner is sexually very exciting.
___ 10. I enjoy the sex techniques that my partner likes or uses.
___ 11. I feel that my partner wants too much sex from me.
___ 12. I think that sex is wonderful.
___ 13. My partner dwells on sex too much.
___ 14. I feel that sex is something that has to be endured in our relationship.
___ 15. My partner is too rough or brutal when we have sex.
___ 16. My partner observes good personal hygiene.
___ 17. I feel that sex is a normal function of our relationship.
___ 18. My partner does not want sex when I do.
___ 19. I feel that our sex life really adds a lot to our relationship.
___ 20. I would like to have sexual contact with someone other than my partner.
___ 21. It is easy for me to get sexually excited by my partner.
___ 22. I feel that my partner is sexually pleased with me.
___ 23. My partner is very sensitive to my sexual needs and desires.
___ 24. I feel that I should have sex more often.
___ 25. I feel that my sex life is boring.

1,2,3,9,10,12,16,17,19,21,22,23

INTENSE AMBIVALENCE SCALE (IAS)

AUTHOR: Michael L. Raulin

PURPOSE: To measure intense ambivalence.

DESCRIPTION: The IAS is a 45-item scale designed to measure intense ambivalence. Ambivalence is defined as the existence of simultaneous or rapidly interchangeable positive and negative feelings toward the same object or activity, with both positive and negative feelings being strong. Although the IAS was developed on the assumption that intense ambivalence is an important feature in schizophrenia, development of the instrument with diverse populations suggests broader utility. The 45 true/false items were chosen from a wide range of potential items. In designing the scale particular attention was placed on minimizing social desirability response set.

NORMS: Several studies were carried out in the development of IAS. The first set involved 384 male and 475 female undergraduate students. The second involved 89 male and 8 female inpatients diagnosed as schizophrenic, 13 male and 18 female inpatients diagnosed as depressed, 66 male and 131 female psychology clinic clients with a range of nonpsychotic disorders, and a normal control group of 104 male and 39 females from the general population. Mean scores on the IAS were 16.23 for the depressed patients, 13.93 for the clinic clients, and 10.82 for the normal controls. For the college students, mean scores ranged from 8.45 to 10.51.

SCORING: The IAS is scored by assigning a score of one to the correct responses and summing them. The correct responses are "true" to items 1, 4, 5, 7–22, 24, 26, 27, 30–32, 34, 35, 37, 38, 40, 42, 43, 45, and "false" for the remainder of the items.

RELIABILITY: The IAS has very good internal consistency with alphas that range from .86 to .94. It also has excellent stability with test-retest correlations involving time periods of ten to twelve weeks of .81.

VALIDITY: The IAS was not correlated with age, education, and social class suggesting these variables do not affect responses. The IAS has good known-groups validity, distinguishing between college students rated as ambivalent or not ambivalent and among depressed, schizophrenic and clinic clients, and normal controls. The IAS also has some concurrent validity, correlating with two other scales of schizotypy (indicating a genetic predisposition for schizophrenia).

PRIMARY REFERENCE: Raulin, M. L. (1984). Development of a scale to measure intense ambivalence, *Journal of Consulting and Clinical Psychology* 52, 63–72. Instrument reproduced with permission of Michael L. Raulin and the American Psychological Association.

AVAILABILITY: Dr. Michael L. Raulin, SUNY-Buffalo, Psychology Department, Julian Park Hall, Buffalo, NY 14260.

192

IAS

Circle either T for true or F for false for each item as it applies to you.

T F 1. Very often, even my favorite pastimes don't excite me.
T F 2. I feel I can trust my friends.
T F 3. Small imperfections in a person are rarely enough to change love into hatred.
T F 4. There have been times when I have hated one or both of my parents for the affection they have expressed for me.
T F 5. Words of affection almost always make people uncomfortable.
T F 6. I don't mind too much the faults of people I admire.
T F 7. Love and hate tend to go together.
T F 8. Honest people will tell you that they often feel chronic resentment toward the people they love.
T F 9. Everything I enjoy has its painful side.
T F 10. Love never seems to last very long.
T F 11. My strongest feelings of pleasure usually seem to be mixed with pain.
T F 12. Whenever I get what I want, I usually don't want it at all any more.
T F 13. I have always experienced dissatisfaction with feelings of love.
T F 14. I worry the most when things are going the best.
T F 15. I often get very angry with people just because I love them so much.
T F 16. I start distrusting people if I have to depend on them too much.
T F 17. I can think of someone right now whom I thought I liked a day or two ago, but now strongly dislike.
T F 18. The people around me seem to be very changeable.
T F 19. It is hard to imagine two people loving one another for many years.
T F 20. The closer I get to people, the more I am annoyed by their faults.
T F 21. I find that the surest way to start resenting someone is to just start liking them too much.
T F 22. Often I feel like I hate even my favorite activities.
T F 23. I usually know when I can trust someone.
T F 24. Everyone has a lot of hidden resentment toward his loved ones.
T F 25. I usually know exactly how I feel about people I have grown close to.
T F 26. I have noticed that feelings of tenderness often turn into feelings of anger.
T F 27. I always seem to be the most unsure of myself at the same time that I am most confident of myself.
T F 28. My interest in personally enjoyed hobbies and pastimes has remained relatively stable.

T F 29. I can usually depend on those with whom I am close.
T F 30. My experiences with love have always been muddled with great frustration.
T F 31. I usually find that feelings of hate will interfere when I have grown to love someone.
T F 32. A sense of shame has often interfered with my accepting words of praise from others.
T F 33. I rarely feel rejected by those who depend on me.
T F 34. I am wary of love because it is such a short-lived emotion.
T F 35. I usually experience doubt when I have accomplished something that I have worked on for a long time.
T F 36. I rarely doubt the appropriateness of praise that I have received from others in the past.
T F 37. I often feel as though I cannot trust people whom I have grown to depend on.
T F 38. I usually experience some grief over my own feelings of pleasure.
T F 39. It is rare for me to love a person one minute and hate them the next minute.
T F 40. I doubt if I can ever be sure exactly what my true interests are.
T F 41. I can't remember ever feeling love and hate for the same person at the same time.
T F 42. Love is always painful for me.
T F 43. Close relationships never seem to last long.
T F 44. I never had much trouble telling whether my parents loved me or hated me.
T F 45. Most people disappoint their friends.

INTERACTION AND AUDIENCE ANXIOUSNESS SCALES
(IAS and AAS)

AUTHOR: Mark R. Leary

PURPOSE: To measure social anxiety.

DESCRIPTION: The IAS (15 items) and AAS (12 items) are designed to measure two forms of social anxiety. These two measures of anxiety deviate from other instruments that assess anxious feelings and anxious behavior. They start from the position that a person who has anxious feelings may still interact socially despite feeling distressed. These instruments define social anxiety as the experiential state of anxiety resulting from being evaluated in social settings. Two classes of social anxiety are measured: interaction anxiety (IA) which concerns social responses that are contingent upon others' behavior, and audience anxiousness (AA), when social responses are not contingent upon others' behaviors. The measures can be used separately or together.

NORMS: A sample of 363 college students was used to develop the IAS and AAS. Demographic data and norms are not reported in the primary reference. Data are reported for a clinical sample of 13 students seeking professional help for interpersonal problems, speech majors (n = 12) and students selected from a pool of volunteers (n = 17). The mean IAS and AAS scores were 54.9 and 43.1, respectively, for those seeking professional help. The speech majors had mean IAS and AAS scores of 33.6 and 28.2, while the third sample's means were 38.1 and 39.3. Little information is available on sampling procedures or demographic characteristics.

SCORING: Each item is rated on a 5-point scale from "uncharacteristic or not true" to "characteristic or true". Items 3, 6, 10, and 15 on the IA and 2 and 8 on the AA are reverse-scored. Scores are the sum of the item ratings. For the 1A, scores range from 15 to 75. For the AA, scores range from 12 to 60.

RELIABILITY: The reliability of these two instruments is excellent. The internal consistency using coefficient alphas was .88 for both the IAs and AAs. Alpha was even higher in a second sample. Both measures had good test-retest reliability, correlating .80 for the IAs and .84 for the AAs over a four-week period.

VALIDITY: These instruments also have strong evidence of validity. Concurrent validity was indicated with IAS scores correlating with the Social Avoidance and Distress Scale, social anxiety, shyness, confidence as a speaker, fear of negative evaluation, sociability, public self-consciousness, and self-esteem. The AAS correlated similarly with these criteria. There is also evidence of known-groups validity with differences between IAS and AAS scores for the clinical sample

and the other two samples mentioned in the section on norms. Scores
are fairly independent of social desirability.

PRIMARY REFERENCE: Leary, M. R. (1983). Social anxiousness: The construct and its measurement, *Journal of Personality Assessment* 47,
66–75. Instruments reproduced with permission of Mark R. Leary.

AVAILABILITY: Journal article.

IAS

Below are fifteen statements. Please read each one and consider how
characteristic it is of you. Rate each statement using the following
scale and record your answer in the space to the left of the statement.

      1 = Uncharacteristic of me or not true
      2 = Somewhat uncharacteristic of me or somewhat not true
      3 = Neither uncharacteristic nor characteristic
      4 = Somewhat characteristic of me or somewhat true
      5 = Characteristic of me or true

____ 1. I often feel nervous even in casual get-togethers.
____ 2. I usually feel uncomfortable when I am in a group of people
     I don't know.
____ 3. I am usually at ease when speaking to a member of the opposite
     sex.
____ 4. I get nervous when I must talk to a teacher or boss.
____ 5. Parties often make me feel anxious and uncomfortable.
____ 6. I am probably less shy in social interactions than most people.
____ 7. I sometimes feel tense when talking to people of my own sex if I
     don't know them very well.
____ 8. I would be nervous if I was being interviewed for a job.
____ 9. I wish I had more confidence in social situations.
____ 10. I seldom feel anxious in social situations.
____ 11. In general, I am a shy person.
____ 12. I often feel nervous when talking to an attractive member of
     the opposite sex.
____ 13. I often feel nervous when calling someone I don't know very
     well on the telephone.
____ 14. I get nervous when I speak to someone in a position of authority.
____ 15. I usually feel relaxed around other people, even people who are
     quite different from me.

AAS

Below are twelve statements. Please read each one and consider how characteristic it is of you. Rate each statement using the following scale and record your answer in the space to the left of the statement.

    1 = Uncharacteristic of me or not true
    2 = Somewhat uncharacteristic of me or somewhat not true
    3 = Neither uncharacteristic nor characteristic
    4 = Somewhat characteristic or somewhat true
    5 = Characteristic of me or true

____ 1. I usually get nervous when I speak in front of a group.
____ 2. I enjoy speaking in public.
____ 3. I tend to experience "stage fright" when I must appear before a group.
____ 4. I would be terrified if I had to appear before a large audience.
____ 5. I get "butterflies" in my stomach when I must speak or perform before others.
____ 6. I would feel awkward and tense if I knew someone was filming me with a movie camera.
____ 7. My thoughts become jumbled when I speak before an audience.
____ 8. I don't mind speaking in front of a group if I have rehearsed what I am going to say.
____ 9. I wish I did not get so nervous when I speak in front of a group.
____ 10. If I was a musician, I would probably get "stage fright" before a concert.
____ 11. When I speak in front of others, I worry about making a fool out of myself.
____ 12. I get nervous when I must make a presentation at school or work.

INTERNAL CONTROL INDEX (ICI)

AUTHOR: Patricia Dutteiler

PURPOSE: To measure locus of control.

DESCRIPTION: The ICI is a 28-item instrument designed to measure where a person looks for, or expects to obtain, reinforcement. An individual with an external locus of control believes that reinforcement is based on luck or chance, while an individual with an internal locus of control believes that reinforcement is based on his or her own behavior. Locus of control is viewed as a personality trait that influences human behavior across a wide range of situations related to learning and achievement. There are two factors contained in the ICI, one that is called self-confidence, and a second that is called autonomous behavior (behavior independent of social pressure).

NORMS: The ICI was developed and tested with several samples of junior college, university undergraduate, and continuing education students. The total N involved 1365 respondents of both sexes. Means are available that are broken down by age, group, sex, race, and educational and socioeconomic level and range from 99.3 and 120.8.

SCORING: Each item is scored on a 5-point scale from A ("rarely") to E ("usually"). Half of the items are worded so that high internally oriented respondents are expected to answer half at the "usually" end of the scale and the other half at the "rarely" end. The "rarely" response is scored as 5 points on items 1, 2, 4, 6, 8, 11, 14, 17, 19, 22, 23, 24, 26, and 27; for the remainder of the items, the response "usually" is scored as 5 points. This produces a possible range of scores from 28 to 140 with higher scores reflecting higher internal locus of control.

RELIABILITY: The ICI has very good internal consistency with alphas of .84 and .85. No test-retest correlations were reported.

VALIDITY: The ICI has fair concurrent validity with a low but significant correlation with Mirels' Factor I of the Rotter I-E Scale.

PRIMARY REFERENCE: Duttweiler, P. C. (1984). The Internal Control Index: A newly developed measure of locus of control, *Educational and Psychological Measurement* 44, 209–221. Instrument reproduced with permission of Patricia Duttweiler and *Educational and Psychological Measurement*.

AVAILABILITY: Journal article.

ICI

Please read each statement. Where there is a blank, decide what your
normal or usual attitude, feeling, or behavior would be:

> A = Rarely (less than 10% of the time)
> B = Occasionally (about 30% of the time)
> C = Sometimes (about half the time)
> D = Frequently (about 70% of the time)
> E = Usually (more than 90% of the time)

Of course, there are always unusual situations in which this would not
be the case, but think of what you would do or feel in most normal
situations.

Write the letter that describes your usual attitude or behavior *in the
space provided on the response sheet.*

1. When faced with a problem I _____ try to forget it.
2. I _____ need frequently encouragement from others for me to keep
    working at a difficult task.
3. I _____ like jobs where I can make decisions and be responsible for
    my own work.
4. I _____ change my opinion when someone I admire disagrees with me.
5. If I want something I _____ work hard to get it.
6. I _____ prefer to learn the facts about something from someone
    else rather than have to dig them out of myself.
7. I will _____ accept jobs that require me to supervise others.
8. I _____ have a hard time saying "no" when someone trys to sell me
    something I don't want.
9. I _____ like to have a say in any decisions made by any group I'm
    in.
10. I _____ consider the different sides of an issue before making any
    decisions.
11. What other people think _____ has a great influence on my behavior.
12. Whenever something good happens to me I _____ feel it is because
    I've earned it.
13. I _____ enjoy being in a position of leadership.
14. I _____ need someone else to praise my work before I am satisfied
    with what I've done.
15. I am _____ sure enough of my opinions to try and influence others.
16. When something is going to affect me I _____ learn as much about
    it as I can.
17. I _____ decide to do things on the spur of the moment.
18. For me, knowing I've done something well is _____ more important
    than being praised by someone else.

19. I _____ let other peoples' demands keep me from doing things I want to do.
20. I _____ stick to my opinions when someone disagrees with me.
21. I _____ do what I feel like doing not what other people think I ought to do.
22. I _____ get discouraged when doing something that takes a long time to achieve results.
23. When part of a group I _____ prefer to let other people make all the decisions.
24. When I have a problem I _____ follow the advice of friends or relatives.
25. I _____ enjoy trying to do difficult tasks more than I enjoy trying to do easy tasks.
26. I _____ prefer situations where I can depend on someone else's ability rather than just my own.
27. Having someone important tell me I did a good job is _____ more important to me than feeling I've done a good job.
28. When I'm involved in something I _____ try to find out all I can about what is going on even when someone else is in charge.

INTERNAL VERSUS EXTERNAL CONTROL
OF WEIGHT SCALE (IECW)

AUTHORS: Lester L. Tobias and Marian L. MacDonald

PURPOSE: To measure locus of control pertaining to weight loss.

DESCRIPTION: The 5-item IECW is similar to other measures of locus of control in that it attempts to measure the degree to which respondents consider achievement of a goal as contingent or noncontingent on their own behavior. The scale was initially developed to test the effectiveness of internal perception to facilitate weight reduction. The instrument is relevant to weight reduction treatment that emphasizes clients' taking responsibility for their treatment. While the IECW registers change toward an internal control orientation as a consequence of experimental manipulation, the perceived responsibility itself is insufficient to facilitate weight loss. Consequently, the IECW needs to be used along with other measures of treatment effectiveness.

NORMS: The IECW was developed on 100 undergraduate females whose weights were at least ten percent more than their desirable weight, who expressed a belief that the weight problem was related to eating and activity patterns, and declared a desire to change. The sample's average age was 19.2 years, ranging from 17 to 26. The average weight of the sample was 161.8 pounds. The average IECW score before any experimental manipulation was approximately 1.04.

SCORING: Items are arranged in a forced-choice format; one alternative reflects an internal orientation and the other reflects an external orientation. External choices (the first alternative in items 1, 3, and 5, the second alternative in items 2 and 4) are scored "1." Total scores are the sum of the internal alternatives selected by the respondent. Scores range from 0 to 5.

RELIABILITY: The reliability of the IECW was determined using test-retest correlations over a ten-week period. The correlation coefficient was .52, which is acceptable, though low, because of the long period between administrations. Internal consistency data were not reported.

VALIDITY: The instrument lacks validity data. Scores did not differ between pre- and postweight reduction program. Criterion validity to determine if scores actually correlate with weight reduction has not been established.

PRIMARY REFERENCE: Tobias, L. L. and MacDonald, M. L. (1977). Internal locus of control and weight loss: An insufficient condition. *Journal of Consulting and Clinical Psychology* 45, 647–653. Instrument reproduced with permission of the American Psychological Association.

AVAILABILITY: Journal article.

IECW

Each item consists of two statements; choose the statement with which
you *agree most*.

1. ___ Overweight problems are mainly a result of hereditary or
   ___ physiological factors.
   ___ Overweight problems are mainly a result of lack of self-
        control.·

2. ___ Overweight people will lose weight only when they can generate
        enough internal motivation.
   ___ Overweight people need some tangible external motivation in
        order to reduce.

3. ___ Diet pills can be a valuable aid in weight reduction.
   ___ A person who loses weight with diet pills will gain the weight
        back eventually.

4. ___ In overweight people, hunger is caused by the expectation of
        being hungry.
   ___ In overweight people, hunger is caused by stomach contractions
        and low blood sugar levels.

5. ___ Overweight problems can be traced to early childhood and are
        very resistant to change.
   ___ Overweight problems can be traced to poor eating habits which
        are relatively simple to change.

INTERPERSONAL DEPENDENCY INVENTORY (IDI)

AUTHORS: Robert M. A. Hirschfield, G. L. Klerman, H. G. Gough, J. Barrett, S. J. Korchin, and P. Chodoff.

PURPOSE: To measure interpersonal dependency.

DESCRIPTION: The IDI is a 48-item instrument designed to measure the thoughts, behaviors, and feelings revolving around need to associate closely with valued people. The theoretical base for the IDI is a blend of psychoanalytic, social learning, and attachment theories emphasizing the importance of excess dependency to a range of emotional and behavioral disorders. Based on an initial pool of 98 items, the 48-item scale was developed using factor analysis. This resulted in three subscales: Emotional reliance on others (items 3, 6, 7, 9, 12, 15, 16, 19, 22, 26, 29, 33, 35, 38, 40, 43, 45, 47), lack of self-confidence (items 2, 5, 10, 13, 17, 19, 20, 23, 24, 27, 30, 32, 36, 29, 41, 44, 46) and assertion of autonomy (items 1, 4, 8, 11, 14, 18, 21, 25, 28, 31, 34, 37, 42, 48).

NORMS: Research on the IDI has involved three samples. The first is a predominantly white group of 88 university males and 132 university females with a mean age of 24. The second involved 76 male and 104 female psychiatric patients, predominantly white. The third involved 19 male and 47 female psychiatric patients (mean age of 31) and 64 male and 57 female nonpsychiatric community residents (mean age of 41). Means for these groups on the IDI ranged from 176.3 to 210.3; however, a new scoring system has replaced the one used in determining these figures so that the mean for normal samples averages around 50.

SCORING: The IDI is scored by summing the responses from each of the three subscales to yield scores for each one. Items 10, 23, and 44 on the self-confidence subscale are rescored by subtracting the item response from 5. The scores on the three subscales can be summed for the overall score. A new, more complicated scoring system for the total score utilizing weighted scores and producing means of around 50 for normal samples is available from the author.

RELIABILITY: The IDI has good internal consistency with split-half reliabilities that range from .72 to .91. No test-retest data were reported.

VALIDITY: The IDI has fairly good concurrent validity with the first two subscales correlating significantly with measures of general neuroticism (the Maudley Personality Inventory) and anxiety, interpersonal sensitivity, and depression (Symptom Checklist–90). The IDI also distinguishes between psychiatric patients and normals. However, the first two subscales are also correlated with the social desirability scale of the MMPI, suggesting that respondents tend to respond based on what they believe is socially desirable.

PRIMARY REFERENCE: Hirschfield, R. M. A., Klerman, G. L., Gough, H. G., Barrett, J., Korchin, S. J., and Chodoff, P. (1977). A measure of interpersonal dependency, *Journal of Personality Assessment* 41, 610–618. Instrument reproduced by permission of the authors and the *Journal of Personality Assessment*.
AVAILABILITY: Dr. Harrison G. Gough, Institute of Personality Assessment and Research, University of California, Berkeley, CA 94720.

IDI

Please read each statement and decide whether or not it is characteristic of your attitudes, feelings, or behavior. Then assign a rating to every statement, using the values given below:

4 = very characteristic of me
3 = quite characteristic of me
2 = somewhat characteristic of me
1 = not characteristic of me

____ 1. I prefer to be by myself.
____ 2. When I have a decision to make, I always ask for advice.
____ 3. I do my best work when I know it will be appreciated.
____ 4. I can't stand being fussed over when I am sick.
____ 5. I would rather be a follower than a leader.
____ 6. I believe people could do a lot more for me if they wanted to.
____ 7. As a child, pleasing my parents was very important to me.
____ 8. I don't need other people to make me feel good.
____ 9. Disapproval by someone I care about is very painful for me.
____ 10. I feel confident of my ability to deal with most of the personal problems I am likely to meet in life.
____ 11. I'm the only person I want to please.
____ 12. The idea of losing a close friend is terrifying to me.
____ 13. I am quick to agree with the opinions expressed by others.
____ 14. I rely only on myself.
____ 15. I would be completely lost if I didn't have someone special.
____ 16. I get upset when someone discovers a mistake I've made.
____ 17. It is hard for me to ask someone for a favor.
____ 18. I hate it when people offer me sympathy.
____ 19. I easily get discouraged when I don't get what I need from others.
____ 20. In an argument, I give in easily.
____ 21. I don't need much from people.
____ 22. I must have one person who is very special to me.
____ 23. When I go to a party, I expect that the other people will like me.
____ 24. I feel better when I know someone else is in command.

___ 25. When I am sick, I prefer that my friends leave me alone.
___ 26. I'm never happier than when people say I've done a good job.
___ 27. It is hard for me to make up my mind about a TV show or movie until I know what other people think.
___ 28. I am willing to disregard other people's feelings in order to accomplish something that's important to me.
___ 29. I need to have one person who puts me above all others.
___ 30. In social situations I tend to be very self-conscious.
___ 31. I don't need anyone.
___ 32. I have a lot of trouble making decisions by myself.
___ 33. I tend to imagine the worst if a loved one doesn't arrive when expected.
___ 34. Even when things go wrong I can get along without asking for help from my friends.
___ 35. I tend to expect too much from others.
___ 36. I don't like to buy clothes by myself.
___ 37. I tend to be a loner.
___ 38. I feel that I never really get all that I need from people.
___ 39. When I meet new people, I'm afraid that I won't do the right thing.
___ 40. Even if most people turned against me, I could still go on if someone I love stood by me.
___ 41. I would rather stay free of involvements with others than to risk disappointments.
___ 42. What people think of me doesn't affect how I feel.
___ 43. I think that most people don't realize how easily they can hurt me.
___ 44. I am very confident about my own judgment.
___ 45. I have always had a terrible fear that I will lose the love and support of people I desperately need.
___ 46. I don't have what it takes to be a good leader.
___ 47. I would feel helpless if deserted by someone I love.
___ 48. What other people say doesn't bother me.

IRRATIONAL VALUES SCALE (IVS)

AUTHOR: A. P. MacDonald

PURPOSE: To measure endorsement of irrational values.

DESCRIPTION: The IVS is a 9-item scale that was designed to measure a respondent's endorsement of nine irrational values that are based on the work of Albert Ellis. The underlying assumption is the belief that high endorsement of certain values or ideas would lead to neurosis. (Although eleven values were studied, two values were dropped because they did not possess adequate psychometric properties.) The IVS was seen as providing construct validity for Ellis's ideas because it was related to several measures of psychopathology. The scale might prove useful in clinical programs where the goal is to challenge and refute the clients' unrealistic, dysfunctional, or irrational ideas.

NORMS: Initial study of the IVS was based on three samples of undergraduates including 101 males and 80 females. No work on standardization was reported.

SCORING: The scores on 9-point Likert scales are totaled, producing a range of 9 to 81.

RELIABILITY: Internal consistency of the IVS is fairly good, with alphas of .73 and .79 reported. No test-retest data were reported.

VALIDITY: The IVS has good concurrent validity, correlating significantly with several measures including the California Personality Inventory, Eysenck Neuroticism Scale, Taylor Manifest Anxiety Scale, and the MacDonald-Tseng Internal-External Locus of Control Scale. Also, the IVS was not correlated with the Marlowe-Crowne Social Desirability Scale, indicating the IVS is free from social desirability response set.

PRIMARY REFERENCE: MacDonald, A. P. and Games, Richard G. (1972). Ellis' irrational values, *Rational Living* 7, 25–28. Instrument reproduced with permission of Dr. A. P. MacDonald.

AVAILABILITY: The Free Press

IVS

People have different opinions. We are interested in knowing your opinions concerning the following issues. There are no right or wrong answers for the items; we are interested in opinions only. Please indicate your own opinion by circling a number from one to nine on the scale provided for each statement. In case of doubt, circle the number which comes closest to representing your true opinion. Please do not leave any blanks.

1. It is essential that one be loved or approved by virtually everyone in his community.

Completely   Completely
disagree   agree
    1   2   3   4   5   6   7   8   9

2. One must be perfectly competent, adequate, and achieving to consider oneself worthwhile.

Completely   Completely
disagree   agree
    1   2   3   4   5   6   7   8   9

3. Some people are bad, wicked, or villainous and therefore should be blamed and punished.

Completely   Completely
disagree   agree
    1   2   3   4   5   6   7   8   9

4. It is a terrible catastrophe when things are not as one wants them to be.

Completely   Completely
disagree   agree
    1   2   3   4   5   6   7   8   9

5. Unhappiness is caused by outside circumstances and the individual has no control over it.

Completely   Completely
disagree   agree
    1   2   3   4   5   6   7   8   9

6. Dangerous or fearsome things are causes for great concern, and their possibility must be continually dwelt upon.

Completely   Completely
disagree   agree
    1   2   3   4   5   6   7   8   9

7. One should be dependent on others and must have someone stronger on whom to rely.

Completely   Completely
disagree   agree
    1   2   3   4   5   6   7   8   9

8. One should be quite upset over people's problems and disturbances.

Completely   Completely
disagree   agree
    1   2   3   4   5   6   7   8   9

9. There is always a right or perfect solution to every problem, and it must be found or the results will be catastrophic.

Completely   Completely
disagree   agree
    1   2   3   4   5   6   7   8   9

LIFE SATISFACTION INDEX–Z (LSIZ)

AUTHORS: Bernice Neugarten, Robert J. Havighurst, and Sheldon S. Tobin

PURPOSE: To measure the psychological well-being of the elderly.

DESCRIPTION: The LSIZ is an 18-item instrument designed to measure the life satisfaction of older people. The LSIZ was developed from a rating scale that was designed to be used by interviewers rating respondents and it may be administered orally or in writing. Items for the LSIZ were selected on the basis of their correlations with the original rating scale and their ability to discriminate between high and low scorers on the rating scale. Based on research on this instrument, it is recommended that the LSIZ be used mainly with individuals over 65.

NORMS: Initial study of the LSIZ was conducted with a sample of 60 reported to represent a wide range of age from 65 years, sex, and social class. The mean score on the original instrument was 12.4; however, this instrument included two more items than the current LSIZ.

SCORING: The LSIZ is easily scored by assigning one point to each item that is "correctly" checked and summing these scores. A correct score is "agree" on items 1, 2, 4, 6, 8, 9, 11, 12, 13, 14, 17. Other items are correct if the respondent answers "disagree."

RELIABILITY: No data were reported, but the rating scales from which the LSIZ was developed had excellent inter-observer agreement.

VALIDITY: The LSIZ showed moderate correlation with the instrument from which it was developed, the Life Satisfaction Rating Scale, indicating some degree of concurrent validity. The LSIZ also demonstrated a form of known-groups validity by successfully discriminating between high and low scores on the Life Satisfaction Rating Scale.

PRIMARY REFERENCE: Neugarten, B. L., Havighurst, R. J., and Tobin, S. S. (1961). The Measurement of Life Satisfaction, *Journal of Gerontology* 16, 134–143. Instrument reproduced with permission of Bernice Neugarten and Robert J. Havighurst.

AVAILABILITY: Journal article.

LSIZ

Here are some statements about life in general that people feel different ways about. Read each statement on the list and indicate at left the number that best describes how you feel about the statement.

1 = Agree
2 = Disagree
3 = Unsure

____ 1. As I grow older, things seem better than I thought they would be.
____ 2. I have gotten more of the breaks in life than most of the people I know.
____ 3. This is the dreariest time of my life.
____ 4. I am just as happy as when I was younger.
____ 5. My life could be happier than it is now.
____ 6. These are the best years of my life.
____ 7. Most of the things I do are boring or monotonous.
____ 8. I expect some interesting and pleasant things to happen to me in the future.
____ 9. The things I do are as interesting to me as they ever were.
____ 10. I feel old and somewhat tired.
____ 11. As I look back on my life, I am fairly well satisfied.
____ 12. I would not change my past life even if I could.
____ 13. Compared to other people my age, I make a good appearance.
____ 14. I have made plans for things I'll be doing in a month or a year from now.
____ 15. When I think back over my life, I didn't get most of the important things I wanted.
____ 16. Compared to other people, I get down in the dumps too often.
____ 17. I've gotten pretty much what I expected out of life.
____ 18. In spite of what some people say, the lot of the average man is getting worse, not better.

LIKING PEOPLE SCALE (LPS)

AUTHOR: Erik E. Filsinger

PURPOSE: To measure interpersonal orientation.

DESCRIPTION: This 15-item instrument measures one aspect of interpersonal orientation, the general liking of other people. Interpersonal orientation plays a significant role in one's social development and adjustment. The theoretical point of departure of the LPS is that the degree of liking people influences whether one approaches or avoids social interaction. The instrument has utility, then, for monitoring intervention in cases of social isolation, shyness, and antisocial behavior. Scores on the instrument do not appear to be significantly different for males and females, although females score slightly higher than males.

NORMS: Normative data are reported for three samples. One hundred and forty college students (57 males and 83 females) from diverse demographic backgrounds had a mean of 59.4 with a standard deviation of 8.14. A second sample of college students had average scores of 57.64 for males (n = 15) and 59.86 for females (n = 58). A third sample of randomly selected adults had a mean score of 52.27 for males and 55.35 for females.

SCORING: Respondents rate each item in terms of their agreement or disagreement. Ratings are quantified from 1 to 5 as follows: a = 1, b = 2, c = 3, d = 4, and e = 5. Items 4, 6, 8, 9, 10, and 15 are reverse-scored; total scores are the sum of all the items, with a range of 15 to 75. High scores indicate more liking of people.

RELIABILITY: The reliability of the LPS was estimated using Cronbach's alpha to test internal consistency. The LPS had very good internal consistency from two samples of college students (.85 and .75 respectively). Coefficient alpha was .78 from the random sample of adults. No data on stability were reported.

VALIDITY: The instrument generally has good validity evidence. In three separate samples the LPS was shown to have good criterion validity, correlating with the amount of time spent alone, the number of close friends, scores on a misanthropy measure, and social anxiety. The instrument has also been shown to correlate with four measures of affiliation motivation. The LPS correlates with social self-esteem and with the ability to judge others.

PRIMARY REFERENCE: Filsinger, E. E. (1981). A measure of interpersonal orientation: The Liking People Scale. *Journal of Personality Assessment* 45, 295–300. Instrument reproduced with permission of Erik E. Filsinger.

AVAILABILITY: Journal article.

LPS

The following questions ask your feeling about a number of things. Since we are all different, some people may think and feel one way; other people think and feel another way. There is no such thing as a "right" or "wrong" answer. The idea is to read each question and then fill out your answer. Try to respond to every question, even if it does not apply to you very well. The possible answers for each question are:

a = Strongly agree
b = Moderately agree
c = Neutral
d = Moderately disagree
e = Strongly disagree

____ 1. Sometimes when people are talking to me, I find myself wishing that they would leave.
____ 2. My need for people is quite low.
____ 3. One of the things wrong with people today is that they are too dependent upon other people.
____ 4. My happiest experiences involve other people.
____ 5. People are not important for my personal happiness.
____ 6. Personal character is developed in the stream of life.
____ 7. I could be happy living away from people.
____ 8. It is important to me to be able to get along with other people.
____ 9. No matter what I am doing, I would rather do it in the company of other people.
____ 10. There is no question about it--I like people.
____ 11. Personal character is developed in solitude.
____ 12. In general, I don't like people.
____ 13. Except for my close friends, I don't like people.
____ 14. A person only has a limited amount of time and people tend to cut into it.
____ 15. People are the most important thing in my life.

LONELINESS RATING SCALE (LRS)

AUTHORS: Joseph J. Scalise, Earl J. Ginter, and Lawrence H. Gerstein

PURPOSE: To measure affective components of loneliness.

DESCRIPTION: The LRS is a 40-item instrument in two parts: Part A measures the frequency of certain affects and Part B measures the intensity or impact of the affective experience. The LRS is composed of four factors derived from factor analysis: depletion (a loss of vigor, exhaustion), isolation (an interpersonal segregation), agitation (restlessness, frustration, antagonism), and dejection (a feeling of discouragement or despondency). The original items for the LRS were based on a list of words solicited from students about how they felt when they were lonely, plus review of the loneliness literature. The LRS thus allows measurement of how often a respondent experiences each of the four dimensions of the measure, and of the impact the experience of those feelings has.

NORMS: The LRS was developed with a sample of 277 males and 486 females, largely university students. The median age was 21 years with a range of 11 to 72 years. Means and standard deviations are reported for all four subscales for both men and women. There is a significant difference between male and female scores on all of the subscales except agitation. In all instances, women scored higher suggesting greater frequency and intensity of the three dimensions when lonely.

SCORING: Eight separate scores are derived from the LRS—four frequency scores and four intensity scores. Scores for each factor are obtained by simply adding up the numbers circled for the items that make up a factor (depletion: 4, 9, 11, 14, 18, 21, 22, 25, 26, 37; isolation: 6, 7, 20, 23, 28, 29, 31, 35, 39, 40; agitation: 3, 8, 12, 13, 15, 17, 24, 32, 33, 34; dejection: 1, 25, 10, 16, 19, 27, 30, 36, 38). If a person circles "never" for frequency, the corresponding intensity (Part B) portion should not be completed. Scores for the frequency dimensions should range from 0 to 30 and scores for intensity from 0 to 50.

RELIABILITY: The frequency dimensions have very good internal consistency with alphas that range from .82 to .89. Stability of the LRS is also good with six-week test-retest reliabilities ranging from .61 to .71 for frequency and .65 to .70 for intensity while four-week test-retest reliability was .72 to .81 for frequency and .73 to .78 for intensity.

VALIDITY: The only validity information available showed correlations of .25 to .46 with the UCLA Loneliness Scale, thus suggesting a moderate degree of concurrent validity.

PRIMARY REFERENCE: Scalise, J. J., Ginter, E. J., and Gerstein, L. H. (1984). A multidimensional loneliness measure: The Loneliness Rating Scale (LRS), *Journal of Personality Assessment* 48, 525–530. Instrument reproduced with permission of J. J. Scalise.

AVAILABILITY: Dr. Joseph J. Scalise, Department of Psychology and Counselor Education, Nicholls State University, Thibodaux, LA 70310.

LRS

This is not a test. We are only interested in finding out how you feel when you experience loneliness.

There are 40 two-part questions. In the first part of the question, several words are used to describe loneliness. Indicate which word most describes how you feel by placing the appropriate number of the following scale to the left of each statement.

0 = Never
1 = Occasionally
2 = Frequently
3 = Always

In the second part, you are asked to indicate on a scale of 1 to 5 how much this feeling affects you by writing the appropriate number on the right hand side of the statement.

1   2   3   4   5

bothersome   overwhelming

If your answer to the first part of the statement is "never," skip the second part of the statement.

____ 1. When I experience loneliness, I feel *low.*
          The feeling of being *low* is: ____

____ 2. When I experience loneliness, I feel *sad.*
          The feeling of being *sad* is: ____

____ 3. When I experience loneliness, I feel *angry.*
          The feeling of being *angry* is: ____

____ 4. When I experience loneliness, I feel *depressed.*
          The feeling of being *depressed* is: ____

____ 5. When I experience loneliness, I feel *drained.*
          The feeling of being *drained* is: ____

____ 6. When I experience loneliness, I feel *unloved.*
          The feeling of being *unloved* is: ____

____ 7. When I experience loneliness, I feel *worthless.*
          The feeling of being *worthless* is: ____

____ 8. When I experience loneliness, I feel *nervous.*
          The feeling of being *nervous* is: ____

____ 9. When I experience loneliness, I feel *empty.*
          The feeling of being *empty* is: ____

___ 10. When I experience loneliness, I feel *blue*.
         The feeling of being *blue* is: ___

___ 11. When I experience loneliness, I feel *hollow*.
         The feeling of being *hollow* is: ___

___ 12. When I experience loneliness, I feel *humiliated*.
         The feeling of being *humiliated* is: ___

___ 13. When I experience loneliness, I feel *guilty*.
         The feeling of being *guilty* is: ___

___ 14. When I experience loneliness, I feel *secluded*.
         The feeling of being *secluded* is: ___

___ 15. When I experience loneliness, I feel *tormented*.
         The feeling of being *tormented* is: ___

___ 16. When I experience loneliness, I feel *self-pity*.
         The feeilng of *self-pity* is: ___

___ 17. When I experience loneliness, I feel *aggressive*.
         The feeling of being *aggressive* is: ___

___ 18. When I experience loneliness, I feel *alienated*.
         The feeling of being *alienated* is: ___

___ 19. When I experience loneliness, I feel *hurt*.
         The feeling of being *hurt* is: ___

___ 20. When I experience loneliness, I feel *hopeless*.
         The feeling of being *hopeless* is: ___

___ 21. When I experience loneliness, I feel *broken*.
         The feeling of being *broken* is: ___

___ 22. When I experience loneliness, I feel *withdrawn*.
         The feeling of being *withdrawn* is: ___

___ 23. When I experience loneliness, I feel *disliked*.
         The feeling of being *disliked* is: ___

___ 24. When I experience loneliness, I feel *hostile*.
         The feeling of being *hostile* is: ___

___ 25. When I experience loneliness, I feel *numb*.
         The feeling of being *numb* is: ___

___ 26. When I experience loneliness, I feel *passive*.
         The feeling of being *passive* is: ___

___ 27. When I experience loneliness, I feel *confused*.
         The feeling of being *confused* is: ___

___ 28. When I experience loneliness, I feel *abandoned*.
The feeling of being *abandoned* is: ___

___ 29. When I experience loneliness, I feel *unacceptable*.
The feeling of being *unacceptable* is: ___

___ 30. When I experience loneliness, I feel *discouraged*.
The feeling of being *discouraged* is: ___

___ 31. When I experience loneliness, I feel *faceless*.
The feeling of being *faceless* is: ___

___ 32. When I experience loneliness, I feel *sick*.
The feeling of being *sick* is: ___

___ 33. When I experience loneliness, I feel *scared*.
The feeling of being *scared* is: ___

___ 34. When I experience loneliness, I feel *tense*.
The feeling of being *tense* is: ___

___ 35. When I experience loneliness, I feel *deserted*.
The feeling of being *deserted* is: ___

___ 36. When I experience loneliness, I feel *miserable*.
The feeling of being *miserable* is: ___

___ 37. When I experience loneliness, I feel *detached*.
The feeling of being *detached* is: ___

___ 38. When I experience loneliness, I feel *unhappy*.
The feeling of being *unhappy* is: ___

___ 39. When I experience loneliness, I feel *excluded*.
The feeling of being *excluded* is: ___

___ 40. When I experience loneliness, I feel *useless*.
The feeling of being *useless* is: ___

MAGICAL IDEATION SCALE (MIS)

AUTHORS: Mark Eckblad and Loren J. Chapman

PURPOSE: To measure magical thinking.

DESCRIPTION: The 30-item instrument was designed to measure the magical ideations characteristic of schizotypical disorders. The MIS is also considered a general measure of a proneness to psychosis. Magical ideation is defined as the belief in what general Western culture would consider invalid causation, such as superstitiousness, clairvoyance, telepathy, and so on. The focus of the MIS is not on the credibility of these forms of causation, but the respondent's personal beliefs and experiences.

NORMS: The MIS has normative data from a total of 1,512 undergraduate college students. The mean score was 8.56 with a standard deviation of 5.24 for males (n = 682). Females (n = 830) have a mean of 9.69 and a standard deviation of 5.93.

SCORING: Respondents indicate whether the item is true or false regarding their personal experience. Items 7, 12, 13, 16 18, 22, 23 are scored 1 if answered false. All other items are scored 1 if answered true. Total scores range from 0 to 30; higher scores reflect more reported experiences of magical ideation.

RELIABILITY: The reliability of this instrument is based on 1,512 college students. It has good internal consistency with correlations of .82 and .85 for males and females respectively.

VALIDITY: The items of the MIS were first judged as whether or not they were congruent with a specified definition of magic ideation; this represents logical content validity. The instrument then went through several revisions in order to make certain it was not associated with social desirability and an acquiescence response set. Validity is also supported with concurrent correlations between scores on the MIS and measures of perceptual aberration, physical anhedonism, and psychoticism. Known-groups validity was evident with differences on psychotic and psychoticlike symptoms for subjects whose MIS scores were two standard deviations above the mean and a control group.

PRIMARY REFERENCE: Eckblad, M. and Chapman, L. J. (1983). Magical ideation as an indicator of schizotypy, *Journal of Consulting and Clinical Psychology* 51, 215–225. Instrument reproduced with permission of Mark Eckblad and Loren Chapman, and the American Psychological Association.

AVAILABILITY: The Free Press

MIS

Indicate whether each item is true or false of your experiences by circling the T or the F to the left of the item.

T F 1. Some people can make me aware of them just by thinking about me.

T F 2. I have had the momentary feeling that I might not be human.

T F 3. I have sometimes been fearful of stepping on sidewalk cracks.

T F 4. I think I could learn to read others' minds if I wanted to.

T F 5. Horoscopes are right too often for it to be a coincidence.

T F 6. Things sometimes seem to be in different places when I get home, even though no one has been there.

T F 7. Numbers like 13 and 7 have no special powers.

T F 8. I have occasionally had the silly feeling that a TV or radio broadcaster knew I was listening to him.

T F 9. I have worried that people on other planets may be influencing what happens on earth.

T F 10. The government refuses to tell us the truth about flying saucers.

T F 11. I have felt that there were messages for me in the way things were arranged, like in a store window.

T F 12. I have never doubted that my dreams are the products of my own mind.

T F 13. Good luck charms don't work.

T F 14. I have noticed sounds on my records that are not there at other times.

T F 15. The hand motions that strangers make seem to influence me at times.

T F 16. I almost never dream about things before they happen.

T F 17. I have had the momentary feeling that someone's place has been taken by a look-alike.

T F 18. It is not possible to harm others merely by thinking bad thoughts about them.

T F 19. I have sometimes sensed an evil presence around me, although I could not see it.

T F 20. I sometimes have a feeling of gaining or losing energy when certain people look at me or touch me.

T F 21. I have sometimes had the passing thought that strangers are in love with me.

T F 22. I have never had the feeling that certain thoughts of mine really belonged to someone else.

T F 23. When introduced to strangers, I rarely wonder whether I have known them before.

T F 24. If reincarnation were true, it would explain some unusual experiences I have had.

T F 25. People often behave so strangely that one wonders if they are part of an experiment.

T F 26. At times I perform certain little rituals to ward off negative influences.

T F   27. I have felt that I might cause something to happen just by
            thinking too much about it.
T F   28. I have wondered whether the spirits of the dead can
            influence the living.
T F   29. At times I have felt that a professor's lecture was meant
            especially for me.
T F   30. I have sometimes felt that strangers were reading my mind.

MATHEMATICS ANXIETY RATING SCALE—REVISED (MARS-R)

AUTHORS: Barbara S. Plake and Clair S. Parker

PURPOSE: To measure anxiety about math.

DESCRIPTION: This 24-item instrument is designed to measure anxiety related to involvement in statistics and mathematic courses. The instrument is a revised version of a 98-item scale by Richardson and Suinn (1972). The current version is more focused on situation-specific (state) anxiety, general (trait) anxiety, and test anxiety. The instrument forms two subscales: learning math anxiety (LMA) which pertains to the process of learning statistics and mathematic evaluation anxiety (MEA) which measures anxiety over being tested about statistics.

NORMS: Data are reported on 170 college students enrolled in three introductory statistics classes at a large, urban, midwestern university. The mean MARS-R score was 59.84 with a standard deviation of 20.55.

SCORING: Respondents rate each item on a 5-point scale from "low anxiety" to "high anxiety." Scores are the sum of the item ratings, and range from 24 to 120 for the total scale.

RELIABILITY: The reliability of the revised form has been tested with internal consistency using coefficient alpha. The scale has excellent reliability with a correlation coefficient of .98. No data are presented on stability.

VALIDITY: There are mixed findings regarding the MARS-R. Scores were not correlated with achievement anxiety, but were correlated with Spielberger's State-Trait Anxiety measures. Concurrent validity was established with correlations between the MARS-R and math achievement, and with significant correlations with the 98-item version.

PRIMARY REFERENCE: Plake, B. S. and Parker, C. S. (1982). The development and validation of a revised version of the Mathematics Anxiety Rating Scale, *Educational and Psychological Measurement* 42, 551–557. Instrument reproduced with permission of Richard M. Suinn, the Rocky Mountain Behavioral Science Institute, Inc., and *Educational and Psychological Measurement*.

AVAILABILITY: Journal article.

MARS-R

Please rate each item in terms of how anxious you feel during the event specified. Use the following scale and record your answer in the space to the left of the item:

> 1 = Low anxiety
> 2 = Some anxiety
> 3 = Moderate anxiety
> 4 = Quite a bit of anxiety
> 5 = High anxiety

Learning Mathematics Anxiety

____ 1. Watching a teacher work an algebraic equation on the blackboard.
____ 2. Buying a math textbook.
____ 3. Reading and interpreting graphs or charts.
____ 4. Signing up for a course in statistics.
____ 5. Listening to another student explain a math formula.
____ 6. Walking into a math class.
____ 7. Looking through the pages in a math text.
____ 8. Starting a new chapter in a math book.
____ 9. Walking on campus and thinking about a math course.
____ 10. Picking up a math textbook to begin working on a homework assignment.
____ 11. Reading the word "statistics."
____ 12. Working on an abstract mathematical problem, such as: "if x = outstanding bills, and y = total income, calculate how much you have left for recreational expenditures."
____ 13. Reading a formula in chemistry.
____ 14. Listening to a lecture in a math class.
____ 15. Having to use the tables in the back of a math book.
____ 16. Being told how to interpret probability statements.

Mathematics Evaluation Anxiety

____ 1. Being given a homework assignment of many difficult problems which is due the next class meeting.
____ 2. Thinking about an upcoming math test one day before.
____ 3. Solving square root problem.
____ 4. Taking an examination (quiz) in a math course.
____ 5. Getting ready to study for a math test.
____ 6. Being given a "pop" quiz in a math class.
____ 7. Waiting to get a math test returned in which you expected to do well.
____ 8. Taking an examination (final) in a math course.

MENSTRUAL SYMPTOM QUESTIONNAIRE (MSQ)

AUTHOR: Margaret Chesney

PURPOSE: To measure spasmodic and congestive menstrual pain.

DESCRIPTION: This 25-item instrument is designed to measure two types of menstrual pain: spasmodic, which begins on the first day of menstruation and is experienced as spasms, and congestive, which occurs during the premenstrual cycle and is experienced as heaviness or dull aching pains in abdomen, breasts, and ankles. The MSQ supports the theory that there are two types of dysmenorrhea. The instrument is very useful in classifying types of menstrual pain and selecting appropriate interventions. Since these two types of menstrual pain occur separately, with few women experiencing both, once the client's pain is classified, the half of the items that assess the particular type of dysmenorrhea should be used.

NORMS: The MSQ was developed on a sample of 56 undergraduate college students who described themselves as having menstrual discomfort. Normative data are not presented.

SCORING: On the first 24 items respondents are asked to indicate the degree to which they experience the symptom by selecting one of the five alternatives. Spasmodic items (2, 4, 6, 7, 8, 10, 12, 14, 15, 18, 21, 24) are scored from 1 to 5 for each alternative as coded on the instrument. Congestive items (1, 3, 5, 9, 11, 13, 16, 17, 19, 20, 22, 23) are reverse-scored. Item 25 is scored by assigning 5 points if the respondent checked Type 1 and 1 point if she checked Type 2. Total scores are the summation of all 25 items. Higher MSQ scores reflect spasmodic menstrual pain, while lower scores reflect congestive menstrual pain. Scores range from 29 to 125 with 77 as a mid-point between the two types of pain. Scores closer to 77 indicate an absence of either type of menstrual pain.

RELIABILITY: Test-retest correlations provide the primary support for reliability. Over a two-week period items 1 through 24 had a test-retest correlation of .78. The test-retest correlation for item 25 was .93. Total MSQ scores correlated .87 for this same period, indicating that the instrument is stable. No internal consistency data were reported.

VALIDITY: The MSQ was developed from a pool of 51 items. Based on factor analysis items were included on the MSQ if they had factor loadings of .35 or greater. Twelve items were related to spasmodic pain and 12 were related to congestive pain. Scores on the forced-choice item, number 25, correlated .49 with spasmodic pain scores and $-.39$ with congestive pain scores, suggesting concurrent validity.

PRIMARY REFERENCE: Chesney, M. A. and Tasto, D. L. (1975). The development of the Menstrual Symptom Questionnaire, *Behaviour Research and Therapy* 13, 237–244. Instrument reproduced with permission of Margaret Chesney.

AVAILABILITY: Journal article.

MSQ

For each of the 24 items below please indicate how often you have had the experience, using the following scale. Please record your answers in the space to the left of the items.

1 = Never
2 = Rarely
3 = Sometimes
4 = Often
5 = Always

____ 1. I feel irritable, easily agitated, and am impatient a few days *before* my period.
____ 2. I have cramps that *begin* on the first day of my period.
____ 3. I feel depressed for several days *before* my period.
____ 4. I have abdominal pain or discomfort which begins one day *before* my period.
____ 5. For several days *before* my period I feel exhausted, lethargic, or tired.
____ 6. I only know that my period is coming by looking at the calendar.
____ 7. I take a prescription drug for the pain *during* my period.
____ 8. I feel weak and dizzy *during* my period.
____ 9. I feel tense and nervous *before* my period.
____ 10. I have diarrhea *during* my period.
____ 11. I have backaches several days *before* my period.
____ 12. I take aspirin for the pain *during* my period.
____ 13. My breasts feel tender and sore a few days *before* my period.
____ 14. My lower back, abdomen, and the inner sides of my thighs *begin* to hurt or be tender on the first day of my period.
____ 15. *During* the first day or so of my period, I feel like curling up in bed, using a hot water bottle on my abdomen, or taking a hot bath.
____ 16. I gain weight *before* my period.
____ 17. I am constipated *during* my period.
____ 18. *Beginning* on the first day of my period, I have pains which may diminish or disappear for several minutes and then reappear.
____ 19. The pain I have with my period is not intense, but a continuous dull aching.
____ 20. I have abdominal discomfort for more than one day *before* my period.
____ 21. I have backaches which *begin* the same day as my period.
____ 22. My abdominal area feels bloated for a few days *before* my period.
____ 23. I feel nauseous *during* the first day or so of my period.
____ 24. I have headaches for a few days *before* my period.

For the final question please read each of the two descriptions and indicate the type most closely experienced by you.

25. TYPE 1

The pain begins on the first day of menstruation, often coming within an hour of the first signs of menstruation. The pain is most severe the first day and may or may not continue on subsequent days. Felt as spasms, the pain may lessen or subside for awhile and then reappear. A few women find this pain so severe as to cause vomiting, fainting or dizziness; some others report that they are most comfortable in bed or taking a hot bath. This pain is limited to the lower abdomen, back and inner sides of the thighs.

TYPE 2

There is advanced warning of the onset of menstruation during which the woman feels an increasing heaviness, and a dull aching pain in the lower abdomen. This pain is sometimes accompanied by nausea, lack of appetite, and constipation. Headaches, backaches, and breast pain are also characteristic of this type of menstrual discomfort.

The type that most closely fits my experience is TYPE _____.

MICHIGAN ALCOHOLISM SCREENING TEST (MAST)

AUTHOR: Melvin L. Selzer

PURPOSE: To detect alcoholism.

DESCRIPTION: The MAST is a 25-item instrument designed to detect alcoholism. The items on the MAST were selected on the basis of review of several other approaches to investigating alcohol abuse. A few items were developed to be sufficiently neutral that persons reluctant to see themselves as problem drinkers may reveal their alcoholic symptoms. The MAST was developed with the understanding that lack of candor of respondents may be a problem, and was validated in a way that attempted to minimize such failures. Although the MAST was originally designed to be administered orally by professionals and nonprofessionals, it may also be completed by the respondent, although it is not known what effect this may have on its validity. The MAST has been found to be superior as a screening device to a search of records from medical, legal, and social agencies. Where the MAST is used for screening purposes, clinical confirmation is suggested.

NORMS: The MAST was administered to several groups: 103 controls, 116 hospitalized alcoholics, 99 people arrested for drunk driving, 110 people arrested for being drunk and disorderly, and 98 people under review for revocation of their driver's licenses because of excessive accidents and moving violations. The groups were largely white and male with mean ages that ranged from 25 to 44 years. Scores on the MAST for all five groups are available in the primary reference.

SCORING: Although the scoring of the MAST appears complicated, it is fairly easy once mastered. Each item on the MAST is assigned a weight of 0 to 5, with 5 considered diagnostic of alcoholism. Weights for the items are listed in the left-hand column of the instrument. Negative responses to items 1, 4, 6, and 8 are considered alcoholic responses, and positive responses to the other items are considered alcoholic responses. An overall score of 3 points or less is considered to indicate nonalcoholism, 4 points is suggestive of alcoholism, and 5 points or more indicates alcoholism.

RELIABILITY: No data have been reported.

VALIDITY: The MAST has excellent known-groups validity, being able to classify most respondents as alcoholic or nonalcoholic; only 15 out of 526 people originally classified as nonalcoholic subsequently were found to be alcoholic. In fact, even when respondents were instructed in advance to lie about their drinking problems, the MAST correctly identified 92% of 99 hospitalized alcoholics as having severe alcoholic problems.

Primary Reference: Selzer, M. L. (1971). The Michigan Alcoholism
Screening Test: The quest for a new diagnostic instrument, *American
Journal of Psychiatry* 127, 89–94. Instrument reproduced with per-
mission of *American Journal of Psychiatry.*
Availability: Journal article.

MAST

Please circle either Yes or No for each item as it applies to you.

Yes	No	(2)	1. Do you feel you are a normal drinker?
Yes	No	(2)	2. Have you ever awakened the morning after some drinking the night before and found that you could not remember a part of the evening before?
Yes	No	(1)	3. Does your wife (or do your parents) ever worry or complain about your drinking?
Yes	No	(2)	4. Can you stop drinking without a struggle after one or two drinks?
Yes	No	(1)	5. Do you ever feel bad about your drinking?
Yes	No	(2)	6. Do friends or relatives think you are a normal drinker?
Yes	No	(0)	7. Do you ever try to limit your drinking to certain times of the day or to certain places?
Yes	No	(2)	8. Are you always able to stop drinking when you want to?
Yes	No	(5)	9. Have you ever attended a meeting of Alcoholics Anonymous (AA)?
Yes	No	(1)	10. Have you gotten into fights when drinking?
Yes	No	(2)	11. Has drinking ever created problems with you and your wife?
Yes	No	(2)	12. Has your wife (or other family member) ever gone to anyone for help about your drinking?
Yes	No	(2)	13. Have you ever lost friends or girlfriends/boyfriends because of drinking?
Yes	No	(2)	14. Have you ever gotten into trouble at work because of drinking?
Yes	No	(2)	15. Have you ever lost a job because of drinking?
Yes	No	(2)	16. Have you ever neglected your obligations, your family, or your work for two or more days in a row because you were drinking?
Yes	No	(1)	17. Do you ever drink before noon?
Yes	No	(2)	18. Have you ever been told you have liver trouble? Cirrhosis?
Yes	No	(5)	19. Have you ever had delirium tremens (DTs), severe shaking, heard voices, or seen things that weren't there after heavy drinking?
Yes	No	(5)	20. Have you ever gone to anyone for help about your drinking?
Yes	No	(5)	21. Have you ever been in a hospital because of drinking?
Yes	No	(2)	22. Have you ever been a patient in a psychiatric hospital or on a psychiatric ward of a general hospital where drinking was part of the problem?
Yes	No	(2)	23. Have you ever been seen at a psychiatric or mental health clinic, or gone to a doctor, social worker, or clergyman for help with an emotional problem in which drinking had played a part?
Yes	No	(2)	24. Have you ever been arrested, even for a few hours, because of drunk behavior?
Yes	No	(2)	25. Have you ever been arrested for drunk driving after drinking?

MILLER SOCIAL INTIMACY SCALE (MSIS)

AUTHORS: Rickey S. Miller and Herbert M. Lefcourt

PURPOSE: To measure the level of social intimacy.

DESCRIPTION: The MSIS is a 17-item instrument designed to measure closeness with others. It is based on the findings of several studies that show intimacy to be an important predictor of healthy psychological and physical functioning, especially in regard to marriage, relationships with others, bereavement, and response to stress. The initial item pool of 30 was generated by intensive interviews with university undergraduates; subsequent tests produced the current 17 items, 6 of which are frequency items and 11 of which measure intensity. The MSIS is structured to permit an assessment of intimacy in the context of friendship or marriage.

NORMS: The 252 respondents who participated in the developmental research on the MSIS included 72 male and 116 female unmarried undergraduate students (mean age 21.3 years) 17 (n = 34) married couples (mean age 24.3), who were also students, and a married clinic sample of 15 couples (n = 30) seeking conjoint marital therapy (mean age 36.3 years). Mean scores for the groups were: unmarried males 134.9, unmarried females 139.3, married males 152.5, married females 156.2, clinic males 124.5, and clinic females 133.8.

SCORING: The original instrument, scored on a 10-point scale, has been revised to the 5-point scale reproduced here. Items 1, 2, 3, 21, and 22 are not scored. Items 5 and 17 are reverse-scored, then the individual items are summed (A = 1, E = 5) to produce an overall score for the MSIS, with higher scores indicating greater amounts of social intimacy.

RELIABILITY: The MSIS has excellent internal consistency, with alphas in two samples of .86 and .91. The MSIS is also extremely stable, with a two-month test-retest correlation of .96 and .84 over a one-month interval.

VALIDITY: The MSIS has good known-groups validity, significantly distinguishing between couples seeking marital therapy and those not seeking it, and between married and unmarried students. It also has established construct validity by correlating or not correlating in predicted directions with several other measures such as the UCLA Loneliness Scale, the Interpersonal Relationship Scale, the Tennessee Self-Concept Scale, and the Personality Research Form. Responses on the MSIS are not affected by social desirability response set.

PRIMARY REFERENCE: Miller, R. S. and Lefcourt, H. M. (1982). The assessment of social intimacy, *Journal of Personality Assessment* 46, 514–518. Instrument reproduced with permission of Rickey S. Miller and Herbert M. Lefcourt.

AVAILABILITY: Dr. Herbert M. Lefcourt, Department of Psychology, University of Waterloo, University Avenue, Waterloo, Ontario, Canada N2L 3G1.

MSIS

A number of phrases are listed below that describe the kind of relationships people have with others. Indicate, by filling in the appropriate letters in the answer field, how you would describe your current relationship with your closest friend. This friend can be of either sex and should be someone whom you consider to be your closest friend at this time. While it is not necessary to specify the name of this friend, please indicate his/her sex in question 1.

Remember that you are to indicate the kind of relationship you have *now* with your *closest friend.*

1. Sex of your closest friend: M_____   F_____

2. Your marital status: single_____   married_____   common-law_____
   separated or divorced_____   widowed_____

3. Is the friend you describe your spouse?   Yes_____   No_____

		Very rarely		Some of the time		Almost always
4.	When you have leisure time how often do you choose to spend it with him/her alone?	A	B	C	D	E
5.	How often do you keep very personal information to yourself and do not share it with him/her?	A	B	C	D	E
6.	How often do you show him/her affection?	A	B	C	D	E
7.	How often do you confide very personal information to him/her?	A	B	C	D	E
8.	How often are you able to understand his/her feelings?	A	B	C	D	E
9.	How often do you feel close to him/her?	A	B	C	D	E

		Not much		A little		A great deal
10.	How much do you like to spend time alone with him/her?	A	B	C	D	E
11.	How much do you feel like being encouraging and supportive to him/her when he/she is unhappy?	A	B	C	D	E
12.	How close do you feel to him/her most of the time?	A	B	C	D	E
13.	How important is it to you to listen to his/her personal disclosures?	A	B	C	D	E
14.	How satisfying is your relationship with him/her?	A	B	C	D	E
15.	How affectionate do you feel towards him/her?	A	B	C	D	E
16.	How important is it to you that he/she understand your feelings?	A	B	C	D	E
17.	How much damage is caused by a typical disagreement in your relationship with him/her?	A	B	C	D	E
18.	How important is it to you that he/she be encouraging and supportive to you when you are unhappy?	A	B	C	D	E
19.	How important is it to you that he/she show you affection?	A	B	C	D	E
20.	How important is your relationship with him/her in your life?	A	B	C	D	E

21. You have just described the relationship you have now with your closest friend. We are interested in knowing *how long* this person has been your closest friend. Please check the appropriate category:
    less than a month_____   1-4 months_____   5-8 months_____
    9-12 months_____   over a year_____

22. Recall your *previous* closest friend. Are you less close____ just as close____ or closer____ with the current friend you described on this scale?

MOBILITY INVENTORY FOR AGORAPHOBIA (MI)

AUTHORS: Dianne L. Chambless, G. Craig Caputo, Susan E. Jasin, Edward J. Gracely, and Christine Williams

PURPOSE: To measure severity of agoraphobic avoidance behavior.

DESCRIPTION: The MI is a 27-item instrument designed to measure agoraphobic avoidance behavior and frequency of panic attacks. Twenty-six of the items measure avoidance, with each item rated for avoidance both when the client is alone and when accompanied. The final item gives a definition of panic and asks the respondent to report the number of panic experiences during the previous week. The MI was developed by using items from the Fear Survey Schedule, items obtained in interviews with agoraphobic clients, and from observations of avoidance behavior and panic attacks in agoraphobic clients. The MI provides clinically useful information both in total score form as well as in interpretation of scores on individual items.

NORMS: Two samples were used in development of the MI. The first consisted of 159 clients applying for treatment at a clinic specializing in agoraphobia and anxiety (88% female, mean age 34.6) and 23 non-agoraphobic controls with similar demographic characteristics. The second sample involved 83 agoraphobic clients, including significantly more males. Norms for all of these groups on each item are available in the primary reference. When averaged across all situations, the mean score for avoidance when accompanied for agoraphobics ranges from 2.41 to 2.64 and the mean score for avoidance when alone ranges from 3.30 to 3.35

SCORING: Each item on the MI is scored on a 1 to 5 basis and each item can be interpreted independently. The MI does not use a mean score averaged across all situations for avoidance when accompanied by another and avoidance when alone. To derive these scores simply add the rating for the "when accompanied" column and divide by the number of items answered. Do the same procedures for the items in the "when alone" column.

RELIABILITY: The MI has excellent internal consistency, with alphas that range from .91 to .97. The MI also has excellent stability, with overall test-retest reliabilities over 31 days of .89 and .90 for avoidance when alone and .75 and .86 for avoidance when accompanied.

VALIDITY: The MI has very good concurrent validity, correlating significantly with the agoraphobic factor of the Fear Questionnaire, the Beck Depression Inventory, and the Trait form of the State-Trait Anxiety Inventory. The MI also has good known-groups validity, significantly distinguishing between agoraphobic and nonclincial and social phobic respondents. Finally, the MI also has been found in two studies to be sensitive to changes following treatment for agoraphobia.

PRIMARY REFERENCE: Chambless, D. L., Caputo, G. C., Jasin, S. E., Gracely, E. J., and Williams, C. (1985). The Mobility Inventory for Agoraphobia, *Behavioral Research and Therapy* 23, 35–44. Instrument reproduced with permission of Pergamon Press.

AVAILABILITY: Journal article.

MI

Please indicate the degree to which you avoid the following places or situations because of discomfort or anxiety. Rate your amount of avoidance when you are with a trusted companion and when you are alone. Do this by using the following scale.

1 = Never avoid
2 = Rarely avoid
3 = Avoid about half the time
4 = Avoid most of the time
5 = Always avoid

(You may use numbers halfway between those listed when you think it is appropriate. For example, 3-1/2 or 4-1/2.)

Write your score in the blanks for each situation or place under both conditions: when accompanied, and when alone. Leave blank those situations that do not apply to you.

Places	When accompanied	When alone
Theatres	_____	_____
Supermarkets	_____	_____
Classrooms	_____	_____
Department stores	_____	_____
Restaurants	_____	_____
Museums	_____	_____
Elevators	_____	_____
Auditoriums or stadiums	_____	_____
Parking garages	_____	_____
High places	_____	_____
Tell how high _____	_____	_____
Enclosed spaces (e.g., tunnels)	_____	_____
Open spaces		
Outside (e.g., fields, wide streets, courtyards)	_____	_____
Inside (e.g., large rooms, lobbies)	_____	_____

Riding In:

  Buses   _____   _____

  Trains   _____   _____

  Subways   _____   _____

  Airplanes   _____   _____

  Boats   _____   _____

Driving or riding in car:

  At any time   _____   _____

  On expressways   _____   _____

Situations:

  Standing in lines _____   _____

  Crossing bridges   _____   _____

  Parties or social
  gatherings   _____   _____

  Walking on the street _____   _____

  Staying at home alone   NA   _____

  Being far way from home _____   _____

  Other (specify)   _____   _____

We define a *panic attack* as:
    (1) a high level of anxiety accompanied by
    (2) strong body reactions (heart palpitations, sweating, muscle tremors, dizziness, nausea) with
    (3) the temporary loss of the ability to plan, think, or reason and
    (4) the intense desire to escape or flee the situation. (Note, this is different from high anxiety or fear alone.)
Please indicate the total number of panic attacks you have had in the last 7 days. _____

MOOD SURVEY (MS)

AUTHORS: Bill Underwood and William J. Froming

PURPOSE: To measure happy and sad moods.

DESCRIPTION: The MS is an 18-item scale that assesses happy and sad moods as traits, that is, as long-term personality characteristics. Happy and sad moods are treated as endpoints on a continuum in an attempt to identify people who differ in average mood level taken over a long period of time. Conceptual analysis of moods suggested three dimensions on which initial construction of the MS was based: the average level of a person's mood, frequency of mood change, and the intensity with which people react to mood experiences. The MS actually possesses two primary subscales: level of mood (LM) and reactivity to situations (RS).

NORMS: Several studies were carried out to identify the psychometric properties of the MS. All were based on undergraduate students in an introductory psychology class (796 females and 591 males). No additional demographic data were reported nor were specific norms.

SCORING: Individual item scores on the 6-point Likert scales are simply totaled along with the responses to three questions asking respondents to estimate mood level, frequency of mood change, and intensity of mood reactions on 99-point scales. The IM subscale consists of items 2, 4, 6, 8, 10, 11, 13, 15, and 16 with items 6, 11, 13 and 15 reverse-scored. The RL subscale consists of items 1, 5, 7, 9, 12, 14, 17 and 18 with items 5, 9 and 14 reverse-scored.

RELIABILITY: Test-retest reliability over three weeks is .80 for the level subscale and .85 for reactivity, indicating good stability. For a seven-week period, test-retest reliability was .63 for level and .83 for reactivity. No data on internal consistency were available.

VALIDITY: The MS has good concurrent validity, correlating significantly with a number of other measures such as the Beck Depression Inventory and the Mood Adjective Checklist. The MS also showed stronger correlations with personality measures than did other, state measures of mood. Further, the subscales of the MS were found to correlate or not correlate in the predicted directions with other mood scales, establishing a form of construct validity.

PRIMARY REFERENCE: Underwood, B. and Froming, W. J. (1980). The Mood Survey: A personality measure of happy and sad moods, *Journal of Personality Assessment* 44, 404–414. Instrument reproduced with permission of William J. Froming and *Journal of Personality Assessment*.

AVAILABILITY: Dr. William J. Froming, Department of Psychology, University of Florida, Gainesville, FL 32611.

MS

Below are a number of statements about your experience of moods. We would like you to consider your usual behavior when you respond. Using the scale, indicate the appropriate number to the left of each question and try to be as honest as you can.

                    1 = Strongly disagree
                    2 = Moderately disagree
                    3 = Somewhat disagree
                    4 = Somewhat agree
                    5 = Moderately agree
                    6 = Strongly agree

_____   1. I may change from happy to sad and back again several times in a single week.
_____   2. I usually feel quite cheerful.
_____   3. I'm frequently "down in the dumps."
_____   4. I generally look at the sunny side of life.
_____   5. Compared to my friends, I'm less up and down in my mood states.
_____   6. I'm not often really elated.
_____   7. Sometimes my moods swing back and forth very rapidly.
_____   8. I usually feel as though I'm bubbling over with joy.
_____   9. My moods are quite consistent; they almost never vary.
_____ 10. I consider myself a happy person.
_____ 11. Compared to my friends, I think less positively about life in general.
_____ 12. I'm a very changeable person.
_____ 13. I am not as cheerful as most people.
_____ 14. I'm not as "moody" as most people I know.
_____ 15. My friends often seem to feel I am unhappy.

_____ 16. If 1 = extremely sad, 50 = neutral, and 99 = extremely happy, how happy are you in general?
_____ 17. If 1 = hardly ever and 99 = extremely frequently, how frequently do your moods change?
_____ 18. If 1 = not at all and 99 = extremely intensely, how intensely do you react to mood experiences?

MULTIDIMENSIONAL HEALTH LOCUS OF CONTROL SCALES (MHLC)

AUTHORS: Kenneth A. Wallston, Barbara Studler Wallston, and Robert DeVellis

PURPOSE: To measure locus of control of health-related behavior.

DESCRIPTION: This 18-item instrument measures three dimensions of locus of control of reinforcement as it pertains to health. Specifically, the MHLC assesses people's belief that their health is or is not determined by their own behavior. These issues of internal and external control have been extensively studied in regard to numerous clinical problems. The MHLC looks at beliefs about three sources of control over health, with each subscale containing six items: internality of health locus of control (IHLC), powerful other locus of control (POLC), and chance locus of control (CHLC). The MHLC has parallel forms (Forms A and B) designed to be alternated for use as repeated measures, or the two forms may be combined to create longer (12 items) and more reliable subscales. Further information on scoring and application of the scales is available from the authors.

NORMS: Normative data are available on samples of chronic patients (n = 609), college students (n = 749), healthy adults (n = 1287) and persons involved in preventive health behaviors (n = 720). The IHLC, CHLC and PHLC scales had average scores of 25.78, 17.64, and 22.54 for the chronic patients, and 26.68, 16.72 and 17.87 for college students. Healthy adults had average scores of 25.55, 16.21 and 19.16 for the IHLC, CHLC and PHLC, respectively, while the sample of persons involved in preventive health behaviors had average scores of 27.38, 15.52 and 18.44.

SCORING: All items are arranged on 6-point Likert scales ranging from "strongly agree" to "strongly disagree." Scores for each subscale are the sums of the following items: IHLC: 1, 6, 8, 12, 13, 17; POLC: 3, 5, 7, 10, 14, 18; CHLC: 2, 4, 9, 11, 15, 16. Higher scores reflect externality.

RELIABILITY: The items were empirically selected from a pool of 88, with fairly stringent criteria. The internal consistency reliability using Cronbach's alpha ranged from .67 to .77 for all six scales, the three dimensions, and two parallel forms. When the parallel forms were combined to make 12-item scales the alphas ranged from .83 to .86 for the three scales.

VALIDITY: The MHLC scales have fairly good criterion validity, correlating with subjects' state of health. The scales also correlate with other measures of locus of control, including the Multidimensional Locus of Control scales for Psychiatric Patients. Except for the chance locus of control scale, the scales were not correlated with social desirability.

PRIMARY REFERENCE: Wallston, K. A., Wallston, B. S., and DeVellis, R. (1978). Development of the Multidimensional Health Locus of Control (MHLC) Scales, *Health Education Monographs* 6, 160–170. Instrument reproduced with permission of Kenneth A. Wallston, Ph.D.
AVAILABILITY: Kenneth A. Wallston, Professor, Health Care Research Project, Vanderbilt University, School of Nursing, Nashville, TN 37240.

MHLC

Form A

This is a questionnaire designed to determine the way in which different people view certain important health-related issues. Each item is a belief statement with which you may agree or disagree. Each statement can be rated on a scale which ranges from strongly disagree (1) to strongly agree (6). For each item we would like you to record the number that represents the extent to which you disagree or agree with the statement. The more strongly you agree with a statement, then the higher will be the number you record. The more strongly you disagree with a statement, then the lower will be the number you record. Please make sure that you answer every item and that you record *only one* number per item. This is a measure of your personal beliefs; obviously, there are no right or wrong answers.

Please answer these items carefully, but do not spend too much time on any one item. As much as you can, try to respond to each item independently. When making your choice, do not be influenced by your previous choices. It is important that you respond according to your actual beliefs and not according to how you feel you should believe or how you think we want you to believe.

$$1 = \text{Strongly disagree}$$
$$2 = \text{Moderately disagree}$$
$$3 = \text{Slightly disagree}$$
$$4 = \text{Slightly agree}$$
$$5 = \text{Moderately agree}$$
$$6 = \text{Strongly agree}$$

____ 1. If I get sick, it is my own behavior which determines how soon I get well again.
____ 2. No matter what I do, if I am going to get sick, I will get sick.
____ 3. Having regular contact with my physician is the best way for me to avoid illness.
____ 4. Most things that affect my health happen to me by accident.
____ 5. Whenever I don't feel well, I should consult a medically trained professional.

____ 6. I am in control of my health.
____ 7. My family has a lot to do with my becoming sick or staying healthy.
____ 8. When I get sick, I am to blame.
____ 9. Luck plays a big part in determining how soon I will recover from an illness.
____ 10. Health professionals control my health.
____ 11. My good health is largely a matter of good fortune.
____ 12. The main thing which affects my health is what I myself do.
____ 13. If I take care of myself, I can avoid illness.
____ 14. When I recover from an illness, it's usually because other people (for example, doctors, nurses, family, friends) have been taking good care of me.
____ 15. No matter what I do, I'm likely to get sick.
____ 16. If it's meant to be, I will stay healthy.
____ 17. If I take the right actions, I can stay healthy.
____ 18. Regarding my health, I can only do what my doctor tells me to do.

Form B

This is a questionnaire designed to determine the way in which different people view certain important health-related issues. Each item is a belief statement with which you may agree or disagree. Each statement can be rated on a scale which ranges from strongly disagree (1) to strongly agree (6). For each item we would like you to record the number that represents the extent to which you disagree or agree with the statement. The more strongly you agree with a statement, then the higher will be the number you record. The more strongly you disagree with a statement, then the lower will be the number you record. Please make sure that you answer every item and that you record *only one* number per item. This is a measure of your personal beliefs; obviously, there are no right or wrong answers.

Please answer these items carefully, but do not spend too much time on any one item. As much as you can, try to respond to each item independently. When making your choice, do not be influenced by your previous choices. It is important that you respond according to your actual beliefs and not according to how you feel you should believe or how you think we want you to believe.

> 1 = Strongly disagree
> 2 = Moderately disagree
> 3 = Slightly disagree
> 4 = Slightly agree
> 5 = Moderately agree
> 6 = Strongly agree

____ 1. If I become sick, I have the power to make myself well again.
____ 2. Often I feel that no matter what I do, if I am going to get sick, I will get sick.
____ 3. If I see an excellent doctor regularly, I am less likely to have health problems.
____ 4. It seems that my health is greatly influenced by accidental happenings.
____ 5. I can only maintain my health by consulting health professionals.

___ 6. I am directly responsible for my health.

___ 7. Other people play a big part in whether I stay healthy or become sick.

___ 8. Whatever goes wrong with my health is my own fault.

___ 9. When I am sick, I just have to let nature run its course.

___ 10. Health professionals keep me healthy.

___ 11. When I stay healthy, I'm just plain lucky.

___ 12. My physical well-being depends on how well I take care of myself.

___ 13. When I feel ill, I know it is because I have not been taking care of myself properly.

___ 14. The type of care I receive from other people is what is responsible for how well I recover from an illness.

___ 15. Even when I take care of myself, it's easy to get sick.

___ 16. When I become ill, it's a matter of fate.

___ 17. I can pretty much stay healthy by taking good care of myself.

___ 18. Following doctor's orders to the letter is the best way for me to stay healthy.

MULTIDIMENSIONAL LOCUS OF CONTROL SCALES
FOR PSYCHIATRIC PATIENTS (MLOCP)

AUTHOR: Hanna Levenson

PURPOSE: To measure locus of control of adjustment and empowerment.

DESCRIPTION: This 24-item multidimensional instrument measures the belief that reinforcement is contingent upon one's own behavior or on events which are not contingent upon one's behavior, such as chance or luck. According to social learning theory, a person who has an internal locus of control is more adjusted than one who considers consequences as the result of external events. Moreover, the author of this instrument believes that one of the goals of treatment is the development of internal control, signifying competence and mastery over one's environment. The three dimensions of locus of control assessed are internal locus of control (ILC), powerful others control (POC) and chance control (CC). Factor analysis has generally supported the dimensionality of the instrument.

NORMS: Normative data are based on 165 consecutively admitted psychiatric patients. Ninety-five were male and 70 were female, and approximately 66 percent of the sample was white, while the rest were black. The average age of the sample was 37 years old. Data are also available on 96 "normal" subjects, although little demographic information is reported. The mean scores for the ICC, POC, and CC were 35.4, 23.8, and 21.7, respectively, for the sample of psychiatric patients. The ICC, POC, and CC average scores were 35.5, 16.7, and 13.9 for the nonclinical sample. Data are also reported for patients' diagnoses. Males and females do not seem to score differently on the subscales.

SCORING: Each item is rated on a 6-point scale from "strongly disagree" to "strongly agree." The three subscales are summed separately, and the items grouped according to scales. Total scale scores range from 8 to 48. Higher scores reflect more externality. Scale items are: ICC: 1, 4, 5, 9, 18, 19, 21, 23; POC: 3, 8, 11, 13, 15, 17, 20, 22; CC: 2, 6, 7, 10, 12, 14, 16, 24.

RELIABILITY: For two of the three scales, the internal consistency reliability was good. Alphas were .67, .82, and .79 for the ILC, POC, and CC, respectively. Test-retest reliability over a five-day interval was .74 and .78 for the POC and CC, but only .08 for the ILC.

VALIDITY: The validity of this instrument is established primarily through known-groups procedures. Scores on the POC and CC scales discriminated between neurotic and psychotic patients, with a range of specific differences occurring between specific types of disorders.

PRIMARY REFERENCE: Levenson, H. (1973). Multidimensional locus of control in psychiatric patients, *Journal of Consulting and Clinical Psychology* 41, 397–404. Instrument reproduced with permission of the American Psychological Association.
AVAILABILITY: Journal article.

MLOCP

Indicate the extent to which you agree with each of the following
statements using the scale:

                1 = Strongly agree
                2 = Moderately agree
                3 = Slightly agree
                4 = Slightly disagree
                5 = Moderately disagree
                6 = Strongly disagree

____ 1. Whether or not I get to be a leader depends mostly on my
         ability.
____ 2. To a great extent my life is controlled by accidental
         happenings.
____ 3. I feel like what happens in my life is mostly determined by
         powerful people.
____ 4. My behavior will determine when I am ready to leave the
         hospital.
____ 5. When I make plans, I am almost certain to make them work.
____ 6. Often there is no chance of protecting my personal interests
         from bad luck happenings.
____ 7. When I get what I want it's usually because I'm lucky.
____ 8. Even if I were a good leader, I would not be made a leader
         unless I play up to those in positions of power.
____ 9. How many friends I have depends on how nice a person I am.
____ 10. I have often found that what is going to happen will happen.
____ 11. My life is chiefly controlled by powerful others.
____ 12. It is impossible for anyone to say how long I'll be in the
         hospital.
____ 13. People like myself have very little chance of protecting our
         interests when they conflict with those of powerful other
         people.
____ 14. It's not always wise for me to plan too far ahead because many
         things turn out to be a matter of good or bad fortune.
____ 15. Getting what I want means I have to please those people above
         me.
____ 16. Whether or not I get to be a leader depends on whether I'm lucky
         enough to be in the right place at the right time.
____ 17. If important people were to decide they didn't like me, I
         probably wouldn't make many friends.
____ 18. I can pretty much determine what will happen in my life.
____ 19. I am usually able to protect my personal interests.
____ 20. How soon I leave the hospital depends on other people who have
         power over me.
____ 21. When I get what I want, it's usually because I worked hard for
         it.
____ 22. In order to have my plans work, I make sure that they fit in
         with the desires of people who have power over me.
____ 23. My life is determined by my own actions.
____ 24. It's chiefly a matter of fate whether or not I have a few
         friends or many friends.

NEGATIVE ATTITUDES TOWARD MASTURBATION INVENTORY (NAMI)

AUTHORS: Paul R. Abramson and Donald L. Mosher

PURPOSE: To measure guilt over masturbation.

DESCRIPTION: This 30-item instrument measures negative attitudes toward masturbation. Negative attitudes can emerge from a lack of information or from inadequate information about sexuality; additionally, negative attitudes may develop from conditioned emotional reactions. Negative attitudes tend to be related to a lower frequency of masturbation and to sexual inexperience. Negative attitudes are considered evidence of guilt over masturbation. Knowledge of negative attitudes toward masturbation can assist in therapeutic work on sexuality and the treatment of some orgasmic disorders. The scores on the NAMI were not influenced by gender.

NORMS: Normative data are reported on 95 male and 99 female college students. The mean NAMI was 72.06 with a standard deviation of 15.29 for males and 72.44 with a standard deviation of 16.36 for females.

SCORING: Each item is rated on a 5-point Likert scale by recording a number from (1) strongly disagree to (5) strongly agree in the space to the left of the item. Items 3, 5, 8, 11, 13, 14-17, 22, 27, 29, are reverse-scored. Total scores are then the sum of all items and range from 30 to 150 with higher scores indicating more negative attitudes.

RELIABILITY: This instrument has acceptable evidence of internal consistency. The reliability, calculated according to the Spearman-Brown formula, was .75. All items except one had significant correlations with total scores. Estimates of test-retest reliability are not available.

VALIDITY: The NAMI shows strong evidence of concurrent validity. Correlations were found between it and sexual guilt, sexual experiences, and frequency of masturbation for females. For males the NAMI only correlated with two of the criteria, sexual guilt and frequency of masturbation.

PRIMARY REFERENCE: Abramson, P. R. and Mosher, D. L. (1975). Development of a measure of negative attitudes toward masturbation, *Journal of Consulting and Clinical Psychology*, 43, 485–490. Instrument reproduced with permission of Dr. Paul R. Abramson and the American Psychological Association.

AVAILABILITY: Dr. Paul R. Abramson, Department of Psychology, UCLA, Los Angeles, CA 90024.

NAMI

Below are thirty statements regarding masturbation. Please indicate the degree to which you agree with each by placing the appropriate number to the left of the statement. The numbers are based on the following scale:

1 = Strongly disagree
2 = Disagree
3 = Neither agree nor disagree
4 = Agree
5 = Strongly agree

____ 1. People masturbate to escape from feelings of tension and anxiety.

____ 2. People who masturbate will not enjoy sexual intercourse as much as those who refrain from masturbation.

____ 3. Masturbation is a private matter which neither harms nor concerns anyone else.

____ 4. Masturbation is a sin against yourself.

____ 5. Masturbation in childhood can help a person develop a natural, healthy attitude toward sex.

____ 6. Masturbation in an adult is juvenile and immature.

____ 7. Masturbation can lead to homosexuality.

____ 8. Excessive masturbation is physically impossible, as it is a needless worry.

____ 9. If you enjoy masturbating too much, you may never learn to relate to the opposite sex.

____ 10. After masturbating, a person feels degraded.

____ 11. Experience with masturbation can potentially help a woman become orgastic in sexual intercourse.

____ 12. I feel guilty about masturbating.

____ 13. Masturbation can be a "friend in need" when there is no "friend in deed."

____ 14. Masturbation can provide an outlet for sex fantasies without harming anyone else or endangering oneself.

____ 15. Excessive masturbation can lead to problems of impotence in men and frigidity in women.

____ 16. Masturbation is an escape mechanism which prevents a person from developing a mature sexual outlook.

____ 17. Masturbation can provide harmless relief from sexual tensions.

____ 18. Playing with your own genitals is disgusting.

____ 19. Excessive masturbation is associated with neurosis, depression, and behavioral problems.

____ 20. Any masturbation is too much.

____ 21. Masturbation is a compulsive, addictive habit which once begun is almost impossible to stop.

____ 22. Masturbation is fun.

___ 23. When I masturbate, I am disgusted with myself.

___ 24. A pattern of frequent masturbation is associated with introversion and withdrawal from social contacts.

___ 25. I would be ashamed to admit publicly that I have masturbated.

___ 26. Excessive masturbation leads to mental dullness and fatigue.

___ 27. Masturbation is a normal sexual outlet.

___ 28. Masturbation is caused by an excessive preoccupation with thoughts about sex.

___ 29. Masturbation can teach you to enjoy the sensuousness of your own body.

___ 30. After I masturbate, I am disgusted with myself for losing control of my body.

OBSESSIVE—COMPULSIVE SCALE (OCS)

AUTHORS: Gerald D. Gibb, James R. Bailey, Randall H. Best and Thomas T. Lambirth

PURPOSE: To measure degree of compulsivity.

DESCRIPTION: This 20-item instrument measures a concept that is widely discussed in clinical practice, but for which there are few systematic measurement tools. The focus of the OCS is on a general tendency toward obsessive thoughts and compulsive behaviors. The scale is a general measure of this disorder, and does not provide separate scores for obsessive thoughts and compulsive behaviors. The true-false format makes the OCS easy to complete, and the instrument has a validity check (see below).

NORMS: The OCS was developed using 114 college students with mean scores of 11.15 and 11.24 for males and females, respectively. The mean for a clinical sample ($N = 57$) was 11.22.

SCORING: Items 1, 2, 4, 6, 7, 8, 16, 17, 18, and 21 are assigned 1 point if answered "true." Items 5, 9, 10, 11, 12, 13, 14, 19, 20, 22 are assigned 1 point if answered "false." Scores range from 0 to 20, with higher scores indicating more compulsivity. Items 3 and 15 are validity checks, and if answered incorrectly, the OCS score should not be considered valid.

RELIABILITY: This instrument has evidence of internal consistency and test-retest reliability. The internal consistency was estimated by correlating each item with the total, and these correlations were significant. The test-retest reliability correlation was .82 over a three-week period indicating good stability.

VALIDITY: The OCS has several estimates of concurrent validity: scores correlated with clinicians' ratings of client's compulsivity, with Comrey's Order Scale, and with a measure of flexibility.

PRIMARY REFERENCE: Gibb, G. D., Bailey, J. R., Best, R. H., and Lambirth, T. T. (1983). The measurement of the obsessive compulsive personality, *Educational and Psychological Measurement* 43, 1233–1237. Instrument reproduced with permission of Gerald D. Gibb.

AVAILABILITY: Lt. Gerald D. Gibb, MSC, USNR, Psychological Sciences Department, Naval Aerospace Medical Research Library, Naval Air Station, Pensacola, FL 32508.

OCS

Please indicate whether each statement below is true or false for you by circling the T or the F to the left of the question.

T F   1. I feel compelled to do things I don't want to do.
T F   2. I usually check things that I know I have already done.
T F   3. I can walk 30 miles in an hour.
T F   4. I often do things I don't want to do because I can not resist doing them.
T F   5. I seldom keep a daily routine.
T F   6. I feel compelled always to complete what I am doing.
T F   7. I often feel the need to double check what I do.
T F   8. I'd rather do things the same way all the time.
T F   9. I seldom have recurring thoughts.
T F 10. I seldom am compelled to do something I don't want to do.
T F 11. I don't feel uncomfortable and uneasy when I don't do things my usual way.
T F 12. If I don't feel like doing something it won't bother me not to do it.
T F 13. I usually never feel the need to be organized.
T F 14. I am uneasy about keeping a rigid time schedule.
T F 15. My birthday comes once a year.
T F 16. I am often compelled to do some things I do not want to do.
T F 17. I like to keep a rigid daily routine.
T F 18. I believe there is a place for everything and everything in its place.
T F 19. I seldom check things I know I have already done.
T F 20. I am not obsessed with details.
T F 21. I often have recurring thoughts.
T F 22. I like to do things differently each time.

PERCEIVED GUILT INDEX (PGI)

AUTHORS: John R. Otterbacher and David C. Munz

PURPOSE: To measure the state and trait of guilt.

DESCRIPTION: The PGI consists of two instruments which measure the emotional experience of guilt as a state at the moment (G-state) and as a generalized self-concept (G-trait). The instrument is quite different from others in this volume as it is scored as a single index and the score value is based on ratings from a sample of college students. The instrument was developed by having undergraduates (n = 80) develop an item pool of adjectives and phrases describing guilt. A second sample of college students rated each item in terms of its intensity of guilt, and 83 items were selected based on the median ratings. A final sample of college students then rated the items on a sematic differential and 11 items were selected as a unidimensional index of the emotional experience of guilt. The instrument is particularly useful in settings where one needs to monitor a client's guilt reaction to specific events or situations, as might occur in marital therapy or with juvenile delinquents. When the G-trait and G-state instruments are used together the trait scale should be administered first.

NORMS: Normative data are not available. The score values for all the items were based on a sample of 55 undergraduate students.

SCORING: There are two ways to score the PGI, as a single index for the specific G-trait and G-state word selected, and as a score assessing one's guilt reaction to a particular situation which is compared to how one "normally" feels. Scores for the G-trait and G-state are determined by assigning the item score value. The score values for each item are: $1 = 6.8$, $2 = 1.1$, $3 = 4.3$, $4 = 9.4$, $5 = 2.0$, $6 = 7.8$, $7 = 5.9$, $8 = 3.4$, $9 = 8.6$, $10 = 5.3$, $11 = 10.4$. Since the respondent is instructed to select one item, the score is simply the item score value corresponding to the item.

The second method of scoring the PGI is more complicated. First assign the respondent the appropriate item scores as described above, then subtract the G-trait from the G-state score, and add 10 to the result. The constant 10 is used to eliminate confusion over minus and positive signs. Moreover, scores above 10 indicate an intensity of guilt greater than what one normally feels, while scores below 10 represent a guilt reaction less than one's usual experience.

RELIABILITY: Reliability for the two scales is reported in terms of test-retest correlations over a four-week period. Scores were not correlated for the G-state scale, as would be expected of a state measurement. The G-trait was only slightly correlated (.30).

VALIDITY: As a measure of one's guilt reaction (i.e. the second scoring

252

method), the PGI has been shown to be sensitive to assessing changes occurring as a consequence of sacramental confession. Concurrent validity is demonstrated by differences in the relationship between state and trait guilt scores for groups where guilt increased and decreased over a four-week period.

PRIMARY REFERENCE: Otterbacher, J. R. and Munz, D. C. (1973). State-trait measure of experiential guilt, *Journal of Consulting and Clinical Psychology* 40, 115–121. Instruments reproduced with permission of David C. Munz and the American Psychological Association.

AVAILABILITY: David C. Munz, Ph.D., Department of Psychology, St. Louis University, St. Louis, MO 63104.

PGI-S

Below is a list of words and phrases people use to describe how they feel at different times. Please check the word or phrase that best describes the way you feel *at this moment*. So that you will become familiar with the general range of feeling that they cover or represent, carefully read the entire list before making your selection. Again, check only *one* word or phrase, that which best describes the way you feel *at this moment*.

____ 1. Reproachable
____ 2. Innocent
____ 3. Pent up
____ 4. Disgraceful
____ 5. Undisturbed
____ 6. Marred
____ 7. Chagrined
____ 8. Restrained
____ 9. Degraded
____ 10. Fretful
____ 11. Unforgivable

PGI-T

Below is a list of words and pharses people use to describe how *guilty* they feel at different times. Please check the word or phrase which best describes the way you *normally feel*. So that you will become familiar with the general range of feeling that they cover or represent, carefully read this entire list before making your selection. Again, check only *one* word or phrase, that which best describes how *guilty* you *normally feel*.

____ 1. Reproachable
____ 2. Innocent
____ 3. Pent up
____ 4. Disgraceful
____ 5. Undistrubed
____ 6. Marred
____ 7. Chagrined
____ 8. Restrained
____ 9. Degraded
____ 10. Fretful
____ 11. Unforgivable

PERSONAL ASSERTION ANALYSIS (PAA)

AUTHORS: Bonnie L. Hedlund and Carol U. Lindquist

PURPOSE: To distinguish among passive, aggressive, and assertive behavior.

DESCRIPTION: The PAA is a 30-item instrument designed to assess passive, aggressive, and assertive behavior and to help determine an individual's need for assertion training. The PAA asks respondents to report what they actually do rather than what they know how to do. A pool of 87 items was collected from a number of available assertion inventories. Through use of factor analysis, the PAA was reduced to 30 items and three factors, each with 10 items; three factor analyses with different samples confirm the presence of the three factors—passive (items 3, 6, 11, 13, 16, 21, 25, 26, 27, 29), aggressive (items 5, 7, 10, 12, 15, 17, 22, 23, 24, 30), and assertive (1, 2, 4, 8, 9, 14, 18, 19, 20, 28).

NORMS: Three separate samples were used in developing and validating the PAA. The first was a sample of 120 undergraduates (mean age 19); the second a sample of 200 undergraduates (mean age 23.3); the third sample of 275 included 68 male and 76 female adolescents (mean age 17.5), 25 male and 32 female alcoholics (mean age 43), 5 females and 7 males involved in spouse abuse, and 10 males and 17 females who reported they were satisfied in their marriages (mean age 40). The means for the second sample were 23.45 for aggression, 18.97 for assertion, and 21.20 for passivity. The means for the third sample were 29.23 for aggression, 22.12 for assertion, and 27.37 for passivity. There were no differences between males and females.

SCORING: The individual items are summed for each subscale; a low score indicates more of that behavior. Each subscale ranges from 0 to 40.

RELIABILITY: The PAA has fairly good stability with a one-week test-retest correlation of .70 for aggression and assertion and .82 for passivity. No internal consistency data were reported.

VALIDITY: The PAA demonstrates a fair degree of construct validity. The PAA subscales correlated in predicted directions with some measures with which they should correlate, including a number of personality tests of assertion and aggression, taped role-play situations, peer ratings, and global self-ratings. There were small but significant correlations between the assertion and aggression subscales and the Marlowe-Crowne Social Desirability Scale, indicating a small effect of social desirability on responses to the PAA.

PRIMARY REFERENCE: Hedlund, B. L. and Lindquist, C. U. (1984). The Development of an inventory for distinguishing among passive, aggressive, and assertive behavior, *Behavioral Assessment* 6, 379–390.

Instrument reproduced with permission of Bonnie L. Hedlund and Carol U. Lindquist.

AVAILABILITY: Dr. Bonnie L. Hedlund or Dr. Carol U. Lindquist, Department of Psychology, California State University, Fullerton, CA 92634.

PAA

Please read the following statements: Each one describes a situation and a response. Try to imagine a situation in your life that is as close to the one described as possible, then rate the response according to its similarity with what you *might* do in the actual situation.

1 = Just like me
2 = Sometimes like me
3 = Not usually like me
4 = Not at all like me

___ 1. You'd like a raise, so you make an appointment with your boss to explain the reasons you feel you should receive one.
___ 2. You usually take the lead when you are in a group of people.
___ 3. Because of a high-pressure salesperson, you buy a camera that meets most but not all of your requirements.
___ 4. You're working on a project with a friend but you seem to be doing all the work. You say, "I'd like to see if we could find a different way to divide the responsibility. I feel I'm doing most of the work."
___ 5. After waiting in a restaurant for 20 minutes, you loudly tell the host of your dissatisfaction and leave.
___ 6. A very important person you have long admired comes to speak in your town. Afterwards you are too hesitant to go and meet him/her.
___ 7. Your parents have been after you to spend more time with them. You tell them to stop nagging you.
___ 8. Your neighbor's stereo is disturbing you. You call and ask if he/she would please turn it down.
___ 9. A repairman overcharges you. You explain that you feel the charges are excessive and ask for the bill to be adjusted.
___ 10. A person cuts in front of you in line, so you push him/her out of line.
___ 11. When you're feeling warm towards your parent/spouse, it is difficult for you to express this to them.
___ 12. You are delayed getting home because you stayed at a friend's too long. When your parent/spouse is angry, you tell him/her it's none of his/her business.
___ 13. When trying to talk to someone of the opposite sex, you get nervous.
___ 14. In a job interview you are able to state your positive points as well as your negative points.
___ 15. You are driving to an appointment with a friend and she/he has a flat tire. While she/he is changing the tire, you tell her/him how dumb it was to let the tires get worn.

____ 16. You accept your boss's opinion about your lack of ability to handle responsibility, but later complain to some friends about his/her unfairness.

____ 17. You are arguing with a person and she/he pushes you, so you push her/him back.

____ 18. In a discussion with a small group of people, you state your position and are willing to discuss it, but you don't feel that you have to win.

____ 19. The person next to you in a movie is explaining the plot of the movie to his/her companion. You ask them to please be quiet because they are distracting you from the movie.

____ 20. When you see a new person you would like to meet, you usually try to start a conversation with him/her.

____ 21. Your neighbor wants to use your car. Even though you'd rather she/he didn't, you say yes.

____ 22. A friend of yours is arguing with someone much larger than she/he is. You decide to help your friend by saying, "I'm really tired of listening to you mouth off."

____ 23. A person cuts in front of you in line, so you say, "Who do you think you are? Get out of my way."

____ 24. You are talking to a friend and she/he doesn't appear to be listening. You tell her/him that you are sick and tired of her/him not listening to you.

____ 25. Speaking before a group makes you so nervous that you have a great deal of trouble speaking clearly.

____ 26. You are waiting for a car to pull out of a parking place so that you can park. Someone comes up behind you and honks. You drive on.

____ 27. You find it hard to express contradictory opinions when dealing with an authority figure.

____ 28. Your spouse/boyfriend/girlfriend is supposed to take you out. Fifteen minutes before you are to leave, she/he calls and cancels. You tell her/him that you are very disappointed.

____ 29. In a group situation, you usually wait to see what the majority of the people want before giving your opinion.

____ 30. You have arranged to meet a friend, but she/he doesn't arrive. At the first opportunity, you call her/him and demand an explanation.

PHYSICAL SELF-EFFICACY SCALE (PSE)

AUTHORS: Richard M. Ryckman, Michael A. Robbins, Billy Thornton, and Peggy Cantrell

PURPOSE: To measure perceived physical competence.

DESCRIPTION: The PSE is a 22-item instrument that is based on the assumption that people's expectations about their own efficacy have important effects on cognitive, affective, and behavioral patterns. The PSE also is based on the assumption that there are a variety of arenas in which individuals must achieve mastery if they are to perceive themselves as efficacious. One of these arenas is physical self-concept. The PSE is designed to measure individual differences in perceived physical competence and feelings of confidence in displaying physical skills to others. The instrument was based on a pool of 90 items; those items that were not highly correlated with social desirability response set but were related to two primary factors were selected to form the PES. The final form has two subscales, perceived physical ability (PPA) (items 1, 2, 4, 6, 8, 12, 13, 19*, 21*, 22*) and physical self-presentation confidence (PSPC) (items 3*, 5, 7, 9*, 10, 11*, 14*, 15, 16, 17*, 18, 20*), plus an overall PES scale. The PES is useful for diagnostic and assessment purposes in medical and clinical settings and in athletic programs.

NORMS: A series of studies was conducted in the development of the PSI, eventually involving some 950 undergraduate students. Demographic data and actual norms were not reported.

SCORING: The PSE is scored by first reverse-scoring the items with asterisks (noted above), then summing the scores on the individual items within each factor for the subscale scores and summing the two subscale scores for the overall PES score. The scores on the PPA range from 10 to 60, on PSPC from 12 to 72, and overall scores from 22 to 132. Higher scores on all three indicate greater self-efficacy.

RELIABILITY: The PSE has good internal consistency with alphas of .84 for PPA, .74 for PSPC, and .81 for the overall PSE. The PSE is also a very stable instrument with six-week test-retest correlations of .89 for PPA, .69 for PSPC, and .80 for the PSE as a whole.

VALIDITY: The PSE has good concurrent validity, correlating significantly with a number of other measures such as the Tennessee Physical Self-Concept Scale, the Texas Social Behavior Inventory (self-esteem), the Self-Consciousness Scale, and the Taylor Manifest Anxiety Scale. The PSE also has good predictive validity, predicting a number of scores on other instruments as well as sports and physically related activities (e.g., respondents with higher PES scores outperform respondents with lower PES scores).

PRIMARY REFERENCE: Ryckman, R. M., Robbins, M. A., Thornton, B., and Cantrell, P. (1982). Development and validation of a Physical Self-Efficacy Scale, *Journal of Personality and Social Psychology* 42, 891–900. Instrument reproduced with permission of Richard M. Ryckman and the American Psychological Association.

AVAILABILITY: Dr. Richard M. Ryckman, Department of Psychology, University of Maine, Orono, ME 04469.

PSE

Please place one number to the left of the column for each item as follows:

1 = Strongly agree
2 = Agree
3 = Somewhat agree
4 = Somewhat disagree
5 = Disagree
6 = Strongly disagree

____ 1. I have excellent reflexes.
____ 2. I am not agile and graceful.
____ 3. I am rarely embarrassed by my voice.
____ 4. My physique is rather strong.
____ 5. Sometimes I don't hold up well under stress.
____ 6. I can't run fast.
____ 7. I have physical defects that sometimes bother me.
____ 8. I don't feel in control when I take tests involving physical dexterity.
____ 9. I am never intimidated by the thought of a sexual encounter.
____ 10. People think negative things about me because of my posture.
____ 11. I am not hesitant about disagreeing with people bigger than I.
____ 12. I have poor muscle tone.
____ 13. I take little pride in my ability in sports.
____ 14. Athletic people usually do not receive more attention than I.
____ 15. I am sometimes envious of those better looking than myself.
____ 16. Sometimes my laugh embarrasses me.
____ 17. I am not concerned with the impression my physique makes on others.
____ 18. Sometimes I feel uncomfortable shaking hands because my hand is clammy.
____ 19. My speed has helped me out of some tight spots.
____ 20. I find that I am not accident prone.
____ 21. I have a strong grip.
____ 22. Because of my agility, I have been able to do things that many others could not do.

THE PROBLEM-SOLVING INVENTORY (PSI)

AUTHOR: P. Paul Heppner

PURPOSE: To assess respondents' perception of their problem-solving behaviors and attitudes.

DESCRIPTION: The PSI is a 35-item instrument designed to measure how individuals believe they generally react to personal problems in their daily lives. The term "problems" refers to personal problems such as getting along with friends, feeling depressed, choosing a career, or deciding whether to get divorced. Although the PSI does not measure actual problem-solving skills, it does measure the evaluative awareness of one's problem solving abilities or style. The PSI comprises three subscales based on factor analysis: problem solving confidence (items 5, 10, 11*, 12, 19, 23, 24, 27, 33, 34*, 35), approach-avoidance style (items 1*, 2*, 4*, 6, 7, 8, 13*, 15*, 16, 17*, 18, 20, 21*, 28, 30, 31), and personal control (3*, 14*, 25*, 26*, 32*). In addition, the total score is viewed as a single, general index of problem-solving perception. This is one of the few standardized measures that addresses this central concern of helping professionals with clients' coping and problem-solving skills.

NORMS: The PSI was developed and tested with several samples of white, introductory psychology students (402 males, 498 females); 25 black male and 59 black female students; 26 male and 42 female counseling center clients; 306 undergraduates across all four academic years; and four populations of adults including 101 "normals," 77 inpatient alcoholic males, 29 elderly, and 90 female university extension staff members. Norms for all these groups are available. The means on the total PSI range from 74.0 for the female extension staff members to 98.0 for male counseling center clients.

SCORING: The PSI can be self-scored by the client, or scored by the practitioner either directly or using a computer (computer answer sheets are available). Items with asterisks (see above) are reverse-scored. Then the scores for the items on each factor are summed. The three factor scores are summed for the total score. Items 9, 22, and 29 are filler items and not scored. Lower scores reflect greater perceived problem-solving abilities.

RELIABILITY: The PSI has good internal consistency with alphas ranging from .72 to .85 on the subscales and .90 for the total measure. The PSI has excellent stability with two-week test-retest correlations for the subscales and total measure that range from .83 to .89.

VALIDITY: Extensive testing of the PSI reveals good validity in several areas. Concurrent validity was established by significant correlations between the PSI and scores on a self-rating scale of one's problem-solving skill. Construct validity has been established in a number of

261

studies by establishing that the PSI is correlated with other measures with which it should be correlated and not with those with which it theoretically should not be. Several personality measures were used in these studies, such as Rotter's Internal-External Scale and the Myers-Briggs Type Indicator. The PSI has been found to distinguish significantly among groups such as clinical and nonclinical, or those with higher and lower scores on measures of psychological disturbance, thus establishing known-groups validity. The PSI is sensitive to clinical changes and also is not affected by social desirability response set.

PRIMARY REFERENCE: Heppner, P. P. and Petersen, C. H. (1982). The development and implications of a personal problem-solving inventory, *Journal of Counseling Psychology* 29, 66–75. Instrument reproduced with permission of P. Paul Heppner.

AVAILABILITY: Dr. P. Paul Heppner, University of Missouri–Columbia, Psychology Department, 210 McAlester Hall, Columbia, MO 65211.

PSI

Read each statement, and indicate the extent to which you agree or disagree with that statement, using the following alternatives:

1 = Strongly agree
2 = Moderately agree
3 = Slightly agree
4 = Slightly disagree
5 = Moderately disagree
6 = Strongly disagree

____ 1. When a solution to a problem was unsuccessful, I did not examine why it didn't work.

____ 2. When I am confronted with a complex problem, I do not bother to develop a strategy to collect information so I can define exactly what the problem is.

____ 3. When my first efforts to solve a problem fail, I become uneasy about my ability to handle the situation.

____ 4. After I have solved a problem, I do not analyze what went right or what went wrong.

____ 5. I am usually able to think up creative and effective alternatives to solve a problem.

____ 6. After I have tried to solve a problem with a certain course of action, I take time and compare the actual outcome to what I think should have happened.

____ 7. When I have a problem, I think up as many possible ways to handle it as I can until I can't come up with any more ideas.

____ 8. When confronted with a problem, I consistently examine my feelings to find out what is going on in a problem situation.

____ 9. When I am confused with a problem, I do not try to define vague ideas or feelings into concrete or specific terms.

____ 10. I have the ability to solve most problems even though initially no solution is immediately apparent.

____ 11. Many problems I face are too complex for me to solve.

____ 12. I make decisions and am happy with them later.

____ 13. When confronted with a problem, I tend to do the first thing that I can think to solve it.

____ 14. Sometimes I do not stop and take time to deal with my problems, but just kind of muddle ahead.

____ 15. When deciding on an idea or possible solution to a problem, I do not take time to consider the chances of each alternative being successful.

____ 16. When confronted with a problem, I stop and think about it before deciding on a next step.

____ 17. I generally go with the first good idea that comes to my mind.

____ 18. When making a decision, I weigh the consequences of each alternative and compare them against each other.

___ 19. When I make plans to solve a problem, I am almost certain that I can make them work.

___ 20. I try to predict the overall result of carrying out a particular course of action.

___ 21. When I try to think up possible solutions to a problem, I do not come up with very many alternatives.

___ 22. In trying to solve a problem, one strategy I often use is to think of past problems that have been similar.

___ 23. Given enough time and effort, I believe I can solve most problems that confront me.

___ 24. When faced with a novel situation I have confidence that I can handle problems that may arise.

___ 25. Even though I work on a problem, sometimes I feel like I am groping or wandering, and am not getting down to the real issue.

___ 26. I make snap judgments and later regret them.

___ 27. I trust my ability to solve new and difficult problems.

___ 28. I have a systematic method for comparing alternatives and making decisions.

___ 29. When I try to think of ways of handling a problem, I do not try to combine different ideas together.

___ 30. When confronted with a problem, I don't usually examine what sort of external things in my environment may be contributing to my problem.

___ 31. When I am confronted by a problem, one of the first things I do is survey the situation and consider all the relevant pieces of information.

___ 32. Sometimes I get so charged up emotionally that I am unable to consider many ways of dealing with my problem.

___ 33. After making a decision, the outcome I expected usually matches the actual outcome.

___ 34. When confronted with a problem, I am unsure of whether I can handle the situation.

___ 35. When I become aware of a problem, one of the first things I do is to try to find out exactly what the problem is.

PROVISION OF SOCIAL RELATIONS (PSR)

AUTHORS: R. Jay Turner, B. Gail Frankel, and Deborah M. Levin

PURPOSE: To measure social support.

DESCRIPTION: The PSR is a 15-item instrument designed to measure components of social support. Based initially on the conceptualization by Weiss of five components of social support (attachment, social integration, reassurance of worth, reliable alliance, and guidance), factor analysis revealed the PSR to have essentially two dimensions, family support (items 4, 7, 10, 11, 12, 14) and friend support (items 1, 2, 3, 5, 6, 8, 9, 13, 15). The PSR is one of the few instruments that examines the environmental variable of social support (or, at least, the respondent's perceptions), a key element for assessment and intervention in many clinical approaches.

NORMS: The PSR was developed in a series of studies involving 200 university students, 523 discharged psychiatric patients in Canada (59% female), and 989 (54% female) psychiatrically disabled community residents located in interviews with 11,000 households in Ontario, Canada. Actual norms are not available.

SCORING: The PSR is scored by reverse-scoring items 7 and 15 and then summing the item scores on each of the subdimensions to get a score for that dimension. A total score can be obtained by summing the scores on the two subdimensions. Higher scores reflect more social support.

RELIABILITY: The PSR has good internal consistency, with alphas that range from .75 to .87. No test-retest correlations were reported.

VALIDITY: The PSR has good concurrent validity correlating significantly with the Kaplan Scale of Social Support. The PSR is negatively correlated with several measures of psychological distress, indicating that the PSR is not confounded by item content measuring psychological distress.

PRIMARY REFERENCE: Turner, R. J., Frankel, B. G., and Levin, D. M. (1983). Social support: Conceptualization, measurement, and implications for mental health, *Research in Community and Mental Health* 3, 67–111. Instrument reproduced with permission of JAI Press, Inc. and B. Gail Frankel.

AVAILABILITY: Journal article.

PSR

We would like to know something about your relationships with other
people. Please read each statement below and decide how well the
statement describes you. For each statement, show your answer by
indicating to the left of the item the number that best describes how
you feel. The numbers represent the following answers.

                    1 = Very much like me
                    2 = Much like me
                    3 = Somewhat like me
                    4 = Not very much like me
                    5 = Not at all like me

____ 1. When I'm with my friends, I feel completely able to relax
         and be myself.
____ 2. I share the same approach to life that many of my friends do.
____ 3. People who know me trust me and respect me.
____ 4. No matter what happens, I know that my family will always be
         there for me should I need them.
____ 5. When I want to go out to do things I know that many of my
         friends would enjoy doing these things with me.
____ 6. I have at least one friend I could tell anything to.
____ 7. Sometimes I'm not sure if I can completely rely on my family.
____ 8. People who know me think I am good at what I do.
____ 9. I feel very close to some of my friends.
____ 10. People in my family have confidence in me.
____ 11. My family lets me know they think I am a worthwhile person.
____ 12. People in my family provide me with help in finding solutions
         to my problems.
____ 13. My friends would take the time to talk over my problems, should
         I ever want to.
____ 14. I know my family will always stand by me.
____ 15. Even when I am with my friends I feel alone.

RATHUS ASSERTIVENESS SCHEDULE (RAS)

AUTHOR: Spencer A. Rathus

PURPOSE: To measure assertiveness.

DESCRIPTION: This 30-item instrument was designed to measure assertiveness, or what the author called social boldness. Respondents are asked to rate 30 social situations according to how characteristic each is of their own experience. This widely used instrument provides the practitioner with clients' impressions of their own assertiveness and frankness, and can be used to provide positive feedback to clients during treatment, which is especially important in working with assertiveness problems. The RAS does not seem to be affected by social desirability.

NORMS: Data are reported for a sample of 68 undergraduates which were used in the reliability analysis. The subjects had an age range from 17 to 27 years. The mean RAS was .294 with a standard deviation of 29.121. At an eight week post test the mean was 1.62 with a standard deviation of 27.632.

SCORING: Items are rated in terms of how descriptive the item is of the respondent. Ratings are from $+3$ to -3. Seventeen items, indicated by an asterisk, are reverse-scored. Scores are determined by summing item ratings, and range from -90 to $+90$. Negative scores reflect nonassertiveness and positive scores reflect assertiveness.

RELIABILITY: The RAS has acceptable evidence of internal consistency and stability. Split-half reliability was .77. Test-retest reliability over an eight-week period was .78.

VALIDITY: The RAS has good criterion validity. Scores on the instrument have been shown to correlate with measures of boldness, outspokenness, assertiveness, aggressiveness, and confidence. Strong concurrent validity is seen in the correlation between RAS scores and trained raters' ranking on assertiveness. Also, the RAS has been shown to possess construct validity: 19 of the 30 items correlated with external measures of assertiveness and 28 were negatively correlated with a measure of niceness.

PRIMARY REFERENCE: Rathus, S. A. (1973). A 30-item schedule for assessing assertive behavior, *Behavior Therapy* 4, 398–406. Instrument reproduced with permission of Academic Press.

AVAILABILITY: Journal article.

RAS

Indicate how characteristic or descriptive each of the following statements is of you by using the code given below.

+3 = Very characteristic of me, extremely descriptive
+2 = Rather characteristic of me, quite descriptive
+1 = Somewhat characteristic of me, slightly descriptive
-1 = Somewhat uncharacteristic of me, slightly nondescriptive
-2 = Rather uncharacteristic of me, quite nondescriptive
-3 = Very uncharacteristic of me, extremely nondescriptive

_____ 1. Most people seem to be more aggressive and assertive than I am.
_____ 2. I have hesitated to make or accept dates because of "shyness."
_____ 3. When the food served at a restaurant is not done to my satisfaction, I complain about it to the waiter or waitress.
_____ 4. I am careful to avoid hurting other people's feelings, even when I feel that I have been injured.
_____ 5. If a salesman has gone to considerable trouble to show me merchandise that is not quite suitable, I have a difficult time saying "No."
_____ 6. When I am asked to do something, I insist upon knowing why.
_____ 7. There are times when I look for a good, vigorous argument.
_____ 8. I strive to get ahead as well as most people in my position.
_____ 9. To be honest, people often take advantage of me.
_____ 10. I enjoy starting conversations with new acquaintances and strangers.
_____ 11. I often don't know what to say to attractive persons of the opposite sex.
_____ 12. I will hesitate to make phone calls to business establishments and institutions.
_____ 13. I would rather apply for a job or for admission to a college by writing letters than by going through with personal interviews.
_____ 14. I find it embarrassing to return merchandise.
_____ 15. If a close and respected relative were annoying me, I would smother my feelings rather than express my annoyance.
_____ 16. I have avoided asking questions for fear of sounding stupid.
_____ 17. During an argument I am sometimes afraid that I will get so upset that I will shake all over.
_____ 18. If a famed and respected lecturer makes a statement which I think is incorrect, I will have the audience hear my point of view as well.
_____ 19. I avoid arguing over prices with clerks and salesmen.
_____ 20. When I have done something important or worthwhile, I manage to let others know about it.
_____ 21. I am open and frank about my feelings.
_____ 22. If someone has been spreading false and bad stories about me, I see him/her as soon as possible to "have a talk" about it.

_____ 23. I often have a hard time saying "No."

_____ 24. I tend to bottle up my emotions rather than make a scene.

_____ 25. I complain about poor service in a restaurant and elsewhere.

_____ 26. When I am given a compliment, I sometimes just don't know what to say.

_____ 27. If a couple near me in a theater or at a lecture were conversing rather loudly, I would ask them to be quiet or to take their conversation elsewhere.

_____ 28. Anyone attempting to push ahead of me in a line is in for a good battle.

_____ 29. I am quick to express an opinion.

_____ 30. There are times when I just can't say anything.

RATIONAL BEHAVIOR INVENTORY (RBI)

AUTHORS: Clayton T. Shorkey and Victor C. Whiteman

PURPOSE: To measure irrational and absolutist beliefs.

DESCRIPTION: The RBI is a 37-item instrument that provides an overall index of irrationality, or the tendency to hold irrational and absolutist beliefs. The RBI is based on the work of Albert Ellis and the assumption that irrational beliefs underlie emotional disorders. The RBI was specifically constructed to be used for assessment, treatment planning, and evaluation in rational-behavior and cognitive-behavior therapy. It has been extensively studied by a number of investigators. The RBI presents one overall score plus 11 factors: (1) catastrophizing, (2) guilt, (3) perfectionism, (4) need for approval, (5) caring and helping, (6) blame and punishment, (7) inertia and avoidance, (8) independence, (9) self-downing, (10) projected misfortune, and (11) control of emotions. Each factor has three or four items, and separate factor scores as well as the overall score give a clear picture of the extent of an individual's irrational or dysfunctional beliefs in several areas.

NORMS: The RBI has been studied with a number of different clinical and nonclinical samples. The initial studies were conducted on 414 undergraduate students and 127 mental health professionals attending workshops by Albert Ellis. For undergraduates, the mean total rationality score was 26.35. There were no statistically significant differences between males and females except on one subscale. For the two groups of mental health professionals, total RBI scores prior to the Ellis workshop were 28.45 and 27.62. Normative data are available for other groups as well (Thyer, Papsdorf, Himle, and Bray, 1981).

SCORING: The RBI is somewhat difficult to score and it is recommended that the scoring guide available with the instrument be used. Basically, each item on the RBI is assigned a cutting point of 3 or 4, and the number of points assigned to that item is based on that cutting point. Once the score for each factor is determined by summing the scores on each item on the factor, the overall score is determined by summing the scores for all eleven factors. This results in a possible range of 0 to 38 with higher scores indicating greater irrationality.

RELIABILITY: The RBI has good internal consistency and homogeneity. Each factor was measured by a Guttman scale with a coefficient of reproducibility of .60 or more. The total RBI had a split-half reliability of .73. The RBI has good stability with a .82 test-retest correlation after three days and .71 after ten days.

VALIDITY: A number of studies have demonstrated good concurrent and known-groups validity for the RBI. The RBI is significantly correlated in predicted directions with several measures of trait and state anxiety in clinical and nonclinical samples. The RBI has been found to be significantly correlated to several other personality measures, such as anomie, authoritarianism, dogmatism, self-esteem, and to measures of psychiatric symptomatology. Further, the RBI has been found to distinguish between clinical and nonclinical samples in several studies, and is also sensitive to changes from both workshops and therapy. Finally, the RBI does not appear to be influenced by social desirability response set.

PRIMARY REFERENCE: Shorkey, C. T. and Whiteman, V. L. (1977). Development of the Rational Behavior Inventory: Initial validity and reliability, *Educational and Psychological Measurement* 37, 527–534. Instrument reproduced with permission of Clayton T. Shorkey.

AVAILABILITY: Educational Testing Service, Princeton, NJ 08540.

RBI

For each of the following questions, please follow the scale and
indicate the numbered response that most clearly reflects your opinion.
Work quickly and answer each question.

                    1 = Strongly disagree
                    2 = Disagree
                    3 = Neutral
                    4 = Agree
                    5 = Strongly agree

____ 1. Helping others is the very basis of life.
____ 2. It is necessary to be especially friendly to new colleagues and
         neighbors.
____ 3. People should observe moral laws more strictly than they do.
____ 4. I find it difficult to take criticism without feeling hurt.
____ 5. I often spend more time trying to think of ways of getting out
         of things than it would take me to do them.
____ 6. I tend to become terribly upset and miserable when things are
         not the way I would like them to be.
____ 7. It is impossible at any given time to change one's emotions.
____ 8. It is sinful to doubt the Bible.
____ 9. Sympathy is the most beautiful human emotion.
____ 10. I shrink from facing a crisis or difficulty.
____ 11. I often get excited or upset when things go wrong.
____ 12. One should rebel against doing unpleasant things, however
         necessary, if doing them is unpleasant.
____ 13. I get upset when neighbors are very harsh with their little
         children.
____ 14. It is realistic to expect that there should be no incompatibility
         in marriage.
____ 15. I frequently feel unhappy with my appearance.
____ 16. A person should be thoroughly competent, adequate, talented, and
         intelligent in all possible respects.
____ 17. What others think of you is most important.
____ 18. Other people should make things easier for us, and help with
         life's difficulties.
____ 19. I tend to look to others for the kind of behavior they approve
         as right or wrong.
____ 20. I find that my occupation and social life tend to make me
         unhappy.
____ 21. I usually try to avoid doing chores which I dislike doing.
____ 22. Some of my family and/or friends have habits that bother and
         annoy me very much.
____ 23. I tend to worry about possible accidents and disasters.
____ 24. I like to bear responsibility alone.
____ 25. I get terribly upset and miserable when things are not the way
         I like them to be.

____ 26. I worry quite a bit over possible misfortunes.
____ 27. Punishing oneself for all errors will prevent future mistakes.
____ 28. One can best help others by criticizing them and sharply pointing out the error of their ways.
____ 29. Worrying about a possible danger will help ward it off or decrease its effects.
____ 30. I worry about little things.
____ 31. Certain people are bad, wicked, or villainous and should be severely blamed and punished for their sins.
____ 32. A large number of people are guilty of bad sexual conduct.
____ 33. One should blame oneself severely for all mistakes and wrongdoings.
____ 34. It makes me very uncomfortable to be different.
____ 35. I worry over possible misfortunes.
____ 36. I prefer to be independent of others in making decisions.
____ 37. Because a certain thing once strongly affected one's life, it should indefinitely affect it.

REACTION INVENTORY INTERFERENCE (RII)

AUTHORS: David R. Evans and Shahe S. Kazarian

PURPOSE: To measure obsessional thoughts and compulsive acts.

DESCRIPTION: The RII is a 40-item scale designed to identify obsessional thoughts and compulsive acts that interfere with an individual's daily activities. Items for the RII were selected empirically by asking students in an introductory psychology class to identify bothersome obsessional ruminations and compulsive acts. Those on which there was agreement were included as items on the RII. Although factor analysis revealed nine factors, the overall score of the scale appears to have the most value for identifying obsessive-compulsive behavior. The RII is considered a state measure in that it does not assume that the obsessive-compulsive thoughts and acts are enduring dispositions.

NORMS: An initial study, used to refine the RII, was conducted with 25 male and 25 female undergraduate students in an introductory psychology class in Canada. A second study was conducted with 172 members of an introductory psychology class in Canada. No other demographic data or norms were presented.

SCORING: The items are rated on a scale of 0 to 4 and those individual scores are simply totaled to produce the "degree of obsessionality" for each respondent. Scores can range from 0 to 160.

RELIABILITY: The RII demonstrates excellent internal consistency using item-test correlations to produce an overall reliability figure of .95. Data on test-retest reliability were not reported.

VALIDITY: The RII was significantly correlated with the Leyton Obsessional Inventory, suggesting good concurrent validity. No other validity data were available.

PRIMARY REFERENCE: Evans, David R. and Kazarian, S. S. (1977). Development of a state measure of obsessive compulsive behavior, *Journal of Clinical Psychology* 33, 436–439. Instrument reproduced with permission of David R. Evans, Shahe S. Kazarian, and the American Psychological Association.

AVAILABILITY: Dr. David R. Evans, Psychology Department, University of Western Ontario, London, Ontario, Canada N6A 5C2.

RII

The items in this questionnaire describe thoughts or acts that may interfere with other things or waste your time. Please indicate how much each problem bothers you by writing the appropriate number in the space next to each item.

1 = Not at all
2 - A little
3 = A fair amount
4 = Much
5 = Very much

___ 1. Eating many times a day
___ 2. Constantly checking your watch
___ 3. Repeatedly worrying about finishing things on time
___ 4. Continually thinking about the future
___ 5. Worrying about your appearance over and over again
___ 6. Repeatedly wondering if you are capable
___ 7. Always worrying about your work piling up
___ 8. Constantly wondering whether you will fail at things
___ 9. Repeatedly worrying about your job situation
___ 10. Continually worrying about catching up with your work
___ 11. Frequently being concerned about how you interact with others
___ 12. Always wasting time wandering around
___ 13. Worrying about everyday decisions over and over again
___ 14. Continually worrying about how well you are doing
___ 15. Worrying about being evaluated all the time
___ 16. Always doubting your intelligence or ability
___ 17. Wondering if you are doing the right thing over and over again
___ 18. Continually pondering about the world at large
___ 19. Repeatedly worrying about how you are performing
___ 20. Always checking several times whether you have done something like locking a door
___ 21. Often worrying about your cleanliness or tidiness
___ 22. Always being indecisive
___ 23. Washing your hands many times each day
___ 24. Repeatedly experiencing a tune (number, word) running through your mind
___ 25. Brooding all the time
___ 26. Constantly counting unimportant things
___ 27. Repeatedly asking people for advice
___ 28. Spending time worrying about trivial details all the time
___ 29. Repeatedly being unable to get started on things
___ 30. Constantly thinking about your family
___ 31. Swearing all the time
___ 32. Continually playing with an object (pen, pencil, keys)
___ 33. Repeatedly thinking about things you don't do well
___ 34. Always thinking about the "rat race"

____ 35. Often worrying about what to do next
____ 36. Constantly worrying about what people above you think about you
____ 37. Frequently thinking about getting to sleep
____ 38. Always being concerned about improving yourself
____ 39. Repeatedly checking to see if you have done something correctly
____ 40. Constantly thinking about yourself

REASONS FOR LIVING INVENTORY (RFL)

AUTHOR: Marsha M. Linehan

PURPOSE: To measure adaptive characteristics in suicide.

DESCRIPTION: This 48-item inventory assesses a range of beliefs that differentiate suicidal from nonsuicidal individuals and can be viewed as a measure of an individual's commitment to various reasons for *not* committing suicide. The RFL is one of the few instruments that approach the topic from the perspective of adaptive coping skills that are absent in the suicidal person. It is based on a cognitive-behavioral theory which assumes that cognitive patterns mediate suicidal behavior. While slightly longer than other instruments in this book, the RFL has six short subscales that are potentially very useful in working with suicidal clients: suicidal and coping belief (SCB), responsibility to family (RF), child-related concerns (CRC), fear of suicide (FS), fear of social disapproval (FSD), and moral objections (MO). Total scores may be used, although more value in guiding intervention is found by using the subscales.

NORMS: The scale was developed on a sample of 193 adults and a sample of 244 psychiatric inpatients. The non-clinical sample had an average age of 36 years. Average scores on the SCB, RF, CRC, FS, FSD and MO were 4.55, 3.86, 3.66, 2.38, 2.34, 3.02, respectively. The clinical sample was categorized into three subsamples according to past suicidal behaviors: nonsuicidal (n = 78), suicidal ideations (n = 89), and parasuicidal (n = 77). The average scores on the SCB, RF, CC, FS, FSD, and MO were as follows for each of the three subsamples: Nonsuicidal subjects: 4.82, 4.49, 3.89, 3.07, 3.13, 3.54; Suicidal ideation: 4.82, 4.49, 3.89, 3.07, 3.13 and 3.54; Parasuicidal: 3.56, 3.55, 2.69, 2.94, 2.82 and 2.73. Mean scores on the total RFL scale were 4.25, 3.28 and 3.28 for the nonsuicidal, suicidal ideation and parasuicidal subsamples. Scores are not significantly different for men and women.

SCORING: Each subscale score is calculated by averaging the individual item ratings within that subscale; for example on the SCB the item total is divided by 24. The total score is obtained by summing each item score and dividing by 44. By using average scores for each subscale comparison across subscales is possible. Subscale items are: SCB: 2, 3, 4, 8, 10, 12, 13, 14, 17, 19, 20, 22, 24, 25, 29, 32, 35, 36, 37, 39, 40, 42, 44, 45; RF: 1, 7, 9, 16, 30, 47, 48; CC: 11, 21, 28; FS: 6, 15, 18, 26, 33, 38, 46; FSD: 31, 41, 43; MO: 5, 24, 27, 34. Higher scores indicate more reasons for living.

RELIABILITY: Reliability was based on a variety of samples, and estimated using Cronbach's alpha. Correlations ranged from .72 to .89, indicating fairly high internal consistency. No data on stability were reported.

277

VALIDITY: Probably the biggest limitation of this inventory is a lack of predictive validity. The subscale with the strongest concurrent validity is the SCB which correlated with suicidal ideation and likelihood of suicide in the normal sample. In the clinical sample the SCB correlated with suicidal ideation, likelihood of suicide, suicidal threats, and suicidal solutions. The RF also correlated with these suicidal behaviors in the clinical sample, but showed less evidence of validity with the nonclinical sample. The CC was correlated with three of the four criteria for the clinical sample. Evidence of known-groups validity also supports the instrument (see Linehan, 1985).

PRIMARY REFERENCE: Linehan, M. M., Goldstein, J. L., Nielsen, S. L., and Chiles, J. A. (1983). Reasons for staying alive when you are thinking of killing yourself: The Reasons for Living Inventory, *Journal of Consulting and Clinical Psychology* 51, 276–286. Instrument reproduced with permission of Marsha M. Linehan, and the American Psychological Association.

AVAILABILITY: Dr. Marsha M. Linehan, Department of Psychology NI-25, University of Washington, Seattle, WA 98195.

RFL

Many people have thought of suicide at least once. Others have never considered it. Whether you have considered it or not, we are interested in the reasons you would have for *not* committing suicide *if* the thought were to occur to you or *if* someone were to suggest it to you.

On the following pages are reasons people sometimes give for *not* committing suicide. We would like to know how important each of these possible reasons would be to you at this time in your life as a reason to *not* kill yourself. Please rate this in the space at the left on each question.

Each reason can be rated from 1 (not at all important) to 6 (extremely important). If a reason does not apply to you or if you do not believe the statement is true, then it is not likely important and you should put a 1. Please use the whole range of choices so as not to rate only at the middle (2, 3, 4, 5) or only at the extremes (1, 6).

Even if you never have considered suicide or firmly believe you never would seriously consider killing yourself, it is still important that you rate each reason. In this case, rate on the basis of why killing yourself is not or would never be an alternative for you.

In each space put a number to indicate the importance to you of each for *not* killing yourself.

> 1 = Not at all *important*
> 2 = Quite *unimportant*
> 3 = Somewhat *unimportant*
> 4 = Somewhat *important*
> 5 = Quite *important*
> 6 = Extremely *important*

____ 1. I have a responsibility and commitment to my family.
____ 2. I believe I can learn to adjust or cope with my problems.
____ 3. I believe I have control over my life and destiny.
____ 4. I have a desire to live.
____ 5. I believe only God has the right to end a life.
____ 6. I am afraid of death.
____ 7. My family might believe I did not love them.
____ 8. I do not believe that things get miserable or hopeless enough that I would rather be dead.
____ 9. My family depends upon me and needs me.
____ 10. I do not want to die.
____ 11. I want to watch my children as they grow.
____ 12. Life is all we have and is better than nothing.
____ 13. I have future plans I am looking forward to carrying out.
____ 14. No matter how badly I feel, I know that it will not last.
____ 15. I am afraid of the unknown.
____ 16. I love and enjoy my family too much and could not leave them.
____ 17. I want to experience all that life has to offer and there are many experiences I haven't had yet which I want to have.

_____ 18. I am afraid that my method of killing myself would fail.

_____ 19. I care enough about myself to live.

_____ 20. Life is too beautiful and precious to end it.

_____ 21. It would not be fair to leave the children for others to take care of.

_____ 22. I believe I can find other solutions to my problems.

_____ 23. I am afraid of going to hell.

_____ 24. I have a love of life.

_____ 25. I am too stable to kill myself.

_____ 26. I am a coward and do not have the guts to do it.

_____ 27. My religious belifs forbid it.

_____ 28. The effect on my children could be harmful.

_____ 29. I am curious about what will happen in the future.

_____ 30. It would hurt my family too much and I would not want them to suffer.

_____ 31. I am concerned about what otherw would think of me.

_____ 32. I believe everything has a way of working out for the best.

_____ 33. I could not decide where, when, and how to do it.

_____ 34. I consider it morally wrong.

_____ 35. I still have many things left to do.

_____ 36. I have the courage to face life.

_____ 38. I am afraid of the actual "act" of killing myself (the pain, blood, violence).

_____ 39. I believe killing myself would not really accomplish or solve anything.

_____ 40. I have hope that things will improve and the future will be happier.

_____ 41. Other people would think I am weak and selfish.

_____ 42. I have an inner drive to survive.

_____ 43. I would not want people to think I did not have control over my life.

_____ 44. I believe I can find a purpose in life, a reason to live.

_____ 45. I see no reason to hrry death along.

_____ 46. I am so inept that my method would not work.

_____ 47. I would not want my family to feel guilty afterwards.

_____ 48. I would not want my family to think I was selfish or a coward.

REID-GUNDLACH SOCIAL SERVICE SATISFACTION SCALE (R-GSSSS)

AUTHORS: P. Nelson Reid and James P. Gundlach

PURPOSE: To assess the extent of consumer satisfaction with social services.

DESCRIPTION: The R-GSSSS is a 34-item scale that provides an overall satisfaction-with-service score plus three subscales dealing with consumers' reactions to social services regarding the following: (1) relevance (the extent to which a service corresponds to the client's perception of his or her problem and needs); (2) impact (the extent to which services reduce the problem); and (3) gratification (the extent to which services enhance the client's self-esteem and contribute to a sense of power and integrity). The relevance subscale consists of items 1 through 11; the impact subscale is composed of items 12 through 21, and the gratification subscale consists of item 22 through 34. The R-GSSSS is designed for use with a wide range of social services. When necessary, the term "social worker" on individual items can be replaced by the appropriate professional designation.

NORMS: The initial study was conducted with 166 heads of households of low-income families who had a high rate of use of social services. The respondents were 81% female, 47% married, and 52.5% were between the ages of 19 and 29. The sample contained fairly equal numbers of white and black respondents; 2.4% were Mexican-American. The scale is relatively new, and no work has yet been reported on actual norms.

SCORING: The instrument is scored by adding the individual item scores and dividing by the number of items in the scale. Thus, the sum of all scores is divided by 34 for the total score, the relevance subscale is divided by 11, the impact subscale is divided by 10, and the gratification subscale is divided by 13. This results in all scales having a range of scores of 1 (minimum satisfaction) to 5 (maximum satisfaction). Items 3, 6, 9, 10, 13, 16, 17, 18, 20, 22, 23, 26, 27, 28, 29, 30, 31 and 33 are reverse-scored.

RELIABILITY: Internal consistency of the scale was very good with a total alpha of .95; the three subscales had alphas ranging from .82 to .86. The authors' analyses reveal the three subscales to be sufficiently independent to justify using all three as measures of different aspects of consumer satisfaction.

VALIDITY: The scales have high face validity. Other forms of validity information are not reported. However, race, marital status, and type of service utilized were significantly related to satisfaction in predictable ways. Blacks and Mexican-Americans, single consumers, and those utilizing AFDS and Medicaid reported lower satisfaction levels.

PRIMARY REFERENCE: P. N. Reid and J. H. Gundlach (1983). A scale for the measurement of consumer satisfaction with social services, *Journal of Social Service Research* 7, 37–54. Instrument reproduced with permission of P. N. Reid and Haworth Press.

AVAILABILITY: Dr. Nelson Reid, North Carolina State University, Department of Social Work, Box 8107, Raleigh, NC 27965-8107.

R-GSSSS

Using the scale from one to five described below, please indicate on the line at the left of each item the number that comes closest to how you feel.

1 = Strongly agree
2 = Agree
3 = Undecided
4 = Disagree
5 = Strongly disagree

_____ 1. The social worker took my problems very seriously.
_____ 2. If I had been the social worker I would have dealt with my problems in just the same way.
_____ 3. The worker I had could never understand anyone like me.
_____ 4. Overall the agency has been very helpful to me.
_____ 5. If a friend of mine had similar problems I would tell them to go to the agency.
_____ 6. The social worker asks a lot of embarrassing questions.
_____ 7. I can always count on the worker to help if I'm in trouble.
_____ 8. The social agency will help me as much as they can.
_____ 9. I don't think the agency has the power to really help me.
_____ 10. The social worker tries hard but usually isn't too helpful.
_____ 11. The problem the agency tried to help me with is one of the most important in my life.
_____ 12. Things have gotten better since I've been going to the agency.
_____ 13. Since I've been using the agency my life is more messed up than ever.
_____ 14. The agency is always available when I need it.
_____ 15. I got from the agency exactly what I wanted.
_____ 16. The social worker loves to talk but won't really do anything for me.
_____ 17. Sometimes I just tell the social worker what I think she wants to hear.
_____ 18. The social worker is usually in a hurry when I see her.
_____ 19. No one should have any trouble getting some help from this agency.

___ 20. The worker sometimes says things I don't understand.
___ 21. The social workers are always explaining things carefully.
___ 22. I never looked forward to my visits to the social agency.
___ 23. I hope I'll never have to go back to tne agency for help.
___ 24. Everytime I talk to my worker I feel relieved.
___ 25. I can tell the social worker the truth without worrying.
___ 26. I usually feel nervous when I talk to my worker.
___ 27. The social worker is always looking for lies in what I tell her.
___ 28. It takes a lot of courage to go to the agency.
___ 29. When I enter the agency I feel very small and insignificant.
___ 30. The agency is very demanding.
___ 31. The social worker will sometimes lie to me.
___ 32. Generally the social worker is an honest person.
___ 33. I have the feeling that the worker talks to other people about me.
___ 34. I always feel well treated when I leave the social agency.

RESTRAINT SCALE (RS)

AUTHOR: C. Peter Herman

PURPOSE: To measure efforts to control eating.

DESCRIPTION: This 10-item instrument measures one aspect of dieting behavior, the ability to restrain from eating in order to maintain a particular weight. The scale ranges from the extreme of someone who has never given a moment's thought about dieting to someone who is overly concerned with dieting. The instrument may be useful with both obese clients attempting to reduce weight and with anorectic and bulimic clients.

NORMS: The instrument was developed on a sample of 57 female college students. Normative data are not presented.

SCORING: The RS score is the sum of all 10 items. For items 1 through 4 and item 10 the alternatives are scored as follows: a = 0, b = 1, c = 2, d = 3, e = 4. Items 5 through 9 are scored as follows: a = 0, b = 1, c = 2, and d = 3. Scores range from zero to 35 with higher scores indicating more concern over dieting.

RELIABILITY: Reliability data are not available from primary reference.

VALIDITY: This instrument was tested for criterion validity by creating two groups, one of restrained eaters and one of nonrestrained eaters. Different eating patterns were then observed for the two groups. The findings tend to be consistent for men and women, with slightly higher scores found for women. Similar differences in eating patterns were found with subjects who were categorized as obese, normal, and skinny according to their scores on the RS. These findings are evidence of known-groups validity. Concurrent validity is evidenced by an association of weight gain with the RS.

PRIMARY REFERENCE: Herman, C. P. (1978). Restrained eating. *Psychiatric Clinics of North America* 1, 593–607. Instrument reproduced with permission of C. P. Herman.

AVAILABILITY: Journal article.

RS

Please answer the following items using the alternatives to the right of the question.

1. How often are you dieting?
   Never   Rarely   Sometimes   Often   Always

2. What is the maximum amount of weight (in pounds) that you have ever lost in one month?
   0-4   5-9   10-14   15-19   20+

3. What is your maximum weight gain within a week?
   0-1   1.1-2   2.1-3   3.1-5   5.1+

4. In a typical week, how much does your weight fluctuate?
   0-1   1.1-2   2.1-3   3.1-5   5.1+

5. Would a weight fluctuation of 5 pounds affect the way you live your life?
   Not at all   Slightly   Moderately   Very Much

6. Do you eat sensibly in front of others and splurge alone?
   Never   Rarely   Often   Always

7. Do you give too much time and thought to food?
   Never   Rarely   Often   Always

8. Do you have feelings of guilt after overeating?
   Never   Rarely   Often   Always

9. How conscious are you of what you are eating?
   Not at all   Slightly   Moderately   Extremely

10. How many pounds over your desired weight were you at your maximum weight?
    0-1   1-5   6-10   11-20   21+

REVISED MARTIN-LARSEN APPROVAL MOTIVATION (MLAM)

AUTHOR: Harry J. Martin

PURPOSE: To measure the need for approval from others.

DESCRIPTION: This 20-item instrument assesses the need for favorable evaluations from others. It is considered revised because the present form controls for an acquiescence response bias, which was a problem with earlier forms of the instrument. It is similar to the Marlowe-Crowne Social Desirability Scale, although the MLAM more directly taps the construct in terms of the desire to receive positive evaluations and social reinforcement (approval), as well as the need to avoid negative evaluations and social punishment (criticism and rejection). The instrument focuses on social situations and interpersonal behaviors. The MLAM also is available in a shorter 10-item form. Scores do not seem to be influenced by gender.

NORMS: Mean and standard deviation scores are available from a sample of college students (n = 123). The average score was 53.6 with a standard deviation of 9.02. The mean and standard deviation for the shorter 10-item version was 26.3 and 5.37, respectively.

SCORING: Items are rated on a 5-point scale from "disagree strongly" to "agree strongly." Items 2, 12, 13, 16, and 19 are reverse-scored. Total scores are the sum of the items and range from 20 to 100; higher scores indicate stronger need for social approval. A shorter version uses only the reverse-scored items, plus items 4, 5, 6, 10, and 18.

RELIABILITY: The reliability of the MLAM was estimated in terms of internal consistency and test-retest reliability. For the long and short forms, alpha was .75 and .67 respectively. Test-retest correlations for a one-week period were .72 and .94 for the two forms.

VALIDITY: Scores on the long version correlated with faking on the MMPI, and clinical defensiveness. The short form correlated with clinical defensiveness but was not associated with faking on the MMPI. Both long and short forms correlated with neuroticism and the Marlowe Crowne Social Desirability Scale.

PRIMARY REFERENCE: Martin, H. J. (1984). A revised measure of approval motivation and its relationship to social desirability, *Journal of Personality Assessment* 48, 508–519. Instrument reproduced with permission of the *Journal of Personality Assessment*.

AVAILABILITY: Journal article.

MLAM

Below are twenty statements. Please rate how much you agree with each using the following scale. Please record your answer in the space to the left of the statement.

> 1 = Disagree strongly
> 2 = Disagree
> 3 = No opinion
> 4 = Agree
> 5 = Agree strongly

____ 1. Depending upon the people involved, I react to the same situation in different ways.

____ 2. I would rather be myself than be well thought of.

____ 3. Many times I feel like just flipping a coin in order to decide what I should do.

____ 4. I change my opinion (or the way that I do things) in order to please someone else.

____ 5. In order to get along and be liked, I tend to be what people expect me to be.

____ 6. I find it difficult to talk about my ideas if they are contrary to group opinion.

____ 7. One should avoid doing things in public which appear to be wrong to others, even though one knows that he/she is right.

____ 8. Sometimes I feel that I don't have enough control over the direction that my life is taking.

____ 9. It is better to be humble than assertive when dealing with people.

____ 10. I am willing to argue only if I know that my friends will back me up.

____ 11. If I hear that someone expresses a poor opinion of me, I do my best the next time that I see this person to make a good impression.

____ 12. I seldom feel the need to make excuses or apologize for my behavior.

____ 13. It is not important to me that I behave "properly" in social situations.

____ 14. The best way to handle people is to agree with them and tell them what they want to hear.

____ 15. It is hard for me to go on with my work if I am not encouraged to do so.

____ 16. If there is any criticism or anyone says anything about me, I can take it.

____ 17. It is wise to flatter important people.

____ 18. I am careful at parties and social gatherings for fear that I will do or say things that others won't like.

____ 19. I usually do not change my position when people disagree with me.

____ 20. How many friends you have depends on how nice a person you are.

REVISED UCLA LONELINESS SCALE (RULS)

AUTHORS: Dan Russell, Letitia Peplau, and Carolyn Cutrona

PURPOSE: To measure loneliness.

DESCRIPTION: The RULS is a 20-item scale designed to measure loneliness in a variety of populations. This and earlier versions have been used in a number of studies that show loneliness is a common and distressing problem for many people. Loneliness has been linked with any number of other problems including personality characteristics (shyness, feelings of alienation), alcohol abuse, adolescent delinquent behavior, suicide, and physical illness. This version of the scale was undertaken to eliminate response bias, social desirability response set, and lack of clarity regarding distinctiveness from related constructs. The RULS has a number of potential uses for practice in identifying lonely individuals whose loneliness is a problem in and of itself or as related to other problems.

NORMS: A number of studies have been carried out with earlier versions of the RULS. With this version, 399 undergraduate students (171 males, 228 females) from three campuses provided the basis for the research. The mean for male students was 37.06 and for females, 128. The mean for students who were not dating was 43.1 which was significantly different from students who were dating casually (34.0) and romantically involved (32.7).

SCORING: After reverse-scoring items 1, 4–6, 9, 10, 15, 16, 19, 20, the scores on all 20 items are summed, producing a possible range of 20 to 80 with higher scores indicating greater loneliness.

RELIABILITY: The RULS has excellent internal consistency with an alpha of .94. No test-retest data are reported.

VALIDITY: The RULS has good concurrent validity correlating with a number of mood and personality measures (e.g., the Beck Depression Inventory, the Texas Social Behavior Inventory), and particularly with a self-labeling loneliness index. In addition, people who were more lonely on the RULS reported more limited social activities and relationships and more emotions theoretically linked to loneliness. Finally, results showed the RULS to be unaffected by social desirability response set as measured by the Marlowe-Crowne Social Desirability Inventory.

PRIMARY REFERENCE: Russell, D., Peplau, L. A., and Cutrona, C. E. (1980). The Revised UCLA Loneliness Scale: Concurrent and discriminant validity evidence, *Journal of Personality and Social Psychology* 39, 472–480. Instrument reproduced with permission of Letitia A. Peplau.

AVAILABILITY: Professor Letitia A. Peplau, Department of Psychology, UCLA, Los Angeles, CA 90024.

RULS

Indicate how often you have felt the way described in each statement using the following scale:

4 = "I have felt this way *often*."
3 = "I have felt this way *sometimes*."
2 = "I have felt this way *rarely*."
1 = I have *never* felt this way."

____ 1. I feel in tune with the people around me.
____ 2. I lack companionship.
____ 3. There is no one I can turn to.
____ 4. I do not feel alone.
____ 5. I feel part of a group of friends.
____ 6. I have a lot in common with the people around me.
____ 7. I am no longer close to anyone.
____ 8. My interests and ideas are not shared by those around me.
____ 9. I am an outgoing person.
____ 10. There are people I feel close to.
____ 11. I feel left out.
____ 12. My social relationships are superficial.
____ 13. No one really knows me well.
____ 14. I feel isolated from others.
____ 15. I can find companionship when I want it.
____ 16. There are people who really understand me.
____ 17. I am unhappy being so withdrawn.
____ 18. People are around me but not with me.
____ 19. There are people I can talk to.
____ 20. There are people I can turn to.

SATISFACTION WITH LIFE SCALE (SWLS)

AUTHORS: Ed Diener, Robert A. Emmons, Randy J. Larsen, and Sharon Griffin

PURPOSE: To assess subjective life satisfaction.

DESCRIPTION: The 5-item SWLS, as part of a body of research on subjective well-being, refers to the cognitive-judgmental aspects of general life satisfaction. Thus, in contrast to measures that apply some external standard, the SWLS reveals the individual's own judgment of his or her quality of life. This instrument is very short and unidimensional. Because satisfaction with life is often a key component of mental well-being, the SWLS may have clinical utility with a wide range of clients, including adolescents undergoing identity crises or adults experiencing midlife crisis.

NORMS: The SWLS was developed on a sample of 176 undergraduates from the University of Illinois. The mean was 23.5 with a standard deviation of 6.43. The researchers also report a mean of 25.8 for a sample of 53 elderly citizens from a midwestern city; the mean age for this sample was 75 years and 32 of the 53 were female.

SCORING: Each item is scored from 1 to 7 in terms of "strongly disagree" to "strongly agree." Item scores are summed for a total score, which ranges from 5 to 35, with higher scores reflecting more satisfaction with life.

RELIABILITY: The 5 items on the SWLS were selected from a pool of 48 based on factor analysis. The instrument's internal consistency has been very good with an alpha of .87. The instrument appears to have excellent test-retest reliability with a correlation of .82 for a two-month period, suggesting it is very stable.

VALIDITY: The SWLS has been tested for concurrent validity using two samples of college students. Scores correlated with nine measures of subjective well-being for both samples. The scale was not correlated with a measure of affect intensity. The SWLS has also been shown to correlate with self-esteem, a checklist of clinical symptoms, neuroticism, and emotionality. Scores on the SWLS also correlated with independent ratings life satisfaction among the elderly.

PRIMARY REFERENCE: Diener, E., Emmons, R. A., Larsen, R. J., and Griffin, S. (1985). The satisfaction with life scale. *Journal of Personality Assessment* 49, 71–75. Instrument reproduced with permission of Ed Diener.

AVAILABILITY: Dr. Ed Diener, Associate Professor, Psychology Department, University of Illinois, 603 E. Daniel, Champaign, IL 61820.

SWLS

Below are five statements with which you may agree or disagree. Using the scale below, indicate your agreement with each item by placing the appropriate number on the line preceding that item. Please be open and honest in your responding.

1 = Strongly disagree
2 = Disagree
3 = Slightly disagree
4 = Neither agree nor disagree
5 = Slightly agree
6 = Agree
7 = Strongly agree

____ 1. In most ways my life is close to my ideal.
____ 2. The conditions of my life are excellent.
____ 3. I am satisfied with my life.
____ 4. So far I have gotten the important things I want in life.
____ 5. If I could live my life over, I would change almost nothing.

SELF-CONSCIOUSNESS SCALE (SCS)

AUTHOR: Michael F. Scheier

PURPOSE: To measure individual differences in private and public self-consciousness and social anxiety.

DESCRIPTION: The SCS is a 22-item scale that was revised from an earlier version (Fenigstein, Scheier, and Buss, 1975) to make it appropriate for non-college student populations. The SCS is focused on the assessment of an individual's self-consciousness in both public and private situations. Public self-consciousness refers to the tendency to think about those aspects of oneself that are matters of public display; private self-consciousness refers to the tendency to think about more covert or hidden aspects of the self. The scale also includes a measure of social anxiety, an apprehensiveness about being evaluated by others. Extensive research on the original instrument shows that public and private self-consciousness mediate a wide range of behaviors and cognitions.

NORMS: Norms for the revised SCS are based on a sample of 213 undergraduate men, 85 undergraduate women, 42 middle-aged men who had recently undergone coronary artery bypass surgery, and 396 women between the ages of 45 and 50 who were involved in a longitudinal study of menopause. For the undergraduate students, means for the men were 15.5 on private self-consciousness, 13.5 on public self-consciousness, and 8.8 on social anxiety. Means for the undergraduate women were 17.3 for private, 14.2 for public and 8.6 for social anxiety. The means were significantly different for men and women on private self-consciousness. For middle-aged men the mean for private self-consciousness was 13.5; for middle-aged women, the mean was 10.8 for public self-consciousness and 7.3 for social anxiety.

SCORING: The SCS is scored by summing scores for each item, which range from 0 to 3. This produces a total possible range of 0 to 66.

RELIABILITY: The SCS has fairly good internal consistency with an alpha of .75 for private self-consciousness, .84 for public self-consciousness, and .79 for social anxiety. The scale also demonstrates good stability with test-retest correlations of .76 for private, .74 for public, and .77 for social anxiety.

VALIDITY: Since the original scale had demonstrated good validity, the main source of validity information to date is a form of concurrent validity, correlations of the revised scale with the original. All three subscales correlate in the low to mid .80s with the original scale.

PRIMARY REFERENCE: Michael F. Scheier and Charles S. Carver (in press). The Self-Consciousness Scale: A revised version for use with general populations, *Journal of Applied Social Psychology.* Instrument reproduced by permission of Dr. Michael F. Scheier.

AVAILABILITY: Dr. Michael F. Scheier, Department of Psychology, Carnegie-Mellon University, Pittsburgh, PA 15213.

SCS

Please put a number next to each item indicating the extent to which that item is like you.

```
0 = Not at all like me
1 = A little like me
2 = Somewhat like me
3 = A lot like me
```

____ 1. I'm always trying to figure myself out.
____ 2. I'm concerned about my style of doing things.
____ 3. It takes me time to get over my shyness in new situations.
____ 4. I think about myself a lot.
____ 5. I care a lot about how I present myself to others.
____ 6. I often daydream about myself.
____ 7. It's hard for me to work when someone is watching me.
____ 8. I never take a hard look at myself.
____ 9. I get embarrassed very easily.
____ 10. I'm self-conscious about the way I look.
____ 11. It's easy for me to talk to strangers.
____ 12. I generally pay attention to my inner feelings.
____ 13. I usually worry about making a good impression.
____ 14. I'm constantly thinking about my reasons for doing things.
____ 15. I feel nervous when I speak in front of a group.
____ 16. Before I leave my house, I check how I look.
____ 17. I sometimes step back (in my mind) in order to examine myself from a distance.
____ 18. I'm concerned about what other people think of me.
____ 19. I'm quick to notice changes in my mood.
____ 20. I'm usually aware of my appearance.
____ 21. I know the way my mind works when I work through a problem.
____ 22. Large groups make me nervous.

SELF-EFFICACY SCALE (SES)

AUTHORS: Mark Sherer, James E. Maddux, Blaise Mercadante, Steven Prentice-Dunn, Beth Jacobs, and Ronald W. Rogers.

PURPOSE: To measure general levels of belief in one's own competence.

DESCRIPTION: The SES is a 23-item scale that measures general expectations of self-efficacy that are not tied to specific situations or behavior. The assumptions underlying this scale are that personal expectations of mastery are a major determinant of behavioral change, and that individual differences in past experiences and attributions of success lead to different levels of generalized self-efficacy expectations. Thus, this scale may be useful in tailoring the course of clinical intervention to the client's needs, and also as an index of progress since expectations of self-efficacy should change during the course of intervention. The SES consists of two subscales, general self-efficacy and social self-efficacy.

NORMS: The initial studies of the SES involved 376 undergraduate students in introductory psychology classes and 150 inpatients from a Veterans Administration alcohol treatment unit. No other demographic data were provided nor were actual norms for these groups.

SCORING: Seven items (1, 5, 9, 13, 17, 21, 25) are filler items and are not scored. After items presented in a negative fashion (3, 6, 7, 8, 11, 14, 18, 20, 22, 24, 26, 29, 30) are reverse-scored, the scores for all items are summed. Before reverse-scoring, the answers are keyed as follows: A = 1, B = 2, C = 3, D = 4, E = 5. The higher the score, the higher the self-efficacy expectations.

RELIABILITY: The SES has fairly good internal consistency with alphas of .86 for the general subscale and .71 for the social subscale. No test-retest data were reported.

VALIDITY: The SES was shown to have good criterion-related validity by accurately predicting that people with higher self-efficacy would have greater success than those who score low in self-efficacy in past vocational, educational, and monetary goals. The SES also has demonstrated construct validity by correlating significantly in predicted directions with a number of measures such as the Ego Strength Scale, the Interpersonal Competency Scale, and the Rosenberg self-esteem scale.

PRIMARY REFERENCE: Sherer, M., Maddox, J. E., Mercandante, B., Prentice-Dunn, S., Jacobs, B., and Rogers, R. W. (1982). The Self-Efficacy Scale: Construction and validation, *Psychological Reports* 51, 663–671. Instrument reproduced with permission of Mark Sherer and Ronald W. Rogers and *Psychological Reports*.

AVAILABILITY: Dr. Mark Sherer, 1874 Pleasant Avenue, Mobile, AL 36617.

SES

This questionnaire is a series of statements about your personal attitudes and traits. Each statement represents a commonly held belief. Read each statement and decide to what extent it describes you. There are no right or wrong answers. You will probably agree with some of the statements and disagree with others. Please indicate your own personal feelings about each statement below by marking the letter that best describes your attitude or feeling. Please be very truthful and describe yourself as you really are, not as you would like to be.

A = Disagree strongly
B = Disagree moderately
C = Neither agree nor disagree
D = Agree moderately
E = Agree strongly

1. I like to grow house plants.
2. When I make plans, I am certain I can make them work.
3. One of my problems is that I cannot get down to work when I should.
4. If I can't do a job the first time, I keep trying until I can.
5. Heredity plays the major role in determining one's personality.
6. It is difficult for me to make new friends.
7. When I set important goals for myself, I rarely achieve them.
8. I give up on things before completing them.
9. I like to cook.
10. If I see someone I would like to meet, I go to that person instead of waiting for him or her to come to me.
11. I avoid facing difficulties.
12. If something looks too complicated, I will not even bother to try it.
13. There is some good in everybody.
14. If I meet someone interesting who is very hard to make friends with, I'll soon stop trying to make friends with that person.
15. When I have something unpleasant to do, I stick to it until I finish it.
16. When I decide to do something, I go right to work on it.
17. I like science.
18. When trying to learn something new, I soon give up if I am not initially successful.
19. When I'm trying to become friends with someone who seems uninterested at first, I don't give up very easily.
20. When unexpected problems occur, I don't handle them well.
21. If I were an artist, I would like to draw children.
22. I avoid trying to learn new things when they look too difficult for me.
23. Failure just makes me try harder.

___ 24. I do not handle myself well in social gatherings.
___ 25. I very much like to ride horses.
___ 26. I feel insecure about my ability to do things.
___ 27. I am a self-reliant person.
___ 28. I have acquired my friends through my personal abilities at making friends.
___ 29. I give up easily.
___ 30. I do not seem capable of dealing with most problems that come up in my life.

SELFISM (NS)

AUTHORS: E. Jerry Phares and Nancy Erskine

PURPOSE: To measure narcissism.

DESCRIPTION: The NS is a 28-item scale designed to measure narcissims, referred to by developers of this instrument as selfism. Selfism is viewed as an orientation, belief, or set affecting how one construes a whole range of situations that deal with the satisfaction of needs. A person who scores high on the NS views a large number of situations in a selfish or egocentric fashion. At the opposite end of the continuum are individuals who submerge their own satisfaction in favor of others. The NS samples beliefs across a broad range of situations and is not targeted toward a specific need area. Based on a review of the literature, impressionistic sources, and the work of cultural observers, the original 100 items were narrowed down to 28 based on low correlations with the Marlowe-Crowne Social Desirability Scale, high correlations with NS total scores, and a reasonable spread over the five response categories.

NORMS: A series of studies was conducted in development of the NS. The respondents included some 548 undergraduate males and 675 undergraduate females, 71 city police, and 11 campus police. No other demographic data are available. Means for 175 college females were 76.50, for 150 college males 77.91, for 71 city police 75.33, and for 11 campus police 74.73. None of these differences was statistically significant.

SCORING: The NS is scored by summing the individual item scores, each of which is on a 5-point Likert scale, to produce a range of 28 to 140. The following are filler items, included to disguise the purpose of the scale, and are not scored: 1, 6, 8, 12, 15, 19, 23, 26, 30, 34, 38, 39.

RELIABILITY: The NS has very good internal consistency, with split-half reliabilities of .84 for males and .83 for females. The NS also has excellent stability with a four-week test-retest correlation of .91.

VALIDITY: The NS has fair concurrent validity, correlating significantly with the Narcissistic Personality Inventory and the Religious Attitude Scale. Also, the NS demonstrated a form of known-groups validity by correlating positively with observers' judgments of their close friends' narcissistic characteristics. The NS also distinguished between respondents who were high and low on cynicism regarding the motives of individuals in need of help.

PRIMARY REFERENCE: Phares, E. J. and Erskine, N. (1984). The measurement of selfism, *Educational and Psychological Measurement* 44, 597–608. Instrument reproduced with permission of E. Jerry Phares.

AVAILABILITY: Dr. E. J. Phares, Department of Psychology, Kansas State University, Manhattan, KS 66506.

NS

Listed below are 40 statements that deal with personal attitudes and feelings about a variety of things. Obviously, there are *no* right or wrong answers--only opinions. Read each item and then decide how *you personally* feel. Mark your answers according to the following scheme:

$$5 = \text{Strongly agree}$$
$$4 = \text{Mildly agree}$$
$$3 = \text{Agree and disagree equally}$$
$$2 = \text{Mildly disagree}$$
$$1 = \text{Strongly disagree}$$

____ 1. The widespread interest in professional sports is just another example of escapism.

____ 2. In times of shortages it is sometimes necessary for one to engage in a little hoarding.

____ 3. Thinking of yourself first is no sin in this world today.

____ 4. The prospect of becoming very close to another person worries me a good bit.

____ 5. The really significant contributions in the world have very frequently been made by people who were preoccupied with themselves.

____ 6. Every older American deserves a guaranteed income to live in dignity.

____ 7. It is more important to live for yourself rather than for other people, parents, or for posterity.

____ 8. Organized religious groups are too concerned with raising funds these days.

____ 9. I regard myself as someone who looks after his/her personal interests.

____ 10. The trouble with getting too close to people is that they start making emotional demands on you.

____ 11. Having children keeps you from engaging in a lot of self-fulfilling activities.

____ 12. Many of our production problems in this country are due to the fact that workers no longer take pride in their jobs.

____ 13. It's best to live for the present and not to worry about tomorrow.

____ 14. Call it selfishness if you will, but in this world today we all have to look out for ourselves first.

____ 15. Education is too job oriented these days; there is not enough emphasis on basic education.

____ 16. It seems impossible to imagine the world without me in it.

____ 17. You can hardly overestimate the importance of selling yourself in getting ahead.

____ 18. The difficulty with marriage is that it locks you into a relationship.

____ 19. Movies emphasize sex and violence too much.

____ 20. If it feels right, it is right.

____ 21. Breaks in life are nonsense. The real story is pursuing your self-interests aggressively.

____ 22. An individual's worth will often pass unrecognized unless that person thinks of himself or herself first.

____ 23. Consumers need a stronger voice in governmental affairs.

____ 24. Getting ahead in life depends mainly on thinking of yourself first.

____ 25. In general, couples should seek a divorce when they find the marriage is not a fulfilling one.

____ 26. Too often, voting means choosing between the lesser of two evils.

____ 27. In striving to reach one's true potential, it is sometimes necessary to worry less about other people.

____ 28. When choosing clothes I generally consider style before matters such as comfort or durability.

____ 29. I believe people have the right to live any damn way they please.

____ 30. Too many people have given up reading to passively watch TV.

____ 31. Owing money is not so bad if it's the only way one can live without depriving oneself of the good life.

____ 32. Not enough people live for the present.

____ 33. I don't see anything wrong with people spending a lot of time and effort on their personal appearance.

____ 34. Physical punishment is necessary to raise children properly.

____ 35. The Peace Corps would be a good idea if it did not delay one's getting started along the road to a personal career.

____ 36. It simply does not pay to become sad or upset about friends, loved ones, or events that don't turn out well.

____ 37. A definite advantage of birth control devices is that they permit sexual pleasure without the emotional responsibilities that might otherwise result.

____ 38. Doctors seem to have forgotten that medicine involves human relations and not just prescriptions.

____ 39. I believe that some unidentified flying objects have actually been sent from outer space to observe our culture here on earth.

____ 40. In this world one has to look out for oneself first because nobody else will look out for you.

SELF-RATING ANXIETY SCALE (SAS)

AUTHOR: William W. K. Zung

PURPOSE: To assess anxiety as a clinical disorder and quantify anxiety symptoms.

DESCRIPTION: The SAS is a 20-item scale consisting of the most commonly found characteristics of an anxiety disorder (5 affective and 15 somatic symptoms). Five of the items are worded symptomatically positive and 15 are worded symptomatically negative; respondents use a 4-point scale to rate how each item applied to him or her during the past week. The author has also developed a rating scale based on the same symptoms to be used by the clinician to rate the client (Anxiety Status Inventory or ASI), thus allowing two sources of data on the same symptoms.

NORMS: The initial study was carried out on 225 psychiatric patients including 152 male inpatients, and 23 male and 50 female outpatients with a mean age of 41 years. An additional 100 male and female "normal" (nonpatient) subjects were part of the study. However, little formal standardization work has been carried out on the SAS.

SCORING: The SAS is scored by summing the values on each item to produce a raw score ranging from 20 to 80. An SAS index is derived by dividing the raw score by 80, producing an index that ranges from .25 to 1.00 (higher scores equal more anxiety).

RELIABILITY: Data are not available.

VALIDITY: The SAS has fair concurrent validity correlating significantly with the Taylor Manifest Anixety Scale and with the clinician rating scale developed by the author (ASI). The SAS also has good known-groups validity, distinguishing between patients diagnosed as having anxiety disorders and those with other psychiatric diagnoses and between nonpatient and patient groups.

PRIMARY REFERENCE: Zung, W. K. (1971). A rating instrument for anxiety disorders, *Psychosomatics* 12, 371–379. Instrument reproduced by permission of W. K. Zung and *Psychosomatics*, all rights reserved.

AVAILABILITY: Psykey, Inc., 7750 Daggett Street, San Diego, CA 92111.

SAS

Below are twenty statements. Please rate each using the following scale:

1 = Some or a little of the time
2 = Some of the time
3 = Good part of the time
4 = Most or all of the time

Please record your rating in the space to the left of each item.

___ 1. I feel more nervous and anxious than usual.
___ 2. I feel afraid for no reason at all.
___ 3. I get upset easily or feel panicky.
___ 4. I feel like I'm falling apart and going to pieces.
___ 5. I feel that everything is all right and nothing bad will happen.
___ 6. My arms and legs shake and tremble.
___ 7. I am bothered by headaches, neck and back pains.
___ 8. I feel weak and get tired easily.
___ 9. I feel calm and can sit still easily.
___ 10. I can feel my heart beating fast.
___ 11. I am bothered by dizzy spells.
___ 12. I have fainting spells or feel like it.
___ 13. I can breathe in and out easily.
___ 14. I get feelings of numbness and tingling in my fingers, toes.
___ 15. I am bothered by stomach aches or indigestion.
___ 16. I have to empty my bladder often.
___ 17. My hands are usually dry and warm.
___ 18. My face gets hot and blushes.
___ 19. I fall asleep easily and get a good night's rest.
___ 20. I have nightmares.

SELF-RATING DEPRESSION SCALE (SDS)

AUTHOR: William W. K. Zung

PURPOSE: To assess depression as a clinical disorder and quantify the symptoms of depression.

DESCRIPTION: The SDS is a 20-item scale developed to examine three basic aspects of depression: (1) pervasive affect, (2) physiological concomitants, and (3) psychological concomitants. The SDS consists of 10 items worded symptomatically positive and 10 items symptomatically negative. Items on the SDS were specifically selected to tap one of the three aspects of depression described above and include cognitive, affective, psychomotor, somatic, and social-interpersonal items. Respondents are asked to rate each of the 20 items on a sliding scale as to how it applies to them at the time of testing. Individual item scores as well as overall scores are considered meaningful. The author suggests the following clinical cutting scores to estimate the degree of depression: 50 to 59 (mild to moderate); 60 to 69 (moderate to severe); 70 and over (severe). A test booklet is available (Zung, 1974).

NORMS: Initial study of the SDS was conducted on 56 patients admitted to the psychiatric service of a hospital with a primary diagnosis of depression and 100 "normal" (nonpatient) subjects. Subsequent study of 22 samples reveals some support for the clinical cutting scores (Blumenthal and Dielman, 1975). However, little formal effort at standardization has been made.

SCORING: The SDS is scored by summing the values obtained on each item to produce a raw score ranging from 20 to 80. An SDS index is produced by dividing the raw score by 80 to produce a range of .25 to 1.00 (higher scores equal greater depression).

RELIABILITY: Data are not available.

VALIDITY: The SDS has good known-groups validity in distinguishing between depressed and nondepressed samples, and has good concurrent validity in regard to correlations with other depression measures. The SDS also is reported to be sensitive to clinical changes (Rehm, 1981).

PRIMARY REFERENCE: Zung, W. K. (1965). A Self-Rating Depression Scale, *Archives of General Psychiatry* 12, 63–70. Instrument reproduced with permission of W. K. Zung, all rights reserved.

AVAILABILITY: Psykey, Inc., 7750 Daggett Street, San Diego, CA 92111.

SDS

Below are twenty statements. Please rate each using the following scale:

> 1 = Some or a little of the time
> 2 = Some of the time
> 3 = Good part of the time
> 4 = Most or all of the time

Please record your rating in the space to the left of each item.

___ 1. I feel down-hearted, blue, and sad.
___ 2. Morning is when I feel the best.
___ 3. I have crying spells or feel like it.
___ 4. I have trouble sleeping through the night.
___ 5. I eat as much as I used to.
___ 6. I enjoy looking at, talking to, and being with attractive women/men.
___ 7. I notice that I am losing weight.
___ 8. I have trouble with constipation.
___ 9. My heart beats faster than usual.
___ 10. I get tired for no reason.
___ 11. My mind is as clear as it used to be.
___ 12. I find it easy to do the things I used to.
___ 13. I am restless and can't keep still.
___ 14. I feel hopeful about the future.
___ 15. I am more irritable than usual.
___ 16. I find it easy to make decisions.
___ 17. I feel that I am useful and needed.
___ 18. My life is pretty full.
___ 19. I feel that others would be better off if I were dead.
___ 20. I still enjoy the things I used to do.

SELF-RIGHTEOUSNESS SCALE (SRS)

AUTHOR: Toni Falbo

PURPOSE: To measure self-righteousness.

DESCRIPTION: This 7-item instrument measures the conviction that one's beliefs or behavior are correct, especially in comparison to alternative beliefs or behaviors. It excludes self-righteousness about political issues and focuses not on specific beliefs, but on the general characteristic of self-righteousness. The SRS is not associated with anxiety, thereby distinguishing it from similar variables such as dogmatism which assumes the presence of anxiety. Two subscales can be formed; one measuring general self-righteousness (SR) and another measuring its opposite, acceptance. The SRS can be reworded to measure self-righteousness about a particular belief or behavior. It is useful in assessing communication style in clinical intervention with families and dyads as well as individuals.

NORMS: One hundred and twenty respondents were involved in the development of the SRS. Fifty-four were male and 66 were female, and the subjects' ages ranged from 17 to 63 years. The total SRS scores ranged from 4 to 18 with a mean of 7.45. A second sample consisted of 70 respondents (45 males and 25 females). This sample had an age range from 17 to 45 and all were involved in a demanding 10-kilometer foot race. Pretest mean scores were 9.82. The average SRS score after completing the race was 9.07.

SCORING: Each item is rated on a 5-point scale, ranging from "strongly agree" to "strongly disagree." The SR items (1, 2, 3, 4) are summed to form a total score ranging from 4 to 20. Items 3 and 4 are reverse-scored. Higher scores reflect more self-righteousness. Items 5, 6, and 7 are summed to obtain an acceptance score. Scores range from 3 to 15 with higher scores indicating more acceptance of others.

RELIABILITY: Reliability was separately determined for the two subscales and was generally only moderate. Internal consistency using coefficient alpha was .60 and .58 for the SR and acceptance subscales, although all items significantly correlated with subscale scores. Stability of the SR was moderate (.54) using test-retest correlations after a ten-kilometer race. While this magnitude of a test-retest reliability coefficient is only moderate, a higher correlation would not be expected since major accomplishments, such as completing a foot race, could impact upon one's level of self-righteousness.

VALIDITY: Items of the SRS were selected from a pool of 100, based on ratings by 15 judges. Items were also selected on the basis of a lack of association with a measure of social desirability. Concurrent validity was evidenced with correlations between the SR and measures of dogmatism, and intolerance for ambiguity and state-trait anxiety. The acceptance subscale was not found to correlate with these validity criteria. Based on the theoretical notion that self-righteousness is a defense mechanism which is utilized less when one has accomplished a goal, scores on the SRS were lower for subjects who were winners in the 10 kilometer race compared to subjects who simply completed the race or lost the race. The change from pretest to posttest for winners in the race was significant, suggesting the SRS is sensitive to measuring change.

PRIMARY REFERENCE: Falbo, T. and Belk, S. S. (1985). A short scale to measure self-righteousness, *Journal of Personality Assessment* 49, 72–77. Instrument reproduced with permission of Toni Falbo and the *Journal of Personality Assessment*.

AVAILABILITY: Journal article.

SRS

Answer each item according to the following scale and record your answer to the left of each statement.

1 = Strongly agree
2 = Agree
3 = Neutral
4 = Disagree
5 = Strongly disagree

____ 1. People who disagree with me are wrong.
____ 2. I can benefit other people by telling them the right way to live.
____ 3. I am excited by the free exchange of ideas.
____ 4. I enjoy having different points of view.
____ 5. One person's opinions are just as valid as the next.
____ 6. Most people naturally do the right thing.
____ 7. People generally make few mistakes because they do know what is right or wrong.

SESSION EVALUATION QUESTIONNAIRE (SEQ)

AUTHOR: William B. Stiles

PURPOSE: To measure the impact of clinical sessions.

DESCRIPTION: The SEQ consists of 24 bipolar adjective scales presented in a 7-point semantic differential format. It is designed to measure clients' perceptions of two dimensions of clinical sessions, depth and smoothness, and two dimensions of post-session mood, positivity and arousal. Depth refers to a session's perceived power and value and smoothness refers to a session's comfort, relaxation, and pleasantness. Positivity refers to feelings of confidence and clarity as well as happiness, while arousal refers to feeling active and excited as opposed to quiet and calm. The four dimensions were constructed on the basis of factor analyses.

NORMS: Several studies have been conducted using several different forms of the SEQ. The most recent included 72 clients and 17 counselors. The clients included 59 undergraduate students, 5 graduate students, and 8 community residents. Of these, 97% were white, 67% were female, and 33% were male. The clients' problems most typically included depression, relationship problems, low self-esteem, and insecurity. The counselors were graduate students in clinical psychology including 9 males and 8 females. Both clients and counselors used the SEQ to rate each session. No real norms are available although means for client and counselor ratings are reported.

SCORING: The four dimensions are scored separately. Scores are the sum of the item ratings, divided by the number of items that make up each dimension. Thus, depth includes four items: deep–shallow, valuable–worthless, full–empty, powerful–weak, and special–ordinary. Smoothness includes smooth–rough, comfortable–uncomfortable, easy–difficult, pleasant–unpleasant, and relaxed–tense. Positivity includes happy–sad, confident–afraid, pleased–angry, definite–uncertain, and friendly–unfriendly. Arousal includes aroused–quiet, fast–slow, moving–still, and excited–calm. Higher scores indicate greater depth, smoothness, positivity, and arousal.

RELIABILITY: The four dimensions of the SEQ have good internal consistency with alphas that range from .78 to .91. No test-retest reliabilities are reported.

VALIDITY: No real validity data are reported although data comparing the dimensions to each other and counselor and client ratings to each other are reported. In essence, the depth and smoothness dimensions are independent of each other, while positivity and arousal were moderately correlated. Both counselor and client ratings varied greatly from session to session.

PRIMARY REFERENCE: Stiles, W. B. and Snow, J. S. (1984). Counseling session impact as seen by novice counselors and their clients, *Journal of Counseling Psychology* 31, 3–12. Instrument reproduced with permission of William B. Stiles and the American Psychological Association.

AVAILABILITY: Dr. William B. Stiles, Department of Psychology, Miami University, Oxford, OH 45056.

SEQ

Please place an "X" on each line to show how you feel about this session.

This session was:

Bad	___:___:___:___:___:___:___	Good
Safe	___:___:___:___:___:___:___	Dangerous
Difficult	___:___:___:___:___:___:___	Easy
Valuable	___:___:___:___:___:___:___	Worthless
Shallow	___:___:___:___:___:___:___	Deep
Relaxed	___:___:___:___:___:___:___	Tense
Unpleasant	___:___:___:___:___:___:___	Pleasant
Full	___:___:___:___:___:___:___	Empty
Weak	___:___:___:___:___:___:___	Powerful
Special	___:___:___:___:___:___:___	Ordinary
Rough	___:___:___:___:___:___:___	Smooth
Comfortable	___:___:___:___:___:___:___	Uncomfortable

Right now I feel:

Happy	___:___:___:___:___:___:___	Sad
Angry	___:___:___:___:___:___:___	Pleased
Moving	___:___:___:___:___:___:___	Still
Uncertain	___:___:___:___:___:___:___	Definite
Calm	___:___:___:___:___:___:___	Excited
Confident	___:___:___:___:___:___:___	Afraid
Wakeful	___:___:___:___:___:___:___	Sleepy
Friendly	___:___:___:___:___:___:___	Unfriendly
Slow	___:___:___:___:___:___:___	Fast
Energetic	___:___:___:___:___:___:___	Peaceful
Involved	___:___:___:___:___:___:___	Detached
Quiet	___:___:___:___:___:___:___	Aroused

SEXUAL AROUSABILITY INVENTORY (SAI) AND SEXUAL AROUSABILITY INVENTORY—EXPANDED (SAI–E)

AUTHORS: Emily Franck Hoon and Dianne L. Chambless

PURPOSE: To measure sexual arousability (SAI) and sexual anxiety (SAI–E).

DESCRIPTION: The SAI is a 38-item instrument designed to measure perceived arousability to a variety of sexual experiences. This instrument was originally designed for use with females. The SAI–E is the same instrument, rated by the respondent on both arousability and anxiety dimensions. This instrument has been used with males and females. The arousability and anxiety dimensions are reported to provide independent information. Both instruments are reproduced here. The SAI has been found to discriminate between a "normal" population and individuals seeking help for sexual functioning and also to be sensitive to therapeutic changes. The SAI-E also can be valuable in helping determine if a client has an arousal or anxiety problem related to sexual dysfunctions. Items 1, 2, 5, 6, 9–12, 14–16, 18, 19, 26 can be used as one short-form version of the SAI, and the remaining items can be used as another short form.

NORMS: The SAI and SAI–E have undergone extensive testing with samples of several hundred heterosexual and homosexual women. The mean age of the samples ranged from 18.91 years to 28.20 years. Mean scores for arousability for samples of heterosexual women range from 78.93 to 99.14 and for lesbians, 92.34. The mean score for 250 heterosexual males for arousability was 90.60. For sexual anxiety, the mean score for 252 undergraduate females was 34.34. A second sample of 90 community women had a mean of 6.36.

SCORING: Both scales are scored by summing the scores on the individual items and subtracting any −1's.

RELIABILITY: The arousability scale has excellent internal consistency with an alpha for women in two samples of .91 and .92 and split-half reliability of .92. The arousability scale is also relatively stable with an eight-week test-retest correlation of .69. The anxiety scale for women also has good internal consistency with a split-half reliability of .94. Reliability data were not available for men.

VALIDITY: The arousability scale has good concurrent validity, correlating significantly with awareness of physiological changes during intercourse, satisfaction with sexual responsiveness, frequency of intercourse, and total episodes of intercourse before marriage. The SAI also demonstrated good known-groups validity, distinguishing between normal and sexually dysfunctional women. Sexual anxiety in the SAI-E also has been shown to demonstrate some degree of concurrent validity, with more sexually experienced women found to be significantly less anxious and with higher frequency of orgasm during intercourse also associated with lower anxiety. Validity data are not yet available for men.

PRIMARY REFERENCE: Hoon, E. F. and Chambless, D. (1986). Sexual Arousability Inventory (SAI) and Sexual Arousability Inventory—Expanded (SAI–E). In C. M. Davis and W. L. Yarber (eds.), *Sexuality-Related Measures: A Compendium*. Syracuse: Graphic Publishing Co. Instrument reproduced with permission of Emily Franck Hoon.

AVAILABILITY: Dr. Emily Franck Hoon, 508 NW 35 Terrace, Gainsville, FL 32607.

SAI

The experiences in this inventory may or may not be sexually arousing to you. There are no right or wrong answers. Read each item carefully, and then indicate at left the number which describes how sexually aroused you feel when you have the experience, or how sexually aroused you think you would feel if you actually experienced it. *Be sure to answer every item.* If you aren't certain about an item, indicate the number that seems about right. Rate feelings of arousal according to the scale below.

```
-1 = Adversely affects arousal; unthinkable, repulsive, distracting
 0 = Doesn't affect sexual arousal
 1 = Possibly causes sexual arousal.
 2 = Sometimes causes sexual arousal; slightly arousing
 3 = Usually causes sexual arousal; moderately arousing
 4 = Almost always sexually arousing; very arousing
 5 = Always causes sexual arousal; extremely arousing
```

1. When a loved one stimulates your genitals with mouth and tongue
2. When a loved one fondles your breasts with his/her hands
3. When you see a loved one nude
4. When a loved one caresses you with his/her eyes
5. When a loved one stimulates your genitals with his/her finger
6. When you are touched or kissed on the inner thighs by a loved one
7. When you caress a loved one's genitals with your fingers
8. When you read a pornographic or "dirty" story
9. When a loved one undresses you
10. When you dance with a loved one
11. When you have intercourse with a loved one
12. When a loved one touches or kisses your nipples
13. When you caress a loved one (other than genitals)
14. When you see pornographic pictures or slides
15. When you lie in bed with a loved one
16. When a loved one kisses you passionately
17. When you hear sounds of pleasure during sex
18. When a loved one kisses you with an exploring tongue
19. When you read suggestive or pornographic poetry
20. When you see a strip show
21. When you stimulate your partner's genitals with your mouth and tongue
22. When a loved one caresses you (other than genitals)
23. When you see a pornographic movie (stag film)
24. When you undress a loved one
25. When a loved one fondles your breasts with mouth and tongue
26. When you make love in a new or unusual place
27. When you masturbate.
28. When your partner has an orgasm.

Now rate each of the items according to how anxious you feel when you have the described experience. The meaning of anxiety is extreme uneasiness and distress. Rate feelings of anxiety according to the scale below:

> -1 = Relaxing, calming
> 0 = No anxiety
> 1 = Possibly causes some anxiety
> 2 = Sometimes causes anxiety; slightly anxiety producing
> 3 = Usually causes anxiety; moderately anxiety producing
> 4 = Almost always causes anxiety; very anxiety producing
> 5 = Always causes anxiety; extremely anxiety producing

____ 1. When a loved one stimulates your genitals with mouth and tongue
____ 2. When a loved one fondles your breasts with his/her hands
____ 3. When you see a loved one nude
____ 4. When a loved one caresses you with his/her eyes
____ 5. When a loved one stimulates your genitals with his/her finger
____ 6. When you are touched or kissed on the inner thighs by a loved one
____ 7. When you caress a loved one's genitals with your fingers
____ 8. When you read a pornographic or "dirty" story
____ 9. When a loved one undresses you
____ 10. When you dance with a loved one
____ 11. When you have intercourse with a loved one
____ 12. When a loved one touches or kisses your nipples
____ 13. When you caress a loved one (other than genitals)
____ 14. When you see pornographic pictures or slides
____ 15. When you lie in bed with a loved one
____ 16. When a loved one kisses you passionately
____ 17. When you hear sounds of pleasure during sex
____ 18. When a loved one kisses you with an exploring tongue
____ 19. When you read suggestive or pornographic poetry
____ 20. When you see a strip show
____ 21. When you stimulate your partner's genitals with your mouth and tongue
____ 22. When a loved one caresses you (other than genitals)
____ 23. When you see a pornographic movie (stag film)
____ 24. When you undress a loved one
____ 25. When a loved one fondles your breasts with mouth and tongue
____ 26. When you make love in a new or unusual place
____ 27. When you masturbate
____ 28. When your partner has an orgasm

SEXUAL BEHAVIOR INVENTORY—FEMALE (SBI–F)

AUTHOR: Peter M. Bentler

PURPOSE: To assess heterosexual behavior in women.

DESCRIPTION: This 21-item instrument measures the extent to which a female has engaged in heterosexual behavior. The SFI-B was developed from 63 items dealing with various types of heterosexual behavior, using the procedure of multidimensional homogeneity scaling to assess the latent ordinal dimensions associated with observed responses to test items. The SBI–F was developed to be similar to the SBI–M (also reproduced in this book), although the SBI–F has a 10-item short form (items with asterisks) which correlates .98 with the 21-item form. This instrument can be useful in cases involving heterosexual anxieties, in developing sexual anxiety hierarchies (e.g., using the technique of systematic desensitization), or as an overall measure of change as a result of therapy. Items 1, 2, 4, 7, 8–10, 13, 14, 16 can be used as a short form.

NORMS: Three samples of college females, totaling 389 and ranging in age from 17 to 29, were used to develop the SBI–F. Means for the three samples were 11.07, 8.01, and 13.27. No other demographic data or norms were reported.

SCORING: The SBI–F is scored by assigning 1 point to each "yes" answer and then summing the scores, producing a range of 0 to 21.

RELIABILITY: The SBI–F has excellent internal consistency with Kuder-Richardson correlations of roughly .95. The SBI–F is also reported as having excellent ordinal scalability with a coefficient of homogeneity of .990.

VALIDITY: No validity data were reported.

PRIMARY REFERENCE: Bentler, P. M. (1968). Heterosexual behavior assessment—II. Females, *Behaviour Research and Therapy* 6, 27–30. Instrument reproduced with permission of Peter M. Bentler.

AVAILABILITY: Dr. P. M. Bentler, Department of Psychology, Franz Hall, UCLA, Los Angeles, CA 90024.

SBI-F

On this page you will find a series of statements which describe various sexual behaviors that a female may have engaged in. Read each statement and decide whether or not you have experienced the sexual behavior described. Then indicate your answer.

If you have engaged in the sexual behavior described in a statement at any time since your 12th birthday, circle Yes. If you have never engaged in the behavior since then, circle No. Most items refer to your behavior with other individuals; you should consider these items as referring to any individuals who were also over 12 years old.

This inventory has been devised for young and sexually inexperienced persons as well as for married and sexually experienced persons. In addition, there are great differences between people in sexual behavior preference. Thus, you will find sexual behaviors described which you have not engaged in. Please note you are asked to indicate only whether or not you have ever taken part in the sexual behavior--you are *not* asked for your attitude or feelings.

Yes No 1. I have kissed the lips of a male for one minute continuously.

Yes No 2. I have engaged in sexual intercourse with a male.

Yes No 3. I have manipulated the genitals of a male with my tongue.

Yes No 4. A male has manipulated my breasts with his hands underneath my clothes.

Yes No 5. I have manipulated the genitals of a male with my hand over his clothes.

Yes No 6. A male has manipulated my genitals with his tongue.

Yes No 7. I have engaged in mutual hand-manipulation of genitals with a male.

Yes No 8. I have had the nipples of my breasts kissed by a male.

Yes No 9. I have engaged in mutual mouth-genital manipulation with a male to the point of my orgasm and his ejaculation.

Yes No 10. I have manipulated the genitals of a male with my hand underneath his clothes.

Yes No 11. I have manipulated a male's genitals with my mouth to the point of his ejaculation.

Yes No 12. A male has manipulated my genitals with his hand over my clothes.

Yes No 13. I have engaged in heterosexual intercourse with the male using rear entry to my vagina.

Yes No 14. I have touched the genitals of a male with my lips.

Yes No 15. A male has touched my genitals with his lips.

Yes No 16. I have engaged in mutual mouth-genital manipulation with a male.

Yes No 17. I have manipulated the genitals of a male with my hand to the point of his ejaculation.

Yes   No   18. A male has manipulated my genitals with his hand to the
             point of massive secretions.
Yes   No   19. A male has manipulated my genitals with his hand underneath
             my clothes.
Yes   No   20. I have engaged in mutual hand-manipulation of genitals with
             a male to the point of my orgasm and his ejaculation.
Yes   No   21. A male has manipulated my breasts with his hands over my
             clothes.

SEXUAL BEHAVIOR INVENTORY—MALE (SBI–M)

AUTHOR: Peter M. Bentler

PURPOSE: To assess heterosexual behavior in men.

DESCRIPTION: This 21-item instrument measures the extent to which a male has engaged in a range of heterosexual behaviors. The SBI-M was developed from 56 items dealing with various types of heterosexual behavior using the procedure of multidimensional homogeneity scaling, which assesses the latent ordinal dimensions associated with observed responses to test items. This instrument can be useful in cases involving heterosexual anxieties, in developing sexual anxiety hierarchies (e.g., using the technique of systematic desensitization), or as an overall measure of change as a result of therapy.

NORMS: The scale was developed using two samples, the first involving 175 college males and the second a sample of 108 males. No other demographic characteristics were reported nor were actual norms, although means for the two samples were 11.14 and 14.48.

SCORING: The SBI–M is scored by assigning 1 point to each "yes" answer and then summing the scores, producing a range of 0 to 21.

RELIABILITY: The SBI–M has excellent internal consistency with Kuder-Richardson correlations of roughly .95. The SBI–M is also reported as having close to perfect ordinal scalability with a coefficient of homogeneity of .987.

VALIDITY: No validity data were reported.

PRIMARY REFERENCE: Bentler, P. M. (1968). Heterosexual behavior —I. Males, *Behavior Research and Therapy* 6, 21–25. Instrument reproduced with permission of Peter M. Bentler.

AVAILABILITY: Dr. P. M. Bentler, Department of Psychology, Franz Hall, UCLA, Los Angeles, CA 90024.

SBI-M

On this page you will find a series of statements which describe various sexual benaviors that a male may have engaged in. Read each statement and decide whether or not you have experienced the sexual behavior described. Then indicate your answer.

If you have engaged in the sexual behavior described in a statement at any time since your 12th birthday, circle Yes. If you have never engaged in the behavior since then, circle No. Most items refer to your behavior with other individuals; you should consider these items as referring to any individuals who were also over 12 years old.

This inventory has been devised for young and sexually inexperienced persons as well as for married and sexually experienced persons. In addition, there are great differences between people in sexual behavior preference. Thus, you will find sexual behaviors described which you have not engaged in. Please note you are asked to indicate only whether or not you have ever taken part in the sexual behavior--you are *not* asked for your attitude or feelings.

Yes No   1. I have kissed the lips of a female for one minute continuously.
Yes No   2. I have engaged in sexual intercourse with a female.
Yes No   3. I have manipulated the genitals of a female with my tongue.
Yes No   4. I have manipulated the breasts of a female with my hands underneath her clothes.
Yes No   5. I have manipulated the genitals of a female with my hand over her clothes.
Yes No   6. A female has manipulated my genitals with her tongue.
Yes No   7. I have engaged in mutual hand-manipulation of genitals with a female.
Yes No   8. I have kissed the nipples of the breasts of a female.
Yes No   9. I have engaged in mutual mouth-genital manipulation with a female to the point of her orgasm and my ejaculation.
Yes No 10. I have manipulated the genitals of a female with my hand underneath her clothes.
Yes No 11. A female has manipulated my genitals with her mouth to the point of my ejaculation.
Yes No 12. A female has manipulated my genitals with her hand over my clothes.
Yes No 13. I have engaged in heterosexual intercourse using rear entry to the vagina.
Yes No 14. I have touched the genitals of a female with my lips.
Yes No 15. A female has touched my genitals with her lips.
Yes No 16. I have engaged in mutual mouth-genital manipulation with a female.
Yes No 17. I have manipulated the genitals of a female with my hand to the point of massive secretions from her genitals.

Yes No 18. A female has manipulated my genitals with her hand to the point of ejaculation.

Yes No 19. A female has manipulated my genitals with her hand underneath my clothes.

Yes No 20. I have engaged in mutual hand-manipulation of genitals with a female to the point of her orgasm and my ejaculation.

Yes No 21. I have manipulated the breasts of a female with my hands over her clothes.

SIMPLE RATHUS ASSERTIVENESS SCHEDULE (SRAS)

AUTHOR: Iain A. McCormick

PURPOSE: To measure assertiveness for persons with low reading ability.

DESCRIPTION: This 30-item measure of assertiveness is based on the Rathus Assertiveness Schedule and is designed for persons with low reading ability. Care was taken to make certain item content was equivalent with that of the original schedule. Because it is shorter and easier to read, the SRAS also is useful in clinical work with adolescents and children. The SRAS is more useful with teenagers than the original RAS.

NORMS: The SRAS was tested on a sample of 116 graduate students. The mean score was 94.6 with a standard deviation of 25.4 for females (n = 82), and 99.8 with a standard deviation of 20.1 for males.

SCORING: Each item is rated on a 6-point scale from "very much like me" to "very unlike me." Items 1, 2, 4, 5, 9, 11, 12–17, 19, 23, 24, 26, 30 are reverse-scored. The total score is the sum of all items, and can range from 30 to 180 with higher scores reflecting more assertion.

RELIABILITY: Reliability of this instrument is very good. Internal consistency was determined with odd-even correlations and was .90. The SRAS correlated .94 with the original, suggesting the two may be used as parallel forms.

VALIDITY: There is very little validity data for this instrument. As a parallel form, much of the validity of the Rathus Assertiveness Schedule would apply. The parallel form reliability correlation can also be seen as concurrent validity data.

PRIMARY REFERENCE: McCormick, I. A. (1984). A simple version of the Rathus Assertiveness Schedule, *Behavioral Assessment 7*, 95–99, Instrument reproduced with permission of Dr. McCormick.

AVAILABILITY: Dr. I. A. McCormick, Psychology Department, Victoria University of Wellington, Private Bay, Wellington, New Zealand.

SRAS

Read each sentence carefully. Write down on each line whatever number is correct for you.

> 6 = Very much like me
> 5 = Rather like me
> 4 = Somewhat like me
> 3 = Somewhat unlike me
> 2 = Rather unlike me
> 1 = Very unlike me

____ 1. Most people stand up for themselves more than I do.

____ 2. At times I have not made or gone on dates because of my shyness.

____ 3. When I am eating out and the food I am served is not cooked the way I like it, I complain to the person serving it.

____ 4. I am careful not to hurt other people's feelings, even when I feel hurt.

____ 5. If a person serving in a store has gone to a lot of trouble to show me something which I do not really like, I have a hard time saying "No."

____ 6. When I am asked to do something, I always want to know why.

____ 7. There are times when I look for a good strong argument.

____ 8. I try as hard to get ahead in life as most people like me do.

____ 9. To be honest, people often get the better of me.

____ 10. I enjoy meeting and talking with people for the first time.

____ 11. I often don't know what to say to good looking people of the opposite sex.

____ 12. I do not like making phone calls to businesses or companies.

____ 13. I would rather apply for jobs by writing letters than by going to talk to the people.

____ 14. I feel silly if I return things I don't like to the store that I bought them from.

____ 15. If a close relative that I like was upsetting me, I would hide my feelings rather than say that I was upset.

____ 16. I have sometimes not asked questions for fear of sounding stupid.

____ 17. During an argument I am sometimes afraid that I will get so upset that I will shake all over.

____ 18. If a famous person were talking in a crowd and I thought he or she was wrong, I would get up and say what I thought.

____ 19. I don't argue over prices with people selling things.

____ 20. When I do something important or good, I try to let others know about it.

____ 21. I am open and honest about my feelings.

___ 22. If someone has been telling false and bad stories about me,
        I see him (her) as soon as possible to "have a talk" about it.
___ 23. I often have a hard time saying "No."
___ 24. I tend not to show my feelings rather than upsetting others.
___ 25. I complain about poor service when I am eating out or in other
        places.
___ 26. When someone says I have done very well, I sometimes just don't
        know what to say.
___ 27. If a couple near me in the theatre were talking rather loudly,
        I would ask them to be quiet or to go somewhere else and talk.
___ 28. Anyone trying to push ahead of me in a line is in for a good
        battle.
___ 29. I am quick to say what I think.
___ 30. There are times when I just can't say anything.

SMOKING SELF-EFFICACY QUESTIONNAIRE (SSEQ)

AUTHORS: Gep Colletti and Jay A. Supnick

PURPOSE: To measure beliefs about one's ability to resist the urge to smoke.

DESCRIPTION: The SSEQ is a 17-item instrument designed to assess the application of self-efficacy theory to smoking, that is, whether a change in one's belief about one's ability to execute a given action successfully can bring about behavior change (smoking reduction or completely quitting). Respondents are asked to read each of 17 situations and then to assess whether they could expect to control their smoking behavior and remain on a smoking reduction program in that situation. The intrument yields a total score indicating the overall strength of the self-efficacy judgment. Although still in an early stage of development, the SSEQ shows potential for clinical and research applications.

NORMS: Initial development of the SSEQ was based on 128 male and female respondents with a mean age of 39.7 who were participants in an ongoing, behaviorally oriented smoking reduction program. Twenty-nine additional respondents participated in earlier stages in the development of the scale. Means for the sample of 128 are available and broken down by sex and pre- and posttreatment scores. The overall pretreatment mean was 42.13 which rose to 72.53 after treatment.

SCORING: The SSEQ is scored by totaling respondents' confidence ratings (on a scale from 10 to 100) on each of the 17 items that apply to that respondent's personal situation. Scores are then divided by the number of items answered. This yields a mean rated confidence score with a range of 0% to 100%.

RELIABILITY: The SSEQ has an alpha coefficient of better than .90, indicating excellent internal consistency. Test-retest reliabilities were lower but significant, ranging from .41 to .62. However, these results were confounded by the fact that respondents were undergoing treatment for smoking at the time.

VALIDITY: Correlations between smoking rate and the SSEQ were statistically significant, suggesting good concurrent and predictive validity.

PRIMARY REFERENCE: Colletti, G., Supnick, J. A. and Payne, T. J. (1985). The Smoking Self-Efficacy Questionnaire (SSEQ): Preliminary scale development and validation, *Behavioral Assessment* 7, 249–260. Instrument reproduced with permission of J. Supnick and G. Colletti.

AVAILABILITY: Dr. Jay Supnick, Department of Psychiatry, University of Rochester, Medical Center, Rochester, NY 14642.

SSEQ

The following paragraphs are descriptions of situations in which people with smoking problems often find it very difficult not to smoke. If you are trying to stop, they may be the situations in which you are likely to give up.

First, read each description and as vividly as possible try to imagine yourself in that situation. Then assess whether you expect that in this situation you could control your smoking behavior and remain on your reduction program. Write down "Yes," meaning "I could control my smoking behavior" or "No," meaning "I could not control my smoking behavior" in the blank marked "Can do."

If you answer "Yes," then please assess how confident you are that you could control your smoking behavior. Using the numbers from the scale 10 to 100 printed below, choose one that expresses your degree of confidence, and write that number down in the blank marked "confidence."

Some of the exact details of a situation may not apply to you -- such as smoking while drinking coffee, but the description may be similar to a situation you do experience, smoking while drinking alcohol. You can assess that instead. If the situation is not one you would ever experience, you can place an X in the "can do" blank and go on to the next item.

Confidence Scale

10	20	30	40	50	60	70	80	90	100
Quite uncertain				Moderately certain					Certain

		Does not apply	Can do	Confidence
1.	You just returned from an important exam and you "know" you have done poorly.	_____	_____	_____
2.	A planned date stands you up. You are disappointed and begin to blame yourself.	_____	_____	_____
3.	You have had a fight with your boyfriend, girlfriend, spouse, or any friend and you are angry and upset.	_____	_____	_____

	Does not apply	Can do	Confidence
4. `You have been out for an evening, you feel relaxed and want to end the evening with a smoke.	___	___	___
5. You have just finished dinner in a good restaurant on a special occasion. Everyone orders coffee and your friends all sit back to enjoy a cigarette.	___	___	___
6. You are out with friends who are smoking a lot. You don't want them to know that you are on a smoking reduction program.	___	___	___
7. You just came home from a really rough day at school or work. The whole day was filled with anxiety, frustration, and failure.	___	___	___
8. You are stting at home alone, in a bad mood, thinking about the problems and failures in your life.	___	___	___
9. Watching television (e.g., sport event).	___	___	___
10. Studying.	___	___	___
11. Reading a novel or magazine.	___	___	___
12. Attending a sports or entertainment event.	___	___	___
13. Talking on the phone.	___	___	___
14. Drinking coffee or other nonalcoholic beverages.	___	___	___
15. After a meal.	___	___	___
16. Talking or socializing.	___	___	___
17. Playing cards.	___	___	___

SOCIAL AVOIDANCE AND DISTRESS SCALE (SAD)

AUTHORS: David Watson and Ronald Friend

PURPOSE: To measure social anxiety.

DESCRIPTION: This 28-item measure was developed to assess anxiety in social situations. The SAD assesses two aspects of anxiety, one's experience of distress, discomfort, fear and anxiety; and the deliberate avoidance of social situations. The SAD, however, is a unidimensional measure and does not have subscales. The items are phrased to reflect anxiety and non-anxiety symptoms in an effort to control for response bias. The SAD is appropriate for general social situations rather than specific problems such as test anxiety or simple phobia.

NORMS: The SAD was developed on a sample of 297 college students. Ninety-two subjects were not included in the analysis because of attrition or incomplete information. Demographic data are not available. The mean for males (n = 60) was 11.2 and for females (n = 145) the mean was 8.24. There was a significant difference between males and females, indicating that females report more social anxiety.

SCORING: Each item is answered either "true" or "false." Items 2, 5, 8, 10, 11, 13, 14, 16, 18, 20, 21, 23, 24, and 26 are keyed for "true" answers, while the other items are keyed "false." Answers which match the keyed response are given the value of 1 and answers which do not match the key are assigned the value of 0. Total scores are the summation of the item values. Scores range from 0 to 28 with higher scores indicating more anxiety.

RELIABILITY: The internal consistency of the instrument was assessed by correlating each item with the total score on the SAD. The average item to total score correlation was .77. Reliability was also determined using Kuder-Richardson Formula 20 and was excellent, .94. Test-retest reliability for a one-month period was .68 using a sample of 154 college students enrolled in summer school and .79 for a separate sample.

VALIDITY: The validity of the SAD was assessed by testing to see if subjects with high scores demonstrated more discomfort in a social situation than did subjects with lower scores. Additionally, comparisons were made to determine if subjects with high scores demonstrated a greater preference for being alone than did subjects with lower scores. Differences were found between the groups on these variables and are evidence of known-groups validity.

PRIMARY REFERENCE: Watson, D. and Friend, R. (1969). Measurement of social-evaluation anxiety, *Journal of Consulting and Clinical Psy-*

chology, 33, 448–457. Instrument reprinted with permission of David Watson and the American Psychological Association.
AVAILABILITY: Journal article.

SAD

For the following statements, please answer each in terms of whether it is true or false for you. Circle T for true or F for false.

T	F	1.	I feel relaxed even in unfamiliar social situations.
T	F	2.	I try to avoid situations which force me to be very sociable.
T	F	3.	It is easy for me to relax when I am with strangers.
T	F	4.	I have no particular desire to avoid people.
T	F	5.	I often find social occasions upsetting.
T	F	6.	I usually feel calm and comfortable at social occasions.
T	F	7.	I am usually at ease when talking to someone of the opposite sex.
T	F	8.	I try to avoid talking to people unless I know them well.
T	F	9.	If the chance comes to meet new people, I often take it.
T	F	10.	I often feel nervous or tense in casual get-togethers in which both sexes are present.
T	F	11.	I am usually nervous with people unless I know them well.
T	F	12.	I usually feel relaxed when I am with a group of people.
T	F	13.	I often want to get away from people.
T	F	14.	I usually feel uncomfortable when I am in a group of people I don't know.
T	F	15.	I usually feel relaxed when I meet someone for the first time.
T	F	16.	Being introduced to people makes me tense and nervous.
T	F	17.	Even though a room is full of strangers, I may enter it anyway.
T	F	18.	I would avoid walking up and joining a large group of people.
T	F	19.	When my superiors want to talk with me, I talk willingly.
T	F	20.	I often feel on edge when I am with a group of people.
T	F	21.	I tend to withdraw from people.
T	F	22.	I don't mind talking to people at parties or social gatherings.
T	F	23.	I am seldom at ease in a large group of people.
T	F	24.	I often think up excuses in order to avoid social engagements.
T	F	25.	I sometimes take the responsibility for introducing people to each other.
T	F	26.	I try to avoid formal social occasions.
T	F	27.	I usually go to whatever social engagement I have.
T	F	28.	I find it easy to relax with other people.

SOCIAL ANXIETY THOUGHTS QUESTIONNAIRE (SAT)

AUTHOR: Lorne M. Hartman

PURPOSE: To measure the cognitive component of social anxiety.

DESCRIPTION: The SAT is a 21-item instrument designed to measure the frequency of cognitions that accompany social distress or anxiety. The basis for this instrument is the notion that cognitive factors (thoughts, images, memories, feelings) such as negative self-evaluations and evaluation of feedback from others play a role in the development, maintenance, and treatment of disorders such as social anxiety. From a pool of 117 self-statements collected from university students, the 21 items that showed the best psychometric properties were selected. Factor analysis revealed four factors, but the overall score on the SAT appears to be the most useful indicator of cognitive components of social anxiety. The four factors are: (1) thoughts of general discomfort and social inadequacy, (2) concern with others' awareness of distress; (3) fear of negative evaluations, and (4) perceptions of autonomic arousal and performance anxiety.

NORMS: Initial study of the SAT involved 28 male and 74 female undergraduates with a mean age of 21.6. No other demographic data or samples were reported. The mean score for those respondents was 42.3.

SCORING: The SAI is scored by summing the individual item scores, producing a range of 21 to 105.

RELIABILITY: The SAT has excellent internal consistency with an alpha of .95. Test-retest correlations were not reported.

VALIDITY: The SAT has fairly good concurrent validity, showing significant correlations with the Social Avoidance and Distress Scale and the Fear of Negative Evaluation Scale. No other forms of validity were reported.

PRIMARY REFERENCE: Hartman, L. M. (1984). Cognitive components of anxiety, *Journal of Clinical Psychology* 40, 137–139. Instrument reproduced with permission of Lorne Hartman.

AVAILABILITY: Dr. L. M. Hartman, Addiction Research Foundation, 33 Russell Street, Toronto, Ontario, Canada.

326

SAT

We are interested in the thoughts people have in social situations.
Listed below are a variety of thoughts that pop into peoples' heads in
situations that involve being with other people or talking to them.
Please read each thought and indicate how frequently, if at all, the
thought occurred to you *over the last week*. Please read each item
carefully and, following the scale, indicate to the left of the question
the number that best applies to you. Please answer each question very
carefully. *In social or interpersonal situations during the past week,
how often did you have the following thoughts?*

1 = Never
2 = Rarely
3 = Sometimes
4 = Often
5 = Always

___ 1. I feel tense and uncertain.
___ 2. I don't know what to say.
___ 3. Maybe I sound stupid.
___ 4. I am perspiring.
___ 5. What will I say first?
___ 6. Can they tell I am nervous?
___ 7. I feel afraid.
___ 8. I wish I could just be myself.
___ 9. What are they thinking of me?
___ 10. I feel shaky.
___ 11. I'm not pronouncing well.
___ 12. Will others notice my anxiety?
___ 13. I feel defenseless.
___ 14. I will freeze up.
___ 15. Now they know I am nervous.
___ 16. I don't like being in this situation.
___ 17. I am inadequate.
___ 18. Does my anxiety show?
___ 19. I feel tense in my stomach.
___ 20. Others will not understand me.
___ 21. What do they think of me?

SOCIAL FEAR SCALE (SFS)

AUTHORS: Michael L. Raulin and Jennifer L. Wee

PURPOSE: To measure social fear.

DESCRIPTION: The SFE is a 36-item scale designed to measure the particular type of social fear that is believed to be a common characteristic of schizotypic individuals, those who have a genetic predisposition to schizophrenia. The SFS was developed to measure interpersonal aversiveness, characteristics such as social inadequacy, and a dearth of interpersonal relationships that might be present in preschizophrenics in the general population. The 36 items were selected from an item pool of 120 items based on descriptions of social fear as a schizotypic symptom.

NORMS: Development of the SFS was carried out with separate samples of undergraduate students, totaling 792 females and 670 males. No actual norms or other demographic information were reported.

SCORING: Respondents are asked to indicate whether each item is true or false as it applies to them. Items 3, 8, 16, 18, 19, 31, and 32 are considered "correct" if marked "false"; all others are "correct" if marked "true." Correct answers are assigned 1 point, and the scores are summed. The higher the score, the greater the degree of social fear.

RELIABILITY: The SFS has excellent internal consistency, with alphas ranging from .85 to .88. No test-retest correlations are reported.

VALIDITY: The SFS has fair concurrent validity, correlating moderately with several other scales measuring schizotypic characteristics (e.g., perceptual aberration, intense ambivalence, somatic symptoms). High, medium, and low scorers on the SFS also significantly distinguished among groups independently rated on social fear and sociability, thus suggesting some degree of known-groups validity. The SFS is slightly correlated with social desirability response bias, so this condition cannot be totally ruled out.

PRIMARY REFERENCE: Raulin, M. L. and Wee, J. L. (1984). The development and validation of a scale to measure social fear, *Journal of Clinical Psychology* 40, 780–784. Instrument reproduced with permission of Michael L. Raulin.

AVAILABILITY: Dr. Michael L. Raulin, SUNY Buffalo, Psychology Department, Julian Park Hall, Buffalo, NY 14260.

SFS

Circle either T for true or F for false for each item as it applies to you.

T F 1. I like staying in bed so that I won't have to see anyone.
T F 2. I enjoy being a loner.
T F 3. I usually prefer being with friends to being by myself.
T F 4. Upon entering a crowded room, I often feel a strong urge to leave immediately.
T F 5. Honest people will admit that socializing is a burden.
T F 6. I find I can't relax unless I am alone.
T F 7. I feel more comfortable being around animals than being around people.
T F 8. I think I would enjoy a job that involved working with a lot of different people.
T F 9. I like to go for days on end without seeing anyone.
T F 10. I stay away from other people whenever possible.
T F 11. All my favorite pastimes are things I do by myself.
T F 12. I often tell people that I am not feeling well just to get out of doing things with them.
T F 13. The only time I feel really comfortable is when I'm off by myself.
T F 14. Being around other people makes me nervous.
T F 15. I would rather eat alone than with other people.
T F 16. I prefer traveling with friends to traveling alone.
T F 17. I really prefer going to movies alone.
T F 18. I almost always enjoy being with people.
T F 19. It is rare for me to prefer sitting home alone to going out with a group of friends.
T F 20. I often dream of being out in the wilderness with only animals as friends.
T F 21. While talking with people I am often overwhelmed with a desire to be alone.
T F 22. Pets are generally safer to be with than people.
T F 23. I usually find that being with people is very wearing.
T F 24. I often feel like leaving parties without saying goodbye.
T F 25. Even when I am in a good mood, I prefer being alone to being with people.
T F 26. Often I can't wait until the day is over so I can be by myself.
T F 27. I wish people would just leave me alone.
T F 28. I feel most secure when I am by myself.
T F 29. When seated in a crowded place I have often felt the urge to get up suddenly and leave.
T F 30. I often need to be totally alone for a couple of days.
T F 31. I feel most comfortable when I am with people.
T F 32. I like spending my spare time with other people.
T F 33. Whenever I make plans to be with people I always regret it later.

T   F   34. The strain of being around people is so unbearable that I have to get away.

T   F   35. I would consider myself a loner.

T   F   36. I wish that I could be alone most of the time.

SOCIAL INTERACTION SELF-STATEMENT TEST (SISST)

AUTHORS: Carol R. Glass, Thomas V. Merluzzi, Joan L. Biever, and Kathryn H. Larsen

PURPOSE: To assess self-statements about social anxiety.

DESCRIPTION: The SISST is a 30-item instrument designed to measure cognitions (self-statements) associated with anxiety about social interaction. This instrument is designed for men and women who tend to have low self-confidence, inappropriate fears, worry over negative experiences, and concern about physical appearance. The SISST is based on the assumption that self-statements in specific stressful social situations are related to anxiety and competence. Thus, the SISST assesses thoughts reported by anxious individuals prior to, during, or after social interaction. The items in the SISST were derived empirically from a sample of individuals who were viewed as having high social anxiety. It consists of 15 positive (facilitative) self-statements (items 2, 4, 6, 9, 10, 12, 13, 14, 17, 18, 24, 25, 27, 28, 30) and 15 negative (inhibitory) self-statements (the remaining items). The gender of pronouns and references to males and females can be changed to produce appropriate forms for men and women.

NORMS: Initial study of the SISST was conducted on two samples. The first consisted of 40 high and 40 low socially anxious undergraduate women and the second included 32 men and 32 women selected on the basis of a random sample of undergraduate introductory psychology students, stratified by scores on the Bem Sex-Role Inventory. Means for the several subcategories of the sample are reported and range from 38.82 to 58.43 on the SISST–positive and 28.43 to 51.91 on the SISST–negative.

SCORING: The SISST is scored by summing up scores (scored from 1 to 5) for the 15 positive and 15 negative items separately. Each subscale has a range of 15 to 75.

RELIABILITY: The SISST has good internal consistency, with split-half reliability coefficients of .73 for the positive and .86 for the negative subscales. No test-retest data were available.

VALIDITY: The SISST has good concurrent validity, with the subscales correlating with the Social Avoidance and Distress Scale and the Survey of Heterosocial Interactions. In addition, the SISST significantly correlated with respondents' self-evaluations of skill and anxiety immediately after role-played situations. The SISST also has good known-groups validity, with both subscales distinguishing between high and low socially anxious respondents based on scores on other measures.

PRIMARY REFERENCE: Glass, C. R., Merluzzi, T. V., Biever, J. O. and Larsen, K. H. (1982). Cognitive assessment of social anxiety: Development and validation of a self-statement questionnaire, *Cognitive Therapy and Research* 6, 37–55. Instrument reproduced with permission of Carol R. Glass and Plenum Publishing Corporation.

AVAILABILITY: Dr. Carol R. Glass, Department of Psychology, Catholic University, Washington, DC 20064.

SISST

It is obvious that people think a variety of things when they are involved in different social situations. Below is a list of things which you may have thought to yourself at some time before, during, and after the interaction in which you were engaged. Read each item and decide how frequently you may have been thinking a similar thought before, during, and after the interaction. Indicate to the left of the item the appropriate number. The scale is interpreted as follows:

1 = Hardly ever had the thought
2 = Rarely had the thought
3 = Sometimes had the thought
4 = Often had the thought
5 = Very often had the thought

Please answer as honestly as possible.

____ 1. When I can't think of anything to say I can feel myself getting very anxious.
____ 2. I can usually talk to women pretty well.
____ 3. I hope I don't make a fool of myself.
____ 4. I'm beginning to feel more at ease.
____ 5. I'm really afraid of what she'll think of me.
____ 6. No worries, no fears, no anxieties.
____ 7. I'm scared to death.
____ 8. She probably won't be interested in me.
____ 9. Maybe I can put her at ease by starting things going.
____ 10. Instead of worrying I can figure out how best to get to know her.
____ 11. I'm not too comfortable meeting women so things are bound to go wrong.
____ 12. What the heck, the worst that can happen is that she won't go for me.
____ 13. She may want to talk to me as much as I want to talk to her.
____ 14. This will be a good opportunity.
____ 15. If I blow this conversation, I'll really lose my confidence.
____ 16. What I say will probably sound stupid.
____ 17. What do I have to lose? It's worth a try.
____ 18. This is an awkward situation but I can handle it.
____ 19. Wow--I don't want to do this.
____ 20. It would crush me if she didn't respond to me.
____ 21. I've just got to make a good impression on her or I'll feel terrible.
____ 22. You're such an inhibited idiot.
____ 23. I'll probably "bomb out" anyway.
____ 24. I can handle anything.
____ 25. Even if things don't go well it's no catastrophe.
____ 26. I feel awkward and dumb; she's bound to notice.
____ 27. We probably have a lot in common.
____ 28. Maybe we'll hit it off real well.
____ 29. I wish I could leave and avoid the whole situation.
____ 30. Ah! Throw caution to the wind.

SPLITTING SCALE (SS)

AUTHOR: Mary-Joan Gerson

PURPOSE: To measure the characterological use of splitting as a defense mechanism.

DESCRIPTION: This 14-item instrument draws from the theories of Kernberg and Kohut who view splitting as a symptom of borderline and narcissistic personality disorders. The function of splitting is to keep ambivalence at bay. Splitting is manifested in radical shifts in evaluations both of self and other, merging of self and other, disassociated grandiosity, and exhibitionism. The defense of splitting is defined as the separation of "good" or idealized objects from "bad" or devalued objects. There does not appear to be a gender difference on the SS, even though females are diagnosed as borderline personality more frequently than males. The SS score is reportedly not associated with age.

NORMS: The SS was developed on a sample of 41 female and 34 male graduate students in psychology. The average age was 27.7 years for men and 30 for women. The mean SS was 52.97 with a standard deviation of 11.46, and ranged from 26 to 79. The SS was also developed on a sample of 113 female and 75 male patients from an urban health clinic. The age of this sample ranged from 21 to 42. Normative data are not presented.

SCORING: All items are phrased to reflect the splitting defense mechanism. Respondents are asked to rate how "true" each item is to him or her. Ratings range from 1, "not at all," to 7, "very true." Scores are the total of each item rating and range from 14 to 98. Higher scores reflect characterological use of splitting.

RELIABILITY: The reliability of the SS has been estimated through internal consistency and test-retest. The alpha coefficient was moderate (.70) but acceptable for an instrument tapping such an illusive concept. The SS was quite stable with a test-retest correlation of .84 over a three-week period.

VALIDITY: The SS has fairly good concurrent validity evidence, with scores correlating positively with a measure of narcissistic personality, and negatively with self-esteem. The negative and positive criterion-related validity coefficients are consistent with the ego-oriented theory of this borderline defense.

PRIMARY REFERENCE: Gerson, M. J. (1984). Splitting: The development of a measure, *Journal of Clinical Psychology* 40, 157–162. Instrument reproduced with permission of Mary-Joan Gerson.

AVAILABILITY: Journal article.

SS

Below are fourteen questions. Please read each question and indicate in the space to the left how true it is for you using the following scale:

1 = Not at all true
2 = A little true
3 = Slightly true
4 = Somewhat true
5 = Moderately true
6 = Considerably true
7 = Very true

____ 1. I hate to hear someone close to me being criticized.
____ 2. When I'm with someone really terrific, I feel dumb.
____ 3. When I'm angry, everyone around me seems rotten.
____ 4. My friends don't know how much I'd like to be admired by people.
____ 5. It's hard for me to get angry at people I like.
____ 6. It's very painful when someone disappoints me.
____ 7. I have absolutely no sympathy for people who abuse their children.
____ 8. Sometimes I feel I could do anything in the world.
____ 9. There are times my wife (husband)/girlfriend (boyfriend) seems as strong as iron, and at other times as helpless as a baby. (Consider your most recent relationship in the absence of an ongoing relationship.)
____ 10. I often feel that I can't put the different parts of my personality together, so that there is one "me."
____ 11. Sometimes I feel my love is dangerous.
____ 12. When I'm in a new situation, there's often one person I really dislike.
____ 13. It's hard for me to become sexually excited when I'm depressed.
____ 14. Some people have too much power over me.

STATE-TRAIT ANGER SCALE (STAS)

AUTHORS: Charles Spielberger and Perry London

PURPOSE: To measure the state and trait of anger.

DESCRIPTION: The 15 items that make up this instrument assess anger both as an emotional state that varies in intensity, and as a relatively stable personality trait. State anger is defined as an emotional condition consisting of subjective feelings of tension, annoyance, irritation, or rage. Trait anger is defined in terms of how frequently a respondent feels state-anger over time. A person high in trait anger would tend to perceive more situations as anger provoking and respond with higher state-anger scores. In this framework, anger differs from hostility, which connotes a set of attitudes that mediate aggressive behavior. The instruments were developed with rigorous psychometric procedures, including the development of long and short forms which were highly correlated, ranging from .95 for state anger to .99 for trait anger. A short form of the state-anger scale is composed of the following items: 1, 2, 3, 7, 8, 9, 10, 11, 12, and 13. A short form of the trait-anger scale is composed of items 1, 2, 3, 5, 6, 7, 8, 9, 11, and 14. Trait anger can also be assessed with two subscales: anger temperament and anger reaction.

NORMS: Extensive normative data are available from samples of high school students (n = 3016), college students (n = 1621), working adults (n = 1252) and military recruits (n = 2360). For a subsample of working adult women who were between 23 and 32 years old the mean scores for the state anger, trait anger, angry temperament and angry reaction were 13.71, 18.45, 5.99, and 9.48, respectively. For a subsample of working adult men with ages ranging from 23 to 32 the mean scores for the same scales were 14.28, 18.49, 5.9 and 9.5.

SCORING: The trait anger items are rated on 4-point scales from "almost never" (1) to "almost always" (4). Scores are the sum of the item ratings. Subscale items are: anger temperament, 1, 2, 3, and 8; anger reaction, 5, 6, 7, and 9. The state anger items are rated on intensity of feelings from "not at all" (1) to "very much so" (4). Scores are the sum of the state anger items. For both state and trait anger, scores range from 10 to 40 for the 10-item short forms.

RELIABILITY: The STAS has excellent reliability. The internal consistency of the original 15-item trait anger measure was .87 for a sample of 146 college students. The trait anger measure had an internal consistency of .87 for male navy recruits and .84 for female navy recruits. The original state anger measure was found to be internally consistent with correlations of .93 for male and female navy recruits. The anger temperament subscale had internal consistency coefficients ranging from .84 to .89 for male and female college students and navy recruits. The angry reaction subscale had internal consistency coefficients ranging from .70 to .75 for the same samples. Internal consistency data are also reported for the 10-item forms using the same samples, are good to excellent. All internal consistency results are based on Cronbach's alpha.

VALIDITY: Concurrent validity support is evidenced by correlations with three measures of hostility, and measures of neuroticism, psychotism, and anxiety. Scores were not associated with state-trait curiosity or extraversion. Additional validity findings are reported in Spielberger et al. (1983).

PRIMARY REFERENCES: Spielberger, C. D., Jacobs, G., Russel, S., and Crane, R. S. (1983). Assessment of anger: The State-Trait Anger Scale. In J. N. Butcher and C. D. Spielberger (eds.), *Advances in Personality Assessment*, Vol. 2, pp. 159–187. Hillsdale, N.J.: Lawrence Erlbaum Associates, Inc. See also London, P. and Spielberger, C. (1983). Job stress, hassles and medical risk, *American Health*, March, 58–63. Instruments reproduced with permission of C. D. Spielberger, *American Health* and Lawrence Erlbaum Associates, Inc.

AVAILABILITY: From primary references.

TAS

A number of statements that people have used to describe themselves are given below. Read the statements below and indicate how you *generally* feel by placing the appropriate number next to each item.

1 = Almost never
2 = Sometimes
3 = Often
4 = Almost always

____ 1. I have a fiery temper.
____ 2. I am quick tempered.
____ 3. I am a hotheaded person.
____ 4. I get annoyed when I am singled out for correction.
____ 5. It makes me furious when I am criticized in front of others.
____ 6. I get angry when I'm slowed down by others' mistakes.
____ 7. I feel infuriated when I do a good job and get a poor evaluation.
____ 8. I fly off the handle.
____ 9. I feel annoyed when I am not given recognition for doing good work.
____ 10. People who think they are always right irritate me.
____ 11. When I get mad, I say nasty things.
____ 12. I feel irritated.
____ 13. I feel angry.
____ 14. When I get frustrated, I feel like hitting someone.
____ 15. It makes my blood boil when I am pressured.

SAS

A number of statements that people have used to describe how they feel are given below. Read the statements below and indicate how you feel *at the moment* by placing the appropriate number next to each item.

1 = Not at all
2 = Somewhat
3 = Moderately so
4 = Very much so

___ 1. I am mad.
___ 2. I feel angry.
___ 3. I am burned up.
___ 4. I feel irritated.
___ 5. I feel frustrated.
___ 6. I feel aggravated.
___ 7. I feel like I'm about to explode.
___ 8. I feel like banging on the table.
___ 9. I feel like yelling at somebody.
___ 10. I feel like swearing.
___ 11. I am furious.
___ 12. I feel like hitting someone.
___ 13. I feel like breaking things.
___ 14. I am annoyed.
___ 15. I am resentful.

STRESS-AROUSAL CHECKLIST (SACL)

AUTHORS: Colin Mackay and Tom Cox

PURPOSE: To measure stress and arousal.

DESCRIPTION: The 30-item SACL consists of adjectives commonly used to describe one's psychological experience of stress. The model of stress is two-dimensional. One dimension consists of feelings ranging from pleasant to unpleasant. This is a general sense of well-being. The second dimension of stress ranges from feelings of wakefulness to drowsiness, or vigorousness. The first dimension is labeled as stress while the second is labeled arousal. The stress dimension is considered a subjective experience in response to the external environment, while the arousal dimension represents ongoing somatic or autonomic activity.

NORMS: The SACL was originally tested with a sample of 145 undergraduates, although no demographic data are reported. Recently, McCormick, Walkey, and Taylor (1985) tested the factor structure of the SACL with 72 male and 131 female second year college students. Normative data were not reported.

SCORING: The respondent rates each adjective in terms of the intensity of his or her feelings about the adjective. For the positive adjectives, the double-plus and plus ratings are scored 1 and the question mark and minus ratings are scored 0. For the negative adjectives the question mark and minus ratings are scored 1 and the plus and double-plus ratings are scored 0. The stress subscale consists of eight negative adjectives (2, 3, 15, 21, 22, 25, 27, 28) and ten positive stress adjectives (1, 5, 6, 9, 10, 11, 12, 13, 18, 23). The arousal subscale consists of seven positive adjectives (4, 7, 14, 19, 20, 29, 30) and five negative adjectives (8, 16, 17, 24, 26). Scores are the sum of negative and positive adjectives. Stress scores range from 0 to 18; arousal scores from 0 to 12. Higher scores reflect more stress and arousal.

RELIABILITY: Reliability data are not available. Evidence of internal consistency is provided, though, by studies using factor analysis, which generally showed adjectives were correlated with other adjectives from the same subscale of stress or arousal.

VALIDITY: The SACL has evidence of known-groups validity such that scores on the stress dimension increased as a consequence of a stressful situation. Additionally, a prolonged, monotonous and repetitive task resulted in increases in stress scores and decreases in arousal scores. The SACL has also been shown to have concurrent validity, with scores correlating with various physiological measures.

PRIMARY REFERENCES: Mackay, C., Cox, T., Burrows, G., and Lazzerini, T. (1978). An inventory for the measurement of self-reported stress and arousal, *British Journal of Social and Clinical Psychology* 17,

340

283–284. McCormick, I. A., Walkey, F. H., and Taylor, A. J. W. (1985). The stress arousal checklist: An independent analysis. *Educational and Psychological Measurement* 45, 143–146. Instrument reproduced with permission of Dr. Tom Cox.

AVAILABILITY: Dr. Tom Cox, Stress Research, Department of Psychology, University of Nottingham, Nottingham, N.G. 7 2 RD, United Kingdom.

SACL

The words shown below describe different feelings and moods. Please use this list to describe your feelings *at this moment.*

If the word *definitely* describes your feelings, circle the double plus (++). If the word *more or less* describes your feelings circle the plus (+). If you do not understand the word, or *you cannot decide* whether or not it describes how you feel, circle the question mark (?). If the word *does not describe* the way you feel, circle the minus (-).

First reactions are most reliable; therefore do not spend too long thinking about each word. Please be as honest and accurate as possible.

1.	Tense	++	+	?	-	16.	Tired	++	+	?	-
2.	Relaxed	++	+	?	-	17.	Idle	++	+	?	-
3.	Restful	++	+	?	-	18.	Up-tight	++	+	?	-
4.	Active	++	+	?	-	19.	Alert	++	+	?	-
5.	Apprehensive	++	+	?	-	20.	Lively	++	+	?	-
6.	Worried	++	+	?	-	21.	Cheerful	++	+	?	-
7.	Energetic	++	+	?	-	22.	Contented	++	+	?	-
8.	Drowsy	++	+	?	-	23.	Jittery	++	+	?	-
9.	Bothered	++	+	?	-	24.	Sluggish	++	+	?	-
10.	Uneasy	++	+	?	-	25.	Pleasant	++	+	?	-
11.	Dejected	++	+	?	-	26.	Sleepy	++	+	?	-
12.	Nervous	++	+	?	-	27.	Comfortable	++	+	?	-
13.	Distressed	++	+	?	-	28.	Calm	++	+	?	-
14.	Vigorous	++	+	?	-	29.	Stimulated	++	+	?	-
15.	Peaceful	++	+	?	-	30.	Activated	++	+	?	-

STRESSFUL SITUATIONS QUESTIONNAIRE (SSQ)

AUTHORS: William F. Hodges and James P. Felling

PURPOSE: To measure apprehension and concern in stressful situations.

DESCRIPTION: This 40-item instrument was originally developed to test hypotheses regarding stress in trait anxious subjects. It measures the level of reported apprehension or concern (anxiety) in various social situations relevant to college students. The situations are those believed to involve a loss of self-esteem. Factor analysis of the instrument produced four factors which may be used as subscales to measure apprehension in physical danger (APD), apprehension in classroom and speech situations (ACSS), apprehension of social and academic failure (ASAF), and apprehension in dating situations (ADS). The last three subscales may be summed to form one measure of apprehension in ego-threatening situations, that is, situations where one fears failure. Females and males score differently only on the APD subscale.

NORMS: The SSQ was developed on a sample of 228 undergraduate college students. One-hundred and forty-one were male and 87 were female. Means and standard deviations are not reported.

SCORING: Each item is rated in terms of degree of apprehensiveness or concern from none (1) to extreme (5). Scores are the sums of the item scores. The subscales and items are: APD: 3, 7, 10, 11, 12, 13, 14, 16, 17, 18, 28, 32, 45; ACSS: 4, 5, 20, 22, 24, 29, 37, 42; ASAD: 6, 9, 44, 15, 19, 21, 23, 25, 27, 33, 35, 38; ADS: 1, 2, 34, 41. Higher scores reflect more apprehension or concern.

RELIABILITY: No reliability data were reported.

VALIDITY: The validity of the SSQ has had some support through concurrent validity procedures. Scores on the APD were not correlated with trait anxiety, but the three subscales concerning ego-threatening situations were moderately correlated. These correlations conform to the predictions of state-trait anxiety theory. A stronger concurrent validity correlation was found between the trait anxiety measure and the combined ego-threatening stressful situations than with the state anxiety measure.

PRIMARY REFERENCE: Hodges, W. F. and Felling, F. P. (1970). Types of stressful situations and their relation to trait anxiety and sex, *Journal of Consulting and Clinical Psychology* 34, 333–337. Instrument reproduced with permission of William F. Hodges and the American Psychological Association.

AVAILABILITY: Journal article.

SSQ

Everyone is faced with situations in life that make them feel more or less apprehensive. Below is a list of situations which you may have experienced, or might be placed in some day. First, read through the entire list; then, for each situation, indicate at left the number that best describes the degree of apprehensiveness or concern you have felt or believe you would feel if in that situation. Do not skip any items. Work rapidly and put down your first impression.

1 = None at all
2 = Slight
3 = Moderate
4 = Considerable
5 = Extreme

1. Going on a blind date.
2. Asking someone for a date to a party.
3. Seeing someone bleed profusely from a cut arm.
4. Asking a teacher to clarify an assignment in class.
5. Giving a speech in front of class.
6. Introducing a friend and forgetting his name.
7. Putting iodine on an open cut.
8. Having someone angry at you.
9. Taking a test that you expect to fail.
10. Seeing a dog run over by a car.
11. Walking in a slum alone at night.
12. Giving blood at the Blood Bank.
13. Riding in an airplane in a storm.
14. Being present at an operation or watching one in a movie.
15. Belching aloud in class.
16. Having a tooth cavity filled.
17. Climbing too steep a mountain.
18. Paying respects at the open coffin of an acquaintance.
19. Being refused membership in a social club.
20. Asking a question in class.
21. Doing poorly in a course that seems easy to others.
22. Reciting a poem in class.
23. Having your date leave a dance with someone else.
24. Reciting in language class.
25. Finding the questions on a test extremely difficult.
26. Having to ask for money that was borrowed from you.
27. Forgetting lines in a school play.
28. Riding a car going 95 miles per hour.
29. Asking a teacher to explain the grading of your test.
30. Getting hurt in a fight.
31. Telling an uninvited guest to leave a party.
32. Passing a very bad traffic accident.
33. Being the only person at a party not dressed up.

___ 34. Introducing yourself to someone attractive of the opposite sex.
___ 35. Spilling your drink on yourself at a formal dinner party.
___ 36. Having an interview for a job.
___ 37. Volunteering an answer to a question in class.
___ 38. Getting back a test you think you may have failed.
___ 39. Skiing out of control.
___ 40. Asking the person behind you to stop kicking your seat.
___ 41. Kissing a date for the first time.
___ 42. Asking a teacher to explain a question during a test.
___ 43. Asking people in a study room to make less noise.
___ 44. Being in a difficult course for which you have inadequate background.
___ 45. Participating in a psychology experiment in which you recieve electric shock.

SURVEY OF HETEROSEXUAL INTERACTIONS (SHI)

AUTHORS: Craig T. Twentyman and Richard M. McFall

PURPOSE: To measure heterosexual avoidance in males.

DESCRIPTION: The SHI is a 20-item instrument designed to evaluate males' ability to handle social situations involving interaction with women. Several studies have shown the SHI to be a useful device for identifying individuals who tend to experience difficulties in heterosocial interactions. It can also be used clinically to examine changes in clients' abilities to deal with specific heterosexual problems.

NORMS: The SHI has been used in a series of studies with samples consisting solely of undergraduate males, mainly from introductory psychology classes, with an N of over 2200. No other demographic data were reported. The mean SHI score for the first 604 respondents was 88.21. However, respondents rated as daters were reported as scoring above 100 on the SHI while nondaters scored below 70.

SCORING: The SHI is scored by summing the individual items (on a 1 to 7 scale) to produce the overall score, which can range from 20 to 140. Higher scores indicate more heterosocial competence or less heterosocial avoidance.

RELIABILITY: The SHI has very good internal consistency, with split-half correlations of .85, and excellent stability with a four-month test-retest correlation of .85.

VALIDITY: The SHI has very good concurrent validity, correlating significantly with reported anxiety in heterosocial situations and with self-reported behavior in social situations. The SHI also has good known-groups validity, distinguishing significantly between dating and nondating and shy and nonshy respondents. The SHI also has been found to be sensitive to changes following counseling.

PRIMARY REFERENCE: Twentyman, C., Boland, T., and McFall, R. M. (1981). Heterosocial avoidance in college males, *Behavior Modification* 5, 523–552. Instrument reproduced with permission of Craig Twentyman and Sage Publications.

AVAILABILITY: Dr. Craig Twentyman, Department of Psychology, University of Hawaii, 2430 Campus Road, Honolulu, HI 96822.

SHI

This questionnaire is concerned with the social behavior of college males. We are interested in what might be broadly defined as "dating behavior." The term "date" used here is to mean any behavior in which some social activity was participated in and planned with a member of the opposite sex. Examples of this type of behavior might include going to the movies, a football game, a party, or even just getting together with some friends.

1. How many "dates" have you had in the last four weeks? Please be exact. _____

2. Estimate the average number of "dates" per month during the past year. _____

3. How many different women have you "dated" during the past year?
_____

4. How would you compare yourself with other persons your age with regard to the amount of social behavior you participate in with the opposite sex?

1	2	3	4	5	6	7
Participate in less than an average amount of social behavior			Participate in an average amount of social behavior		Participate in more than an average amount of social behavior	

ITEMS

1. You want to call a woman up for a date. This is the first time you are calling her up as you only know her slightly. When you get ready to make the call, your roommate comes into the room, sits down on his bed, and begins reading a magazine. In this situation you would

1	2	3	4	5	6	7
be unable to call in every case			be able to call in some cases		be able to call in every case	

2. You are at a dance. You see a very attractive woman whom you do not know. She is standing *alone* and you would like to dance with her. You would

1	2	3	4	5	6	7
be unable to ask her in every case			be able to ask her in some cases		be able to ask her in every case	

3. You are at a party and you see two women talking. You do not know these women but you would like to know one of them better. In this situation you would

1	2	3	4	5	6	7
be unable to initiate a conversation			be able to initiate a conversation in some cases		be able to initiate a conversation in every case	

4. You are at a bar where there is also dancing. You see a couple of women sitting in a booth. One, whom you do not know, is talking with a fellow who is standing by the booth. These two go over to dance leaving the other woman sitting alone. You have seen this woman around, but do not really know her. You would like to go over and talk with her (but you wouldn't like to dance). In this situation you would

1	2	3	4	5	6	7
be unable to go over and talk to her			be able to go over and talk to her in some cases		be able to go over and talk to her in every case	

5. On a work break at your job you see a woman who also works there and is about your age. You would like to talk to her, but you do not know her. You would

1	2	3	4	5	6	7
be unable to talk to her in every case			be able to talk to her in some cases		be able to talk to her in every case	

6. You are on a crowded bus. A woman you know only *slightly* is sitting in front of you. You would like to talk to her but you notice that the fellow sitting next to her is watching you. You would

1	2	3	4	5	6	7
be unable to talk to her in every case			be able to talk to her in some cases		be able to talk to her in every case	

7. You are at a dance. You see an attractive woman whom you do not know, standing *in a group* of four women. You would like to dance. In this situation you would

1	2	3	4	5	6	7
be unable to ask in every case			be able to ask in some cases		be able to ask in every case	

8. You are at a drugstore counter eating lunch. A woman whom you do
   not know sits down beside you. You would like to talk to her.
   After her meal comes she asks you to pass the sugar. In this
   situation you would pass the sugar

1	2	3	4	5	6	7
but be unable to initiate a conversation with her			and in some cases be able to initiate a conversation		and be able to initiate a conversation	

9. A friend of yours is going out with his girlfriend this weekend.
   He wants you to come along and gives you the name and phone number
   of a woman he says would be a good date. You are not doing anything
   this weekend. In this situation you would

1	2	3	4	5	6	7
be unable to call in every case			be able to call in some cases		be able to call in every case	

10. You are in the library. You decide to take a break, and as you
    walk down the hall you see a girl whom you know only casually.
    She is sitting at a table and appears to be studying. You decide
    that you would like to ask her to get a coke with you. In this
    situation you would

1	2	3	4	5	6	7
be unable to ask her in every case			be able to ask her in some cases		be able to ask her in every case	

11. You want to call a woman for a date. You find this woman attractive
    but you do not know her. You would

1	2	3	4	5	6	7
be unable to call in very case			be able to call in some cases		be able to call in every case	

12. You are taking a class at the university. After one of your classes
    you see a woman whom you know. You would like to talk to her;
    however, she is walking with a couple of other women you do not
    know. You would

1	2	3	4	5	6	7
be unable to talk to her in every case			be able to talk to her in some cases		be able to talk to her in every case	

13. You have been working on a committee for the past year. There is
     a banquet at which you are assigned a particular seat. On one side
     of you there is a woman you do not know, on the other is a man you
     do not know. In this situation you would

1	2	3	4	5	6	7
be unable to initiate a conversation with the woman and talk only with the man			be able to initiate a conversation with the woman in some cases but talk mostly to the man		be able to initiate a conversation in every case and be able to talk equally as freely with the woman as with the man	

14. You are in the lobby of a large apartment complex waiting for a
     friend. As you are waiting for him to come down, a woman whom you
     know well walks by with another woman whom you have never seen
     before. The woman you know says hello and begins to talk to you.
     Suddenly she remembers that she left something in her room. Just
     before she leaves you she tells you the other woman's name. In
     this situation you would

1	2	3	4	5	6	7
find it very difficult to initiate a conversation with the other woman			find it only slightly difficult		find it easy to initiate and continue a conversation	

15. You are at a party at a friend's apartment. You see a woman who
     has come alone. You don't know her, but you would like to talk to
     her. In this situation you would

1	2	3	4	5	6	7
be unable to go over and talk to her			be able to go over and talk to her in some cases		be able to go over and talk to her in every case	

16. You are walking to your mailbox in the large apartment building
     where you live. When you get there you notice that two women are
     putting their names on the mailbox of the vacant apartment beneath
     yours. In this situation you would

1	2	3	4	5	6	7
be unable to go over and initiate a conversation			be able to go over and initiate a conversation		be able to go over and initiate a conversation in every case	

17. You are at a record store and see a woman that you once were introduced to. That was several months ago and now you have forgotten her name. You would like to talk to her. In this situation you would

1	2	3	4	5	6	7
be unable to start a conversation with her in every case			be able to start a conversation with her in some cases		be able to start a conversation with her in every case	

18. You are at the student union or local cafeteria where friends your age eat lunch. You have gotten your meal and are now looking for a place to sit down. Unfortunately, there are no empty tables. At one table, however, there is a woman sitting alone. In this situation you would

1	2	3	4	5	6	7
wait until another place was empty and then sit down			ask the woman if you could sit at the table but not say anything more to her		ask the woman if you could sit at the table and then initiate a conversation	

19. A couple of weeks ago you had a first date with a woman you now see walking on the street toward you. For some reason you haven't seen each other since then. You would like to talk to her but you aren't sure of what she thinks of you. In this situation you would

1	2	3	4	5	6	7
walk by without saying anything			walk up to her and say something in some cases		walk up to her and say something in every case	

20. Generally, in most social situations involving women whom you do not know, you would

1	2	3	4	5	6	7
be unable to initiate a conversation			be unable to initiate a conversation in some cases		be able to initiate a conversation in some cases	

VERBAL AGGRESSIVENESS SCALE (VAS)

AUTHORS: Dominic A. Infante and Charles J. Wigley, III

PURPOSE: To measure verbal aggressiveness.

DESCRIPTION: The VAS is a 20-item scale designed to measure verbal aggressiveness as a trait that predisposes people to attack the self-concepts of others instead of, or in addition to, their positions on topics of communication. The VAS is undimensional, with 10 items worded negatively. Its main focus is interpersonal; verbal aggressiveness is viewed as an exchange of messages between two people where at least one person in the dyad attacks the other in order to hurt him or her psychologically. Thus, the VAS appears to hold promise in the area of family and couple counseling.

NORMS: Research on the VAS was conducted on approximately 660 undergraduate students in communication courses. Other demographic information and actual norms were not reported. However, in one study, the mean of 51.97 for males (N = 195) was significantly different from the mean of 46.38 for females (N = 202).

SCORING: The VAS is scored by reverse-scoring items 1, 3, 5, 8, 10, 12, 14, 15, 17, and 20 and then totaling the scores. This produces a range of 20 to 100.

RELIABILITY: The VAS has good internal consistency, with an alpha of .81. The VAS also has excellent stability, with a four-week test-retest correlation of .82.

VALIDITY: The VAS has fairly good concurrent validity, correlating at moderate levels with five other trait measures. Further, the VAS was significantly correlated with predicted performance for verbally aggressive messages in a variety of social influence situations, suggesting good predictive validity.

PRIMARY REFERENCE: Infante, D. A. and Wigley, C. J., III. (1986). Verbal aggressiveness: An interpersonal model and measure, *Communication Monographs* 53, 61–69. Instrument reproduced with permission of Dominic A. Infante.

AVAILABILITY: Journal article.

VAS

This survey is concerned with how we try to get people to comply with our wishes. Indicate how often each statement is true for you personally when you try to influence other persons. Use the following scale:

1 = Almost never true
2 = Rarely true
3 = Occasionally true
4 = Often true
5 = Almost always true

____ 1. I am extremely careful to avoid attacking individuals' intelligence when I attack their ideas.

____ 2. When individuals are very stubborn, I use insults to soften the stubbornness.

____ 3. I try very hard to avoid having other people feel bad about themselves when I try to influence them.

____ 4. When people refuse to do a task I know is important, without good reason, I tell them they are unreasonable.

____ 5. When others do things I regard as stupid, I try to be extremely gentle with them.

____ 6. If individuals I am trying to influence really deserve it, I attack their character.

____ 7. When people behave in ways that are in very poor taste, I insult them in order to shock them into proper behavior.

____ 8. I try to make people feel good about themselves even when their ideas are stupid.

____ 9. When people simply will not budge on a matter of importance I lose my temper and say rather strong things to them.

____ 10. When people criticize my shortcomings, I take it in good humor and do not try to get back at them.

____ 11. When individuals insult me, I get a lot of pleasure out of really telling them off.

____ 12. When I dislike individuals greatly, I try not to show it in what I say or how I say it.

____ 13. I like poking fun at people who do things that are very stupid in order to stimulate their intelligence.

____ 14. When I attack peoples' ideas, I try not to damage their self-concepts.

____ 15. When I try to influence people, I make a great effort not to offend them.

____ 16. When people do things that are mean or cruel, I attack their character in order to help correct their behavior.

____ 17. I refuse to participate in arguments when they involve personal attacks.

____ 18. When nothing seems to work in trying to influence others, I yell and scream in order to get some movement from them.

___ 19. When I am not able to refute others' positions, I try to make them feel defensive in order to weaken their positions.

___ 20. When an argument shifts to personal attacks, I try very hard to change the subject.

INSTRUMENTS FOR CHILDREN

ASSERTIVENESS SCALE FOR ADOLESCENTS (ASA)

AUTHORS: Dong Yul Lee, Ernest T. Hallberg, Alan G. Slemon, and Richard F. Haase

PURPOSE: To measure the assertiveness of adolescents in specific situations.

DESCRIPTION: The ASA is a 33-item scale designed for children in grades 6 through 12. It describes 33 interpersonal situations and provides the respondent with three options as to what he or she would usually do in each situation. The three options are classified as assertive, unassertive, and aggressive or passive-aggressive. The instrument has three purposes: (1) to obtain children's reports about their typical behavior that could be used by practitioners to identify interpersonal problem areas, (2) to be used as a screening device for intervention or prevention programs, and (3) to be used as a research tool in investigating assertiveness.

NORMS: Initial studies used 682 students in grades 6 through 12 in Canada. The children included 323 boys and 359 girls and were from two elementary and three secondary schools. Means are available for boys and girls at each grade level and range from 19.81 to 23.48.

SCORING: One of each of the three options for each situation has been designated as the ("appropriate") assertive response. Each of these responses is assigned 1 point and the scores are summed, producing an overall assertiveness score that can range from 0 to 33 (higher scores reflect greater assertiveness). "A" is the assertive response for items 6, 10, 14, 20, 21, 23, 26, 28, 29, 31, 32; "B" is assertive for items 1, 7, 9, 12, 15, 18, 19, 22, 25, 27, 30, 33; and "C" is assertive for items 2, 3, 4, 5, 8, 11, 13, 16, 17, and 24.

RELIABILITY: Based on a subsample of 55 children, the Kuder-Richardson formula 20, indicating fairly good internal consistency, was .76, while the test-retest reliability (stability) was quite good with a correlation over a four-week interval of .84.

VALIDITY: Although the instrument is in an early stage of development, it appears to have fair validity in several areas. Concurrent validity based on correlations with two other measures was rather low (.33 for selected items from the Gambrill-Richey Assertiveness Inventory and .55 with the Children's Action Tendency Scale) although both were statistically significant. However, the SAS did distinguish between known-groups on several dimensions (e.g., leaders versus non-leaders), appears to be sensitive to the effects of group assertion training sessions, and does not appear to be confounded with aggression or social desirability response set (based on lack of a significant relationship with the Crowne-Marlowe Social Desirability Scale). The SAS also was negatively correlated with irrational beliefs (the more assertive, the less respondents held irrational beliefs based on the Irrational Belief Questionnaire).

PRIMARY REFERENCE: Lee, D. Y., Hallberg, E. T., Slemon, A. G., and Haase, R. F. (1985). An Assertiveness Scale for Adolescents, *Journal of Clinical Psychology* 41, 51–57. Instrument reproduced by permission of D. Y. Lee.

AVAILABILITY: Dr. Dong Yul Lee, Department of Educational Psychology, Faculty of Education, University of Western Ontario, London, Ontario, Canada N6G 1G7.

ASA

On the next few pages, you will see several situations that you may or may not have met in the past. We would like to know *what you would usually do in each situation*.

Please circle the letter of the response that best describes what you would do in this situation.

1. You and your best friend have four tickets for the football game. Your other two friends do not show up, leaving you both with an extra ticket. Your best friend says, "If you give me your extra ticket, I will try to sell both." Your best friend does sell both, but doesn't give you your share of the money.
    A. You accept your friend's actions because you think that your friend earned the extra money by selling your ticket.
    B. You say calmly, "Give me my money."
    C. You say, "You crook. I am telling you now that if you don't give me the money it will be the end of our friendship."

2. Your mother has sent you shoping for food. The supermarket is busy and you are waiting patiently at the check-out. Your mother has told you to hurry. Suddenly a woman behind you pushes you with her shopping cart and says, "Hey, you don't mind if I go first, do you? I'm in a hurry."
    A. You are not happy with the way she treats you, but you calm yourself down and say, "Okay," and let the woman go first.
    B. You push the woman's cart and say, "You've got your nerve butting in like that," and refuse to give her your place in the line.
    C. You say, "Yes, I can see that, but I am in a hurry too. Please wait your turn or go to another check-out."

3. A school friend of yours has been spreading lies about you. As a result, most of your other friends now avoid you and talk about you behind your back. Today you happen to run into your school friend in the cafeteria. You are greeted as if nothing has happened.
    A. You talk with your friend, and pretend that you do not know about the lies your friend has told.
    B. You say, "Well, well, I'm glad I have finally caught up with you. We have a little matter to settle, liar."
    C. You say, "I am hurt by the rumors that you have been spreading about me. I thought you were my friend, and I am surprised that you did this to me. If you have a reason, I would like you to tell me so that we can get this matter sorted out."

4. You often do favors for your friends. One of your friends, however,
    requests many more favors than the others. In fact, you think that
    some of this friend's requests are unreasonable, and that you are
    being used. Today this friend again asks for a favor.
    A. You do the favor because friendship is very important to
        you.
    B. You make up an excuse and tell your friend that you are too
        busy to help today.
    C. You say to your friend, "Lately you have been asking for a
        lot of favors and some of them have been unreasonable. This
        time I will say no. Friendship is a two-way street."

5. You are a member of the school basketball team. The coach has
    promised that everyone will get a chance to play in this game. There
    are only five minutes left to play in the game and the coach hasn't
    put you in yet.
    A. You get up, walk over to the coach, swear, and stomp out.
    B. You stay on the bench. You think that you can learn a lot
        of things by watching the others play.
    C. You approach the coach and remind him that you haven't been
        in the game yet.

6. Today you got back your graded test paper. After talking to your
    classmates, you feel that one of your answers was not graded fairly.
    Later in the day your teacher greets you in the corridor.
    A. You say, "Hello. By the way, I believe that one of my
        answers was not graded fairly. Could we go over it
        together?"
    B. You say, "Hello, I think you have been very unfair to me."
    C. You don't think this is the time to argue over the grade so
        you simply say, "Hi," and continue walking.

7. A classmate of yours missed a test and asks you for your test paper
    when you are walking home together. You both know that the teacher is
    going to give the same test to those who missed the first one. You
    don't think it is fair to allow your friend to get a good grade by
    studying only the answers to the questions on the test.
    A. You refuse to give your test paper to your friend and say
        that you are no longer friends.
    B. You refuse to give your test paper to your friend and
        explain why you think it would be wrong for your friend to
        use it.
    C. Keeping a good friendship means a lot to you, so you give
        your classmate your test paper.

8. Your favorite teacher asks you to volunteer one or two hours a day to help with an extracurricular project. You are doing well in his class, but are behind in some of your other subjects and are afraid that you might fail.
   - A. You say, "I will think about it," and then do your best to avoid that teacher.
   - B. You are not happy about doing it, but you are afraid that the teacher's feelings will be hurt if you refuse. You agree to work on the project.
   - C. You say "No," and explain that you would like to help, but you need the time to catch up on your other subjects.

9. You are having dinner at a friend's house. After sitting down at the table you discover that everything is served on your plate, including a vegetable you hate. This vegetable has made you sick in the past. Your friend's mother says, "The rule in this house is that you eat everything on your plate."
   - A. You don't wish to cause any embarrassment at your friend's house, so you force yourself to eat the vegetable.
   - B. You tell her that in the past this vegetable has made you sick and that you don't think it would be wise for you to eat it now.
   - C. You say nothing, but to show your displeasure you get up quietly, leave the table, and go home.

10. You are standing in a line at the popcorn booth in the movie theater. The show is going to start in a few minutes and you don't want to miss the beginning. Finally you get to the counter. As the girl is about to serve you, a man behind you shouts his order and the girl starts to serve him first.
    - A. You simply say, "Sorry, I was next," and proceed to order your popcorn.
    - B. You say to the man, "You've got your nerve pushing in like that," and then say to the girl, "What's the idea of serving him first?"
    - C. You are upset, but you wait until the girl asks for your order. You decide that you'll never go back to that movie theater again.

11. You buy a game at a store. When you get home you discover that some of the pieces are missing. You go back to the store to ask for a refund or a replacement. When you talk to the cashier about it, she says "That's too bad," but does nothing about it.
    - A. You say nothing, leave the store, and decide never to go back there again.
    - B. You get angry at the cashier, throw the game on the floor, and walk out.
    - C. You say, "I know it's too bad, but I insist that the game be replaced or that a refund be given."

12. Your teacher singles you out in class by saying loudly, "Your answers to these problems are very similar to those of one of your classmates. I'll let it pass this time, but don't let it happen again." You didn't copy anybody's work and your teacher is wrong in suggesting that you cheated.

    A. You don't say anything, pick up a book, and start reading it as if you had never been spoken to.

    B. You say, "I didn't cheat, and I resent the suggestion that I did."

    C. You are angry, but don't say anything, hoping you will be able to get back at the teacher later.

13. You are traveling by bus to another city. The bus is crowded and you are sitting in the no smoking section. The man sitting beside you is smoking one cigarette after another. You are beginning to feel sick.

    A. You do nothing, fight off the smoke and hope that the driver will come and give him a warning.

    B. You angrily stare at him and hope that he will get the message soon.

    C. You say to the man, "I would appreciate it if you would stop smoking because it is making me sick. You know this is a no smoking section."

14. It is Saturday and you have just finished doing your chores. Now you would like to go out and play with your friends. Your mother, however, tells you that you are to babysit your younger sister for the afternoon.

    A. You say, "I would like to go out and play with my friends."

    B. You don't want to babysit, but you say, "Yes, mother."

    C. You ignore your mother's request and walk out of the house.

15. During an exam the student behind you asks for a kleenex. Since you have some, you pass one back. The teacher sees this and accuses you of cheating.

    A. You are upset, but say, "I'm sorry," and continue working on the exam.

    B. You tell the teacher that the student behind you asked for a Kleenex and that you passed one back.

    C. Realizing that only your friend can help you, you look back at your friend hoping that he will speak on your behalf.

16. Your best friend has continually borrowed money from you for several days and hasn't paid you back. Today you don't have the money and need a dollar to buy lunch. You ask your best friend for some money and are refused.

    A. Although you are hurt, you say nothing and decide that this is the end of your friendship.

    B. You say, "Isn't it great when you continually ask me for money and I give it to you? Well, from now on you can forget about asking me for any more money."

    C. You say, "I've been lending money to you for several days and it bugs me that you can't return the favor just once."

17. You are waiting in line at a store. The customer in front of you has been chatting to the cashier for at least five minutes. It is almost supper time and you are in a hurry to get home.
    A. You say nothing, and walk out of the store, without getting what you came for.
    B. You interrupt the cashier and the other customer and say, "Hey, don't you people think it's about time that you shut up? Can't you see that I've been waiting here for more than five minutes?"
    C. You say, "Excuse me, I have waited quite some time and would like to be served now."

18. Today is Wednesday and your science notebook is due on Friday. One of your friends who is behind in this subject asks to borrow your notebook to catch up. You need to do some more work on the notebook yourself.
    A. You lend your notebook for the sake of your friendship even though you have more work to do on it yourself.
    B. You say, "No, you may not have it. I still have work to do on it before Friday."
    C. You say, "Let me think about it," and then try to avoid him, hoping he will not ask you again.

19. You are waiting at the bus stop with a lot of packages. When the bus arrives it is almost full and you are lucky to get the last seat. After you sit down you notice that you have dropped one of your packages. When you leave your seat to pick it up, someone else takes your seat.
    A. You don't want to make a big fuss over a seat, so you say nothing and stand up in the aisle.
    B. You say, "Excuse me, that's my seat."
    C. You stare angrily at the person, hoping the person will get the message and give up the seat.

20. You and your classmate have just completed a school project together. You, however, have done most of the work. The teacher is very pleased, especially with the drawings you did. The teacher asks which one of you did the drawings. Before you can say anything, your classmate claims credit for doing them.
    A. You say, "That's not true. I did the drawings."
    B. You ignore what has been said because you don't want to embarrass your classmate in front of your teacher.
    C. You say to your teacher, "He is a liar," and say to your classmate, "I will never work on another project with you again."

21. Your teacher has told you that you have been doing very well in class
    lately, and that your grade will go up from the B you received on your
    first report card. She has said that you might get an A. Today you
    receive your final mark and discover with disbelief that it is still a
    B.
    A. You ask the teacher why you were given a B when you were told
       that your grade would be higher.
    B. You accept the fact that you received only a B, because you
       feel that you must have done something recently to change the
       teacher's mind.
    C. You say nothing to your teacher, but spread the word among
       your friends that your teacher lied to you.

22. You have agreed to babysit for your neighbor for 75¢ an hour. You
    don't really like the neighbor's kids because they always give you a
    hard time at bedtime. Tonight is worse than usual. When your neighbor
    comes home, he says that he will pay you only 50¢ an hour.
    A. You say nothing, take the 50¢ an hour, and decide that you
       will never babysit his kids again.
    B. You say, "You promised me 75¢ an hour. It is only fair that
       you give it to me."
    C. You accept the 50¢ an hour because it is better than nothing,
       and go home very unhappy.

23. You are playing baseball with your friends in the backyard. One of
    them accidentally breaks a neighbor's window. Later, when the neighbor
    comes home, you are called over and blamed for breaking the window.
    Your neighbor says, "I know you did it. Be more careful next time."
    A. You tell her that it was an accident, but that you didn't do
       it.
    B. You say nothing, but the next day break another window on
       purpose.
    C. You say, "Okay," and accept the blame so that your friend
       will not get in trouble.

24. Your mother's friend comes over to your house and asks you to run an
    errand for her. It's time to go to your swimming lesson and if you do
    this errand you will be late. To make matters worse, your mother
    supports her friend's request.
    A. You refuse to do the errand, and tell your mother's friend
       that she should do it herself.
    B. You say nothing and do the errand, even though you'll be late
       for your swimming lesson.
    C. You tell your mother and her friend that you have a swimming
       lesson, and that you will be late if you run this errand.

25. You and your two friends are hungry, so you go to the nearest snack
bar. The waitress takes your orders -- two hamburgers with the works,
and one without onion. You hate onions. When she brings back the
hamburgers, all three have onions on them.
    A. You say nothing, and scrape the onion off the hamburger.
    B. You call the waitress over and tell her that you ordered a
hamburger without onion. You ask her to get another one with
no onions.
    C. You get angry at the waitress and say, "You are dumb, lady.
I told you I didn't want any onions."

26. Your best friend has asked to borrow the ring that your parents gave
you for doing well in school last year. You value this ring very much
and don't want to lend it, even to your best friend.
    A. You say, "No, this ring is very special to me and I wouldn't
lend it to anyone."
    B. You don't want to hurt your friend, so you let your best
friend borrow the ring.
    C. You say, "Well, let me think about it," and then try your
best to avoid your friend so that you won't have to lend the
ring.

27. You are at the beach. It is very crowded but you find a very good spot
and place your towel there while you go swimming. When you get back to
your spot you find that someone has moved your towel and two people are
lying there.
    A. You say nothing, pick up your towel, and look for another
spot.
    B. You tell the people that you were there first, and ask them
to move to another spot.
    C. You say nothing but angrily stare at them, hoping that they
get the message and move to a different place.

28. After school you stop at the corner store to buy some candy. As soon
as you get outside, you realize that you have not been given the
correct change. You go back into the store and tell the cashier, but
are not believed.
    A. You say to the cashier, "You should believe me. I know that
you don't have to give me the five cents but I would
appreciate it."
    B. You tell the cashier that you will never come back to this
store again, and that you will tell your friends not to come
here, either.
    C. You forget about trying to correct the error, and tell
yourself that you won't let this happen again.

29. Your parents have just given you a new book. You proudly show it to your sister who immediately wants to borrow it for a day. You don't want to lend it at this time because you have not had a chance to read it yourself. Your sister, however, insists on borrowing it.
    A. You tell your sister that you don't want to lend it to her until you have had a chance to read it yourself.
    B. You say nothing and give the book to your sister, because you do not wish to argue with her.
    C. You get angry at your sister for asking to borrow something that is yours.

30. You went with your friend to the hospital after school because your friend sprained an ankle in Phys. Ed class. You are late for dinner and your father asks you for an explanation. You tell him the truth. He calls you a liar, and tells you to go to your room without supper.
    A. You go to your room, thinking that this is the only way to keep peace in your family.
    B. You again tell your father what happened and suggest that he call the hospital and your teacher.
    C. You say to your father, "I've had enough. I don't deserve this type of treatment. I won't go to my room."

31. You and your friend go over to a classmate's home. You don't know the classmate that well and her/his parents are not home. While watching TV the classmate offers you and your friend cigarettes. Your friend accepts and they light up. You don't want to smoke, but your friend and classmate tease you and laugh.
    A. You stand firm by simply saying, "No, I don't want to smoke, but I guess you're in the mood for some jokes."
    B. You don't really want to, but you do because you don't want them to laugh at you.
    C. You don't say anything, but get up and leave the house, not wanting to return.

32. A close friend of yours is nominated to be captain of the basketball team. Another player, whom you believe would make a better captain, is also nominated. You are to vote by raising your hand. If you do not vote for your friend, you may hurt your friend's feelings.
    A. You vote for the player who you believe will be the best captain.
    B. You don't want your close friend to feel hurt, so you say, "This is dumb, I'm not going to vote."
    C. All of a sudden you remember that you have something else to do, excuse yourself, and say, "Go ahead and vote without me."

33. You have been looking forward to going to your friend's place after school to listen to a new record, and your mother has given you her permission. You rush home from school, drop off your books, and are about to leave when you mother says, "I'd like you to vacuum the living room. We're going to have company tonight and I'm very busy."
    A. You pretend that you did not hear what your mother said and walk out.
    B. You say to your mother, "You told me I could go out. It's not fair to ask me to stay home at the last minute."
    C. You say to your mother, "You're always interrupting my plans," and rush out the door.

BEHAVIORAL SELF-CONCEPT SCALE (BSCS)

AUTHORS: Robert L. Williams and Edward A. Workman

PURPOSE: To measure children's self-concept.

DESCRIPTION: The BSCS is a 36-item instrument designed to measure children's school-related self-concept. The rationale for this instrument is that experiences in the classroom have a significant impact on the child's self-concept. The BSCS is actually a measure of behavioral self-concept in that children are asked to specify which member of 36 pairs of academic behaviors they are better at. The BSCS can be administered orally or in writing.

NORMS: The BSCS was initially developed on 86 male and female fourth and fifth grade students. No other demographic information or norms are provided.

SCORING: The respondent's self-concept for a specific activity is determined by summing the number of times a student ranks that activity over other activities. There appear to be four major activities—reading, mathematics, spelling and writing, and play, which includes drawing and singing. Higher scores indicate higher self-concept for that particular activity.

RELIABILITY: The BSCS has fair stability, with three-week test-retest correlations that range from .59 to .90. No data on internal consistency are available.

VALIDITY: No validity data were reported although the BSCS appears to have fair face and content validity for the specific academic areas selected.

PRIMARY REFERENCE: William, R. L. and Workman, E. A. (1978). The development of a behavioral self-concept scale, *Behavior Therapy* 9, 680–681. Instrument reproduced with permission of Robert L. Williams.

AVAILABILITY: Dr. Robert L. Williams, University of Tennessee, Educational and Counseling Psychology, Knoxville, TN 37996-3400.

BSCS

Instructions to be read to students: "All of us are better at some things than we are at others. The sheets I have given you describe activities we do at school. Each item lists two of those activities. As I read each item, underline the activity you're better at. For example, for item 1 if you are better at solving math problems in class than you are reading the language book at school, you would underline solving math problems in class. However, if you are better at reading the language book at school, what would you underline for that item? . . . That's correct. Now, do you have any questions as to what you are to do? . . . All right, let's actually do item 1."

1.	Solving math problems in class	Reading the language book at school
2.	Spelling	Writing school assignments
3.	Drawing in art class	Reading the science book at school
4.	Playing games during gym or recess	Singing in music class
5.	Reading the social studies book at school	Spelling
6.	Writing school assignments	Drawing in art class
7.	Reading the language book at school	Playing games during gym or recess
8.	Singing in music class	Solving math problems in class
9.	Reading the science book at school	Reading the social studies book at school
10.	Spelling	Drawing in art class
11.	Playing games during gym or recess	Writing school assignments
12.	Reading the language book at school	Singing in music class
13.	Solving math problems in class	Reading the science book at school
14.	Reading the social studies book at school	Playing games during gym or recess

15. Drawing in art class   Reading the language book at school

16. Singing in music class   Spelling

17. Writing school assignments   Solving math problems in class

18. Reading the science book at   Playing games during gym or recess
    school

19. Reading the language book at Reading the social studies book at
    school   school

20. Drawing in art class   Singing in music class

21. Spelling   Reading the science book at school

22. Solving math problems in class Reading the social studies book at
                                  school

23. Singing in music class   Writing school assignments

24. Playing games during gym or   Drawing in art class
    recess

25. Reading the science book at   Reading the language book at school
    school

26. Reading the social studies   Singing in music class
    book

27. Playing games during gym or   Spelling
    recess

28. Drawing in art class   Solving math problems in class

29. Reading the science book   Writing school assignments
    at school

30. Reading the language book at Spelling
    school

31. Reading the social studies   Drawing in art class
    book at school

32. Solving math problems in   Playing games during gym or recess
    school

33. Writing school assignments   Reading the language book at school

34. Singing in music class   Reading the science book at school

35. Spelling   Solving math problems in class

36. Writing school assignments   Reading the social studies book at
                                  school

CHILDREN'S ACTION TENDENCY SCALE (CATS)

AUTHOR: Robert H. Deluty

PURPOSE: To measure assertion in children.

DESCRIPTION: This 39-item instrument measures assertiveness, aggressiveness, and submission in children. The scale was originally developed with three pairs of possible responses to each of the 13 conflict situations; the three pairs of responses represent all combinations of assertive, aggressive, or submissive ways of behaving in the conflict. For each of the pairs of alternatives the child is asked to select one which best describes how he or she would behave. For young children, below a fourth or fifth grade level, the items can be read aloud, although this may require frequent repetition of the items. A valid short version can be created by eliminating situations "C," "L" and "M."

NORMS: The CATS was originally tested on a sample of 46 parochial school children from grades three, four and six. There was a total of 27 boys and 19 girls. The mean aggressiveness score for boys was 7.93 and 5.05 for girls. The average assertiveness scores were 14.48 for boys and 16.21 for girls. The average submissiveness score was 7.59 for boys and 8.74 for girls.

SCORING: The respondent is instructed to read both alternatives in each item and circle the one alternative from each pair that is most like how they would behave. Scores on each of the three dimensions are the total number of aggressive, assertive, and submissive alternatives circled as coded in parentheses next to each stituation. Since each situation has all possible combinations of aggressive, assertive and submissive responses, a child could select any one type of alternative twice. For this reason scores on the scales range from 0 to 29, but all three scales must total 39 for the long form. Higher scores reflect more aggression, assertion, and submission.

RELIABILITY: Reliability has been estimated with internal consistency and test-retest reliability methods. The coefficients of internal consistency using split-half reliability were .77, .63, and .72 for the aggressiveness, assertiveness, and submission scales. Test-retest reliability over a four-week interval was .48, .60, and .57. While the test-retest reliability may seem low, for a children's measure over a four-week period, this is acceptable.

VALIDITY: The CATS generally has very good validity data. Concurrent validity is demonstrated in correlations with scores on a self-esteem measure, and peer and teacher rating of interpersonal behavior. Scores also discriminate between samples of clinically aggressive and normal subjects. Behavioral observations also provide validity support.

PRIMARY REFERENCE: Deluty, R. H. (1979). Children's Action Tendency Scale: A self reported measure of aggressiveness, assertiveness, and submissiveness in children, *Journal of Consulting and Clinical Psychology* 47, 1061–1071. Instrument reproduced with permission of Robert Deluty and the American Psychological Association.

AVAILABILITY: Robert H. Deluty, Ph.D., Division of Child Psychiatry, Children's Memorial Hospital, 2300 Children's Plaza, Chicago, IL 60614

CATS

Below are thirteen situations. After each you are asked what you would
do in that situation by selecting *one* of the two pairs of answers.
Indicate your answer by circling either alternative "a" or alternative "b."
Remember to select one answer for each of the 36 pairs of choices. We
are concerned with what you *would* do and not with what you *should* do.
There are no "right" or "wrong" answers. You are not going to be graded
on this, so please be honest.

A. You're playing a game with your friends. You try your very best but
    you keep making mistakes. Your friends start teasing you and calling
    you names. What would you do?

    1. a. Punch the kid who's teasing me the most, *or* (Agg)
        b. Quit the game and come home (Sub)

    2. a. Tell them to stop because they wouldn't like it if I did it (As)
           to them, *or*
        b. Punch the kid who's teasing me the most

    3. a. Quit the game and come home, *or*
        b. Tell them to stop because they wouldn't like it if I did it
           to them

B. You and a friend are playing in your house. Your friend makes a big
    mess, but your parents blame you and punish you. What would you do?

    4. a. Ask my friend to help me clean up the mess, *or* (As)
        b. Refuse to talk to or listen to my parents the next day (Agg)

    5. a. Clean up the mess, *or* (Sub)
        b. Ask my friend to help me clean up the mess

    6. a. Refuse to talk to or listen to my parents the next day, *or*
        b. Clean up the mess

C. One morning before class, a friend comes over to you and asks if they
    can copy your homework. They tell you that if you don't give them
    your answers, they'll tell everyone that you're really mean. What
    would you do?

    7. a. Tell them to do their own work, *or* (As)
        b. Give them the answers (Sub)

    8. a. Tell them that I'll tell everyone they're a cheater, *or* (Agg)
        b. Tell them to do their own work

    9. a. Give them the answers, *or*
        b. Tell them that I'll tell everyone they're a cheater.

D. You're standing in line for a drink of water. A kid your age and size walks over and just shoves you out of line. What would you do?

   10. a. Push the kid back out of line, *or* (Agg)
        b. Tell the kid, "You've no right to do that." (As)

   11. a. I'd go to the end of the line, *or* (Sub)
        b. Push the kid back out of line

   12. a. Tell the kid, "You've no right to do that," *or*
        b. I'd go to the end of the line

E. You lend a friend your favorite book. A few days later it is returned, but some of the pages are torn and the cover is dirty and bent out of shape. What would you do?

   13. a. Ask my friend, "How did it happen?" *or* (As)
        b. Call the kid names (Agg)

   14. a. Ignore it, *or* (Sub)
        b. Ask my friend, "How did it happen?"

   15. a. Call the kid names, *or*
        b. Ignore it.

F. You're coming out of school. A kid who is smaller and younger than you are throws a snowball right at your head. What would you do?

   16. a. Beat the kid up, *or* (Agg)
        b. Ignore it (Sub)

   17. a. Tell the kid that throwing at someone's head is very dangerous, *or*
        b. Beat the kid up

   18. a. Ignore it, *or*
        b. Tell the kid that throwing at someone's head is very dangerous

G. You see some kids playing a game. You walk over and ask if you can join. They tell you that you can't play with them because you're not good enough. What would you do?

   19. a. Ask them to give me a chance, *or* (As)
        b. Walk away, feeling hurt (Sub)

   20. a. Interfere with their game so that they won't be able to play, *or* (A
        b. Ask them to give me a chance

   21. a. Walk away, feeling hurt, *or*
        b. Interfere with their game so that they won't be able to play

H. You're watching a really terrific show on television. In the middle of the show, your parents tell you that it's time for bed and turn off the TV. What would you do?

22. a. Scream at them, "I don't want to!" *or* (Agg)
    b. Start crying (Sub)

23. a. Promise to go to bed early tomorrow night if they let me stay (As) up late tonight, *or*
    b. Scream at them, "I don't want to!"

24. a. Start crying, *or*
    b. Promise to go to bed early tomorrow night if they let me stay up late tonight.

I. You're having lunch in the cafeteria. Your friend has a big bag of delicious chocolates for dessert. You ask if you can have just one, but your friend says, "No." What would you do?

25. a. Offer to trade something of mine for the chocolate, *or* (As)
    b. Call the kid mean and selfish (Agg)

26. a. Forget about it and continue eating my lunch, *or* (Sub)
    b. Offer to trade something of mine for the chocolate

27. a. Call the kid mean and selfish, *or*
    b. Forget about it and continue eating my lunch

J. A kid in your class brags that they're much smarter than you. However, you know for sure that the kid is wrong and that really you're smarter. What would you do?

28. a. Tell the kid to shut up, *or* (Agg)
    b. Suggest that we ask each other questions to find out who is smarter (As)

29. a. Ignore the kid and just walk away, *or* (Sub)
    b. Tell the kid to shut up

30. a. Suggest that we ask each other questions to find out who is smarter, *or*
    b. Ignore the kid and just walk away

K. You and another kid are playing a game. The winner of the game will win a really nice prize. You try very hard, but lose by just one point. What would you do?

31. a. Tell the kid that they cheated, *or* (Agg)
     b. Practice, so I'll win the next time (As)

32. a. Go home and cry, *or* (Sub)
     b. Tell the kid that they cheated

33. a. Practice, so I'll win the next time, *or*
     b. Go home and cry

L. Your parents do something that really bugs you. They know that it bugs you, but they just ignore how you feel and keep doing it anyway. What would you do?

34. a. Get back at them by doing something that bugs them, *or* (Agg)
     b. Tell them that they are bugging me (As)

35. a. Try to ignore it, *or* (Sub)
     b. Get back at them by doing something that bugs them

36. a. Tell them that they are bugging me, *or*
     b. Try to ignore it

M. You're playing with a friend in your house and you're making a lot of noise. You parents get really angry and start yelling at you for making so much noise. What would you do?

37. a. Find something else to do, *or* (Sub)
     b. Ignore their yelling and continue to make noise (Agg)

38. a. Tell them, "I'm sorry, but I can't play the game without making noise," *or* (As)
     b. Find something else to do

39. a. Ignore their yelling and continue to make noise, *or*
     b. Tell them, "I'm sorry, but I can't play the game without making noise."

CHILDREN'S COGNITIVE ASSESSMENT QUESTIONNAIRE (CCAQ)

AUTHORS: Sheri Zatz and Laurie Chassin

PURPOSE: To measure the cognitions associated with test anxiety.

DESCRIPTION: This 40-item instrument measures self-defeating and self-enhancing cognitions associated with test anxiety. The instrument was originally developed for hypothesis testing on the relationship of cognition to test anxiety and task performance. The theoretical perspective asserts that self-defeating thoughts inhibit one's performance while self-enhancing thoughts facilitate performance. The CCAQ focuses on negative evaluations (NSE) and positive evaluations (PSE) as reflecting self-defeating and self-enhancing cognitions, respectively. It also assesses self-distracting thoughts (called off-task thoughts; OFFT) and cognitions which focus one's attention to the task (called on-task thoughts; ONT). The four aspects of the CCAQ are to be used as subscales. The CCAQ is particularly useful for practitioners in school settings or residential programs where academic performance is frequently found to be an antecedent to clinical problems and in cognitive therapy.

NORMS: The CCAQ was developed on a sample of 294 fifth and sixth grade children. Fifty-seven percent were female, 89 percent were white, and 55 were from working class families. Subjects were screened for test anxiety and were categorized into three groups: low anxiety (n = 69), moderate anxiety (n = 106) and high anxiety (n = 119). The mean scores on the negative evaluation subscale were .6, 1.4 and 2.7 for the low, moderate and high anxious subsamples, respectively. Off-task thought means were 2.2, 3.5, and 4.4 for the three respective groups. Mean scores on the positive evaluation subscale were 6.1, 5.7, and 5.2 for the three groups. The mean scores on the on-task thoughts subscale were 5.8, 6.9, and 6.4 for the low, moderate, and high anxious subsamples.

SCORING: Each of the 40 items is answered True or False. Total scores for the four subscales are the number of times answered "true," and they range from 0 to 10. Higher scores reflect more thoughts associated with test anxiety.

RELIABILITY: The subscales had moderate to good internal consistency: PSE .74, NSE .82, ONT .67, OFFT .72. Test-retest reliability correlations for a six-week period were PSE .71, NSE .69, ONT .69, OFFT .63, which are fairly strong for a children's instrument measured over such a long period.

VALIDITY: The validity of the CCAQ was tested with known-groups procedures. The group of highly anxious children scored differently from less anxious children on all four subscales of the CCAQ. In general, the more anxious children revealed more negative evaluation and off-task thought, and less anxious children scored higher on positive evaluation. The CCAQ subscales have good concurrent validity, with subscales correlating with test anxiety. For the sample of females, only the NSE and OFFT scores correlated with test anxiety.

PRIMARY REFERENCE: Zatz, S. and Chassin, L. (1983). Cognitions of test-anxious children, *Journal of Consulting and Clinical Psychology* 51, 526–534. Instrument reproduced with permission of the American Psychological Association.

AVAILABILITY: Journal article.

CCAQ

Listed below are four sets of statements. Indicate whether each is true or false of your thoughts while taking the test by circling T or F.

Negative evaluations

T	F	The others probably think I'm dumb.
T	F	I have a bad memory.
T	F	I'm doing poorly.
T	F	I can't do this--I give up.
T	F	Everyone usually does better than me.
T	F	I must be making many mistakes.
T	F	I don't do well on tests like this.
T	F	I am too dumb to do this.
T	F	I'm doing worse than the others.
T	F	I really feel stupid.

Off-task thoughts

T	F	I wish I were playing with my friends.
T	F	I am nervous and worried.
T	F	I wish I were home.
T	F	I wish this was over.
T	F	My mind keeps wandering.
T	F	I keep on daydreaming.
T	F	I wonder what the examiner is going to find out about me.
T	F	I can't seem to sit still.
T	F	Pretty soon I'll get to do something else.
T	F	I am hungry.

Positive evaluations

T F   I am fast enough to finish this.
T F   I do well on tests like this.
T F   I usually do better than the others.
T F   I am bright enough to do this.
T F   This test is easy for me to do.
T F   I am doing the best that I can.
T F   I usually catch on quickly to new things.
T F   I am doing better than the others.
T F   I am sure to do fine on this.
T F   I am able to do well on different things.

On-task thoughts

T F   Stay calm and relaxed.
T F   The harder it gets, the more I need to try.
T F   Try a different plan.
T F   One step at a time.
T F   I have a plan to solve this.
T F   Keep looking for a solution.
T F   Work faster.
T F   Pay attention.
T F   I've almost got it now--keep working.
T F   Don't think about anything but solving the problem.

CHILDREN'S LONELINESS QUESTIONNAIRE (CLQ)

AUTHOR: Steven R. Asher

PURPOSE: To measure children's feelings of loneliness.

DESCRIPTION: The CLQ includes 16 primary items focused on children's feelings of loneliness, feelings of social adequacy versus inadequacy, and subjective estimations of peer status. Eight "filler" items that ask about children's hobbies and other activities are included to help children feel more relaxed and open about expressing their feelings. Specific instructions, including the way children are taught to use the 5-point scale, are available in Asher et al. (1984). In addition to identifying children who feel lonely, this instrument may be used to examine variables related to that loneliness.

NORMS: A study of an earlier version of the questionnaire was conducted on third to sixth grade children. After modifying the questionnaire, more recent data were collected from 200 children in the third to sixth grades in one elementary school. These children included 89 girls and 111 boys; 80% were white, 16% black, and 4% Asian or Hispanic. All socioeconomic groups seemed represented. No actual norms have been reported yet.

SCORING: Items 2, 5, 7, 11, 13, 15, 19 and 23 are the "filler" items and are not scored. Scores for the 16 5-point items are totaled, producing a potential range of 16 to 80. Items 6, 9, 12, 14, 17, 18, 20, 21 and 24 are reverse-scored. Higher scores reflect more loneliness.

RELIABILITY: The CLQ has excellent internal consistency with an alpha of .90 for the 16 primary items. A one year test-retest correlation of .55 suggests fairly good long-term stability.

VALIDITY: The major form of validity reported on the CLQ is a type of known-groups validity: the CLQ was significantly and negatively correlated with positive social status (lower loneliness associated with higher status) and positively correlated with negative status. In addition, the CLQ distinguished between rejected children and children from other status groups (neglected, controversial, and popular).

PRIMARY REFERENCE: Asher, S. R. and Wheeler, V. A. (1985). Children's loneliness: A comparison of rejected and neglected peer status, *Journal of Consulting and Clinical Psychology* 53, 500–505. Instrument reproduced with permission of Steven R. Asher and the American Psychological Association.

AVAILABILITY: Dr. Steven R. Asher, University of Illinois, Bureau of Educational Research, 1310 South Sixth Street, Champaign, IL 61820.

CLQ

Below are 24 statements. Please read each statement and indicate how true it is for you using the following rating scale:

> 1 = That's always true about me
> 2 = That's true about me most of the time
> 3 = That's sometimes true about me
> 4 = That's hardly ever true about me
> 5 = That's not true at all about me

Please record your answer in the space to the left of each item.

___ 1. It's easy for me to make new friends at school.
___ 2. I like to read.
___ 3. I have nobody to talk to in my class.
___ 4. I'm good at working with other children in my class.
___ 5. I watch TV a lot.
___ 6. It's hard for me to make friends at school.
___ 7. I like school.
___ 8. I have lots of friends in my class.
___ 9. I feel alone at school.
___ 10. I can find a friend in my class when I need one.
___ 11. I play sports a lot.
___ 12. It's hard to get kids in school to like me.
___ 13. I like science.
___ 14. I don't have anyone to play with at school.
___ 15. I like music.
___ 16. I get along with my classmates.
___ 17. I feel left out of things at school.
___ 18. There are no other kids I can go to when I need help in school.
___ 19. I like to paint and draw.
___ 20. I don't get along with other children in school.
___ 21. I'm lonely at school.
___ 22. I am well liked by the kids in my class.
___ 23. I like playing board games a lot.
___ 24. I don't have any friends in class.

CHILDREN'S PERCEIVED SELF-CONTROL (CPSC) SCALE

AUTHOR: Laura Lynn Humphrey

PURPOSE: To measure children's perceptions of their self-control.

DESCRIPTION: This 11-item instrument measures self-control from a cognitive-behavioral perspective. The theory asserts that self-control is a personal competency which can solidify treatment gains and promote health and adjustment in children. Self-control includes problem recognition, commitment, protracted self-regulation, and habit reorganization. The instrument has subscales which measure three aspects of self-control: interpersonal self control (ISC), personal self-control (PSC), and self evaluation (SE). Total scores on the CPSC can also be used. The measure has a similar form developed for teachers' assessment of a child's self-control.

NORMS: The CPSC was developed on a sample of suburban, middle class, fourth and fifth graders (372 boys and 391 girls). For boys, the mean scores were 4.96, 2.12, and 1.37 on the ISC, PSC and SE subscales; the mean on the total CPSC was 5.34 with a standard deviation of 3.08. For girls the mean scores were 5.92, 2.32, and 1.39 on the ISC, PSC and SE; the mean of the total scale was 5.82 with a standard deviation of 2.17.

SCORING: Each item is answered as either 1, "usually yes" or 0, "usually no," according to whether the content describes the child. Items reflecting poor self-control are reverse-scored. Total scores range from 0 to 11, with higher scores reflecting more self-control. Subscale items are: ISC: 1, 2, 3, 4; PSC: 5, 6, 7; SE: 8 and 9 and ranges are 0 to 4, 0 to 3, and 0 to 2, respectively.

RELIABILITY: Reliability is reported in terms of test-retest correlations over a two to three-week period. Total scores correlated .71, while the subscales were correlated as follows: ISC .63, PSC .63, SE. 56. No data on internal consistency were reported.

VALIDITY: The concurrent validity evidence has been minimal. Scores on the total CPSC were not correlated with several expected criteria. Correlations were high, however, between the ISC and naturalistic observations, although scores were uncorrelated with the Child Behavior Rating Score on academic achievement.

PRIMARY REFERENCE: Humphrey, L. L. (1982). Children's and teachers' perspectives on children's self-control: The development of two rating scales, *Journal of Consulting and Clinical Psychology* 50, 624–633. Instrument reproduced with permission of Laura Humphrey and the American Psychological Association.

AVAILABILITY: Laura Humphrey, Ph.D., Department of Psychiatry, Northwestern University Medical School, 320 E. Huron, Chicago, IL 60611.

CPSC

Below are eleven statements. Please consider each in terms of whether it is usually true for you or not. Answer each according to the following scale:

1 = Usually yes
0 = Usually no

Record your answer in the space to the left of the statement.

___ 1. If someone bothers me when I'm busy I ignore him/her.
___ 2. When the teacher is busy I talk to my friends.
___ 3. When someone pushes me I fight them.
___ 4. I think about other things while I work.
___ 5. It's hard to keep working when my friends are having fun.
___ 6. It's hard to wait for something I want.
___ 7. I make mistakes because I work too fast.
___ 8. I know when I'm doing something wrong without someone telling me.
___ 9. If my work is too hard I switch to something else.
___ 10. After I do something it's hard to tell what will happen next.
___ 11. It's hard for me to finish my work if I don't like it.

COMMON BELIEF INVENTORY FOR STUDENTS (CBIS)

AUTHORS: Stephen R. Hooper and C. Clinton Layne

PURPOSE: To measure rationality in children.

DESCRIPTION: The CBIS is a 44-item instrument that was developed to measure the eleven irrational beliefs that Albert Ellis suggests are commonly held by people in general. Although total scores on this instrument can be used, each of the eleven beliefs is related to four items on the scale and each of the eleven can be scored separately. The numbers in parentheses on the instrument correspond with each of the eleven beliefs. (To summarize, the beliefs are as follows: 1. the idea one must be loved by everyone; 2. the idea one must be thoroughly competent; 3. the belief that certain people are wicked and warrant punishment; 4. the belief that it is awful and catastrophic when things do not go your way; 5. the idea that human happiness is determined by external events and not within human control; 6. the idea that if something is dangerous or fearsome, one should be concerned about it; 7. the belief that it is easier to avoid than to face certain of life's difficulties; 8. the belief that one should be dependent on others; 9. the idea that one's past history determines one's present behavior; 10. the belief that one should be quite upset over others' problems or disturbances; 11. the idea that there are perfect solutions to human problems and that it is catastrophic if the solutions are not found.) Although the CBIS is a relatively new instrument, it appears to hold much promise for standardized clinical assessment of rational thinking in children. All of the items are constructed so that the more one adheres to any of the statements (the higher the score), the more irrational the thinking. The authors are currently in the process of examining the factor structure of the CBIS, with plans to transform the scores on the CBIS into standard score units, thus allowing practitioners to compare CBIS scores with other standardized measures.

NORMS: The CBIS was initially developed using two groups of fourth through seventh graders totaling several thousand boys and girls. Newer data have been collected on a sample of 1500 fourth through seventh graders to further examine and perhaps standardize the CBIS. Actual norms are not available, but for one sample of 1226 students, the mean overall score was 74.4, with means on the individual beliefs ranging from 4.4 to 8.1.

SCORING: Each item is scored on a scale from 0 to 4; the 4 items pertaining to each of the eleven beliefs are summed to obtain the score for that belief, and all 44 items are summed to obtain the total score. Total scores can range from 0 to 176.

RELIABILITY: The CBIS has excellent internal consistency, with an alpha of .85 for the total scale and split-half reliability of .88. The CBIS also has excellent stability with test-retest correlations of .84 over a six-week period.

VALIDITY: The CBIS has demonstrated fair concurrent validity in correlating significantly with the FCMAS which measures trait anxiety in children. The CBIS also was found in two studies to be sensitive to clinical changes following treatment using rational therapy techniques.

PRIMARY REFERENCE: Hooper, S. R. and Layne, C. C. (1983). The Common Belief Inventory for Students: A measure of rationality in children, *Journal of Personality Assessment*, 47, 85–90. Instrument reproduced with permission of Stephen R. Hooper. The authors would appreciate correspondence from other investigators using the CBI and would be happy to serve as consultants.

AVAILABILITY: Dr. Stephen R. Hooper, Bradley Hospital, Department of Psychology, 1011 Veterans Memorial Parkway, East Providence, RI 02915.

CBIS

The following are common beliefs which most people your age think.   Please
indicate the number that shows how often you think that belief. Remember,
this is about how you usually think. Please take your time and answer every
question.

> 0 = Never (0%)
> 1 = Sometimes (25%)
> 2 = Half the time (50%)
> 3 = Almost always (75%)
> 4 = Always (100%)

___ 1. If a person doesn't have any friends, that means that nobody likes him. (1)
___ 2. I believe I should be different from what I am. (9)
___ 3. I should be a better person. (7)
___ 4. I believe I need to change some things about myself. (9)
___ 5. I believe I should be smarter than I am. (7)
___ 6. I believe that I should be better looking. (7)
___ 7. A person who doesn't have any friends has got to be unhappy. (1)
___ 8. I worry about many things. (6)
___ 9. It's only human to be upset when things don't go my way. (5)
___ 10. I believe that it helps to worry about some things. (6)
___ 11. I am unlucky. (11)
___ 12. I believe I need to always think of other peoples' feelings first instead of my own. (10)
___ 13. I believe I need more confidence in myself. (2)
___ 14. I feel bad about many things that I have done. (4)
___ 15. I feel bad when I fail at something. (2)
___ 16. I believe I would like myself better if I had more friends. (2)
___ 17. I worry about what other people are thinking about me. (1)
___ 18. I always get upset if something important doesn't go the way I want. (4)
___ 19. I believe some people don't treat me the way they ought to. (5)
___ 20. Most of the time when I get upset it's because someone else made me mad or hurt my feelings. (5)
___ 21. I believe that how other people treat me makes a difference in how much I like myself. (5)
___ 22. I believe that I am selfish because I usually please myself first and other people second. (10)
___ 23. If a close friend has his feelings hurt, and if I feel badly too, then that tells me how much I really like that person. (10)
___ 24. I believe that everyone should always know what they want to do in life. (11)
___ 25. I believe that what a person does tells me everything about that person. (9)
___ 26. Sometimes things happen to me that just shouldn't happen. (11)
___ 27. When I make a mistake I feel awful. (2)
___ 28. People have no right to make me feel bad. (3)
___ 29. It's terrible when people make fun of me. (1)
___ 30. People who do bad things should always be punished. (3)

___ 31. Children who don't do their school work should always be punished. (3)
___ 32. Kids who do bad things are bad people. (3)
___ 33. I feel awful if I don't get what I want. (4)
___ 34. School is terrible if I don't do well. (4)
___ 35. I always worry about how well I am doing in school. (10)
___ 36. I am always afraid that dogs will bite me. (6)
___ 37. I can't work alone. (8)
___ 38. It's easier to quit a game I am losing than to finish it. (8)
___ 39. I believe that it is better for my parents to do the things that are hard for me to do. (8)
___ 40. I always have trouble doing things by myself. (8)
___ 41. I always need other people to tell me how to do things. (8)
___ 42. I feel terrible when my friends get yelled at in school. (11)
___ 43. Things should always turn out the way I plan them. (11)
___ 44. Life isn't as good as it should be because of things that happened when I was little. (9)

COMPULSIVE EATING SCALE (CES)

AUTHORS: Dona M. Kagan and Rose L. Squires

PURPOSE: To measure uncontrollable eating.

DESCRIPTION: This 8-item instrument measures compulsive eating which is associated with obesity. More specifically, the CES assesses the inability to control one's eating behaviors in terms of overeating and eating during times when one is not necessarily hungry. The CES is one of the few instruments on eating which was developed for high school students and for males and females, alike. It is also appropriate for adults.

NORMS: The CES was developed on a sample of over 2000 high school students. Normative data were not reported.

SCORING: All items are rated on 5-point scales, but have different categories for various items. The letters used in the rating are converted to numbers as follows: a = 1, b = 2, c = 3, d = 4 and e = 5. Scores are the sum of the item ratings, and range from 8 to 40. Higher scores indicate more compulsivity in one's eating.

RELIABILITY: The CES was tested for internal consistency using Cronbach's alpha. The coefficient was .75 which is only fair. There is no evidence of test-retest reliability.

VALIDITY: The CES was first utilized in research on the prevalence of eating disorders among high school students. The measure predicted differences among subjects categorized as normal eaters, borderline eaters and disordered eaters. Support for the instrument's concurrent validity is found with correlations with self-discipline and rebelliousness.

PRIMARY REFERENCE: Kagan, D. M. and Squires, R. L. (1984). Eating disorders among adolescents: Patterns and prevalence. *Adolescence* 19, 15–29. Instrument reproduced with permission of Dona M. Kagan and Libra Publishers.

AVAILABILITY: Journal article.

CES

How often do you do each of the following activities? Circle the one answer for each question that comes closest to describing you.

1. Eat because you are feeling lonely.
   a. Never   b. Once or twice a year   c. Once a month   d. Once a week
   e. More than once a week

2. Feel completely out of control when it comes to food.
   a. Never   b. Once or twice a year   c. Once a month   d. Once a week
   e. More than once a week

3. Eat so much that your stomach hurts.
   a. Never   b. Once or twice a year   c. Once a month   d. Once a week
   e. More than once a week

4. Eat too much because you are upset or nervous.
   a. Never   b. Once or twice a year   c. Once a month   d. Once a week
   e. More than once a week

5. Eat too much because you are bored.
   a. Never   b. Once or twice a year   c. Once a month   d. Once a week
   e. More than once a week

6. Go out with friends just for the purpose of over-stuffing yourselves with food.
   a. Never   b. Once or twice a year   c. Once a month   d. Once a week
   e. More than once a week

7. Eat so much food so fast that you don't know how much you ate or how it tasted.
   a. Never   b. Once or twice a year   c. Once a month   d. Once a week
   e. More than once a week

8. Get out of bed at night, go into the kitchen, and finish the remains of some delicious food, because you knew it was there.
   a. Never   b. Once or twice a year   c. Once a month   d. Once a week
   e. More than once a week

CONCERN OVER WEIGHT AND DIETING SCALE (COWD)

AUTHORS: Dona M. Kagan and Rose L. Squires

PURPOSE: To measure dieting behavior.

DESCRIPTION: This 14-item instrument measures concerns over weight and dieting as symptoms of eating disorders. The instrument was originally developed in a study of the prevalence rate of eating disorders in high school students, and its clinical utility has yet to be established. The COWD was found to be independent of compulsive eating, suggesting a concern over one's weight and dieting are not a consequence of compulsive eating. The COWD is most useful with bulimic and anorectic clients, or clients who self-impose restrictive diets.

NORMS: The COWD was developed on a sample of over 2000 high school students. Normative data are not available.

SCORING: All items are rated on 5-point scales, although there are different response categories for various items. The letters used in rating one's responses are converted to the following numeric values: a = 1, b = 2, c = 3, d = 4 and e = 5. Scores are the sum of all item responses and range from 14 to 70. Higher scores indicate greater concern over one's weight and diet.

RELIABILITY: The COWD was tested for internal consistency using Cronbach's alpha. The instrument has very good reliability, with a correlation coefficient of .88. There is no reported evidence of test-retest reliability.

VALIDITY: Evidence of known-groups validity is found with differences in COWD scores for subjects categorized as normal eaters, borderline eaters, and disordered eaters. The COWD also has good evidence of concurrent validity correlating with self-discipline and rebelliousness.

PRIMARY REFERENCE: Kagan, D. M. and Squires, R. L. (1984). Eating disorders among adolescents: Patterns and prevalence, *Adolescence* 19, 15–29. Instrument reproduced with permission of Dona Kagan and Libra Publications.

AVAILABILITY: Journal article.

COWD

For the following questions please answer each by circling the alternative that is most true for you.

1. The worst thing about being fat is:
   a. No opinion   b. Getting teased   c. Feeling unsexy
   d. Being unpopular   e. Feeling bad about yourself

2. What is the greatest amount of weight you ever lost on a diet?
   a. Never on a diet   b. 10 lbs   c. 11-19 lbs   d. 20-29 lbs.
   e. 30 lbs or more

3. Do you think you are overweight now?
   a. Don't know   b. No   c. Yes: by less than 10 lbs   d. Yes: 10-19 lbs
   e. Yes: by 20 lbs or more

4. How often do you skip one meal so you will lose weight?
   a. Never   b. Once or twice a year   c. Once a month   d. Once a week
   e. More than once a week

5. How often do you avoid eating fattening foods like candy so you will lose weight?
   a. Never   b. Once or twice a year   c. Once a month   d. Once a week
   e. More than once a week

6. How often do you hate yourself or feel guilty because you cannot stop overeating?
   a. Never   b. Once or twice a year   c. Once a month   d. Once a week
   e. More than once a week

7. How often do you go without eating solid food for 24 hours or more so you will lose weight?
   a. Never   b. Once or twice a year   c. Once a month   d. Once a week
   e. More than once a week

8. If a special weight-control course were offered at this school, would you take it?
   a. No opinion   b. No   c. Probably no   d. Probably yes
   e. Definitely yes

9. How often do you feel guilty after eating?
   a. Never   b. Once in a while   c. Frequently   d. Very frequently
   e. All the time

10. How often are you aware of the calorie content of the food you eat?
    a. Never   b. Once in a while   c. Frequently   d. Very frequently
    e. All the time

11. How old were you when you first started worrying about your weight?
     a. Never   b. 12 years or less   c. 13-14 years   d. 15-16 years
     e. 17-18 years

How many times have you tried each of the weight-loss methods listed
below?

12. Diet medicine (pills, liquids, or powders).
     a. Never   b. Once   c. Twice   d. Three times
     e. More than three times

13. Health spa or exercise class (including aerobic dancing).
     a. Never   b. Once   c. Twice   d. Three times
     e. More than three times

14. Diet published in a book or magazine or recommended by a friend or
     relative.
     a. Never   b. Once   c. Twice   d. Three times
     e. More than three times

DEPRESSION SELF-RATING SCALE (DSRS)

AUTHOR: Peter Birleson

PURPOSE: To measure the extent and severity of depression in children.

DESCRIPTION: The DSRS is an 18-item scale designed specifically to measure depression in children between the ages of 7 and 13. Because of the age group, the items on the scale are written in particularly simple language and responses categories are not complicated. Initial items were developed by identifying from the literature items associated with depressive symptomatology in childhood. Bias due to response set is avoided by wording some items positively and some negatively. The scale includes items dealing with mood, physiological and somatic complaints, and cognitive aspects of depression. The DSRS has a rough cutting score of 13 which was found to discriminate between depressed and nondepressed children.

NORMS: The initial study (referenced below) was conducted on four groups of children (N = 53), including depressed and nondepressed children from a child psychiatric clinic, and children from a residential school for "maladjusted children" and a "normal" school in Britain. A second study (Asarnow and Carlson, 1985) was conducted on 85 consecutively admitted child psychiatric inpatients in the United States (this study used a modified scale with additional items but analyzed data based on the original 18-item scale). The intial study was divided fairly evenly between boys and girls across the range of all income groups. The second study contained 22 girls and 60 boys from a wide range of socioeconomic levels (63 white, 9 black, and 10 Hispanic respondents).

SCORING: The DSRS items are scored on a 3-point scale, with positively worded items ranging from 0 to 2 and negatively worded items ranging from 2 to 0. These responses are totaled, so the range of possible scores is 0 to 36.

RELIABILITY: Alphas in the two studies were .86 and .73, indicating fair internal consistency. The test-retest reliability coefficient was .80, showing good stability.

VALIDITY: The DSRS has good concurrent validity correlating .81 with the Children's Depression Inventory. In both studies, the DSRS showed good known-groups validity, significantly discriminating between depressed and nondepressed children with very few false positive errors (classifying nondepressed children as depressed).

PRIMARY REFERENCE: Birlsen, Peter (1981). The validity of depression disorders in childhood and the development of a self-rating scale: A research report, *Journal of Child Psychology and Psychiatry* 22, 73–88. Instrument reproduced with permission of Peter Birleson and Pergamon Press.

AVAILABILITY: Dr. Peter Birleson, Royal Children's Hospital, Fleminton Road, Parkville, Victoria 3052, Australia

DSRS

Please answer as honestly as you can by indicating at left the number that best refers to how you have felt over the past week. There are no right answers; it is important to say how *you* have felt.

1 = Most of the time
2 = Sometimes
3 = Never

____ 1. I look forward to things as much as I used to.
____ 2. I sleep very well.
____ 3. I feel like crying.
____ 4. I like to go out to play.
____ 5. I feel like running away.
____ 6. I get tummy aches.
____ 7. I have lots of energy.
____ 8. I enjoy my food.
____ 9. I can stick up for myself.
____ 10. I think life isn't worth living.
____ 11. I am good at things I do.
____ 12. I enjoy the things I do as much as I used to.
____ 13. I like talking with my family.
____ 14. I have horrible dreams.
____ 15. I feel very lonely.
____ 16. I am easily cheered up.
____ 17. I feel so sad I can hardly stand it.
____ 18. I feel very bored.

HARE SELF-ESTEEM SCALE (HSS)

AUTHOR: Bruce R. Hare

PURPOSE: To measure self-esteem in school age children.

DESCRIPTION: The HSS is a 30-item instrument that measures self-esteem of school age children 10 years old and above. The HSS consists of three 10-item subscales that are arena-specific (peer, school, and home) and presented as distinct units. The sum of all 30 items is viewed as a general self-esteem measure. Items were chosen to include both self-evaluative and other-evaluative items. The items are also intended to induce respondents to report a general sense of the self-feeling within each arena. The rationale for concluding that the sum of the three subscales produces an overall measure of self-esteem is that peer, home, and school are the major areas of interaction for the child in which he or she develops a sense of self-worth. Thus, they represent something close to the child's universe for self-evaluation. The HSS can be administered individually or in groups, orally or in writing.

NORMS: The HSS was tested on fifth and eighth graders. Subsamples included 41 blacks and 207 whites, 115 boys and 137 girls. Means for all the subsamples are available; the mean ranges from 90.4 to 95 with a group mean of 91.1 for all subsamples.

SCORING: After reverse-scoring negatively worded items, the items for the subscales are summed using the following scale: a = 1, b = 2, c = 3, d = 4. The three subscale scores are totaled to produce the score for the general self-esteem scale. Higher scores indicate higher self-esteem.

RELIABILITY: No internal consistency data are reported. Test-retest correlations indicate fair stability with three-month correlations ranging from .56 to .65 for the three subscales and .74 for the general scale.

VALIDITY: The HSS general scale correlated .83 with both the Coopersmith Self-Esteem Inventory and the Rosenberg Self-Esteem Scale, indicating excellent concurrent validity. The HSS subscales also correlate significantly with changes in life status and with predicted arena-specific activities (e.g., reading achievement scores with school subscale). This suggests that changes in arena-specific sources of self-esteem do not result in changes in the level of general self-esteem.

PRIMARY REFERENCE: Hare, B. R. (1985). The HARE general and area-specific (school, peer, and home) self-esteem scale. Unpublished manuscript, Department of Sociology, SUNY Stony Brook, Stony Brook, New York (mimeo.). Instrument reproduced with permission of Bruce R. Hare.

AVAILABILITY: The Free Press

HSS

Peer Self-Esteem Scale

In the blank provided, please write the letter of the answer that best describes how you feel about the sentence. These sentences are designed to find out how you generally feel when you are with other people your age. There are no right or wrong answers.

> a = Strongly disagree
> b = Disagree
> c = Agree
> d = Strongly agree

____ 1. I have at least as many friends as other people my age.
____ 2. I am *not* as popular as other people my age.
____ 3. In the kinds of things that people my age like to do, I am at least as good as most other people.
____ 4. People my age often pick on me.
____ 5. Other people think I am a lot of fun to be with.
____ 6. I usually keep to myself because I am *not* like other people my age.
____ 7. Other people wish that they were like me.
____ 8. I wish I were a different kind of person because I'd have more friends.
____ 9. If my group of friends decided to vote for leaders of their group I'd be elected to a high position.
____ 10. When things get tough, I am *not* a person that other people my age would turn to for help.

Home Self-Esteem Scale

In the blank provided, please write the letter of the answer that best describes how you feel about the sentence. These sentences are designed to find out how you generally feel when you are with your family. There are no right or wrong answers.

> a = Strongly disagree
> b = Disagree
> c = Agree
> d = Strongly agree

____ 1. My parents are proud of the kind of person I am.
____ 2. No one pays much attention to me at home.
____ 3. My parents feel that I can be depended on.
____ 4. I often feel that if they could, my parents would trade me in for another child.
____ 5. My parents try to understand me.
____ 6. My parents expect too much of me.
____ 7. I am an important person to my family.
____ 8. I often feel unwanted at home.
____ 9. My parents believe that I will be a success in the future.
____ 10. I often wish that I had been born into another family.

School Self-Esteem Scale

In the blank provided, please write the letter of the answer that best describes how you feel about the sentence. These sentences are designed to find out how you generally feel when you are in school. There are no right or wrong answers.

a = Strongly disagree
b = Disagree
c = Agree
d = Strongly agree

____ 1. My teachers expect too much of me.
____ 2. In the kinds of things we do in school, I am at least as good as other people in my classes.
____ 3. I often feel worthless in school.
____ 4. I am usually proud of my report card.
____ 5. School is harder for me than most other people.
____ 6. My teachers are usually happy with the kind of work I do.
____ 7. Most of my teachers do *not* understand me.
____ 8. I am an important person in my classes.
____ 9. It seems that no matter how hard I try, I never get the grades I deserve.
____ 10. All and all, I feel I've been very fortunate to have had the kinds of teachers I've had since I started school.

HOPELESSNESS SCALE FOR CHILDREN (HSC)

AUTHOR: Alan E. Kazdin

PURPOSE: To measure hopelessness in children.

DESCRIPTION: This 17-item instrument measures cognitions of hopelessness, a construct pertinent to depression and suicidal ideation. Hopelessness is defined as negative expectations about oneself and the future. The HSC was modeled after the Hopelessness Scale for Adults by Beck, Weissman, Lester and Trexler (1974). It has a second-grade reading comprehension level, making it useful for children 7 years and older. Scores on the HSC have been shown to be associated with severity of depression and self-esteem. Moreover, the well established correlation between depression and suicidal intent is minimized when hopelessness is statistically controlled, suggesting the HSC is an important measure to use when working with suicidal clients.

NORMS: The HSC was developed on a sample of 66 children from an inpatient psychiatric unit. The research protocol required these subjects show no evidence of a confused state, uncontrollable seizures, or dementia. The average IQ score was 92.9. Fifty-three children were white, and thirteen were female. The age range for the sample was 5 to 13 with a mean age of 10.5. The mean score on the HSC was 5.2 with a standard deviation of 3.2.

SCORING: Items are answered "true" or "false." Items keyed for true answers are 2, 8, 9, 10, 12, 13, 14, 15, and 17. The remaining items are keyed "false." Scores are the number of items answered in agreement with the key, and range from 0 to 17, with higher scores reflecting greater hopelessness.

RELIABILITY: Reliability is reported in terms of coefficient alpha, .71, and split-half reliability, .70. These coefficients are low but acceptable for a children's measure.

VALIDITY: Validity is demonstrated by concurrent correlations between the HSC and three measures of depression. Scores were inversely correlated with self-esteem. Research on known-groups validity indicated scores discriminated between suicidal and nonsuicidal children.

PRIMARY REFERENCE: Kazdin, A. E., French, N. H., Unis, A. S., Esveldt-Dawson, K., and Sherick, R. B. (1983). Hopelessness, depression, and suicidal intent among psychiatrically disturbed children, *Journal of Consulting and Clinical Psychology* 51, 504–510. Instrument reproduced with permission of Alan Kazdin and the American Psychological Association.

AVAILABILITY: Alan E. Kazdin, Ph.D. Professor of Psychiatry and Psychology, Western Psychiatric Institute and Clinic, 3811 O'Hara Street, Pittsburgh, Pa. 15213.

HSC

Instructions to be read to the child: "These sentences are about
how some kids feel about their lives. Your answers let us know about
how kids feel about things.

I am going to read each sentence to you. I'd like you to tell me if
the sentence is *true* for you or *false* for you. If the sentence is
how you feel, you would say it is *like you* or *true*. If the sentence is
not how you think you feel, you would say it is not like you or *false*.

There are no right or wrong answers. Just tell me if the sentence is
like you or not like you--true or false."

T F   1. I want to grow up because I think things will be better.
T F   2. I might as well give up because I can't make things better
         for myself.
T F   3. When things are going badly, I know that they won't be bad
         all of the time.
T F   4. I can imagine what my life will be like when I'm grown up.
T F   5. I have enough time to finish the things I really want to do.
T F   6. Some day, I will be good at doing the things that I really
         care about.
T F   7. I will get more of the good things in life than most other
         kids.
T F   8. I don't have good luck and there's no reason to think I
         will when I grow up.
T F   9. All I can see ahead of me are bad things, not good things.
T F 10. I don't think I will get what I really want.
T F 11. When I grow up, I think I will be happier than I am now.
T F 12. Things just won't work out the way I want them to.
T F 13. I never get what I want, so it's dumb to want anything.
T F 14. I don't think I will have any real fun when I grow up.
T F 15. Tomorrow seems unclear and confusing to me.
T F 16. I will have more good times than bad times.
T F 17. There's no use in really trying to get something I want
         because I probably won't get it.

IMPULSIVITY SCALE (IS)

AUTHORS: Paul P. Hirschfield, Brian Sutton-Smith, and B. G. Rosenberg

PURPOSE: To measure impulsivity in children.

DESCRIPTION: This 19-item instrument assesses impulsivity, and is arranged in a true-false format for easy administration. The instrument defines impulsivity as the tendency toward restlessness, rule-breaking, and indulgence in horseplay. Each item is phrased one way with another parallel item worded in the reverse. Only one set of the 19 items should be used; the other may serve as a parallel form. The instrument has potential use with children with problems in control or oppositional and acting out disorders.

NORMS: The instrument was developed on 127 fifth and sixth grade students. The mean score was 8.24.

SCORING: When a respondent's item answer corresponds to the item key, it is given a score of 1. The nonparenthetical items are scored True while those within parentheses are keyed False. Total scores range from 0 to 19.

RELIABILITY: Internal consistency data were not reported. Stability was good with test-retest correlations of .85.

VALIDITY: This instrument has criterion-referenced validity, correlating significantly with teacher ratings of school children. Scores are also correlated with behavioral observations by teachers and the researcher in the classroom.

PRIMARY REFERENCE: Hirschfield, P. P. (1965). Response set in impulsive children, *Journal of Genetic Psychology* 107, 117–126. Instrument reproduced with permission of Paul P. Hirschfield.

AVAILABILITY: Dr. Paul P. Hirschfield, Hirschfield and Associates, 529 Pharr Road, Atlanta, GA 30305.

IS

Decide whether each statement is true as applied to you or false as applied to you. If a statement is True or Mostly True as applied to you, circle T. If a statement is False or Mostly False as applied to you, circle F.

T F   1. I like to keep moving around.
           (I don't like to keep moving around.)
T F   2. I make friends quickly.
           (I don't make friends quickly.)
T F   3. I like to wrestle and to horse around.
           (I don't like to wrestle and to horse around.)
T F   4. I like to shoot with bows and arrows.
           (I don't like to shoot with bows and arrows.)
T F   5. I must admit I'm a pretty good talker.
           (I must admit that I'm not a good talker.)
T F   6. Whenever there's a fire engine going someplace, I like to
           follow it.
           (If there's a fire engine going someplace, I don't usually
           like to follow it.)
T F   7. My home life is not always happy.
           (My home life is always happy.)
T F   8. When things get quiet, I like to stir up a little fuss.
           (I usually don't like to stir up a little fuss when things
           get quiet.)
T F   9. I am restless.
           (I am not restless.)
T F 10. I don't think I'm as happy as other people.
           (I think I'm as happy as other people.)
T F 11. I get into tricks at Halloween.
           (I don't get into tricks at Halloween.)
T F 12. I like being "it" when we play games of that sort.
           (I don't like being "it" when we play games of that sort.)
T F 13. It's fun to push people off the edge into the pool.
           (It's not fun to push people off the edge into the pool.)
T F 14. I play hooky sometimes.
           (I never play hooky.)
T F 15. I like to go with lots of other kids, not just one.
           (I usually like to go with one kid, rather than lots of them.)
T F 16. I like throwing stones at targets.
           (I don't like throwing stones at targets.)
T F 17. It's hard to stick to the rules if you're losing the game.
           (It's not hard to stick to the rules even if you are losing
           the game.)
T F 18. I like to dare kids to do things.
           (I don't like to dare kids to do things.)
T F 19. I'm not known as a hard and steady worker.
           (I'm known as a hard and steady worker.)

INDEX OF PEER RELATIONS (IPR)

AUTHOR: Walter W. Hudson

PURPOSE: To measure problems with peers.

DESCRIPTION: The IPR is a 25-item scale designed to measure the extent, severity or magnitude of a problem the respondent has with peers. The IPR can be used as a global measure of relationship problems with peers or one or more specific peer reference groups can be considered. A note stating which reference group is being used should be placed at the top of the questionnaire. The IPR has a cutting score of 35 ($\pm$ 5), with scores above 35 indicating the respondent has a clinically significant problem and scores below 35 indicating the individual has no such problem. Another advantage of the IPR is that it is one of 9 scales of the Clinical Measurement Package (Hudson, 1982) reproduced here, all of which are administered and scored the same way.

NORMS: The norms for the IPR were developed with a sample of 107 clients currently engaged in counseling of whom 50 were evaluated by their therapists as not having problems with peers. Means for these groups on the IPR are 55.9 and 20.8, respectively. No other demographic information was provided, although the sample was described as diverse with respect to gender, ethnicity, and social class.

SCORING: The IPR is scored by reverse-scoring the items listed at the bottom of the scale, totaling these and the other item scores, and subtracting 25. This gives a range of 0 to 100 with higher scores indicating more evidence of presence of problems with peers. For scoring questionnaires with missing items, see Hudson (1982) or the instructions for scoring the Index of Family Relations in this book.

RELIABILITY: The IPR has a mean alpha of .94 indicating excellent internal consistency, and an excellent (low) Standard Error of Measurement of 4.44. Test-retest data are not available.

VALIDITY: The IPR has excellent known-groups validity, significantly distinguishing between clients judged by themselves and their therapists as either having or not having peer relationship problems.

PRIMARY REFERENCE: Hudson, W. W., Nurius, P. S., Daley, J. G., and Newsome, R. D. (1986). A short-form scale to measure peer relations dysfunction (submitted for publication). Instrument reproduced with permission of Walter W. Hudson and the Dorsey Press.

AVAILABILITY: The Dorsey Press, 224 South Michigan Avenue, Suite 440, Chicago, IL 60604

IPR

This questionnaire is designed to measure the way you feel about the people you work, play, or associate with most of the time; your peer group. It is not a test so there are no right or wrong answers. Answer each item as carefully and as accurately as you can by placing a number beside each one as follows:

1 = Rarely or none of the time
2 = A little of the time
3 = Some of the time
4 = A good part of the time
5 = Most or all of the time

_____ 1. I get along very well with my peers.
_____ 2. My peers act like they don't care about me.
_____ 3. My peers treat me badly.
_____ 4. My peers really seem to respect me.
_____ 5. I don't feel like I am "part of the group."
_____ 6. My peers are a bunch of snobs.
_____ 7. My peers really understand me.
_____ 8. My peers seem to like me very much.
_____ 9. I really feel "left out" of my peer group.
_____ 10. I hate my present peer group.
_____ 11. My peers seem to like having me around.
_____ 12. I really like my present peer group.
_____ 13. I really feel like I am disliked by my peers.
_____ 14. I wish I had a different peer group.
_____ 15. My peers are very nice to me.
_____ 16. My peers seem to look up to me.
_____ 17. My peers think I am important to them.
_____ 18. My peers are a real source of pleasure to me.
_____ 19. My peers don't seem to even notice me.
_____ 20. I wish I were not part of this peer group.
_____ 21. My peers regard my ideas and opinions very highly.
_____ 22. I feel like I am an important member of my peer group.
_____ 23. I can't stand to be around my peer group.
_____ 24. My peers seem to look down on me.
_____ 25. My peers really do not interest me.

1,4,7,8,11,12,15,16,17,18,21,22

NOWICKI-STRICKLAND LOCUS OF CONTROL SCALE (N-SLCS)

AUTHORS: Stephen Nowicki, Jr. and Bonni R. Strickland

PURPOSE: To measure locus of control in children.

DESCRIPTION: The N-SLCS is a 40-item instrument designed to measure whether or not a child believes that reinforcement comes to him or her by chance or fate (external locus of control) or because of his or her own behavior (internal locus of control). Locus of control in children is important because a number of studies have shown that it is related to several other behaviors and attitudes including some involving academic achievement. Thus, a child who is relatively high on internal locus of control will view himself or herself as more in control of his or her life. The N-SLCS has been used with children from the third grade up. It also has been modified for use by college age and adult respondents by changing the word "kids" to "people" and deleting items about parents.

NORMS: The N-SLCS was developed in a series of studies involving over 1000 male and female children from the third to the twelfth grade. The students were primarily white with representation from all socioeconomic levels. Means for males and females are available and range from 11.01 to 18.80, with students' responses becoming more internal with age.

SCORING: The N-SLCS is scored by adding up the number of items that are scored "correctly." The correct responses are "yes" for items 1, 3, 5, 7, 8, 10–12, 14, 16–19, 21, 23, 24, 27, 29, 31, 33, 35–39, and "no" for the remainder. Higher scores reflect more external locus of control.

RELIABILITY: The N-SLCS has only fair internal consistency overall with split-half reliabilities of .32 for grades 3 through 5, .68 for grades 6 through 8, .74 for grades 9 through 11, and .81 for grade 12. Stability of the instrument is fair with six-week test-retest correlations of .63 for third grade, .66 for seventh grade, and .71 for tenth grade.

VALIDITY: The N-SLCS has fair concurrent validity, correlating significantly with three other measures of locus of control. The N-SLCS also has been shown to correlate with a number of other academic and nonacademic behaviors, although race, socioeconomic level, and sex tend to mediate some of those findings. Further, the N-SLCS has also been found to be sensitive to change due to a therapeutically designed camping experience. The N-SLCS was found not to be affected by social desirability response set.

PRIMARY REFERENCE: Nowicki, S. and Strickland, B. R. (1973). A locus of control scale for children, *Journal of Consulting and Clinical Psychology* 40, 148–154. Instrument reproduced with permission of Stephen Nowicki and the American Psychological Association.

AVAILABILITY: Dr. Stephen Nowicki, Department of Psychology, Emory University, Atlanta, GA 30322.

N-SLCS

Please circle Yes or No for each question as it applies to you.

Yes No   1. Do you believe that most problems will solve themselves if you just don't fool with them?

Yes No   2. Do you believe that you can stop yourself from catching a cold?

Yes No   3. Are some kids just born lucky?

Yes No   4. Most of the time do you feel that getting good grades means a great deal to you?

Yes No   5. Are you often blamed for things that just aren't your fault?

Yes No   6. Do you believe that if somebody studies hard enough he or she can pass any subject?

Yes No   7. Do you feel that most of the time it doesn't pay to try hard because things never turn out right anyway?

Yes No   8. Do you feel that if things start out well in the morning it's going to be a good day no matter what you do?

Yes No   9. Do you feel that most of the time parents listen to what their children have to say?

Yes No 10. Do you believe that wishing can make good things happen?

Yes No 11. When you get punished does it usually seem it's for no good reason at all?

Yes No 12. Most of the time do you find it hard to change a friend's opinion?

Yes No 13. Do you think that cheering more than luck helps a team to win?

Yes No 14. Do you feel that it's nearly impossible to change your parent's mind about anything?

Yes No 15. Do you believe that your parents should allow you to make most of your own decisions?

Yes No 16. Do you feel that when you do something wrong there's very little you can do to make it right?

Yes No 17. Do you believe that most kids are just born good at sports?

Yes No 18. Are most of the other kids your age stronger than you are?

Yes No 19. Do you feel that one of the best ways to handle most problems is just not to think about them?

Yes No 20. Do you feel that you have a lot of choice in deciding who your friends are?

Yes No 21. If you find a four-leaf clover do you believe that it might bring you good luck?

Yes No 22. Do you often feel that whether you do your homework has much to do with what kind of grades you get?

Yes No 23. Do you feel that when a kid your age decides to hit you, there's little you can do to stop him or her?

Yes No 24. Have you ever had a good luck charm?

Yes No 25. Do you believe that whether or not people like you depends on how you act?

Yes No 26. Will your parents usually help you if you ask them to?

Yes No 27. Have you felt that when people were mean to you it was usually for no reason at all?

Yes No 28. Most of the time, do you feel that you can change what might happen tomorrow by what you do today?

Yes No 29. Do you believe that when bad things are going to happen they just are going to happen no matter what you try to do to stop them?

Yes No 30. Do you think that kids can get their own way if they just keep trying?

Yes No 31. Most of the time do you find it useless to try to get your own way at home?

Yes No 32. Do you feel that when good things happen they happen because of hard work?

Yes No 33. Do you feel that when somebody your age wants to be your enemy there's little you can do to change matters?

Yes No 34. Do you usually feel that it's easy to get friends to do what you want them to?

Yes No 35. Do you usually feel that you have little to say about what you get to eat at home?

Yes No 36. Do you feel that when someone doesn't like you there's little you can do about it?

Yes No 37. Do you usually feel that it's almost useless to try in school because most other children are just plain smarter than you are?

Yes No 38. Are you the kind of person who believes that planning ahead mades things turn out better?

Yes No 39. Most of the time, do you feel that you have little to say about what your family decides to do?

Yes No 40. Do you think it's better to be smart than to be lucky?

PERSONAL ATTRIBUTE INVENTORY FOR CHILDREN AND NONSEXIST PERSONAL ATTRIBUTE INVENTORY (PAIC)

AUTHOR: Thomas S. Parish

PURPOSE: To measure children's self concept.

DESCRIPTION: This 48-item adjective checklist is designed to measure children's self concept. While slightly longer than most instruments in this volume, the checklist format allows it to be completed quickly. The focus of the PAI is on evaluative and affective descriptions of either one's self or another, such as a parent. The instrument does not evaluate cognitions or behaviors. The instructions for the PAIC have a blank at the end. Consequently, the measure can also be used to assess a child's impression of someone else, such as a parent or sibling. This is accomplished by replacing the word "you" in the blank with the other person's name. Thus, the scale has potential for use in family therapy or in parent-child conflicts. A shorter 32-adjective form is also available. This form is considered nonsexist as many of the adjectives reflecting either gender are removed.

NORMS: The PAIC has been tested on over 1000 children (450 males and 586 females). The mean score was 12.01 with a standard deviation of 3.02 for males and 12.41 with a standard deviation of 2.75 for females. Additional normative data are available from the author.

SCORING: The child is asked to put an X in the box next to the 15 adjectives that best describes him or her or the other person he or she is rating. Twenty-four of the adjectives are positive (marked with asterisks here) and 24 are negative. The PAIC scores are the total number of positive adjectives and range from 1 to 15.

RELIABILITY: Especially for a children's measure, this instrument has excellent test-retest reliability, .73 for a sample of school children, over a four-week period. The instrument was less stable for third graders, (.66) than for sixth graders (.87) over the same period. The evidence of stability is good, as children change so quickly that lower coefficients are anticipated. Evidence of interval consistency is not reported.

VALIDITY: The PAIC has good concurrent validity, demonstrated by significant correlations with the Piers-Harris Children's Self-Concept Scale. While the magnitude of the concurrent validity correlations was less for third than for sixth graders, the evidence is generally supportive.

PRIMARY REFERENCE: Parish, T. S. and Taylor, J. C. (1978). The personal attribute inventory for children: A report on its validity and reliability as a self-concept scale, *Educational and Psychological Measurement* 38, 565–569. For the adult form, see Parish, T. S., Bryant, W., and Shirazi, A. (1976). The personal attribute inventory, *Perceptual and Motor Skills* 42, 715–720. Instruments reprinted with permission of T. S. Parish.

AVAILABILITY: Thomas S. Parish, Professor, College of Education, Kansas State University, Manhattan, KS 66506.

PAIC

Read through this list of words, then put an X on the line beside the 15 words that best describe you.

____ Afraid	____ Happy*
____ Angry	____ Healthy*
____ Awkward	____ Helpful*
____ Bad	____ Honest*
____ Beautiful*	____ Jolly*
____ Bitter	____ Kind*
____ Brave*	____ Lazy
____ Calm*	____ Lovely*
____ Careless	____ Mean
____ Cheerful*	____ Nagging
____ Complaining	____ Nice*
____ Cowardly	____ Polite*
____ Cruel	____ Pretty*
____ Dirty	____ Rude
____ Dumb	____ Selfish
____ Fairminded*	____ Show-off
____ Foolish	____ Strong*
____ Friendly*	____ Sweet*
____ Gentle*	____ Ugly
____ Gloomy	____ Unfriendly
____ Good*	____ Weak
____ Great*	____ Wise*
____ Greedy	____ Wonderful*
____ Handsome*	____ Wrongful

NPAIC

Read through this list of words, then put an X on the line beside the 10 words that best describe you.

___ Angry	___ Helpful*
___ Awkward	___ Honest*
___ Calm*	___ Jolly*
___ Careless	___ Kind*
___ Complaining	___ Lazy
___ Cowardly	___ Lovely*
___ Dirty	___ Mean
___ Dumb	___ Nagging
___ Fairminded*	___ Nice*
___ Foolish	___ Polite*
___ Friendly *	___ Rude
___ Gentle*	___ Ugly
___ Good*	___ Unfriendly
___ Greedy	___ Wise*
___ Happy*	___ Wonderful*
___ Healthy*	___ Wrongful

ROSENBERG SELF-ESTEEM SCALE (RSE)

AUTHOR: Morris Rosenberg

PURPOSE: To measure self-esteem.

DESCRIPTION: The RSE is a 10-item Guttman scale with one dimension that was originally designed (1962) to measure the self-esteem of high school students. Since its development, the scale has been used with a number of other groups including adults with a variety of occupations. One of its greatest strengths is the amount of research that has been conducted with a wide range of groups on this scale over the years.

NORMS: The original research on the RSE was conducted on some 5000 high school students of varying ethnic backgrounds. Subsequent research involved thousands of college students and other adults from a range of professions and occupations. Norms are available for many of those groups.

SCORING: As a Guttman scale, scoring is based on a somewhat complicated method of combined ratings. Low self-esteem responses are "disagree" or "strongly disagree" on items 1, 3, 4, 7, 10, and "strongly agree" or "agree" on items 2, 5, 6, 8, 9. Two or three out of three correct responses to items 3, 7, and 9 are scored as one item. One or two out of two correct responses for items 4 and 5 are considered as a single item, items 1, 8, and 10 are scored as individual items, and combined correct responses (one or two out of two) to items 2 and 6 are considered to be a single item. The scale might also be scored by a simple totaling of the individual 4-point items after reverse-scoring the negatively worded items.

RELIABILITY: The RSE has a Guttman scale coefficient of reproducibility of .92, indicating good internal consistency. Two studies of two-week test-retest reliability show correlations of .85 and .88, indicating excellent stability.

VALIDITY: A great deal of research demonstrates the concurrent, known-groups, predictive, and construct validity of the RSE. The RSE correlates significantly with other self-esteem measures such as the Coopersmith Self-Esteem Inventory. Similarly, the RSE correlates in predicted directions with measures of depression, anxiety, and peer-group reputation, demonstrating good construct validity by correlating with measures with which it should theoretically correlate and not correlating with those with which it should not.

PRIMARY REFERENCE: Rosenberg, M. (1979). *Conceiving the Self.* New York: Basic Books. Instrument reproduced with permission of Morris Rosenberg.

AVAILABILITY: Dr. Morris Rosenberg, Department of Sociology, University of Maryland, College Park, MD. 20742

RSE

Please record the appropriate answer per item, depending on whether you strongly agree, agree, disagree, or strongly disagree with it.

1 = Strongly agree
2 = Agree
3 = Disagree
4 = Strongly disagree

____ 1. On the whole, I am satisfied with myself.
____ 2. At times I think I am no good at all.
____ 3. I feel that I have a number of good qualities.
____ 4. I am able to do things as well as most other people.
____ 5. I feel I do not have much to be proud of.
____ 6. I certainly feel useless at times.
____ 7. I feel that I'm a person of worth, at least on an equal plane with others.
____ 8. I wish I could have more respect for myself.
____ 9. All in all, I am inclined to feel that I am a failure.
____ 10. I take a positive attitude toward myself.

SELF-CONCEPT SCALE FOR CHILDREN (SC)

AUTHOR: Lewis P. Lipsitt

PURPOSE: To measure the self-concept of children.

DESCRIPTION: The SC consists of 22 descriptive adjectives tapping children's feelings about themselves, which are responded to on 5-point scales. Three of these adjectives, items 10, 17, and 20 are considered negative while the rest are positives. The SC is one of the few self-report measures available that can be used with children from approximately the fourth grade up. Higher scores on the SC reflect higher self-concept (i.e., less self-disparagement).

NORMS: The original study involved 138 boys and 160 girls in the fourth through sixth grades. No real norms are available although the mean score for all children was 86.75. There were no differences based on grade or sex.

SCORING: After the three negatively worded items are reverse-scored, the scores on the individual 22 items are totaled, producing a potential range of 22 to 110.

RELIABILITY: No data on internal consistency are reported. However, two-week test-retest correlations range from .73 to .91, indicating good stability.

VALIDITY: The only validity data reported show that the SC correlates significantly and in predicted directions with scores on the Children's Manifest Anxiety Scale. Thus, the greater the anxiety level, the lower the score on the SC.

PRIMARY REFERENCE: Lipsitt, L. P. (1958). A Self-Concept Scale for Children and its relationship to the children's form of the Manifest Anxiety Scale, *Child Development* 29, 463–472. Instrument reproduced with permission of L. P. Lipsitt.

AVAILABILITY: Journal article or Dr. L. P. Lipsitt, Department of Psychology, Brown University, Providence, RI 02912.

SC

Select the phrase that comes closest to the way you are by recording the
appropriate number to the left of each statement. Select only one of
them. Do the best you can.

1 = Not at all
2 = Not very often
3 = Some of the time
4 = Most of the time
5 = All of the time

____ 1. I am friendly.
____ 2. I am happy.
____ 3. I am kind.
____ 4. I am brave.
____ 5. I am honest.
____ 6. I am likable.
____ 7. I am trusted.
____ 8. I am good.
____ 9. I am proud.
____ 10. I am lazy.
____ 11. I am loyal.
____ 12. I am cooperative.
____ 13. I am cheerful.
____ 14. I am thoughtful.
____ 15. I am popular.
____ 16. I am courteous.
____ 17. I am jealous.
____ 18. I am obedient.
____ 19. I am polite.
____ 20. I am bashful.
____ 21. I am clean.
____ 22. I am helpful.

YOUNG CHILDREN'S SOCIAL DESIRABILITY SCALE
(YCSD)

AUTHORS: LeRoy H. Ford and Barry M. Rubin

PURPOSE: To measure need for social approval in young children.

DESCRIPTION: The 26-item forced-choice YCSD considers social desirability as a form of defensive denial. The research indicates the instrument is a measure of general motivation to comply with social demands. The instrument may be administered in writing or read aloud to young children or respondents with limited reading ability. The forced-choice format helps control for an acquiescence response set.

NORMS: Normative data are available on three samples of preschool children with a total sample size of 437. A mean score of 16.36 and a standard deviation of approximately 4.85 are reported for the combined sample. Additional normative data are available from the primary reference.

SCORING: In selecting the alternative when verbally presented, the child must repeat at least one word or phrase from the statement. The key words are identified by italics. The first two items are warm-up items and are not to be scored. The socially desirable response is the second alternative in items 3, 6, 7, 10, 11, 14, 15, 17, 18, 22–24, 27, and the first alternative in the remainder. Scores are the total number of socially desirable responses. Scores range from 0 to 28.

RELIABILITY: The reliability data tend to be very dependent on the age of the children. For example, the internal consistency was .48 and .51 for young boys and girls, respectively. For older children it was .79 for boys and .84 for girls. In a third sample, internal consistency using Kuder-Richardson was .83 for boys and .85 for girls. Over a five-week period, the test-retest correlation was. 58.

VALIDITY: The criterion validity of the YCSD was tested using concurrent procedures. Scores correlated with vocabulary IQ suggesting that children with higher verbal intelligence are more likely to idealize social norms and indicate adherence to them. Validity was also demonstrated in three experiements. In general, the results indicate that children who score high on the YCSD respond more positively to interpersonal demands than children who score low on the measure.

PRIMARY REFERENCE: Ford, L. H. and Rubin, B. M. (1970). A social desirability questionnaire for young children, *Journal of Consulting and Clinical Psychology* 35, 195–204. Instrument reproduced with persmission of the American Psychological Association.

AVAILABILITY: Journal article.

YCSD

Below are twenty-eight sets of statements. Indicate which is most true for you by circling the number to the left of the choice.

1. 1. Do you *sometimes* play with toys? or
    2. Do you *never* play with toys?

2. 1. Do you *always* play all by yourself? or
    2. Do you *sometimes* play with other children?

3. 1. Do you *sometimes* argue with your mother? or
    2. Do you *never* argue with your mother?

4. 1. Are you *always polite* to older people? or
    2. Are you *sometimes not polite* to older people?

5. 1. Do you *never shout* when you feel angry? or
    2. Do you *sometimes shout* when you feel angry?

6. 1. Do you *sometimes* tell a little *lie*? or
    2. Do you *never* tell a little *lie*?

7. 1. Do you *sometimes hit* another boy or girl?
    2. Do you *never hit* another boy or girl?

8. 1. Do you *always help* people? or
    2. Do you *sometimes not help* people?

9. 1. Do you *never show off* to your friends? or
    2. Do you *sometimes show off* to your friends?

10. 1. Do you *sometimes say mean things* to people? or
    2. Do you *never say mean things* to people?

11. 1. Do you *sometimes feel like throwing* or *breaking* things? or
    2. Do you *never feel like throwing* or *breaking* things?

12. 1. Do you feel that your parents are *always right*? or
    2. Do you sometimes feel that your parents are *not always right*?

13. 1. Do you *never* act *naughty*? or
    2. Do you *sometimes* act *naughty*?

14. 1. Do you *sometimes do other things* instead of what your teacher tells you to do? or
    2. Do you *always do what* your *teacher tells* you to do?

15. 1. Do you *sometimes do things* you're *not supposed to do*? or
    2. Do you *never do things* you're *not supposed to* do?

16. *1.* Do you think your *teachers know more* than you do? or
     2. Do you think you *know more* than your teacher does? (*I know more*)

17. *1.* Do you *sometimes want things* your *parents don't want* you to have?
         or
     2. Do you *never want things* your *parents don't want* you to have?

18. *1.* Does it *sometimes bother* you *when* you *don't get* your *way?* or
     2. Does it *never bother* you *when* you *don't get* your *way?*

19. *1.* Do you *always listen* to your parents? or
     2. Do you *sometimes not listen* to your parents?

20. *1.* Do you *always wash* your *hands* before every meal? or
     2. Do you *sometimes not wash* your *hands* before every meal?

21. *1.* Do you *never feel like making fun* of other people? or
     2. Do you *sometimes feel like making fun* of other people?

22. *1.* Do you *sometimes forget* to say "please" and thank you"? or
     2. Do you *never forget* to say "please" and "thank you"?

23. *1.* Does it *sometimes bother* you *to share things* with your friends?
         or (*bothers me*)
     2. Does it *never bother* you *to share things* with your friends?

24. *1.* Do you *sometimes want to do things* your *parents tell* you *not to do?*
     2. Do you *never want to do things* your *parents tell* you *not* to do?

25. *1.* Do you *never get angry?* or
     2. Do you *sometimes get angry?*

26. *1.* Are you *always nice* to people? or
     2. Are you *sometimes not nice* to people?

27. *1.* Do you *sometimes not do the right things?* or
     2. Do you *always do the right things?*

28. *1.* Do you *always tell the truth?* or
     2. Do you *sometimes not tell the truth?*

INSTRUMENTS FOR COUPLES AND FAMILIES

ADULT-ADOLESCENT PARENTING INVENTORY (AAPI)

AUTHOR: Stephen J. Bavolek

PURPOSE: To assess the parenting and child rearing attitudes of adolescents and adults.

DESCRIPTION: The AAPI is a 32-item scale, written in simple language, designed to help professionals assess parenting and child rearing strengths and weaknesses in four areas: (1) inappropriate developmental expectations of children, (2) lack of empathy toward children's needs, (3) belief in the use of corporal punishment, and (4) reversing parent-child roles. The AAPI can be used to assess attitudes of prospective parents, to assess changes in parenting attitudes before and after treatment, to screen and train foster parent applicants, and to assess attitudes of professionals and paraprofessionals. Two forms are used when pre- and posttesting is called for. An excellent handbook describing all details of the psychometric properties, administration, and scoring is available.

NORMS: Extensive norms are available based on 782 abusive adults, 1239 nonabusive adults, 305 abused adolescents, and 6480 nonabused adolescents. These respondents come from geographic areas all over the United States and include both males and females and blacks and whites. These norms allow easy comparison of individual scores with norms from these groups. The AAPI is designed specifically for adolescents aged 12 to 19 and adults 20 and over.

SCORING: The AAPI requires the use of scoring stencils for each test form. Raw scores are easily converted into standard scores by using the tables in the handbook. These tables give information on the four

415

parenting subscales noted above and provide standard scores for abusive and nonabusive adults and abused and nonabused adolescents.

RELIABILITY: The internal consistency of the AAPI, based on coefficient alpha, ranges from .70 for the construct of inappropriate expectations of children (for adolescents) to .86 for the construct of family role-reversal (for adults). Test-retest reliability (stability) is .39 for inappropriate expectation of children, .65 for empathic awareness of children's needs, .85 for family role-reversal, and .89 for empathic awareness. Total test-retest correlation is .76, indicating fairly good stability.

VALIDITY: Extensive validity information is available including excellent content validity based on expert judgments, construct validity data based on several different types of analyses, and excellent concurrent and known-groups validity indicating that the AAPI was clearly able to discriminate among different groups in a number of studies.

PRIMARY REFERENCE: Bavolek, S. J. (1984). *Handbook for the Adult-Adolescent Parenting Inventory.* Eau Claire, Wisconsin: Family Development Associates, Inc. Instrument reproduced with permission of S. J. Bavolek.

AVAILABILITY: Family Development Resources, Inc., 767 Second Avenue, Eau Claire, WI 54703.

AAPI

There are 32 statements in this questionnaire. They are statements about parenting and raising children. You decide the degree to which you agree or disagree with each statement by indicating the appropriate number at the left. If you strongly support the statement, or feel this statement is true most or all the time, indicate *strongly agree*. If you support the statement or feel this statement is true some of the time, indicate *agree*. If you feel strongly against the statement or feel this statement is not true most or all the time, indicate *strongly disagree*. If you feel you cannot support the statement or that the statement is not true some of the time, indicate *disagree*. Use *uncertain* only when it is absolutely impossible to decide on one of the other choices.

Please keep these four points in mind:

1. Answer the questions frankly and truthfully. There is no advantage in giving an untrue answer because you think it is the right thing to say.

2. Answer the questions as quickly as you can. Don't spend too much time thinking about what to answer. Give the first natural answer that comes to mind.

3. Don't skip any questions or provide two answers to any question. Make sure you respond to every statement with only one answer.

4. Although some questions may seem much like others, there are no two statements exactly alike so make sure you respond to every statement.

If there is anything you don't understand, please ask your questions now. If you come across a word you don't know while answering a question, ask the examiner for help.

> 1 = Strongly agree
> 2 = Agree
> 3 = Uncertain
> 4 = Disagree
> 5 = Strongly disagree

____ 1. Young children should be expected to comfort their mother when she is feeling blue.

____ 2. Parents should teach their children right from wrong by sometimes using physical punishment.

____ 3. Children should be the main source of comfort and care for their parents.

____ 4. Young children should be expected to hug their mother when she is sad.

____ 5. Parents will spoil their children by picking them up and comforting them when they cry.

____ 6. Children should be expected to verbally express themselves before the age of one year.

___ 7. A good child will comfort both of his/her parents after the parents have argued.

___ 8. Children learn good behavior through the use of physical punishment.

___ 9. Children develop good, strong characters through very strict discipline.

___ 10. Parents should expect their children who are under three years to begin taking care of themselves.

___ 11. Young children should be aware of ways to comfort their parents after a hard day's work.

___ 12. Parents should slap their chld when she/he has done something wrong.

___ 13. Children should always be spanked when they misbehave.

___ 14. Young children should be responsible for much of the happiness of their parents.

___ 15. Parents have a responsibility to spank their child when she/he misbehaves.

___ 16. Parents should expect children to feed themselves by twelve months.

___ 17. Parents should expect their children to grow physically at about the same rate.

___ 18. Young children who feel secure often grow up expecting too much.

___ 19. Children should always "pay the price" for misbehaving.

___ 20. Children should be expected at an early age to feed, bathe, and clothe themselves.

___ 21. Parents who are sensitive to their children's feelings and moods often spoil their children.

___ 22. Children deserve more discipline than they get.

___ 23. Children whose needs are left unattended will often grow up to be more independent.

___ 24. Parents who encourage communication with their children only end up listening to complaints.

___ 25. Children are more likely to learn appropriate behavior when they are spanked for misbehaving.

___ 26. Children will quit crying faster if they are ignored.

___ 27. Children five months of age ought to be capable of sensing what their parents expect.

___ 28. Children who are given too much love by their parents will grow up to be stubborn and spoiled.

___ 29. Children should be forced to respect parental authority.

___ 30. Young children should try to make their parent's life more pleasurable.

___ 31. Young children who are hugged and kissed often will grow up to be "sissies."

___ 32. Young children should be expected to comfort their father when he is upset.

BEIER-STERNBERG DISCORD QUESTIONNAIRE (DQ)

AUTHORS: Ernest G. Beier and Daniel P. Sternberg

PURPOSE: To measure marital conflict and unhappiness.

DESCRIPTION: The DQ is a 10-item instrument designed to measure two dimensions of a marital relationship: discord or conflict and the degree of unhappiness attached to such discord. The items on the DQ were selected based on a review of literature that revealed these topics to be major sources of marital disagreement. Each respondent first scores each topic with regard to the amount of conflict it generates in the marriage and then evaluates the extent to which such discord produces unhappiness. The items are scored individually. Although there is not a great deal of psychometric information available about the DQ, its utility stems from the ability to analyze separately each relevant dimension of a couple's relationship.

NORMS: The data for the DQ were generated from a series of studies involving newly married couples who responded to letters soliciting their cooperation. The couples were heterogenous in background, and were contacted shortly after marriage and one year later. Means are available for each item in the DQ for these couples at both time periods. There was a slight increase in conflict for the couples over the period of a year with an overall conflict mean of 33.92 shortly after marriage and 36.55 a year later.

SCORING: Each item is scored separately on a 7-point scale with higher scores indicating more conflict and more unhappiness. The individual items can be summed for a total score, but the meaning of that score is not clear.

RELIABILITY: No information is available.

VALIDITY: The DQ has some degree of concurrent validity in that conflict ratings are significantly correlated with unhappiness ratings, and there is some correlation between scores on the DQ and a range of intimate behavior ratings. Also, there is a significant change over the first year of marriage for wives (total mean moved from 19 to 25.33), suggesting some degree of predictive validity for the DQ.

PRIMARY REFERENCE: Beier, E. G. and Sternberg, D. P. (1977). Marital Communication, *Journal of Communication* 27, 92–100. Instrument reproduced with permission of Ernest G. Beier and Daniel P. Sternberg.

AVAILABILITY: Dr. Daniel P. Sternberg, Psychiatric Associates, 3540 South 4000 West, Suite 310, West Valley City, UT 84120.

DQ

With these scales, we want to find out what you believe are the areas of agreement or disagreement in your marriage. We also want to find out if these areas of agreement and disagreement make you feel happy, sad, or indifferent. For example, if money is a topic of much disagreement in your marriage, you could make a mark in *Scale 1: Degree of Agreement* under the numbers 5, 6, or 7 depending on the extent of your disagreement. If you were to make a mark under the number 7, this would mean that you feel there is much disagreement about money in your marriage. If you were to mark under the number 5, this means you feel there is some disagreement about money.

With *Scale 1* we want to find out how you differ from your spouse in looking at things. In *Scale 2* we want to find out how you feel about these differences. If, for example, a disagreement were to make you very unhappy, as in the "Money" example given above, you would mark 6 or 7 on *Scale 2: Results of Agreement or Disagreement*. Please check each item in both scales. Remember, the *higher* the number the *more* disagreement or conflict over a particular topic, the *lower* the number, the *more* agreement.

	Scale 1: Degree of Agreement							Scale 2: Results of Agreement or Disagreement						
	Agree						Disagree	Happy						Unhappy
	1	2	3	4	5	6	7	1	2	3	4	5	6	7
1. Money														
2. Children														
3. Sex														
4. Concern and love														
5. Doing things together (in spare time)														
6. Friends and social life														
7. Getting ahead, ambition														
8. Politics														
9. Children's education														
10. Religion														
Other(s): please specify														

CHILD'S ATTITUDE TOWARD FATHER (CAF) AND MOTHER (CAM) SCALES

AUTHOR: Walter W. Hudson

PURPOSE: To measure problems children have with their parents.

DESCRIPTION: The CAF and CAM are 25-item scales designed to measure the extent, degree, or severity of problems a child has with his or her father or mother. The instruments are identical with the exception of the interchangeable use of the word "father" or "mother". These are two of the few instruments available for assessing parent-child relationship problems from the child's point of view. The CAF and CAM have cutting scores of 30 (± 5), with scores above 30 indicating the respondent has a clinically significant problem and scores below 30 indicating the individual has no such problem. Another advantage of these instruments is that they are two of nine scales of the Clinical Measurement Package (Hudson, 1982) reproduced here, all of which are administered and scored the same way.

NORMS: The CAF and CAM were developed using 1072 students of heterogenous backgrounds from the seventh through twelfth grades. Respondents were Caucasian, Japanese and Chinese Americans, and a smaller number of members of other ethnic groups. The scales are not recommended for use with children under the age of 12.

SCORING: The CAF and CAM are scored by first reverse-scoring the items listed at the bottom of each scale, totaling these and the other items scores, and subtracting 25. This gives a range of 0 to 100 with higher scores giving more evidence of the presence of problems with parents. For scoring questionnaires with missing items, see Hudson (1982) or instructions for scoring the Index of Family Relations in this book.

RELIABILITY: The CAF has a mean alpha of .95 and an excellent (low) S.E.M. of 4.56; the CAM has a mean alpha of .94 and a Standard Error of Measurement of 4.57; both possess excellent internal consistency. Both measures also have excellent stability with one-week test-retest correlations of .96 (CAF) and .95 (CAM).

VALIDITY: The CAF and CAM have excellent known-groups validity, both significantly distinguishing between children who rate themselves as having relationship problems with their parents and those who don't. The CAF and CAM also have good predictive validity, significantly predicting children's responses to questions regarding problems with their parents.

PRIMARY REFERENCE: Hudson, W. W. (1982). *The Clinical Measurement Package: A Field Manual*. Chicago: Dorsey Press. Instrument reproduced with permission of Walter W. Hudson and the Dorsey Press.

AVAILABILITY: The Dorsey Press, 224 South Michigan Avenue, Suite 440, Chicago, IL 60604.

CAF

This questionnaire is designed to measure the degree of contentment you have in your relationship with your father. It is not a test, so there are no right or wrong answers. Answer each item as carefully and accurately as you can by placing a number beside each one as follows:

1 = Rarely or none of the time
2 = A little of the time
3 = Some of the time
4 = Good part of the time
5 = Most or all of the time

____ 1. My father gets on my nerves.
____ 2. I get along well with my father.
____ 3. I feel that I can really trust my father.
____ 4. I dislike my father.
____ 5. My father's behavior embarrasses me.
____ 6. My father is too demanding.
____ 7. I wish I had a different father.
____ 8. I really enjoy my father.
____ 9. My father puts too many limits on me.
____ 10. My father interferes with my activities.
____ 11. I resent my father.
____ 12. I think my father is terrific.
____ 13. I hate my father.
____ 14. My father is very patient with me.
____ 15. I really like my father.
____ 16. I like being with my father.
____ 17. I feel like I do not love my father.
____ 18. My father is very irritating.
____ 19. I feel very angry toward my father.
____ 20. I feel violent toward my father.
____ 21. I feel proud of my father.
____ 22. I wish my father was more like others I know.
____ 23. My father does not understand me.
____ 24. I can really depend on my father.
____ 25. I feel ashamed of my father.

2,3,8,12,14,15,16,21,24

CAM

This questionnaire is designed to measure the degree of contentment you have in your relationship with your mother. It is not a test, so there are no right or wrong answers. Answer each item as carefully and accurately as you can by placing a number beside each one as follows:

1 = Rarely or none of the time
2 = A little of the time
3 = Some of the time
4 = Good part of the time
5 = Most or all of the time

_____ 1. My mother gets on my nerves.
_____ 2. I get along well with my mother.
_____ 3. I feel that I can really trust my mother.
_____ 4. I dislike my mother.
_____ 5. My mother's behavior embarrasses me.
_____ 6. My mother is too demanding.
_____ 7. I wish I had a different mother.
_____ 8. I really enjoy my mother.
_____ 9. My mother puts too many limits on me.
_____ 10. My mother interferes with my activities.
_____ 11. I resent my mother.
_____ 12. I think my mother is terrific.
_____ 13. I hate my mother.
_____ 14. My mother is very patient with me.
_____ 15. I really like my mother.
_____ 16. I like being with my mother.
_____ 17. I feel like I do not love my mother.
_____ 18. My mother is very irritating.
_____ 19. I feel very angry toward my mother.
_____ 20. I feel violent toward my mother.
_____ 21. I feel proud of my mother.
_____ 22. I wish my mother was more like others I know.
_____ 23. My mother does not understand me.
_____ 24. I can really depend on my mother.
_____ 25. I feel ashamed of my mother.

2,3,8,12,14,15,16,21,24

DYADIC ADJUSTMENT SCALE (DAS)

AUTHOR: Graham B. Spanier

PURPOSE: To assess the quality of marriage or similar dyads.

DESCRIPTION: This 32-item instrument is designed to assess the quality of the relationship as perceived by married or cohabiting couples. The instrument was designed to serve a number of needs. It can be used as a general measure of satisfaction in an intimate relationship by using total scores. Factor analysis indicates that the instrument measures four aspects of the relationship: dyadic satisfaction (DS), dyadic cohesion (DCoh), dyadic consensus (DCon) and affectional expression (AE). The instrument may be adapted for use in interviews.

NORMS: The DAS was developed on a sample of married (n = 218) and divorced persons (n = 94). The average age of the married people was 35.1 years, while the divorced sample was slightly younger, 30.4 years. The married sample had been married an average of 13.2 years while the average length of the marriages for the divorced sample was 8.5 years. The mean score on the total DAS was 114.8 with a standard deviation of 17.8 for the married sample. The mean for the divorced sample was 70.7 with a standard deviation of 23.8.

SCORING: Three different types of rating scales are used with the DAS. Total scores are the sum of all items, ranging from 0–151. Higher scores reflect a better relationship. The factor items are as follows: DS: 16, 17, 18, 19, 20, 21, 22, 23, 31, 32; DCoh: 24, 25, 26, 27, 28; DCon: 1, 2, 3, 5, 7, 8, 9, 10, 11, 12, 13, 14, 15; AE: 4, 6, 29, 30.

RELIABILITY: As a total score, the DAS has impressive internal consistency, with an alpha of .96. The subscales have fair to excellent internal consistency: DS .94, DCoh .81, DCon .90, and AE .73.

VALIDITY: The instrument was first checked with logical content validity procedures. The DAS also has shown known-groups validity by discriminating between married and divorced couples on each item. The instrument also has evidence of concurrent validity, correlating with the Locke-Wallace Marital Adjustment Scale.

PRIMARY REFERENCE: Spanier, G. B. (1976). Measuring dyadic adjustment: New scales for assessing the quality of marriage and similar dyads, *Journal of Marriage and the Family* 38, 15–28. Instrument reproduced with permission of Graham B. Spanier.

AVAILABILITY: Journal article.

424

DAS

Most persons have disagreements in their relationships. Please indicate below the approximate extent of agreement or disagreement between you and your partner for each item on the following list.

1 = Always agree
2 = Almost always agree
3 = Occasionlly disagree
4 = Frequently disagree
5 = Almost always disagree
6 = Always disagree

____ 1. Handling family finances
____ 2. Matters of recreation
____ 3. Religious matters
____ 4. Demonstrations of affection
____ 5. Friends
____ 6. Sex relations
____ 7. Conventionality (correct or proper behavior)
____ 8. Philosophy of life
____ 9. Ways of dealing with parents or in-laws
____ 10. Aims, goals, and things believed important
____ 11. Amount of time spent together
____ 12. Making major decisions
____ 13. Household tasks
____ 14. Leisure time interests and activities
____ 15. Career decisions

1 = All the time
2 = Most of the time
3 = More often than not
4 = Occasionally
5 = Rarely
6 = Never

____ 16. How often do you discuss or have you considered divorce, separation, or terminating your relationship?
____ 17. How often do you or your mate leave the house after a fight?
____ 18. In general, how often do you think that things between you and your partner are going well?
____ 19. Do you confide in your mate?
____ 20. Do you ever regret that you married? (*or lived together*)
____ 21. How often do you and your partner quarrel?
____ 22. How often do you and your mate "get on each other's nerves?"

23. Do you kiss your mate?

	Almost	Occa-		
Every day	Every day	sionally	Rarely	Never
4	3	2	1	0

24. Do you and your mate engage in outside interests together?

All of	Most of	Some of	Very few	None of
them	them	them	of them	them
4	3	2	1	0

How often would you say the following events occur between you and your mate?

        0 = Never
        1 = Less than once a month
        2 = Once or twice a month
        3 = Once a day
        4 = More often

___ 25. Have a stimulating exchange of ideas
___ 26. Laugh together
___ 27. Calmly discuss something
___ 28. Work together on a project

These are some things about which couples sometimes agree and sometimes disagree. Indicate if either item below caused differences of opinions or problems in your relationship during the past few weeks. (Check yes or no)

Yes No 29. Being too tired for sex
Yes No 30. Not showing love

31. The numbers on the following line represent different degrees of happiness in your relationship. The middle point, "happy," represents the degree of happiness of most relationships. Please circle the number that best describes the degree of happiness, all things considered, of your relationship.

0	1	2	3	4	5	6
Extremely	Fairly	A Little	Happy	Very	Extremely	Perfect
Unhappy	Unhappy	Unhappy		Happy	Happy	

32. Please circle one of the following statements that best describes how you feel about the future of your relationship.

    <u>5</u> I want desperately for my relationship to succeed, and *would go to almost any length* to see that it does.

    <u>4</u> I want very much for my relationship to succeed, and *will do all I can* to see that it does.

    <u>3</u> I want very much for my relationship to succeed, and *will do my fair share* to see that it does.

    <u>2</u> It would be nice if my relationship succeeded, but *I can't do much more than I am doing* now to help it succeed.

    <u>1</u> It would be nice if it succeeded, but I *refuse to do any more than I am doing* now to keep the relationship going.

    <u>0</u> My relationship can never succeed, and *there is no more that I can do* to keep the relationship going.

FAMILY ADAPTABILITY AND COHESION EVALUATION SCALE (FACES–III)

AUTHORS: David H. Olson, Joyce Portner, Yoav Lavee

PURPOSE: To measure family cohesion and family adaptability.

DESCRIPTION: FACES–III is a 20-item instrument designed to measure two main dimensions of family functioning: cohesion and adaptability. FACES–III is based on the Circumplex Model of family functioning which asserts that there are three central dimensions of family behavior: cohesion, adapability (ability to change), and communication. FACES–III is the third in a series of instruments designed to measure two out of three of these dimensions. The instrument is designed to place families within the Circumplex Model and does so by assessing how family members see their family (perceived) and how they would like it to be (ideal). Thus, the same 20 items on the FACES–III are responded to in two different ways. FACES–III can also be used with couples simply by changing the wording on some of the items (e.g., the first item becomes, "We ask each other for help"). Clinical rating scales for therapists are also available for each of the three dimensions of family functioning.

NORMS: Extensive research on FACES–III has involved 2453 adults across the life cycle and 412 adolescents. Norms are available for families, families with adolescents, and young couples in different stages of the life cycle. Cutting scores also are available that distinguish among rigid, structured, flexible, and chaotic families on the adaptability dimension, and among disengaged, separated, connected, and enmeshed families on the cohesion dimension.

SCORING: FACES–III is scored by summing all items to obtain the total score, summing odd items to obtain the cohesion score, and summing even items to obtain the adaptability score. The higher the cohesion score, the more enmeshed the family is said to be. The higher the adaptability score, the more chaotic it is.

RELIABILITY: FACES–III has only fair internal consistency with an overall alpha of .68 for the total instrument, .77 for cohesion, and .62 for adaptability. Test-retest data are not available but for FACES–II, there was a four to five-week test-retest correlation of .83 for cohesion and .80 for adaptability showing very good stability.

VALIDITY: FACES–III appears to have good face validity, but data are not yet available demonstrating any other type of validity. On the other hand, a number of studies have shown FACES–II to have fair known-groups validity in being able to discriminate among extreme, mid-range, and balanced families in several problem categories. A good deal of research currently is being conducted on FACES–III which might generate more information on validity.

PRIMARY REFERENCE: Olson, D. H., Portner, J., and Lavee, Y. (1985). FACES–III, Family Social Science, University of Minnesota, 290 McNeal Hall, St. Paul, Minnesota, 55108. Instrument reproduced with permission of David H. Olson.

AVAILABILITY: Dr. David H. Olson, Family Social Science, University of Minnesota, 290 McNeal Hall, 1985 Buford Avenue, St. Paul, MN 55108.

FACES-III

Please use the following scale to answer both sets of questions:

1 = Almost never
2 = Once in a while
3 = Sometimes
4 = Frequently
5 = Almost always

DESCRIBE YOUR FAMILY NOW:

____ 1. Family members ask each other for help.
____ 2. In solving problems, the children's suggestions are followed.
____ 3. We approve of each other's friends.
____ 4. Children have a say in their discipline.
____ 5. We like to do things with just our immediate family.
____ 6. Different persons act as leaders in our family.
____ 7. Family members feel closer to other family members than to people outside the family.
____ 8. Our family changes its way of handling tasks.
____ 9. Family members like to spend free time with each other.
____ 10. Parent(s) and children discuss punishment together.
____ 11. Family members feel very close to each other.
____ 12. The children make the decisions in our family.
____ 13. When our family gets together for activities, everybody is present.
____ 14. Rules change in our family.
____ 15. We can easily think of things to do together as a family.
____ 16. We shift household responsibilities from person to person.
____ 17. Family members consult other family members on their decisions.
____ 18. It is hard to identify the leader(s) in our family.
____ 19. Family togetherness is very important.
____ 20. It is hard to tell who does which household chores.

IDEALLY, HOW WOULD YOU LIKE YOUR FAMILY TO BE:

____ 21. Family members would ask each other for help.
____ 22. In solving problems, the children's suggestions would be followed.
____ 23. We would approve of each other's friends.
____ 24. The children would have a say in their discipline.
____ 25. We would like to do things with just our immediate family.
____ 26. Different persons would act as leaders in our family.
____ 27. Family members would feel closer to each other than to people outside the family.
____ 28. Our family would change its way of handling tasks.
____ 29. Family members would like to spend free time with each other.
____ 30. Parent(s) and children would discuss punishment together.

___ 31. Family members would feel very close to each other.
___ 32. Children would make the decisions in our family.
___ 33. When our family got together, everybody would be present.
___ 34. Rules would change in our family.
___ 35. We could easily think of things to do together as a family.
___ 36. We would shift household responsibilities from person to person.
___ 37. Family members would consult each other on their decisions.
___ 38. We would know who the leader(s) was (were) in our family.
___ 39. Family togetherness would be very important.
___ 40. We could tell who does which household chores.

FAMILY ASSESSMENT DEVICE (FAD)

AUTHORS: Nathan B. Epstein, Lawrence M. Baldwin, Duane S. Bishop

PURPOSE: To evaluate family functioning.

DESCRIPTION: The FAD is a 60-item questionnaire designed to evaluate family functioning according to the McMaster Model. This model describes structural, occupational, and transactional properties of families and identifies six dimensions of family functioning: problem solving, communication, roles, affective responsiveness, affective involvement, and behavior control. Accordingly, the FAD is made up of six subscales to measure each of these dimensions plus a seventh subscale dealing with general functioning. A clinical rating scale, used by clinicians in evaluating family functioning, is also available.

NORMS: The FAD was developed on the basis of responses of 503 individuals of whom 294 came from a group of 112 families. The bulk (93) of these families had one member who was an inpatient in an adult psychiatric hospital. The remaining 209 individuals in the sample were students in an introductory psychology course. No other demographic data were presented. Means and standard deviations for clinical and nonclinical samples are:

Scale	Clinical	Non-Clinical
Problem Solving	2.20	2.38
Communication	2.15	2.37
Roles	2.22	2.47
Affective Responsiveness	2.23	2.42
Affective Involvement	2.05	2.23
Behavior Control	1.90	2.02
General Functioning	1.96	2.26

Although the current version of the scale has 60 items, the original studies were based on a 53-item measure. Seven items were added which are reported to increase reliability of the subscales to which they were added.

SCORING: Each item is scored on a 1 to 4 basis using the following key: SA = 1, A = 2, D = 3, SD = 4. Items describing unhealthy functioning are reverse-scored. Lower scores indicate healthier functioning. Scored responses to the items are averaged to provide seven scale scores, each having a possible range from 1.0 (healthy) to 4.0 (unhealthy). Scoring sheets and keys are available to make the scoring process relatively simple and to indicate the items of each subscale.

RELIABILITY: The FAD demonstrates fairly good internal consistency

432

with alphas for the subscales ranging from .72 to .92. No reliability figures are reported for the overall measure; test-retest reliability data are not available.

VALIDITY: When the general functioning subscale is removed from the analysis, the six other subscales appear relatively independent. The FAD demonstrates some degree of concurrent and predictive validity. In a separate study of 178 couples in their sixties, the FAD was moderately correlated with the Locke-Wallace Marital Satisfaction Scale and showed a fair ability to predict scores on the Philadelphia Geriatric Morale Scale. Further, the FAD has good known-groups validity, with all seven subscales significantly distinguishing between individuals from clinical families and those from nonclinical families.

PRIMARY REFERENCE: Epstein, N. B., Baldwin, L. M., and Bishop, D. S. (1983). The McMaster Family Assessment Device, *Journal of Marital and Family Therapy,* 9, 171–180. Instrument reproduced with permission of Nathan Epstein and Duane Bishop.

AVAILABILITY: Family Research Program, Butler Hospital, 345 Blackstone Boulevard, Providence, RI 92906.

FAD

The following pages contain a number of statements about families. Please read each statement carefully, and decide how well it describes your own family. You should answer according to how you see your family.

For each statement there are four (4) possible reponses:

1 = Strongly agree   Select 1 if you feel that the statement describes your family very accurately.

2 = Agree   Select 2 if you feel that the statement describes your family for the most part.

3 = Disagree   Select 3 if you feel that the statement does not describe your family for the most part.

4 = Strongly disagree   Select 4 if you feel that the statement does not describe your family at all.

Try not to spend too much time thinking about each statement, but respond as quickly and as honestly as you can. If you have trouble with one, answer with your first reaction. Please be sure to answer *every* statement and mark all your answers in the *space provided to the left* of each statement.

____ 1. Planning family activities is difficult because we misunderstand each other.
____ 2. We resolve most everyday problems around the house.
____ 3. When someone is upset the others know why.
____ 4. When you ask someone to do something, you have to check that they did it.
____ 5. If someone is in trouble, the others become too involved.
____ 6. In times of crisis we can turn to each other for support.
____ 7. We don't know what to do when an emergency comes up.
____ 8. We sometimes run out of things that we need.
____ 9. We are reluctant to show our affection for each other.
____ 10. We make sure members meet their family responsibilities.
____ 11. We cannot talk to each other about the sadness we feel.
____ 12. We usually act on our decisions regarding problems.
____ 13. You only get the interest of others when something is important to them.
____ 14. You can't tell how a person is feeling from what they are saying.
____ 15. Family tasks don't get spread around enough.
____ 16. Individuals are accepted for what they are.
____ 17. You can easily get away with breaking the rules.
____ 18. People come right out and say things instead of hinting at them.
____ 19. Some of us just don't respond emotionally.

___ 20. We know what to do in an emergency.
___ 21. We avoid discussing our fears and concerns.
___ 22. It is difficult to talk to each other about tender feelings.
___ 23. We have trouble meeting our bills.
___ 24. After our family tries to solve a problem, we usually discuss whether it worked or not.
___ 25. We are too self-centered.
___ 26. We can express feelings to each other.
___ 27. We have no clear expectations about toilet habits.
___ 28. We do not show our love for each other.
___ 29. We talk to people directly rather than through go-betweens.
___ 30. Each of us has particular duties and responsibilities.
___ 31. There are lots of bad feelings in the family.
___ 32. We have rules about hitting people.
___ 33. We get involved with each other only when something interests us.
___ 34. There's little time to explore personal interests.
___ 35. We often don't say what we mean.
___ 36. We feel accepted for what we are.
___ 37. We show interest in each other when we can get something out of it personally.
___ 38. We resolve most emotional upsets that come up.
___ 39. Tenderness takes second place to other things in our family.
___ 40. We discuss who is to do household jobs.
___ 41. Making decisions is a problem for our family.
___ 42. Our family shows interest in each other only when they can get something out of it.
___ 43. We are frank with each other.
___ 44. We don't hold to any rules or standards.
___ 45. If people are asked to do something, they need reminding.
___ 46. We are able to make decisions about how to solve problems.
___ 47. If the rules are broken, we don't know what to expect.
___ 48. Anything goes in our family.
___ 49. We express tenderness.
___ 50. We confront problems involving feelings.
___ 51. We don't get along well together.
___ 52. We don't talk to each other when we are angry.
___ 53. We are generally dissatisfied with the family duties assigned to us.
___ 54. Even though we mean well, we intrude too much into each others' lives.
___ 55. There are rules about dangerous situations.
___ 56. We confide in each other.
___ 57. We cry openly.
___ 58. We don't have reasonable transport.
___ 59. When we don't like what someone has done, we tell them.
___ 60. We try to think of different ways to solve problems.

FAMILY AWARENESS SCALE (FAS)

AUTHORS: Michael S. Kolevzon and Robert G. Green

PURPOSE: To measure family competence.

DESCRIPTION: The FAS is a 14-item instrument designed to measure family competence as described in the Beavers-Timberlawn Model of Family Competence. This model proposes that optimally functioning families can be distinguished from less competent families on the basis of several dimensions: family structure, mythology (how the family views itself), goal-directed negotiation, autonomy of its members, and the nature of family expression. The FAS can be administered to all members of a family able to understand the questions. As a new instrument, the FAS does not have a great deal of psychometric data available, but it does appear to be one means of providing an overall view of family competence.

NORMS: The FAS was initially studied with 157 families who participated in a family therapy research project. All families had one child under supervision of the Corrections Department of the State of Virginia. The families were mainly white (79%), 36.9 single-parent, with a broad range of income levels. No actual norms are reported.

SCORING: Items 1 and 2 are scored on a 5-point scale while items 3 through 14 are scored on 9-point scales. Negatively worded items are reverse-scored and then all the items are summed to produce a range of 14 to 118, with higher scores meaning greater family competence.

RELIABILITY: The FAS has very good internal consistency, with alphas of .85 for children, .87 for mothers, and .88 for fathers. No test-retest data were reported.

VALIDITY: The FAS has some degree of concurrent validity, correlating at low but significant levels with trained raters of family competence who also used the Beavers-Timberlawn model. The FAS is also significantly correlated with the Parent-Adolescent Communication Inventory and the Dyadic Adjustment Scale. No other validity data were reported.

PRIMARY REFERENCE: Green, R. G., Kolevzon, M. S. and Vosler, N. R. (1985). The Beavers-Timberlawn Model of Family Competence and the Circumplex Model of Family Adaptability and Cohesion: Separate, but equal? *Family Process*, 24, 385–398. Instrument reproduced with permission of Michael S. Kolevzon and Robert G. Green.

AVAILABILITY: Dr. Michael S. Kolevzon, Florida International University School of Public Affairs and Services, Social Work Department, North Miami Beach, FL 33181.

FAS

PART I

Questions 1 and 2 each contain a group of statements that describe families. For each question please check the blank for the statement that *most accurately describes* your family.

1. a.___ No one person is really strong enough to be the leader in our family.
   b.___ Our family has one strong leader. The leader always makes the rules and enforces them.
   c.___ Although we have a strong leader, *at times* we talk over decisions.
   d.___ We *frequently* talk things over, but in the end one person is usually in charge.
   e.___ Leadership is always shared between the adults in our family depending on the situation.

2. a.___ In our family it seems that a parent and a child are always "teaming or ganging" up against other family members.
   b.___ Frequently a parent and a child team up against other family members.
   c.___ The adults are usually on the same side, but they are not a strong team.
   d.___ The adults are usually on the same side and generally they make a good learning team.
   e.___ There is always a strong adult team in our family.

PART II

Questions 3 to 14 describe certain characteristics of all families on a 9-point scale. Please *circle* the number on the scale that best describes your family. *Please circle only one number for each item.*

3. How difficult is it for someone outside of your family to figure out which family members have power over other family members?

   Very
   difficult 1   2   3   4   5   6   7   8   9 Very
                                                                 easy

4. How good a judge are individual family members of their own behaviors within your family?

   Very
   good   1   2   3   4   5   6   7   8   9 Very
   judge   poor
                                                                 judge

5. How good is your family at taking over and solving problems?

Very
good   1   2   3   4   5   6   7   8   9 bad   Very

6. How *clearly* do the members of your family tell one another about their feelings and thoughts?

Very
clear   1   2   3   4   5   6   7   8   9 clear   Not

7. How frequently do the members of your family say or admit that they are responsible for their own past and present behavior?

Always   Never
            1   2   3   4   5   6   7   8   9

8. How often do the members of your family speak for one another or act like they can read each other's minds?

Fre-
quently   Never
            1   2   3   4   5   6   7   8   9

9. How often are family members open and willing to listen to the statements of other family members?

Usually   Prac-
                                                             tically
            1   2   3   4   5   6   7   8   9 Never

10. How often do family members share their feelings with one another?

Always   Never
            1   2   3   4   5   6   7   8   9

11. How would you describe your family?

Warm,   Cynical,
Humorous,   Hopeless,
Opti-   1   2   3   4   5   6   7   8   9 Pessi-
mistic   mistic

12. How much conflict is there generally in your family?

Always   Never
            1   2   3   4   5   6   7   8   9

13. How often are family members sensitive to, and understanding of, each others' feelings?

Always   Never
            1   2   3   4   5   6   7   8   9

14. How many emotional problems does your family have compared *to most families?*

Far more   _____   Far fewer

       1   2   3   4   5   6   7   8   9

INDEX OF FAMILY RELATIONS (IFR)

AUTHOR: Walter W. Hudson

PURPOSE: To measure family relationship problems.

DESCRIPTION: The IFR is a 25-item scale designed to measure the extent, severity, or magnitude of problems that family members have in their relationships with one another. The IFR allows the respondent to characterize the severity of family problems in a global fashion and can be regarded as an overall measure of intrafamilial stress. It can be used with one client or with two or more family members who each evaluate the overall family environment. The IFR has a cutting score of 30 (± 5), with scores above 30 indicating that the respondent has a clinically significant problem and scores below 30 indicating no such problem. Another advantage of the GCS is that it is one of nine scales of the Clinical Measurement Package (Hudson, 1982) reproduced here, all of which are administered and scored the same way.

NORMS: The IFR was developed with 518 respondents, including single and married individuals, clinical and nonclinical populations, and college students and nonstudents. Respondents were primarily Caucasian, but also included Japanese and Chinese Americans, and a smaller number of other ethnic groups. The IFR is not recommended for use with children under the age of 12.

SCORING: The IFR is scored by first reverse-scoring the items listed at the bottom of the scale, then totaling these and the other item scores, and subtracting 25. This gives a range of 0 to 100 with higher scores giving more evidence of the presence of family relationship problems. For scoring questionnaires with missing items, the procedure is as follows: If the client omits up to four items, reverse-score and sum scores as on the fully completed scale. Subtract from that number the number of items completed. Multiply this figure by 100. Divide the results by the number of items completed times four. This will produce a score between 0 and 100 (Hudson, 1982).

RELIABILITY: The IFR has a mean alpha of .95, indicating excellent internal consistency, and an excellent (low) Standard Error of Measurement of 3.65. Test-retest data are not available.

VALIDITY: The IFR has excellent known-groups validity, significantly distinguishing respondents designated by themselves and their counselors as having family relationships problems. The IFR also has good construct validity, correlating poorly with measures with which it should not correlate, and correlating well with other measures with which it should correlate such as other parent-child and family relationship ratings.

440

IFR

This questionnaire is designed to measure the way you feel about your family as a whole. It is not a test, so there are no right or wrong answers. Answer each item as carefully and accurately as you can by placing a number beside each one as follows:

1 = Rarely or none of the time
2 = A little of the time
3 = Some of the time
4 = A good part of the time
5 = Most or all of the time

_____ 1. The members of my family really care about each other.
_____ 2. I think my family is terrific.
_____ 3. My family gets on my nerves.
_____ 4. I really enjoy my family.
_____ 5. I can really depend on my family.
_____ 6. I really do not care to be around my family.
_____ 7. I wish I was not part of this family.
_____ 8. I get along well with my family.
_____ 9. Members of my family argue too much.
_____ 10. There is no sense of closeness in my family.
_____ 11. I feel like a stranger in my family.
_____ 12. My family does not understand me.
_____ 13. There is too much hatred in my family.
_____ 14. Members of my family are really good to one another.
_____ 15. My family is well respected by those who know us.
_____ 16. There seems to be a lot of friction in my family.
_____ 17. There is a lot of love in my family.
_____ 18. Members of my family get along well together.
_____ 19. Life in my family is generally unpleasant.
_____ 20. My family is a great joy to me.
_____ 21. I feel proud of my family.
_____ 22. Other families seem to get along better than ours.
_____ 23. My family is a real source of comfort to me.
_____ 24. I feel left out of my family.
_____ 25. My family is an unhappy one.

1,2,4,5,8,14,15,17,18,20,21,23

PRIMARY REFERENCE: Hudson, W. W. (1982). *The Clinical Measuremer Package: A Field Manual*. Chicago: Dorsey Press. Instrument repro duced with permission of Walter W. Hudson and the Dorsey Press.
AVAILABILITY: The Dorsey Press, 224 South Michigan Avenue, Suite 440 Chicago, IL 60604

INDEX OF MARITAL SATISFACTION (IMS)

AUTHOR: Walter W. Hudson

PURPOSE: To measure problems in the marital relationship.

DESCRIPTION: The IMS is a 25-item instrument designed to measure the degree, severity, or magnitude of a problem one spouse or partner has in the marital relationship. It does not characterize the relationship as a unitary entity but measures the extent to which one partner perceives problems in the relationship. The IMS does not measure marital adjustment since a couple may have arrived at a good adjustment despite having a high degree of discord or dissatisfaction. The IMS has a cutting score of 30 (± 5), with scores above 30 indicating the respondent has a clinically significant problem and scores below 30 indicating no such problem. Another advantage of the IMS is that it is one of nine scales of the Clinical Measurement Package (Hudson, 1982) reproduced here, all of which are administered and scored the same way.

NORMS: The 1803 respondents who participated in the development of this scale included single and married individuals, clinical and nonclinical populations, high school and college students and nonstudents. Respondents were primarily Caucasian, but also included Japanese and Chinese Americans, and a smaller number of members of other ethnic groups.

SCORING: The IMS is scored by first reverse-scoring the items listed at the bottom of the scale, totaling these and the other item scores, and subtracting 25. This gives a range of 0 to 100 with higher scores giving more evidence of the presence of marital dissatisfaction. For scoring questionnaires with missing items, see Hudson (1982) or instructions for scoring the Index of Family Relations in this book.

RELIABILITY: The IMS has a mean alpha of .96, indicating excellent internal consistency, and an excellent (low) Standard Error of Measurement of 4.00. The IMS also has excellent stability with a two-hour test-retest correlation of .96.

VALIDITY: The IMS has excellent concurrent validity, correlating significantly with the Locke-Wallace Marital Adjustment Test. The IMS also has very good known-groups validity discriminating significantly between couples known to have marital problems and those known not to. The IMS also has good construct validity, correlating poorly with measures with which it should not correlate, and correlating significantly with several measures with which it should correlate, such as sexual satisfaction and marital problems.

PRIMARY REFERENCE: Hudson, W. W. (1982). *The Clinical Measurement Package: A Field Manual*. Chicago: Dorsey Press. Instrument reproduced with permission of Walter W. Hudson and the Dorsey Press.

AVAILABILITY: The Dorsey Press, 224 South Michigan Avenue, Suite 440, Chicago, IL 60604.

IMS

This questionnaire is designed to measure the degree of satisfaction you have with your present marriage. It is not a test, so there are no right or wrong answers. Answer each item as carefully and as accurately as you can by placing a number beside each one as follows:

1 = Rarely or none of the time
2 = A little of the time
3 = Some of the time
4 = Good part of the time
5 = Most or all of the time

____ 1. I feel that my partner is affectionate enough.
____ 2. I feel that my partner treats me badly.
____ 3. I feel that my partner really cares for me.
____ 4. I feel that I would not choose the same partner if I had it to do over.
____ 5. I feel that I can trust my partner.
____ 6. I feel that our relationship is breaking up.
____ 7. I feel that my partner doesn't understand me.
____ 8. I feel that our relationship is a good one.
____ 9. I feel that ours is a very happy relationship.
____ 10. I feel that our life together is dull.
____ 11. I feel that we have a lot of fun together.
____ 12. I feel that my partner doesn't confide in me.
____ 13. I feel that ours is a very close relationship.
____ 14. I feel that I cannot rely on my partner.
____ 15. I feel that we do not have enough interests in common.
____ 16. I feel that we manage arguments and disagreements very well.
____ 17. I feel that we do a good job of managing our finances.
____ 18. I feel that I should never have married my partner.
____ 19. I feel that my partner and I get along very well together.
____ 20. I feel that our relationship is very stable.
____ 21. I feel that my partner is pleased with me as a sex partner.
____ 22. I feel that we should do more things together.
____ 23. I feel that the future looks bright for our relationship.
____ 24. I feel that our relationship is empty.
____ 25. I feel there is no excitement in our relationship.

1,3,5,8,9,11,13,16,17,19,20,21,23

INDEX OF PARENTAL ATTITUDES (IPA)

AUTHOR: Walter W. Hudson

PURPOSE: To measure a parent's relationship problems with a child.

DESCRIPTION: The IPA is a 25-item scale designed to measure the extent, severity, or magnitude of parent-child relationship problems as seen and reported by a parent. The child may be of any age, from infant to adult. The IPA has a cutting score of 30 (± 5), with scores above 30 indicating the respondent has a clinically significant problem and scores below 30 indicating no such problem. Another advantage of the IPA is that it is one of nine scales of the Clinical Measurement Package (Hudson, 1982) reproduced here, all of which are administered and scored the same way.

NORMS: The 93 respondents who participated in the development of this scale all were seeking counseling services for personal or interpersonal problems. No other demographic data are available.

SCORING: The IPA is scored by first reverse-scoring items listed at the bottom of the scale, totaling these and the other item scores, and subtracting 25. This gives a range of 0 to 100 with higher scores giving more evidence of the presence of relationship problems with a child. For scoring questionnaires with missing items, see Hudson (1982) or instructions for scoring the Index of Family Relations in this book.

RELIABILITY: The IPA has a mean alpha of .97, indicating excellent internal consistency, and an excellent (low) Standard Error of Measurement of 3.64. Test-retest data are not available.

VALIDITY: The IPA has excellent known-groups validity, significantly distinguishing between groups of clients designated by themselves and their counselors as having or not having relationship problems with their children. The IPA also has fair construct validity, correlating moderately with variables with which it is predicted it would correlate moderately, and correlating highly with other measures with which it should correlate including other measures of parent-child and family relationships.

PRIMARY REFERENCE: Hudson, W. W. (1982). *The Clinical Measurement Package: A Field Manual*. Chicago: Dorsey Press. Instrument reproduced with permission of Walter W. Hudson and the Dorsey Press.

AVAILABILITY: The Dorsey Press, 224 South Michigan Avenue, Suite 440, Chicago, IL 60604.

IPA

This questionnaire is designed to measure the degree of contentment you have in your relationship with your child. It is not a test, so there are no right or wrong answers. Answer each item as carefully and accurately as you can by placing a number beside each one as follows:

1 = Rarely or none of the time
2 = A little of the time
3 = Some of the time
4 = Good part of the time
5 = Most or all of the time

___ 1. My child gets on my nerves.
___ 2. I get along well with my child.
___ 3. I feel that I can really trust my child.
___ 4. I dislike my child.
___ 5. My child is well behaved.
___ 6. My child is too demanding.
___ 7. I wish I did not have this child.
___ 8. I really enjoy my child.
___ 9. I have a hard time controlling my child.
___ 10. My child interferes with my activities.
___ 11. I resent my child.
___ 12. I think my child is terrific.
___ 13. I hate my child.
___ 14. I am very patient with my child.
___ 15. I really like my child.
___ 16. I like being with my child.
___ 17. I feel like I do not love my child.
___ 18. My child is irritating.
___ 19. I feel very angry toward my child.
___ 20. I feel violent toward my child.
___ 21. I feel very proud of my child.
___ 22. I wish my child was more like others I know.
___ 23. I just do not understand my child.
___ 24. My child is a real joy to me.
___ 25. I feel ashamed of my child.

2,3,5,8,12,14,15,16,21,24

INDEX OF SPOUSE ABUSE (ISA)

AUTHOR: Walter W. Hudson

PURPOSE: To measure the degree or severity of abuse.

DESCRIPTION: The ISA is a 30-item scale designed to measure the severity or magnitude of physical or nonphysical abuse inflicted on a woman by her spouse or partner. Each item on the ISA represents some behavior or interaction that is considered abusive. Some items represent more serious types of abuse than others, and this is taken into account in scoring and interpretation. The ISA comprises two subscales, an ISA-P that measures the severity of physical abuse, and an ISA-NP that measures the severity of nonphysical abuse. The ISA also contains two clinical cutting scores, one for each subscale. For the ISA-P, scores above 10 indicate the respondent is very likely a victim of serious physical abuse, and for the ISA-NP, scores above 25 indicate the respondent is likely a victim of serious nonphysical abuse. As one of the few, and perhaps the only, available measure for clinical evaluation of spouse or partner abuse, the ISA is a very important instrument for the helping professions.

NORMS: A series of studies was conducted in developing and evaluating the ISA. The first involved 398 graduate and undergraduate female students who were married to, residing with, or involved with a male partner. The second involved 108 female graduate and undergraduate students in social work and psychology (no other demographic data are available). The third involved a clinical sample of 107 women obtained from social agencies and protective shelters. Although complete norms are not available for the ISA, mean scores for a group identified by others as abused was 45.2 on the ISA-P and 58.9 on the ISA-NP; for the nonabused group, means were only 3.8 on the ISA-P and 8.3 on the ISA-NP.

SCORING: Scoring of the ISA is fairly complicated because the two subscales are scored separately and because each item is weighted according to the seriousness of the abusive behavior. (For a description of the development of item weights, see primary reference). Item weights are in parentheses following each item. The following general scoring procedures are carried out separately for the ISA-P and ISA-NP; items relating to each are listed at the bottom of the instrument. First, if any item is not answered, disregard it. Second, multiply the item score (from 1 to 5) by the item weight and place it in the margin next to the item; sum these scores. Third, add up all the item weights to obtain the minimum score a person could obtain. Finally, subtract that minimum score from the sum of other scores (item times weight), multiply by 100, and divide that by the minimum score times 4. This produces scores that conveniently range from 0 to 100 for each subscale.

RELIABILITY: The ISA has excellent internal consistency, with alphas that range from .90 to .94 for the ISA-P and .91 to .97 for the ISA-NP. The Standard Errors of Measurement were also very low, ranging from 2.68 to 4.67 for the ISA-P and 3.27 to 3.33 for the ISA-NP. Thus, the ISA appears to have relatively little measurement error. No data are available for test-retest reliability.

VALIDITY: The ISA has good known-groups validity, accurately discriminating between women known to be abuse victims and women known not to be victims. The ISA also has good construct validity, showing predicted low correlations with a group of personal and social problems believed to have little or no direct correlation with abuse and high correlations with personal and social problems believed to be related to abuse (e.g., depression, low self-esteem, sexual satisfaction, marital relationship problems).

PRIMARY REFERENCE: Hudson, W. W. and McIntosh, S. R. (1981). The assessment of spouse abuse: Two quantifiable dimensions, *Journal of Marriage and the Family* 43, 873–888. Instrument reproduced by permission of Walter W. Hudson.

AVAILABILITY: Dr. Walter W. Hudson, University of Arizona, School of Social Work, Tempe, AZ 95287.

ISA

This questionnaire is designed to measure the degree of abuse you have experienced in your relationship with your partner. It is not a test, so there are no right or wrong answers. Answer each item as carefully and accurately as you can by placing a number beside each one as follows:

1 = Never
2 = Rarely
3 = Occasionally
4 = Frequently
5 = Very frequently

____ 1. My partner belittles me. (1)
____ 2. My partner demands obedience to his whims. (17)
____ 3. My partner becomes surly and angry if I tell him he is drinking too much. (15)
____ 4. My partner makes me perform sex acts that I do not enjoy or like. (50)
____ 5. My partner becomes very upset if dinner, housework, or laundry is not done when he thinks it should be. (4)
____ 6. My partner is jealous and suspicious of my friends. (8)
____ 7. My partner punches me with his fists. (75)
____ 8. My partner tells me I am ugly and unattractive. (26)
____ 9. My partner tells me I really couldn't manage or take care of myself without him. (8)
____ 10. My partner acts like I am his personal servant. (20)
____ 11. My partner insults or shames me in front of others. (41)
____ 12. My partner becomes very angry if I disagree with his point of view. (15)
____ 13. My partner threatens me with a weapon. (82)
____ 14. My partner is stingy in giving me enough money to run our home. (12)
____ 15. My partner belittles me intellectually. (20)
____ 16. My partner demands that I stay home to take care of the children. (14)
____ 17. My partner beats me so badly that I must seek medical help. (98)
____ 18. My partner feels that I should not work or go to school. (21)
____ 19. My partner is not a kind person. (13)
____ 20. My partner does not want me to socialize with my female friends. (18)
____ 21. My partner demands sex whether I want it or not. (52)
____ 22. My partner screams and yells at me. (38)
____ 23. My partner slaps me around my face and head. (80)
____ 24. My partner becomes abusive when he drinks. (65)
____ 25. My partner orders me around. (29)
____ 26. My partner has no respect for my feelings. (39)
____ 27. My partner acts like a bully towards me. (44)

___ 28. My partner frightens me. (55)
___ 29. My partner treats me like a dunce. (29)
___ 30. My partner acts like he would like to kill me. (80)

P: 3,4,7,13,17,22-24,27,28,30.
NP: 1,2,5,6,8-12,14-16,18-21,25,26,29.

LOCKE-WALLACE MARITAL ADJUSTMENT TEST (LWMAT)

AUTHORS: Harvey J. Locke and Karl M. Wallace

PURPOSE: To measure marital adjustment

DESCRIPTION: This 15-item instrument was one of the first short measures of marital adjustment. Marital adjustment is defined as the accommodation of partners to each other at any given time. The first item is a general index of marital happiness and is given extra weight in scoring. Scores of 100 or less are considered cutting scores, indicating maladjustment in the marital relationship. The instrument is rather global and may not be very helpful in treatment planning where behavioral specificity is important.

NORMS: Normative data are available on a sample of 236 married couples. The sample was predominantely white and was approximately 30 years old. A subsample of adjusted respondents had a mean score of 135.9 while a subsample of maladjusted respondents had a mean of 71.7.

SCORING: Items are scored with different weights, as indicated on the instrument. Item 12 is scored 10 points if respondents indicate both spouses prefer to "stay at home," 3 points if both spouses prefer to be "on the go" and 2 points if the preferences for the spouses are different from each other. Scores are the sum of each item and range from 2 to 158.

RELIABILITY: The internal consistency was estimated using the Spearman-Brown formula and was very good, with a correlation of .90. No information is available for test-retest reliability.

VALIDITY: The LWMAT has evidence of known-groups validity with scores discriminating between adjusted and maladjusted couples. Concurrent validity is suggested as scores on the instrument correlate with the Locke-Wallace Marital Predictions Test, a measure of predicted future adjustment.

PRIMARY REFERENCE: Locke, H. J. and Wallace, K. M. (1959). Short marital-adjustment and prediction tests: Their reliability and validity, *Marriage and Family Living* 21, 251–255. Instrument reproduced with permission of Harvey J. Locke and Karl M. Wallace.

AVAILABILITY: Journal article.

LWMAT

1. Check the dot on the scale line below which best describes the degree of happiness, everything considered, of your present marriage. The middle point, "happy," represents the degree of happiness which most people get from marriage, and the scale gradually ranges on one side to those few who are very unhappy in marriage, and on the other, to those few who experience extreme joy or felicity in marriage.

0	2	7	15	20	25	35
•	•	•	•	•	•	•

Very   Perfectly
unhappy   happy

State the approximate extent of agreement or disagreement between you and your mate on the following items. Please check each column.

	Always agree	Almost always agree	Occasionally disagree	Frequently disagree	Almost always disagree	Always disagree
2. Handling family finances	5	4	3	2	1	0
3. Matters of recreation	5	4	3	2	1	0
4. Demonstration of affection	8	6	4	2	1	0
5. Friends	5	4	3	2	1	0
6. Sex Relations	15	12	9	4	1	0
7. Conventionality (right, good, or proper conduct)	5	4	3	2	1	0
8. Philosophy of life	5	4	3	2	1	0
9. Ways of dealing with in-laws	5	4	3	2	1	0

10. When disagreements arise, they usually result in:
    - 0 husband giving in
    - *2* wife giving in
    - 10 agreement by mutual give and take

11. Do you and your mate engage in outside interests together?
    - 10 All of them
    - 8 some of them
    - 3 very few of them
    - 0 none of them

12. In leisure time do you generally prefer: to be "on the go" ___
                                                 to stay at home? ___

    Does your mate generally prefer: to be "on the go" ___
                                            to stay at home? ___

13. Do you ever wish you had not married?
    - 0 Frequently
    - 3 occasionally
    - 8 rarely
    - 15 never

14. If you had your life to live over, do you think you would:
    - 15 marry the same person
    - 0 marry a different person
    - 1 not marry at all

15. Do you confide in your mate:
    - 0 almost never
    - 2 rarely
    - 10 in most things
    - 10 in everything

MARITAL COMPARISON LEVEL INDEX (MCLI)

AUTHORS: Ronald M. Sabatelli

PURPOSE: To assess spouses' perceptions of their marital relationship.

DESCRIPTION: The MCLI is a 32-item instrument designed to measure an individual's perception of the degree to which his or her marital relationship is living up to his or her expectations. The MCLI can be viewed as a global assessment of the respondent's complaints about his or her marital relationship. It is based on the notion that one complains about some aspect of the marriage only when that aspect fails to meet one's expectations. The items were initially generated from theory based on comprehensive review of the marital satisfaction/adjustment literature. Through factor analysis, with the elimination of four items, the MCLI was found to be unidimensional. In order to assess marital outcomes relative to expectations, each item was scored on a 7-point scale with the midpoint on the scale reflecting the respondent's expectation level. This allows respondents to indicate the degree to which their relationship outcomes fall above or below expectations.

NORMS: A sample of 300 married couples was selected from a Wisconsin university. The sample had a mean age of 36.1 for women and 38 for men, and consisted primarily of upper middle-class, professional families. Means on the MCLI for men were 144.7 and for women 149.7.

SCORING: The MCLI is scored by assigning 1 point to an answer of −3, 4 points when a person circled "0" (the midpoint), and 7 when a person circled +3. The individual item scores are then summed with higher scores indicating more favorable evaluation of outcomes relative to expectations.

RELIABILITY: The MCLI has excellent internal consistency with an alpha of .93. A very low Standard Error of Measurement of 1.38 also indicates excellent reliability. No test-retest data were reported.

VALIDITY: The MCLI has good concurrent validity, correlating significantly with scores on measure of relational equity and marital commitment.

PRIMARY REFERENCE: Sabatelli, R. M. (1984). The Marital Comparison Level Index: A measure for assessing outcomes relative to expectations, *Journal of Marriage and the Family* 46, 651–662. Instrument reproduced with permission of Ronald M. Sabatelli.

AVAILABILITY: Dr. Ronald M. Sabatelli, Human Development Center, U-117, Storrs, CT 06268.

MCL I

Indicate by circling the appropriate number how your current experiences compare to your expectations.

-3	-2	-1	0	+1	+2	+3

Worse than I expect	About what I expect	Better than I expect

1. The amount of companionship you experience   -3   -2   -1   0   +1   +2   +3

2. The amount your partner is trusting of you   -3   -2   -1   0   +1   +2   +3

3. The amount of sexual activity that you experience   -3   -2   -1   0   +1   +2   +3

4. The amount of confiding that occurs between you and your spouse   -3   -2   -1   0   +1   +2   +3

5. The amount of conflict over daily decisions that exists   -3   -2   -1   0   +1   +2   +3

6. The amount of time you spend together   -3   -2   -1   0   +1   +2   +3

7. The amount of affection your partner displays   -3   -2   -1   0   +1   +2   +3

8. The amount of the responsibility for household tasks is shared   -3   -2   -1   0   +1   +2   +3

9. The amount your partner is willing to listen to you   -3   -2   -1   0   +1   +2   +3

10. The amount of relationship equality you experience   -3   -2   -1   0   +1   +2   +3

11. The amount of conflict over money you experience   -3   -2   -1   0   +1   +2   +3

12. The amount of compatibility that you experience   -3   -2   -1   0   +1   +2   +3

13. The amount of conflict over the use of leisure time that you experience   -3   -2   -1   0   +1   +2   +3

14. The amount of disagreement over   -3 -2 -1   0 +1 +2 +3
    friends that you experience

15. The amount of interest in sex   -3 -2 -1   0 +1 +2 +3
    your partner expresses

16. The fairness with which money is   -3 -2 -1   0 +1 +2 +3
    spent

17. The amount of criticism your   -3 -2 -1   0 +1 +2 +3
    partner expresses

18. The amount of mutual respect you   -3 -2 -1   0 +1 +2 +3
    experience

19. The degree to which your   -3 -2 -1   0 +1 +2 +3
    interpersonal communications
    are effective

20. The amount of love you experience   -3 -2 -1   0 +1 +2 +3

21. The degree to which your needs   -3 -2 -1   0 +1 +2 +3
    are met

22. The amount of freedom you   -3 -2 -1   0 +1 +2 +3
    experience in pursuing other
    friendships

23. The amount of responsibility   -3 -2 -1   0 +1 +2 +3
    your partner accepts for
    household chores

24. The amount that you and your   -3 -2 -1   0 +1 +2 +3
    partner discuss sex

25. The amount of privacy you   -3 -2 -1   0 +1 +2 +3
    experience

26. The amount to which your spouse   -3 -2 -1   0 +1 +2 +3
    supports your choice of an
    occupation

27. The amount to which you and your   -3 -2 -1   0 +1 +2 +3
    spouse agree on your life-style

28. The amount to which you and your   -3 -2 -1   0 +1 +2 +3
    spouse agree on the number of
    children to have

29. The degree of physical   -3 -2 -1   0 +1 +2 +3
    attractiveness of your partner

30.	The amount of arguing over petty issues that you experience	-3	-2	-1	0	+1	+2	+3
31.	The amount of jealousy your partner expresses	-3	-2	-1	0	+1	+2	+3
32.	The amount of commitment you experience from your spouse	-3	-2	-1	0	+1	+2	+3

MARITAL HAPPINESS SCALE (MHS)

AUTHORS: Nathan H. Azrin, Barry T. Naster, and Robert Jones

PURPOSE: To measure current levels of marital happiness.

DESCRIPTION: This 10-item instrument was originally designed to test the effects of reciprocity counseling, a behavioral approach to marital counseling. The MHS assesses marital happiness in nine different areas of interaction with a global single item index measuring general happiness. Attention is given to the content of each item separately. The instrument seems particularly useful for couples dealing with the distribution of responsibility.

NORMS: Normative data are not available. The instrument was originally tested with 24 couples.

SCORING: Each item can be treated as a separate index of marital happiness for specific areas of marital interaction. Scores, thus, are the item responses having a range from 1 to 10. Scores on all items can be summed to produce a general index of marital happiness, with scores ranging from 10 to 100.

RELIABILITY: Data are not presented in primary reference.

VALIDITY: The couples used in the development of the MHS participated first in catharsis counseling and then in reciprocity counseling. Scores during the first treatment condition were lower than scores during the reciprocity counseling, suggesting the instrument is sensitive to measuring change. No other validity evidence is available.

PRIMARY REFERENCE: Azrin, N. H., Naster, B. J. and Jones, R. (1973). Reciprocity counseling: A rapid learning-based procedure for marital counseling. *Behavioral Research and Therapy* 11, 365–382. Instrument reproduced with permission of Dr. N. Azrin.

AVAILABILITY: Dr. N. Azrin, 5151 Bayview Drive, Ft. Lauderdale, FL 33308.

MHS

This scale is intended to estimate your *current* happiness with your
marriage on each of the ten dimensions listed. You are to circle one of
the numbers (1-10) beside each marriage area. Numbers toward the left end
of the ten-unit scale indicate some degree of unhappiness and numbers toward
the right end of the scale reflect varying degrees of happiness. Ask
yourself this question as you rate each marriage area: "If my partner
continues to act in the future as he (she) is acting *today* with respect to
this marriage area, how happy will I be *with this area of our marriage?*"
In other words, state according to the numerical scale (1-10) exactly how
you feel today. Try to exclude all feelings of yesterday and concentrate
only on the feelings of today in each of the marital areas. Also try not
to allow one category to influence the results of the other categories.

	Completely unhappy									Completely happy
Household responsibilities	1	2	3	4	5	6	7	8	9	10
Rearing of children	1	2	3	4	5	6	7	8	9	10
Social activities	1	2	3	4	5	6	7	8	9	10
Money	1	2	3	4	5	6	7	8	9	10
Communication	1	2	3	4	5	6	7	8	9	10
Sex	1	2	3	4	5	6	7	8	9	10
Academic (or occupational) progress	1	2	3	4	5	6	7	8	9	10
Personal independence	1	2	3	4	5	6	7	8	9	10
Spouse independence	1	2	3	4	5	6	7	8	9	10
General happiness	1	2	3	4	5	6	7	8	9	10

PRIMARY COMMUNICATION INVENTORY (PCI)

AUTHORS: H. J. Locke, F. Sabaght, and Mary M. Thomes

PURPOSE: To measure marital communication.

DESCRIPTION: The PCI is a 25-item instrument designed to assess marital communication. The overall score on the PCI appears to be a good indicator of the soundness of communication between two members of a couple. Various subscales have been used by different investigators, including verbal and nonverbal communication subscales determined by face validity, and two subscales determined by factor analysis: (1) the individual's perception of his or her own communication ability, and (2) the partner's perceptions of the individual's communication abilities (Beach and Arias, 1983). In view of the discrepancies regarding the subscales and problems in interpreting them, it is recommended that the overall score be used. It is necessary for both members of a couple to fill out the PCI for the instrument to be scored accurately since the PCI requires the respondent to complete items dealing with his or her own communication and the partner's communication.

NORMS: Several studies of the PCI have been conducted with distressed and nondistressed couples. In an early study 24 unhappy married couples were compared with 24 happily married couples. All the couples were from the same socioeconomic class (union workers and their spouses) and their mean age was in the mid-thirties. Mean scores for the happily married husbands and wives were virtually identical, 105.1 and 105.4 respectively. Means for the unhappily married husbands and wives were also similar, 81.6 and 81.1.

SCORING: The PCI is scored by reverse-scoring items 8, 15, and 17, transposing items 5, 6, 7, 9, 11, 13, 15, 21, and 24 from the partner's questionnaire (i.e., an individual's score for each of these items is the rating given by the partner), and then summing all these items for the individual score. Higher scores mean better or more positively viewed communication. (It is also possible to subtract a partner's ratings from the other person's self-ratings to determine dyadic disagreement in the perceptions of the other person's communication ability.)

RELIABILITY: Data are not available.

VALIDITY: The PCI has excellent concurrent validity, correlating strongly and significantly with the Locke-Wallace Marriage Relationship Inventory. The PCI also has excellent known-groups validity, distinguishing in several studies between distressed and nondistressed couples and couples seeking marital therapy and nonclinic couples. The PCI also has been found to be sensitive to changes due to therapeutic interventions.

PRIMARY REFERENCE: Navran, L. (1967). Communication and adjustment in marriage, *Family Process* 6, 173–184. Instrument reproduced with permission of *Family Process*.
AVAILABILITY: Journal article.

PCI

Below is a list of items on communication between you and your spouse. Using the scale described here, fill in the blank space next to each item with the number which best represents the extent to which you and your spouse behave in the specified way.

> 1 = Never
> 2 = Seldom
> 3 = Occasionally
> 4 = Frequently
> 5 = Very frequently

___ 1. How often do you and your spouse talk over pleasant things that happen during the day?

___ 2. How often do you and your spouse talk over unpleasant things that happen during the day?

___ 3. Do you and your spouse talk over things you disagree about or have difficulties over?

___ 4. Do you and your spouse talk about things in which you are both interested?

___ 5. Does your spouse adjust what he/she says and how he/she says it to the way you seem to feel at the moment?

___ 6. When you start to ask a question, does your spouse know what it is before you ask it?

___ 7. Do you know the feelings of your spouse from his/her facial and bodily gestures?

___ 8. Do you and your spouse avoid certain subjects in conversation?

___ 9. Does your spouse explain or express himself/herself to you through a glance or gesture?

___ 10. Do you and your spouse discuss things together before making an important decision?

___ 11. Can your spouse tell what kind of day you have had without asking?

___ 12. Your spouse wants to visit some close friends or relatives. You don't particularly enjoy their company. Would you tell him/her this?

___ 13. Does your spouse discuss matters of sex with you?

___ 14. Do you and your spouse use words which have a special meaning not understood by outsiders?

___ 15. How often does your spouse sulk or pout?

___ 16. Can you and your spouse discuss your most sacred beliefs without feelings of restraint or embarrassment?

___ 17. Do you avoid telling your spouse things that put you in a bad light?

___ 18. You and your spouse are visiting friends. Something is said by the friends which causes you to glance at each other. Would you understand each other?

___ 19. How often can you tell as much from the tone of voice of your spouse as from what he/she actually says?

___ 20. How often do you and your spouse talk with each other about personal problems?

___ 21. Do you feel that in most matters your spouse knows what you are trying to say?

___ 22. Would you rather talk about intimate matters with your spouse than with some other person?

___ 23. Do you understand the meaning of your spouse's facial expressions?

___ 24. If you and your spouse are visiting friends or relatives and one of you starts to say something, does the other take over the conversation without the feeling of interrupting?

___ 25. During marriage, have you and your spouse, in general, talked most things over together?

SELF-REPORT FAMILY INSTRUMENT (SFI)

AUTHORS: W. Robert Beavers, Robert B. Hampson, and Yosef F. Hulgus

PURPOSE: To measure family competence.

DESCRIPTION: The SFI is a 36-item instrument based on the Beavers-Timberlawn Model of Family Competence in which several dimensions of family functioning are proposed to distinguish competent from less competent families. These dimensions include family structure, mythology, goal-directed negotiation, autonomy of family members, the nature of family expression, and family style. All members of the family who can understand the items can be administered the SFI. Factor analysis reveals five subdimensions of the SFI: family conflict (items 5, 6, 7, 8, 10, 14, 18, 24, 25, 30, 31, and 34), family communication (items 11, 23, 26, and 29) family cohesion (items 2, 15, 19, 27, and 36), directive leadership (items 8, 16, and 32), and family health (all remaining items except 1, 9, 13, 20 and 22). A sixth dimension is composed of items 1, 9, 13, 20, and 22, although this subscale was not empirically determined. The SFI can be used as a total scale or the subscales can be used separately.

NORMS: Data are based on two nonclinical samples of college students (n = 279 and n = 205). Additionally, 71 families who had previously been in treatment completed the measure. No other demographic or normative data are available.

SCORING: The following items are reverse-scored: 5, 6, 7, 8, 10, 14, 18, 19, 23, 24, 25, 27, 29, 30, 31, 34. The scores on the six factors are summed and then divided by the number of items included in the particular factor; subscale scores can be summed for an overall score.

RELIABILITY: The internal consistency of the SFI is reported for the two samples of college students. For the larger sample the internal consistency was good, .85 using Cronbach's alpha. For the other sample, the alpha coefficient was .78.

VALIDITY: The SFI has a fair amount of concurrent validity, with subscales of the SFI correlating with the subscales of FACES–II, several factors of the Bloom Family Functioning Scale, and ratings of a clinical sample of 71 families. There is also some preliminary information on known-groups validity, with the subscales of health and expressiveness able to distinguish between outside-rated groups of high and low functioning families.

PRIMARY REFERENCE: Beavers, W. R., Hampson, R. B., and Hulgus, Y. F. (1985). Commentary: The Beavers systems approach to family assessment, *Family Process* 24, 398–405. Instrument reproduced with permission of Yosaf F. Hulgus and *Family Process*.

AVAILABILITY: W. Robert Beavers, M. D., Southwest Family Institute, 12532 Nuestra, Dallas, Texas, 75230.

SFI

For each question, mark the answer that best fits how you see your family now. If you feel that your answer is between two of the labeled numbers (the odd numbers), then choose the even number that is between them.

		YES: Fits our family very well		SOME: Fits our family some		NO: Does not fit our family
1.	Family members pay attention to each other's feelings.	1	2	3	4	5
2.	Our family would rather do things together than with other people.	1	2	3	4	5
3.	We all have a say in family plans.	1	2	3	4	5
4.	The grownups in this family understand and agree on family decisions.	1	2	3	4	5
5.	The grownups in the family compete and fight with each other.	1	2	3	4	5
6.	There is closeness in my family but each person is allowed to be special and different.	1	2	3	4	5
7.	We accept each other's friends.	1	2	3	4	5
8.	There is confusion in our family because there is no leader.	1	2	3	4	5
9.	Our family members touch and hug each other.	1	2	3	4	5
10.	Family members put each other down.	1	2	3	4	5
11.	We speak our minds, no matter what.	1	2	3	4	5

		YES: Fits our family very well		SOME: Fits our family some		NO: Does not fit our family
12.	In our home, we feel loved.	1	2	3	4	5
13.	Even when we feel close, our family is embarrassed to admit it.	1	2	3	4	5
14.	We argue a lot and never solve problems.	1	2	3	4	5
15.	Our happiest times are at home.	1	2	3	4	5
16.	The grownups in this family are strong leaders.	1	2	3	4	5
17.	The future looks good to our family.	1	2	3	4	5
18.	We usually blame one person in our family when things aren't going right.	1	2	3	4	5
19.	Family members go their own way most of the time.	1	2	3	4	5
20.	Our family is proud of being close.	1	2	3	4	5
21.	Our family is good at solving problems together.	1	2	3	4	5
22.	Family members easily express warmth and caring towards each other.	1	2	3	4	5
23.	It's okay to fight and yell in our family.	1	2	3	4	5
24.	One of the adults in this family has a favorite child.	1	2	3	4	5
25.	When things go wrong we blame each other.	1	2	3	4	5
26.	We say what we think and feel.	1	2	3	4	5

		YES: Fits our family very well	SOME: Fits our family some		NO: Does not fit our family
27.	Our family members would rather do things with other people than together.	1	2	3	4	5
28.	Family members pay attention to each other and listen to what is said.	1	2	3	4	5
29.	We worry about hurting each other's feelings.	1	2	3	4	5
30.	The mood in my family is usually sad and blue.	1	2	3	4	5
31.	We argue a lot.	1	2	3	4	5
32.	One person controls and leads our family.	1	2	3	4	5
33.	My family is happy most of the time.	1	2	3	4	5
34.	Each person takes responsibility for his/her behavior.	1	2	3	4	5

---

35. On a scale of 1 to 5, I would rate my family as:

1	2	3	4	5
My family functions very well together				My family does not function well together at all. We really need help.

36. On a scale of 1 to 5, I would rate the independence in my family as:

1	2	3	4	5
(No one is independent. There are no open arguments. Family members rely on each other for satisfaction rather than on outsiders.)		(Sometimes independent. There are some dis-agreements. Family members find satis-faction both within and outside of the family.)		(Family members usually go their own way. Dis-agreements are open. Family members look outside of the family for satisfaction.)

REFERENCES

Adorno, T. W., Frenkel-Brunswick, E., Levinson, D. J., and Sanford, R. N. (1950). *The Authoritarian Personality.* New York: Harper.

American Psychiatric Association (1980). *Diagnostic and Statistical Manual, Third Edition.* Washington, D.C.

American Psychological Association (1974). *Standards for Educational and Psychological Tests.* Washington, D.C.

Anastasi, A. (1976). *Psychological Testing,* 5th edition. New York: Macmillan.

Asarnow, J. R. and Carlson, G. A. (1982). Depression self-rating: Utility with child psychiatric inpatients, *Journal of Consulting and Clinical Psychology* 53, 491–499.

Asher, D. R., Hymel, S., and Renshaw, P. D. (1984). Loneliness in Children, *Child Development* 55, 1457–1464.

Austin, C. D. (1981). Client assessment in context. *Social Work Research and Abstracts* 17, 4–12.

Babbie, E. (1983). *The Practice of Social Research,* 3rd edition. Belmont, California: Wadsworth.

Barlow, D. H. (ed.). (1981). *Behavioral Assessment of Adult Disorders.* New York: Guilford Press.

—— (1985). *Clinical handbook of Psychological Disorders.* New York: Guilford Press.

——, Hayes, S. C., and Nelson, R. O. (1984). *The Scientist Practitioner: Research and Accountability in Clinical and Educational Settings.* New York: Pergamon Press.

—— and Hersen, M. (1984). *Single Case Experimental Designs: Strategies for Studying Behavior Change.* 2nd edition. New York: Pergamon Press.

Beach, S. R. H. and Arias, I. (1983). Assessment of perceptual discrepancy: Utility of the primary communication inventory, *Family Process* 22, 309–316.

467

Beck, A. T., Ward, C. H., Mendelson, M., Mock, J., and Erbaugh, J. (1961). An inventory for measuring depression. *Archives of General Psychiatry* 4, 561–571.

———, Weissman, A., Lester, D. and Trexler, L. (1974) The measurement of pessimism: The Hopelessness Scale, *Journal of Consulting and Clinical Psychology* 42, 861–865.

Beere, C. A. (1979). *Women and Women's Issues: A Handbook of Tests and Measures*. San Francisco: Jossey-Bass.

Bellack, A. S. and Hersen, M. (1977). The use of self-report inventories in behavioral assessment. In J. D. Cone and R. P. Hawkins (eds.), *Behavioral Assessment: New Directions in Clinical Psychology*, pp. 52–76. New York: Brunner/Mazel.

Bernstein, D. A., and Allen, G. J. (1969). Fear Survey Schedule (II): Normative data and factor analyses based upon a large college sample. *Behavioral Research and Therapy*, 1969, 7, 403–407.

Bloom, M. (1975). *The Paradox of Helping. Introduction to the Philosophy of Scientific Practice*. New York: John Wiley.

——— and Fischer, J. (1982). *Evaluating Practice: Guidelines for the Accountable Professional*. Englewood Cliffs, N.J.: Prentice-Hall.

Blumenthal, M. and Dielman, T. (1975). Depression symtomatology and role function in a general population, *Archives of General Psychiatry* 32, 985–991.

Buros, O. K. (ed.) (1978). *The Eighth Mental Measurements Yearbook*, Vols. I and II. Highland Park, N.J.: Gryphon Press.

Cattell, R. B. (1966). The scree test for the number of factors, *Multivariate Behavioral Research* 1, 245–276.

Cautela, J. R. (1977). *Behavior Analysis Forms for Clinical Intervention*. Champaign, Ill.: Research Press.

——— (1981). *Behavior Analysis Forms for Clinical Intervention*, Vol. 2. Champaign, Ill.: Research Press.

Chun, K.-T., Cobb, S. and French, J. R., Jr. (1975). *Measures for Psychological Assessment: A Guide to 3,000 Original Sources and Their Application*. Ann Arbor, Mich.: Institute for Social Research.

Ciminero, A. R., Calhoun, K. S., and Adams, H. E. (eds.). (1977). *Handbook of Behavioral Assessment*. New York: John Wiley.

Colby, K. M. (1980). Computer Psychotherapists. In J. B. Sidowski, J. H. Johnson, and T. A. Williams (eds.), *Technology in Mental Health Care Delivery Systems*, pp. 109–117. Norwood, N.J.: Ablex.

Comrey, A. L. et al. (1973). *A Sourcebook for Mental Health Measures*. Los Angeles: Human Interaction Research Institute.

———— (1978). Common methodological problems in factor analytic studies, *Journal of Consulting and Clinical Psychology* 46, 648–659.

Cone, J. D. and Hawkins, R. P. (eds.) (1977). *Behavioral Assessment: New Directions in Clinical Psychology.* New York: Brunner/Mazel.

Conway, J. B. (1977). Behavioral self-control of smoking through aversion conditioning and self-management, *Journal of Consulting and Clinical Psychology* 45, 348–357.

Corcoran, K. J. (1988). Selecting a measuring instrument. In R. M. Grinnell, Jr. *Social Work Research and Evaluation,* 3rd edition. Itasca, ILL.: F. E. Peacock.

Cronbach, L. J. (1970). *Essentials of Psychological Testing,* 3rd edition. New York: Macmillan.

Epstein, L. H. (1976). Psychophysiological measurement in assessment, in M. Hersen and A. S. Bellack (eds.), *Behavioral Assessment: A Practical Handbook,* pp. 207–232. New York: Pergamon Press.

Erdman, H. P., Klein, M. H., and Greist, J. H. (1985). Direct patient computer interviewing, *Journal of Consulting and Clinical Psychology* 53(6), 760–773.

Fenigstein, A., Scheier, M. F., and Buss, A. H. (1975). Public and private self-consciousness: Assessment and theory, *Journal of Consulting and Clinical Psychology* 43, 522–527.

Fischer, J. (1981). The Social Work Revolution, *Social Work* 26, 199–207.

———— and Gochros, H. (1975). *Planned Behavior Change: Behavior Modification in Social Work.* New York: The Free Press.

Fowler, D. (1985). Landmarks in Computer-Assisted Psychological Assessment, *Journal of Consulting and Clinical Psychology* 53(6), 748–759.

Gambrill, E. (1983). *Casework: A Competency-Based Approach.* Englewood Cliffs, N.J.: Prentice-Hall.

Gottman, J. M. and Leiblum, S. R. (1974). *How to Do Psychotherapy and How to Evaluate It.* New York: Holt.

Gerson, M. J. (1984). Splitting: The development of a measure, *Journal of Clinical Psychology* 40, 157–162.

Golden, C. J., Sawicki, R. F., and Franzen, M. D. (1984). Test construction. In G. Goldstein and M. Hersen (eds.), *Handbook of Psychological Assessment,* pp. 19–37. New York: Pergamon Press.

Goldman, B. A. and Busch, J. C. (1978). *Directory of Unpublished Experimental Mental Measures,* Vol. II. New York: Human Sciences Press.

Goldman, B. A. and Busch, J. C. (1982). *Directory of Unpublished Ex-*

perimental Mental Measures, Vol. III. New York: Human Sciences Press.

Goldman, B. A. and Sanders, J. L. (1974). *Directory of Unpublished Experimental Mental Measures*, Vol. I. New York: Behavioral Publications.

Goldman, J., Stein, C. L., and Guerry, S. (1983). *Psychological Methods of Clinical Assessment*. New York: Pergamon Press.

Goldstein, G. and Hersen, M. (eds.) (1984). *Handbook of Psychological Assessment*, New York: Pergamon Press.

Haynes, S. N. (1978). *Principles of Behavioral Assessment*. New York: Gardner Press.

—— (1983). Behavioral assessment. In M. Hersen, A. E. Kazdin, and A. S. Bellack (eds.), *The Clinical Psychology Handbook*, pp. 397–425. New York: Pergamon Press.

—— and Wilson, C. C. (1979). *Behavioral Assessment*. San Francisco: Jossey-Bass.

Hersen, M. and Bellack, A. S. (eds.) (1981). *Behavioral Assessment: A Practical Handbook*. 2nd edition. New York: Pergamon Press.

Hoon, E. F. and Chambless, D. (1987). Sexual Arousability Inventory (SAI) and Sexual Arousability Inventory—Expanded (SAI-E). In C. M. Davis and W. L. Yarber (eds.), *Sexuality-Related Measures: A Compendium*. Syracuse, N.Y.: Graphic Publishing.

Hudson, W. W. (1978). First axioms of treatment, *Social Work* 23, 65–66.

—— (1981). Development and use of indexes and scales. In R. M. Grinnell (ed.), *Social Work Research and Evaluation*. Itasca, Ill.: F. E. Peacock, 130–155.

—— (1982). *The Clinical Measurement Package: A Field Manual*. Chicago: Ill.: Dorsey Press.

—— (1985). *The Clinical Assessment System*. University of Arizona, School of Social Work, Tempe, Arizona 85287 (computer program).

Humphrey, L. L. (1982). Children's and teachers' perceptions on children's self-control: The development of two rating scales. *Journal of Consulting and Clinical Psychology* 50, 624–633.

Jayaratne, S. and Levy, R. L. (1979). *Empirical Clinical Practice*. New York: Columbia University Press.

Johnson, S. M. and Bolstad, O. D. (1973). Methodological issues in natural observation: Some problems and solutions for field research. In L. A. Hammerlynck, L. C. Handy, and E. J. Mash (eds.), *Behavior*

Change: Methodology, Concepts, and Practice. Champaign, Ill.: Research Press.

Johnson, O. G. and Bommarito, J. W. (1971). *Tests and Measurements in Child Development: A Handbook.* San Francisco: Jossey-Bass.

Kallman, W. M. and Feuerstein, M. (1977). Psychophysiological Procedures. In A. R. Ciminero, C. S. Calhoun, and H. E. Adams (eds.), *Handbook of Behavioral Assessment,* pp. 329–366. New York: John Wiley.

Kazdin, A. F. (1979). Situational specificity: The two-edged sword of behavioral assessment, *Behavioral Assessment* 1, 57–76.

—— (1980). *Research design in clinical psychology.* New York: Harper and Row.

—— (1982). Observer effects: Reactivity of direct observation. In D. P. Hartman (ed.), *Using Observers to Study Behavior: New Directions for Methodology of Social and Behavioral Science,* pp. 5–19. San Francisco: Jossey-Bass.

—— (1982). *Single-Case Research Designs: Methods for Clinical and Applied Settings.* New York: Oxford University Press.

Kendall, P. C. and Hollon, S. D. (eds.) (1981). *Assessment Strategies for Cognitive-Behavioral Interventions.* New York: Academic Press.

Kratochwill, T. R. (ed.) (1978). *Single-Subject Research: Strategies for Evaluating Change.* New York: Academic Press.

Lake, D. G., Miles, M. B. and Earle, R. B., Jr. (1973). *Measuring Human Behavior: Tools for the Assessment of Social Functioning.* New York: Teachers College Press.

Lambert, M. J., Christensen, E. R., and DeJulio, S. S. (eds.) (1983). *The Assessment of Psychotherapy Outcome.* New York: Wiley and Sons.

Lang, P. J. (1977). Physiological assessment of anxiety and fear, in D. D. Cone and R. P. Hawkins (eds.), *Behavioral Assessment: New Directions in Clinical Psychology,* pp. 178–195. New York: Brunner/Mazel.

Lauffer, A. (1982). *Assessment Tools for Practitioners, Managers, and Trainers.* Beverly Hills, Calif.: Sage Publications.

Levitt, J. L. and Reid, W. J. (1981). Rapid-assessment instruments for practice, *Social Work Research and Abstracts* 17, 13–19.

Levy, L. H. (1983). Trait approaches. In M. Hersen, A. E. Kazdin, and A. S. Bellack (eds.), *The Clinical Psychology Handbook,* pp. 123–142. New York: Pergamon Press.

Linehan, Marsha M. (1985). The reason for living scale. In P. A. Keller and L. G. Ritt (eds.), *Innovations in Clinical Practice: A Source Book* (vol. 4). Sarasota, FL.: Professional Resource Exchange.

Mash, E. and Terdal, L. (eds.) (1981). *Behavioral Assessment of Childhood Disorders*. New York: Guildford Press.

Mathews, A. M., Gelder, M. G., and Johnston, D. W. (1981). *Agoraphobia: Nature and Treatment*. New York: Guilford Press.

McCormick, I. A. (1984). A simple version of the Rathus Assertiveness Schedule, *Behavior Assessment* 7, 95–99.

McDonald, A. P. and Games, R. G. (1972). Ellis's irrational values, *Rational Living* 7, 25–28.

McReynolds, P. (1981) (ed.). *Advances in Psychological Assessment*, Vol. V, San Francisco: Jossey-Bass.

Merluzzi, T. V., Glass, C. R., and Genest, M. (eds.) (1981). *Cognitive Assessment*. New York: Guilford Press.

Miller, D. C. (1977). *Handbook of Research Design and Social Measurement*, 3rd edition. New York: Longman.

Minuchin, S. (1974). *Families and Family Therapy*. Cambridge, Mass.: Harvard University Press.

Mischel, W. (1968). *Personality and Assessment*. New York: John Wiley.

—— (1981). *Introduction to Personality*. New York: Holt.

Moos, R. H. (1974). *Evaluating Treatment Environments: A Social Ecological Approach*. New York: John Wiley.

—— (1975a). Assessment and impact of social climate. In P. McReynolds (ed.), *Advances in Psychological Assessment*, Vol. 3. San Francisco: Jossey-Bass.

—— (1975b). *Evaluating Correctional and Community Settings*. New York: John Wiley.

—— (1979). *Evaluating Educational Environments*. San Francisco: Jossey-Bass.

Mosher, D. L. and Sirkin, M. (1984). Measuring a macho personality constellation, *Journal of Research in Personality* 18, 150–163.

Nay, W. R. (1979). *Multimethod Clinical Assessment*. New York: Gardner Press.

Nelsen, J. C. (1985). Verifying the independent variable in single-subject research, *Social Work Research and Abstracts* 21, 3–8.

Nelson, R. O. (1981). Realistic dependent measures for clinical use, *Journal of Consulting and Clinical Psychology* 49, 168–182.

—— and Barlow, D. H. (1981). Behavioral assessment: Basic strategies and initial procedures. In D. H. Barlow (ed.), *Behavioral Assessment of Adult Disorders*, pp. 13–43. New York: Guilford Press.

Nunnally, J. C. (1978). *Psychometric Theory*, 2nd edition. New York: McGraw-Hill.

Phares, E. J. and Erskine, N. (1984). The measurement of selfism, *Educational and Psychological Measurement* 44, 597–608.

Rathus, S. A. (1973). A 30-item schedule for assessing assertive behavior, *Behavior Therapy* 4, 398–406.

Ray, W. J. and Raczynski, J. M. (1981). Psychophysiological assessment. In M. Hersen and A. S. Bellack (eds.), *Behavioral Assessment: A Practical Handbook*, 2nd edition. New York: Pergamon Press.

Reckase, M. D. (1984). Scaling techniques. In G. Goldstein and M. Hersen (eds.), *Handbook of Psychological Assessment*, pp. 38–53. New York: Pergamon Press.

Rehm, L. P. (1981). Assessment of depression. In M. Hersen and A. S. Bellack (eds.), *Behavioral Assessment: A Practical Handbook*, pp. 246–295. New York: Pergamon Press.

Richardson, F. C. and Suinn, R. M. (1972). The Mathematics Anxiety Rating Scale: Psychometric data, *Journal of Counseling Psychology* 19, 551–554.

Roberts, R. E. and Attkisson, C. C. (1984). Assessing client satisfaction among Hispanics, *Evaluation and Program Planning* 6, 401–413.

Robinson, J. P. and Shaver, P. R. (1973). *Measures of Social Psychological Attitudes*, revised edition. Ann Arbor, Mich.: Institute for Social Research.

Rugh, J. D. and Schwitzgebel, R. L. (1977). Instrumentation for behavioral assessment. In A. R. Ciminero, K. S. Calhoun, and H. E. Adams (eds.), *Handbook of Behavioral Assessment*, pp. 79–116. New York: John Wiley.

Scholl, G. and Schnur, R. (1976). *Measures of Psychological, Vocational and Educational Functioning in the Blind and Visually Handicapped*. New York: American Foundation for the Blind.

Schwartz, A. and Goldiamond, I. (1975). *Social Casework: A Behavioral Approach*. New York: Columbia University Press.

Shelton, J. L. and Levy, R. L. (1981). *Behavioral Assignments and Treatment Compliance: A Handbook of Clinical Strategies*. Champaign, Ill.: Research Press.

Shorkey, C. T. and Whiteman, V. (1977). Development of the Rational Behavior Inventory: Initial validity and reliability, *Educational and Psychological Measurement* 37, 527–534.

Slack, W. V., Hicks, G. P., Reed, C. Z., and Van Cura, L. J. (1966). A computer-based medical history system, *New England Journal of Medicine* 274, 194–198.

Smith, M. C. and Thelen, M. N. (1984). Development and validation of a test for bulimia, *Journal of Consulting and Clinical Psychology* 52, 863–872.

Southworth, L. E., Burr, R. L., and Cox, A. E. (1981). *Screening and Evaluating the Young Infant: A Handbook of Instruments to Use from Infancy to Six Years.* Springfield, Ill.: C. C. Thomas.

Spielberger, C. D., Jacobs, G., Russel, S., and Crane, R. S. (1983). Assessment of anger: The state-trait anger scale. In J. N. Butcher and C. D. Spielberger (eds.), *Advances in Personality Assessment,* Vol. 2, pp. 159–187. Hillsdale, N.J.: Lawrence Erlbaum Associates.

Stiles, W. B. (1980). Measurement of the impact of psychotherapy sessions, *Journal of Consulting and Clinical Psychology* 48, 176–185.

Sundberg, N. D. (1977). *Assessment of Persons.* Englewood Cliffs, N.J.: Prentice-Hall.

Sweetland, R. C. and Keyser, D. J. (1983). *Tests: A Comprehensive Reference.* Kansas City, Mo.: Test Corporation of America.

Tan, A. L., Kendis, R. J., Fine, J. T., and Porac, J. (1977). A short measure of Eriksonian ego identity, *Journal of Personality Assessment* 41, 279–284.

Thomas, E. J. (1978). Research and service in single-case experimentation: Conflicts and choices, *Social Work Research and Abstracts* 14, 20–31.

Thyer, B., Papsdorf, J., Himle, D., and Bray, H. (1981). Normative data on the Rational Behavior Inventory: A further study, *Educational and Psychological Measurement* 41, 757–760.

Toseland, R. W. and Reid, W. J. (1985). Using rapid assessment instruments in a family service agency, *Social Casework* 66, 547–555.

Waskow, I. E. and Parloff, M. B. (eds.) (1975). *Psychotherapy Change Measures.* Rockville, Md.: National Institute of Mental Health.

Webb, E. J., Campbell, D. T., Schwartz, R. D., and Sechrest, L. (1966). *Unobtrusive Measures: Nonreactive Research in the Social Sciences.* Chicago: Rand McNally.

—— Campbell, D. T., Schwartz, R. D., Sechrest, L., and Grove, J. B. (1981). *Nonreactive Measures in the Social Sciences.* 2nd edition. Boston: Houghton Mifflin.

Wicker, A. W. (1981). Nature and assessment of behavior settings: Recent contributions from the ecological perspective. In P. Mc-

Reynolds (ed.), *Advances in Psychological Assessment,* Vol. V, pp. 22–61. San Francisco: Jossey-Bass.

Wincze, J. P. and Lange, J. D. (1982). Assessment of sexual behavior. In D. H. Barlow (ed.), *Behavioral Assessment of Adult Disorder,* pp. 301–328. New York: Guilford Press.

Wittenborn, J. R. (1984). Psychological assessment in treatment. In G. Goldstein and M. Hersen (eds.), *Handbook of Psychological Assessment.* Elmsford, NY: Pergamon Press, 405–420.

Woody, R. H. (ed.) (1980). *Encyclopedia of Clinical Assessment,* Vols. I and II. San Francisco: Jossey-Bass.

Zung, W. K. (1965). A self-rating depression scale. *Archives of General Psychiatry* 12, 63–70.

—— (1974). *The Measurement of Depression.* Milwaukee: Lakeside Laboratories.

INDEX